Straight Talk About
College Costs and Prices

Straight Talk About College Costs and Prices

Report of
The National Commission on the Cost of Higher Education

CONTRIBUTING AUTHORS

James Harvey
Roger M. Williams
James Harvey and Associates

Rita J. Kirshstein
Amy Smith O'Malley
American Institutes for Research

Jane V. Wellman
Institute for Higher Education Policy

Published at the request of The National Commission on the Cost of Higher Education by the American Council on Education and The Oryx Press.

*The rare Arabian Oryx is believed to have inspired the myth of the unicorn. This desert
antelope became virtually extinct in the early 1960s. At that time several groups of
international conservationists arranged to have 9 animals sent to the Phoenix Zoo
to be the nucleus of a captive breeding herd. Today the Oryx population
is over 1,000, and over 500 have been returned to the Middle East.*

Published by The Oryx Press
4041 North Central at Indian School Road
Phoenix, Arizona 85012-3397

Printed and Bound in the United States of America

♾ The paper used in this publication meets the minimum requirements of
American National Standard for Information Science—Permanence
of Paper for Printed Library Materials, ANSI Z39.48, 1984.

Cover Design: Levine & Associates—Washington, DC

ISBN 1-57356-225-4

Contents

Members of the National Commission on the Cost of Higher Education

Foreword

It has been my privilege to serve as Chairman of the National Commission on the Cost of Higher Education. In the words of the Honorable Howard R. McKeon, Chairman of the House Subcommittee on Post Secondary Education, Training, and Life-Long Learning, the Commission was charged with the task of presenting "a clear understanding of what is truly happening with respect to the cost of a college education and what steps can or should be taken to ensure a quality post secondary education remains affordable." The Commission has worked hard to achieve these ends.

Despite our brief six month tenure, the Commission reached broad agreement on major themes and issues. In short, we believe that it is time for straight talk about college expenses. Key to this discussion is the distinction between cost and price. By cost we mean the expense an institution of higher education incurs to deliver education to a student; by price we mean the portion of those costs students and families are asked to pay. Confusion abounds about cost and price and the general subsidy that goes to all students regardless of what type of institution they attend. The distinction between these terms must be recognized and become common place in all attempts to understand higher education finance and to keep higher education affordable. From the Commission's perspective, rising costs are just as troubling a policy issue as rising prices.

Although the major responsibility for controlling costs and prices is a shared responsibility among institutions of higher education, government at all levels, families and students, and other patrons, the major onus rests with the higher education community. The Commission, though, was deeply concerned that most institutions of higher education have permitted a veil of obscurity to settle over their financial operations and many have yet to take seriously basic strategies for reducing costs. Furthermore, the Commission was also concerned with the possibility that continued inattention to issues of cost and price threatens to create a gulf of ill will between institutions of higher education and the public they serve. Such a development would be dangerous for higher education and the larger society. Unless academic institutions attend to these problems now, policy makers at both the state and federal levels could impose unilateral solutions that are likely to be heavy handed and regulatory. The Commission, though, believes that a heavy handed, regulatory approach will not work and would be destructive of academic quality in higher education.

Finally, this Commission has tried to speak directly to students and their families. Their concern about rising college prices is real. We understand the anxiety involved when families face the prospect of paying for a college education. We do not dismiss it. In no way do we minimize it. On the contrary, all the recommendations in this document were developed with one goal in mind: to keep open the door of higher education by maintaining access at prices students and families can afford.

The Commission calls upon everyone to take up their share of the work involved in implementing the recommendations of this report. We believe that the institutions of higher education should take the lead in this process. We believe, further, that this will lead to increased public confidence and support of our nation's institutions of higher education.

William E. Troutt
Commission Chairman
President, Belmont University
Nashville, Tennessee
February, 1998

Introduction

This volume brings together two items: the final report of the National Commission on the Cost of Higher Education and the supplementary research material produced for the Commission's deliberations. The report contains the Commission's analysis of college costs and prices; its assessment of the major reasons advanced for increases in college costs and prices; and its convictions and recommendations on how to keep higher education affordable. The supplementary collection is organized using the eleven issues that Congress charged the Commission with investigating.

This volume is produced with the cooperation of the American Council on Education (ACE), Oryx Press, and the American Institutes for Research (AIR). The Commission approached ACE about making the Commission's report and research available in a volume that could be used by those interested in the issues which the Commission investigated. The result is this volume, published for the Commission by ACE in collaboration with Oryx Press. AIR served as the Commission's researcher contractor. Special thanks to the following whose assistance has led to the production of this volume: James Murray (ACE), Susan Slesinger (Oryx Press), and David Rhodes (AIR).

Bruno V. Manno
Executive Director
National Commission on the Cost of Higher Education

Letter of Transmittal

January 21, 1998

The Honorable William Jefferson Clinton
President of the United States

The Honorable Albert Gore
President
United States Senate

The Honorable Newt Gingrich
Speaker
United States House of Representatives

Gentlemen:

Public Law 105-18 (Title IV, Cost of Higher Education Review, 1997) established the National Commission on the Cost of Higher Education as an independent advisory body and called for a comprehensive review of college costs and prices.

The legislation created an 11-member Commission — three each to be appointed by the Speaker of the House of Representatives and the Majority Leader of the U.S. Senate; two each to be appointed by the Minority Leader of the House and the Minority Leader of the Senate; and one to be appointed by the Secretary of Education.

Noting that public concern about college affordability was at a 30-year high and that tuition increases at four-year public institutions had outpaced growth in median household income and the cost of consumer goods since 1980, the statute directed the Commission to submit a report to the President and Congress by February 1998. We are pleased to submit this final report.

Our Congressional charter asked that we examine eleven specific factors related to costs. These included:

1. The increase in tuition compared with other commodities and services.

2. Innovative methods of reducing or stabilizing tuition.

3. Trends in college and university administrative costs, including administrative staffing, ratio of administrative staff to instructors, ratio of administrative staff to students, remuneration of administrative staff, and remuneration of college and university presidents and chancellors.

4. Trends in faculty workload and remuneration (including the use of adjunct faculty); faculty-to-student ratios; number of hours spent in the classroom by faculty; and tenure practices, and the impact of such trends on tuition.

5. Trends in the construction and renovation of academic and other collegiate facilities, the modernization of facilities to access and utilize new technologies, and the impact of such trends on tuition.

6. The extent to which increases in institutional financial aid and tuition discounting have effected tuition increases, including the demographics of students receiving such aid, the extent to which such aid is provided to students with limited need in order to attract such students to particular institutions or major fields of study, and the extent to which Federal financial aid, including loan aid, has been used to offset such increases.

7. The extent to which Federal, state and local laws, regulations or other mandates contribute to increasing tuition, and recommendations on reducing those mandates.

8. The establishment of a mechanism for a more timely and widespread distribution of data on tuition trends and other costs of operating colleges and universities.

9. The extent to which student financial aid programs have contributed to changes in tuition.

10. Trends in state fiscal policies that have affected college costs.

11. The adequacy of existing Federal and state financial aid programs in meeting the costs of attending colleges and universities.

Despite our brief tenure, we had little difficulty reaching broad agreement on major themes and directions. We believe that it is time for straight talk about college expenses and that the distinction between cost and price must be recognized and respected. By "cost" we mean the expense an institution of higher education incurs to deliver education to a student; by "price" we mean the portion of those costs students and families are asked to pay. Against that backdrop, the conclusions in this document speak for themselves:

- The United States has a world-class system of higher education, and a college degree has become a key requirement for economic success in today's world.

- This Commission is convinced that American higher education remains an extraordinary value.

- Institutions, families and students, and other patrons share responsibility for maintaining quality and reducing costs.

- Tuition price controls will not work and would be destructive of academic quality in higher education.

- Nevertheless, the Commission is also deeply concerned that most academic institutions have permitted a veil of obscurity to settle over their financial operations and many have yet to take seriously basic strategies for reducing their costs.

- Unless academic institutions attend to these problems now, policymakers at both the state and Federal levels could impose unilateral solutions that are likely to be heavy-handed and regulatory.

To deal with these concerns, this report presents a five-part action agenda. The Commission's recommendations, several dozen in all, emphasize shared responsibility to

(1) strengthen institutional cost control; (2) improve market information and public accountability; (3) deregulate higher education; (4) rethink accreditation; and (5) enhance and simplify Federal student aid.

We have been straightforward in our discussions with each other and in our recommendations about what needs to be done. We are unanimous in supporting the broad themes and recommendations in this document.

We want to thank each of you for your confidence that we could complete this challenging assignment. Your support helped us complete the task on schedule.

Finally, we want to acknowledge the work of our staff, under the able leadership of its executive director, Bruno Manno, which unfailingly served us well.

William E. Troutt
Commission Chairman

Barry Munitz
Commission Vice Chairman

Straight Talk About College Costs and Prices

The phenomenon of rising college tuition evokes a public reaction that is sometimes compared to the "sticker shock" of buying a new car. Although this reference to automobile prices may irritate some within the higher education community, it serves to remind all of us that higher education is a product, a service and a life-long investment bought and paid for, like others.

Rising college tuitions are real. In the 20 years between 1976 and 1996, the average tuition at public universities increased from $642 to $3,151 and the average tuition at private universities increased from $2,881 to $15,581. Tuitions at public two-year colleges, the least expensive of all types of institutions, increased from an average of $245 to $1,245 during this period.[1]

Public anxiety about college prices has risen along with increases in tuition. It is now on the order of anxiety about how to pay for health care or housing, or cover the expenses of taking care of an elderly relative.[2] Financing a college education is a serious and troublesome matter to the American people.

Each member of this Commission understands this anxiety. We treat it seriously. We do not take lightly the public concern generated by increases in tuition. Worry about college prices, the difficulty of planning for them, and the amount of debt they entail dominated a discussion group of parents convened by the Commission in Nashville in November 1997. Members of the Commission are equally convinced that if this public concern continues, and if colleges and universities do not take steps to reduce their costs, policymakers at the Federal and state levels will intervene and take up the task for them.

What concerns this Commission is the possibility that continued inattention to issues of cost and price threatens to create a gulf of ill will between institutions of higher education and the public they serve. We believe that such a development would be dangerous for higher education and the larger society.

In the end, academic institutions must be affordable and more accountable. The Commission is worried that many academic institutions have not seriously confronted the basic issues involved with reducing their costs—and that most of them have also permitted a veil of obscurity to settle over their basic financial operations.

This report addresses these issues. It provides straight talk about college costs and about college prices. While this Commission's ultimate goal is ensuring the affordability of higher education, achieving that goal requires an understanding of what it costs colleges and universities to educate students, the prices academic institutions charge students to attend, and the relationship between the two. Moreover, the role of financial aid is considered since many students do not pay the full price they are charged for their education. This report, therefore, is divided into three main sections: the first provides a review of significant facts about higher education and the current situation with regard to higher education costs and prices. The second outlines our review and assessment of the major reasons advanced for increases in college costs and prices. The third presents our convictions about the college cost and price crisis and our recommendations to keep higher education affordable.

FACTS ABOUT HIGHER EDUCATION, ITS COST, AND ITS PRICE

The diversity of American higher education is unequaled in the world and is, without question, one of this nation's great strengths. Approximately 3,700 not-for-profit colleges and universities which vary in terms of size, geography, sector, selectivity, and mission comprise the academic spectrum: flagship state universities expanding the boundaries of human knowledge; four-year public institutions providing access at very low prices; private universities, many of them among the most prestigious in the world; liberal arts colleges proud of their tradition of encouraging intellectual development in small, intimate settings; and two-year community colleges offering everything from high school and transfer programs to retirement planning and technical training.

Although there are more private colleges and universities than public ones, more than three quarters (78 percent) of all students—and 81 percent of all undergraduates—are enrolled in public two- and four-year institutions. In recent years, the number of part-time students has increased substantially. Indeed, the student profile has changed radically in recent decades profoundly affecting the way colleges look at and do their jobs. In addition to the traditional 18-to-22 year-old full-time students, higher education enrollments now include large numbers of older, married individuals, many of them parents, with limited means, demanding personal schedules, and a tendency to move in and out of the student population on a part-time basis. Current students are the most racially and ethnically diverse group ever served by any nation's system of higher education. A high percentage of these students, including many undergraduates, are financially independent of their parents. In fact, the percentage of undergraduates enrolled part-time increased from 28 percent of all enrollments (two- and four-year) in 1980 to 42 percent in 1994, with the greatest concentration of part-time students in two-year institutions. (See Table 1.)

TABLE 1

Number of Institutions and Enrollment by Status and Age, by Type of Institution

	Public		Private		Total
	Four-year	Two-year	Four-year	Two-year	
Number of Insitutions[1]	608	1,047	1,636	415	3,706
Total Enrollments (thousands)[2]	5,825	5,308	2,924	221	14,278
Full-Time (thousands)	4,065	1,885	2,041	146	8,138
Part-time (thousands)	1,760	3,423	883	75	6,141
Percent Undergraduate Enrollment	80%	100%	72%	100%	86%

Source: *Digest of Education Statistics*, 1996. Tables 237, 192, 194, and 174.
[1]1995-96 Academic year
[2]Fall 1994

The diversity within American higher education is also reflected in the prices institutions charge students to attend. The average undergraduate tuition ranged from $1,245 in public two-year colleges in the Fall of 1996 to $15,581 in private universities.[3] Tuition, however, generally does not cover the full cost of the students' education. This means that *all* students—both those in public and private institutions—receive a subsidy.

Posted tuition does not include other education-related costs borne by students such as books, special laboratory fees, and living expenses (room and board if living on campus, or rent or related housing costs if the student lives off campus). Furthermore, for a large percentage of students and families, the price actually paid to attend college bears little resemblance to the tuition charged and other education-related expenses. This occurs because many students receive some form of financial aid (See Table 2.) In 1995-96, for example, 80 percent of full-time undergraduates at private four-year institutions (and 70 percent of part-time students) received aid. For public four-year institutions, 66 and 48 percent respectively received aid, and for two-year institutions, 63 and 36 percent.

Finally, since financial aid awards are often based on financial need, students from lower income families tend to pay less to attend the same institution than students from higher income families. In 1995-96, full-time undergraduates who were financially dependent on their parents and whose family incomes were less than $40,000 paid, on average, $5,412 to attend a public university (this estimate subtracts all financial aid awards from tuition and other education-related expenses). Undergraduates whose family incomes exceeded $80,000 paid almost twice as much, $10,376. Indeed, while much of the public attention focuses on increases in tuition, tuition is but one element of the price of attending college.

TABLE 2

Percentage of Undergraduates Receiving Financial Aid, by Type of Institution: 1995-96

	Public		Private	
	Four-year (%)	Two-year (%)	Four-year (%)	Two-year (%)
Full-Time Students				
Percent receiving any financial aid49	66	63	80	82
Percent receiving grants	44	72	63	
Percent obtaining loans	45	16	57	56
Percent participating in work-study	8	6	26	6
Part-Time Students				
Percent receiving any fiancial aid	48	36	70	49
Percent receiving grants	34	31	47	34
Percent obtaining loans	30	8	29	30
Percent participating in work-study	4	1	4	0

Source: National Postsecondary Student Aid Study, 1996.'
Student Aid Study, 1996.
Note: Percents for specific types of financial aid do not sum to the percent receiving any financial aid because students often receive more than one form of aid.

DEFINING TERMS AND THE SCOPE OF OUR REVIEW

Understanding the Commission's review of costs and prices requires defining terms such as *cost, price,* and *general subsidy.* Defining these terms is not just a technical sidenote, of interest only to policy analysts; a major semantic challenge exists in our national discussion of college costs. The term "cost" is used interchangeably to mean at least four different things: it can mean the *production cost,* or the cost of delivering education to a single student. It can also mean the "sticker" price, or the posted *nominal price* students are asked to pay in tuition and fees. It is also used to describe the *cost to the student* to attend college—including not just tuition and fees, but room, board, books, supplies, and transportation. Finally, it can mean the *net price* paid by the student after financial aid awards are subtracted from the full cost to the student.

Despite their obvious differences, these concepts are often discussed as if they were the same thing. This Commission believes the confusion arising from the careless use of these terms—as well as inattention within higher education to the relationships between cost and price—to be so serious that we have devoted considerable time and attention to distinguishing among them.

It is important to make a clear distinction between expenditures that *institutions incur* in order to provide education (costs) and expenses that *students and families face* (prices). Furthermore, there is another factor not considered in most conversations on these issues: what students pay is not the total cost of education. There is a *general subsidy* that goes to all students, regardless of the institution they attend or whether they receive any financial aid. Therefore, the Commission makes a major effort to define its terms carefully, and to use the terms "cost," "price," and "subsidy" consistently. (See Figure 1.)

FIGURE 1

Definitions of Cost, Price, and General Subsidy

Costs: What institutions spend to provide education and related educational services to students

> **Cost per student:** The average amount spent annually to provide education and related services to each full-time equivalent student

Price: What students and their families are charged and what they pay

> **Sticker price:** The tuition and fees that institutions charge

> **Total price of attendance**: The tuition and fees that institutions charge students as well as other expenses related to obtaining a higher education. These expenses could include housing (room and board if the student lives on campus, or rent or related housing costs if the student does not live on campus), books, transportation, etc. (This term typically is referred to by other higher education analysts as the "cost of attendance.")

> **Net price:** What students pay after financial aid is subtracted from the total price of attendance. Financial aid comes in different forms: *grants* are scholarships or "gifts" to the student that do not have to be repaid; *loans* are borrowed money that must be paid back, typically after the student leaves school; *work study* entails working to receive financial assistance. Because of the very different nature of grants vs. loans and work study, the Commission uses two different concepts of net price:

> • The first measure subtracts *only grants* from the total price of attendance. This concept provides a measure of *affordability*, or the amount of money a student actually pays to attend college.

> • The second measure subtracts *all financial aid* awarded—grants, loans, and work study—from the total price of attendance, to measure the amount of money a student needs in order to enter the college or university. This concept provides a measure of *access*, because, even though loans must be repaid, they allow a student to attend college, just like car loans allow many to buy a car who otherwise may not be able to afford one.

General Subsidy: The difference between the cost to the institution of providing an education ("cost per student") and the tuition and fees charged to students ("sticker price"). Students who attend institutions of higher education, regardless of whether they attend public or private colleges or universities, or whether they receive financial aid, typically receive a general subsidy. This general subsidy does not include subsidies some students receive from scholarships and other types of financial aid.

The Commission has also found that the traditional disregard of capital assets in discussions of educational expenditures is a major barrier to understanding the true costs of higher education. For this reason, the Commission has included capital expenditures and assets in its estimates of the cost of education per student, and urges all colleges and universities to include its capital expenditures when estimating the cost of educating students.

The Commission also struggled with ways to classify and present the approximately 3,700 not-for-profit colleges and universities so as best to capture their diversity and character. In discussions of price, certainly the most important distinction to be made is that between private and public institutions. Because the nation's public colleges and universities receive considerable, but varying, support from the states in which they are located, tuitions at public institutions are typically much lower than those at private institutions. And, tuitions at public two-year colleges tend to be even lower than those at four-year institutions.

For the sake of simplicity, and given available data and their limitations, our analysis presents findings for three groups of institutions: public four-year colleges and universities; private four-year colleges and universities; and public two-year colleges (often referred to as community colleges). Moreover, our analysis is limited to one category of students—full-time undergraduates who are financially dependent on their parents and who attend schools in the not-for-profit sector.

Of course, the Commission understands the limitations in its work. There are many ways to group institutions of higher education and the categories chosen do not reflect all institutions: it does not consider proprietary (i.e., profit-making) institutions. It also knows that it is not only full-time dependent undergraduates who experience difficulty covering their expenses. The Commission is concerned about students experiencing financial difficulty, whatever their status and wherever they go to school. However, given available data and their limitations, the Commission feels most confident drawing conclusions about full-time undergraduates in the not-for-profit sector using these institutional categories.

TRENDS IN COSTS, PRICES, AND SUBSIDIES

Although most public discussion of the affordability of higher education focuses on tuition charges and increases, tuition (i.e., "sticker price") is but one component of the college cost/price picture. As noted, the total price (tuition plus other educational expenses), net price, and instructional cost per student—and the complex interrelationships among these concepts—should all be included in discussions of why the price of attending college may be increasing. Below we present what we have learned about costs, prices, and generalized subsidy for our three types of institutions and how they have changed over time. (See Figure 2.)

Public four-year colleges and universities. Between 1987 and 1996,[4] the instructional cost per student increased from $7,922, on average, to $12,416, an increase of 57 percent. During this same period, the sticker price increased considerably faster, 132 percent, from an average of $1,688 to $3,918. The general subsidy, which averaged $6,234 in 1987, increased 36 percent, to approximately $8,500 in 1996. Thus, the sticker price, or tuition, increased much faster than either instructional costs or the subsidy. During part of this period—between fiscal years 1990-91 and 1992-93—state appropriations in 16 states declined and tuitions in many of these states increased much higher than in previous years. In most of these states, appropriations began to increase again in 1994. Thus, declines in state appropriations to higher education during a small portion of this period cannot totally account for the rate at which public four-year tuitions rose between 1987 and 1996. In public four-year colleges and universities, the percentage of total student costs covered by the general subsidy declined from 79 percent to 68 percent.

Private four-year colleges and universities. In these institutions, the cost per student increased between 1987 and 1996 from an average of $10,911 to $18,387. This represents a 69 percent increase. Tuition, or sticker price, increased by 99 percent—lower in percentage terms than for the public four-year colleges, but higher in real-money terms because of the higher base, from $6,665 to $13,250. Even in the private sector, the percentage of per-student costs covered by the general subsidy declined by 11 percentage points, from 39 percent in 1987 to 28 percent in 1996. The Commission does not understand the sources of subsidies in private institutions as well as it does subsidies in public institutions; endowment income cannot be a complete explanation since it only represents a significant contribution to a relatively small number of colleges and universities.

Public two-year colleges. For these institutions, total costs per student increased by 52 percent between 1987 and 1996, from an average of $5,197 to $7,916. Sticker prices increased 85 percent, from $710 to $1,316. Similar to the situation for public four-year colleges and universities, subsidies to public two-year colleges declined for part of this period. Among all three institutional types, the decrease in the general subsidy was lowest for public two-year colleges; here the percentage of total costs covered by the general subsidy declined only from 86 to 83 percent.

FIGURE 2

Cost, Tuition, and General Subsidy: 1987 to 1996

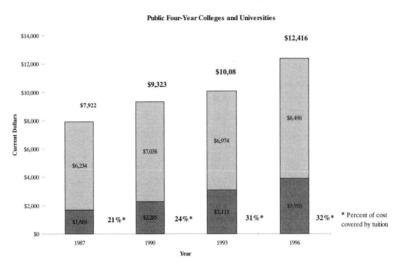

Public Four-Year Colleges and Universities

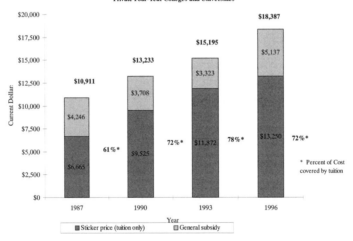

Private Four-Year Colleges and Universities

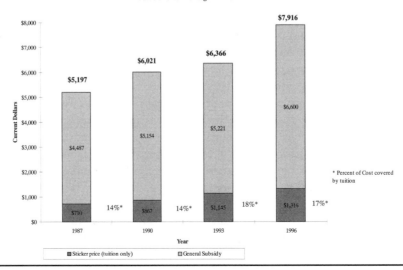

Public Two-Year Colleges and Universities

In all three institutional categories, tuition (or sticker price) increased faster than cost per student between 1987 and 1996. It may be tempting to conclude that institutions acted irresponsibly, by charging students and their families higher tuition but not spending the additional revenue to improve or maintain the quality of the education provided. However, tuition is not the sole source of institutional revenue, and if other revenues declined, institutions may have been forced to increase their tuition revenue. We know that state appropriations to public higher education declined during part of this period and tuitions in many state institutions escalated even faster at that time. At best we can conclude that tuition appears to have increased faster than institutional costs in all types of colleges and universities. We believe that institutions themselves should explain to the public why this occurs.

TRENDS IN COLLEGE AFFORDABILITY

The above discussion sheds light on the relationship between trends in higher education costs and sticker prices; however, it says little about the affordability of higher education for those who pay for it. If tuition had doubled over the past decade but incomes tripled during that same time, the general public may not be nearly as concerned about the affordability of higher education. However, the fact is that by two common measures of income— median household income and per capita disposable income—college tuition increased faster than income.

Before turning to a comparison of tuition and income, it is important to reiterate that a discussion of college affordability must account for the fact that many students do not pay the total price to attend college. Not only does total price not reflect the full *cost* of higher education, because of the subsidies described above, many students do not pay the total price of attendance, because they receive financial aid. A discussion of college affordability, therefore, must examine the prices that students *actually* pay for their education (i.e., after financial aid), which we refer to in this report as the *net price*.

Income and net price. Two calculations of net price are presented here since they represent two fairly different concepts. The first calculation only subtracts grants from the total price. The result represents a measure of *affordability*, the actual amount a student has to pay. The second calculation subtracts all financial aid (grants, loans, and work-study) from the total price. The Commission believes that this measure represents *access* to higher education, because, even though the loans must be repaid eventually and the student must work to receive work-study money, without this aid, the student might not be able to get in the door of any institution.

Between 1987 and 1996, median family income rose 37 percent and disposable per-capita income rose 52 percent. During this same period, both measures of net price rose considerably faster. (See Table 3.) Specifically, the price of attendance minus grants rose 114 percent at public four-year institutions, 81 percent at private four-year institutions, and 159 percent at public two-year institutions. Total price minus all financial aid (grants, loans, and work-study) demonstrates a similar pattern: this measure of net price increased 95 percent at four-year institutions, 64 percent at private four-year institutions, and 169 percent at public two-year institutions.

TABLE 3						
Changes in Total Price of Attendance and Net Prices, 1987 to 1996						
	Public Four-year		**Private Four-year**		**Public Two-year**	
	1987	1996	1987	1996	1987	1996
Total per-student price	$5,146	$10,759	$10,896	$20,003	$2,808	$6,761
Percent change		(109%)		(84%)		(141%)
Total price minus grants	$4,385	$9,365	$8,307	$15,069	$2,345	$6,067
Percent change		(114%)		(81%)		(159%)
Total price minus all aid	$3,715	$7,262	$6,823	$11,205	$2,125	$5,717
Percent change		(95%)		(64%)		(169%)

Source: National Postsecondary Student Aid Study, 1996.

It is important to note, however, that changes in net price appear to have moderated between 1993 and 1996. Indeed, for students attending public four-year institutions, our measure of affordability (total price minus grants) increased only 10 percent for this time period and our measure of access (total price minus all aid) actually did not increase. Private four-year institutions followed a similar pattern, with total price minus grants only increasing by 4 percent between 1993 and 1996 and total price minus all aid declining slightly, by approximately 7 percent. These changes should be interpreted cautiously; sticker price did not increase as fast relative to median family income or disposable per capita income across this time period as it did in earlier time periods, but increases nonetheless occurred. The apparent moderation in net price can more likely be attributed to increased availability of financial aid, particularly loans.

Over the total time period examined, 1987 to 1996, total student aid from all sources increased by 128 percent. Although three-quarters of all aid comes from Federal sources, the largest *rate* of increase in aid during this period came from institutional sources, which went up by 178 percent.[5] Within the Federal programs, the lion's share of the increase was in loan volume under the guaranteed student-loan programs—the Federal Family Education Loan and Federal Direct Student Loan (FFEL/FDSL). The number of recipients obtaining loans under these programs increased by 87 percent between 1987 and 1996.[6] Because a greater number of students received aid, Federal aid per recipient was less than the increase in aid spending. Average Pell grant awards, for example, increased 21 percent, and the FFEL/FDSL awards by 41 percent.[7]

REFERENCES

[1] U.S. Department of Education, *Digest of Education Statistics 1996*, Table 309.

[2] James Harvey and John Immerwahr, *Goodwill and Growing Worry: Public Perceptions of Higher Education*. (Washington: American Council on Education, 1994.)

[3] Appendix G, Exhibit 1-1a.

[4] These years are examined because our basic financial aid data come from the National Postsecondary Student Aid Study, which was conducted in 1987, 1990, 1993, and 1997.

[5] Appendix G, Exhibit 6-1.

[6] Appendix G, Exhibit 6-3.

[7] Appendix G, Exhibit 6-3.

"Cost and Price Drivers" in Higher Education

What lies behind increases in tuition? Several of the issues that Congress asked the Commission to address point to potential explanations for rising college costs with the assumption that rising costs result in rising prices. The "cost drivers" that the Commission reviewed can be grouped into six categories: (1) financial aid, (2) people, (3) facilities, (4) technology, (5) regulations, and (6) expectations.

Financial Aid. The Commission reviewed a number of studies on the connection between student financial aid in public and private non-profit institutions of higher education and costs and prices, and it commissioned two analyses of its own. (Figure 3 describes the major programs of Federal student aid—grants and work-study, loans, and newly-enacted tax incentives.)

The Commission finds no evidence to suggest any relationship between the availability of Federal grants and the costs or prices in these institutions. Less than one student in four receives a Federal grant, which pays for less than 10 percent of the total price of attendance in either sector. And, although the methodology of financial need analysis is tuition-sensitive, the maximum Pell grant award is capped at $3,000.

The Commission has found no conclusive evidence that loans have contributed to rising costs and prices. One commissioned paper suggests that Federal loan availability has helped contribute to rising prices.

Another paper suggests that the capital available through loans has allowed colleges to increase their charges—and allowed independent colleges in particular to maintain enrollment—in ways that would not have been possible otherwise.

The Commission knows of other studies which come to conclusions opposite to these. This question should be studied in greater detail and with much greater attention to empirical facts.

The members of the Commission are, however, unanimously concerned about sharp increases in student borrowing. What is unclear is whether these increases have occurred because (1) higher loan limits and the new "un-subsidized" program permit more borrowing; (2) more families are choosing to finance college expenses through loans rather than from savings or current income; or (3) the price of attending higher education has increased. The Commission's judgment is that all three factors are probably involved.

Finally, the Commission looked at the relationship between institutional financial aid and increases in student prices. In this instance, there is slightly stronger evidence that increases in institutional aid have been one of the cost and price drivers, as institutional aid grew by 178 percent between 1987 and 1996. Since most of the revenue for institutional aid comes from tuition dollars, it seems reasonable to conclude that tuitions could have increased slightly less had institutions not been putting these revenues into institutional aid. At the same time, however, had institutions not generated revenue to pay for institutional aid, student borrowing would have had to increase to maintain access, or access would have had to diminish.

FIGURE 3

The Complex Picture of Student Financial Aid

The major Federal programs providing financial assistance to students can be thought of in three categories: grants, loans and tax incentives of various kinds. Most of these are directed to low- and middle-income students with financial need.

Grants and Work Study

The Pell Grant Program provides awards of between $400 and $3,000 for low-income students, most of whom are from families with annual incomes below $20,000. This program is funded at $7.34 billion in Fiscal Year 1998.

The Supplemental Educational Opportunity Grant Program provides additional grant aid to students from extremely low-income families. This program is funded at $614 million in Fiscal Year 1998.

FIGURE 3 (continued)

The Federal Work Study Program helps to pay for jobs on- and off-campus as part of need-based financial aid packages. Unlike the Pell and supplemental grant programs, which are available only to undergraduate students, Federal Work Study aid also assists graduate and professional students. This program is funded at $830 million in Fiscal Year 1998.

Loan Programs

A variety of loan programs, many with interest subsidized and deferred, exist to help cover college tuition and other expenses for undergraduate, graduate, and professional students. The Perkins Loan Program (formerly the National Defense Loan Program) provides low-interest loans to low-income students. Perkins Loan funds, which are a combination of Federal and institutional capital contributions, are administered on campus. Additional loan capital is generated as collections on prior loans are deposited into the institution's revolving fund.

Stafford Loans are available to students from all income levels. Students who demonstrate financial need are eligible for interest subsidies; students who do not demonstrate need, while not eligible for interest subsidies, may defer loan and interest payments while in school and under certain other circumstances. PLUS Loans provide assistance to parents of students of dependent undergraduate students in an amount up to the cost of college attendance less other financial aid. Both the Stafford and Plus loan programs are available through financial institutions (Federal Financial Education Loan Program) or directly through the Federal Government (William D. Ford Direct Loan Program). Roughly two-thirds of $30 billion in current annual loan volume is provided through the former, the remaining loan capital is provided by the latter.

Tax Incentives

The budget agreement hammered out by Congressional and White House negotiators in August 1997 provided about $40 billion over five years in tax breaks to help students pay for higher education. They include:

Hope Scholarships, aimed at making two years of college universally available, provide a dollar for dollar nonrefundable tax credit for 100 percent of the first $1,000 of tuition and fees and 50 percent of the second $1,000. Available for college enrollment after January 1, 1998, the credit phases out for joint filers with incomes between $80,000 and $100,000, and for single filers between $40,000 and $50,000.

College juniors, seniors and graduate students may receive a nonrefundable 20 percent tax credit on the first $5,000 of tuition and fees through 2002 (and the first $10,000, thereafter). To encourage lifelong learning, the credit is also available to working Americans. The credit, effective after July 1, 1998, is phased out at the same income levels as the Hope Scholarship. Unlike the Hope Scholarship, the Lifetime Learning Credit is calculated on a per family, rather than a per student, basis.

Education and Retirement Savings Accounts allow penalty-free IRA withdrawals for undergraduate and graduate programs and postsecondary vocational programs. In addition, eligible taxpayers can deposit $500 annually into an education IRA which will accumulate earnings tax-free, with no taxes due until withdrawal for approved purposes.

Other Major Provisions: Workers can exclude $5,250 of employer provided education benefits from taxable incomes; eligible taxpayers can deduct up to $2,500 per year of interest paid on education loans and exclude from taxable income loan amounts forgiven for participating in community service jobs; and taxpayers are exempt from taxation on some earnings on pre-paid tuition plans.

People. Three groups of people are associated with higher education costs: students, administrators, and faculty. Changes in the composition of—or policies regarding—these groups can contribute to rising costs.

Students. Changes in the students who now attend our nation's colleges and universities have the potential for increasing institutional costs. In recent years, college campuses have found themselves populated with more part-time and older students. Between 1980 and 1994, the percentage of undergraduates enrolled part-time, for example, increased from 28 percent to 42 percent of all students enrolled.

"Nontraditional" students bring with them some nontraditional needs, such as child care, re-entry counseling, and tutoring, to name but a few possibilities. Since tuition structures typically do not reflect differing student needs and use of services, the cost of educating part-time and older students could be increasing costs. Furthermore, standard practices of estimating the educational costs per full-time-equivalent student (e.g., three part-time students are considered equivalent to one full-time student) probably do not capture the real costs of educating part-time students.

The need to offer remedial courses to students could also contribute to rising costs. Approximately 78 percent of all colleges and universities that enroll freshmen offered some type of remedial course (typically reading, writing, or mathematics) in the fall of 1995. Although it is difficult to provide national estimates of the costs, data for individual institutions exists. For example, in 1993-94, California spent $9.3 million to provide remedial courses for students on the 22 campuses of the California State University system, representing just under one percent of the system's total budget.

A Florida legislative report said that, with nearly 70 percent of community college freshmen requiring remedial education courses, Florida community colleges are spending $53 million a year providing this type of instruction.

Increasing accessibility for students with disabilities is also a potential cost driver. While no one argues the necessity of providing access and related services, the cost is relatively new and it is real. Estimates of the cost of complying with the Americans with Disabilities Act (ADA) range from an average of $694,000 for public two-year institutions to $12,867,000 for public research institutions.

Administrators. The need to employ more administrators to cover both expanded services and larger numbers of Federal, state, and local regulations combined with higher administrative salaries is thought to drive up administrative costs.

This contention may be true for the first half of the 1980s, when administrative expenditures increased as a share of total educational and general (E&G) expenditures, but, between 1987 and 1994, administrative expenditures either remained the same or fell, as a percentage of total E&G expenditures. Another way of looking at rising administrative costs is that administrative expenditures per full-time-equivalent (FTE) student increased over 22 percent between 1979 and 1986, but less than 1 percent between 1986 and 1993, after adjusting for inflation. The expenditures for student services costs increased 16 percent during each of the two time periods in question.

Faculty. Many believe that the labor structure and tenure system of college faculty drive up college costs. It is true that higher education is a labor-intensive industry and that changes in policies that affect the number of faculty required to teach courses as well as the types of faculty hired (part-time vs. full-time, tenured vs. non-tenured) have an impact on an institution's cost of providing education.

There is little evidence to suggest, however, that changes in faculty hiring practices or workload have driven up college costs in the past decade. In fact, there has been movement in the opposite direction. In an effort to control costs, institutions have hired more part-time and non-tenured faculty and increased the number of hours faculty spend in the classroom: the proportion of part-time faculty and staff employed by colleges and universities increased from 33 percent of all instructional faculty and staff in 1987 to 42 percent in 1992. In the same period, the percentage of instructional faculty and staff with tenure declined from 58 to 54 percent. And, the reported number of student contact hours at all institutions increased from 300 in 1987 to 337 in 1992.

Facilities. Growth in higher education enrollments over the past 30 years has meant that colleges and universities have had to construct new classrooms, laboratories, and dormitories to accommodate students. Serving students with special needs has also meant that higher education institutions have had to redesign classrooms, dormitories, and other public spaces.

Looking to the future with regard to campus facilities' needs does not provide a rosy picture. A 1997 study completed by the Association of Higher Education Facilities Officers, the National Association of College and University Business Officers, and Sallie Mae estimates deferred maintenance costs for all campus facilities to be approximately $26 billion.

Facilities could thus become a major cost driver in the next decade.

Technology. The percentages of courses using technology in a variety of capacities has risen significantly just since 1994.

Institutions must provide equipment for faculty and students as well as the infrastructure to accommodate it. Given the age of many campus buildings and the state of the infrastructure to support this equipment, this expense is substantial.

To cover the costs of technology, some campuses have instituted mandatory computer/instructional technology fees, thus passing on some of the costs to students. These fees ranged from an average of $55 per student in community colleges to $140 in public universities.

It appears that increasing costs for technology almost certainly translate into higher prices charged to students.

Although technology holds promise for making educational operations more efficient and less costly, there is no evidence to date to indicate that the use of technology in higher education has resulted in cost savings to colleges and universities.

Regulations. The number and types of regulations with which colleges and universities are asked to comply have grown rapidly in recent years. Complying with these regulations costs money. The Federal government regulates colleges and universities through a maze of mandates covering personnel, students, laboratory animals, buildings, and the environment. Stanford University, for example, estimates that the university incurs approximately $20 million a year (or 7.5 cents of every tuition dollar) in costs related to complying with a range of regulations.

The cost of accreditation has also increased in recent years. There has been significant growth in the number of accrediting bodies, particularly specialized ones. Currently, accrediting activities are undertaken by approximately 60 specialized agencies overseeing more than 100 different types of academic programs. Institutions report that the self-study procedures involved with these accrediting efforts overlap and duplicate one another and absorb large amounts of faculty and administrator time.

Expectations. Less concrete than the other cost and price drivers are changing expectations about quality. Prospective students visiting college campuses today expect to see gyms with state-of-the-art exercise equipment. Students also expect a complete range of course offerings, dormitories that are wired for computers as well as stereo equipment, and specialized counselors who can advise on personal as well as career and job placement matters. The changing student population has also brought changing expectations to campus. Parents look for child care on campus; older students returning to college anticipate counseling relevant to their interests; and part-time students who work during the day expect courses (and administrative services) to be available on evenings and weekends. These changing expectations cost money.

The expectations of faculty and administrators have also been changing. The curriculum has become more specialized and institutions now support entire disciplines that did not exist a generation or two ago. Many faculty also prefer to teach only certain courses, or to restrict their undergraduate teaching to upper-division courses. And, in many institutions, faculty also expect the university to provide space, equipment, and time for their research.

Many of these expectations—from parents and students and administrators and faculty members—are perfectly reasonable standing alone. But in combination, the accumulated effect of these expectations is continual institutional pressure to increase spending.

THE OPAQUE RELATIONSHIP BETWEEN COSTS AND PRICES

A number of different factors contribute to increasing higher education costs. However, linking specific cost increases to price increases is a tricky matter: Quite simply, the available data on higher education expenditures and revenues make it difficult to ascertain direct relationships among cost drivers and increases in the price of higher education.

Institutions of higher education, even to most people in the academy, are financially opaque. Academic institutions have made little effort, either on campus or off, to make themselves more transparent, to explain their finances. As a result, there is no readily available information about college costs and prices—nor is there a common national reporting standard for either. (National does not mean Federal; it means a standard that is understood and commonly accepted in the profession.) Indeed, differences in financial reporting standards that have evolved in the current environment of quasi-self-regulation contribute to confusion about how to measure costs in a straightforward way. Colleges report on financial standards using one methodology; report expenditures using another; and conform to government cost-recovery principles with yet a third.

What the Commission can assert, however, is a basic fact about academic finance: Virtually no activity, other than self-supporting auxiliary enterprises such as dormitories and cafeterias, generates enough revenue to pay for itself. Everything is "subsidized" to a greater or lesser extent, either through tax revenues, endowment income, or private giving.

In addition, there are wide disparities in expenditure levels between and among different instructional levels and disciplines. For example, courses in the "hard" sciences typically are more expensive to offer than courses in the humanities or social sciences. Yet most institutions do not charge higher tuition for higher cost programs, and lab fees (when assessed) barely begin to cover the costs. Or, to take another example, it is clear that on most campuses undergraduate instruction usually, but not always, costs less to provide than graduate education. But differences in tuition and fee levels for undergraduate and graduate courses of study generally do not reflect the true cost differential.

The truth is that institutions prefer not to look too hard at these matters, both because a broad-based curriculum is a desirable thing in and of itself and because of a desire to base decisions on quality and not on costs.

This Commission, therefore, finds itself in the discomfiting position of acknowledging that the nation's academic institutions, justly renowned for their ability to analyze practically every other major economic activity in the United States, have not devoted similar analytic attention to their own internal financial structures. Blessed, until recently, with sufficient resources that allowed questions about costs or internal cross-subsidies to be avoided, academic institutions now find themselves confronting hard questions about whether their spending patterns match their priorities and about how to communicate the choices they have made to the public.

Convictions and Recommendations

Based on its review of college affordability, this Commission has arrived at five key convictions about the college cost and price crisis:

Conviction 1: The concern about rising college prices is real. The Commission has observed the anxiety in parents' faces as they talk about the price of sending their children to college. People consider a college degree as essential to their children's future, as something of great value because it promises their children a better life. And, they also worry that access and opportunity are slipping away. These are genuine public fears to which academic institutions must respond.

Although concerns and perceptions about price are not entirely wrong, they are not always based on sound factual information. Moreover, as we have noted, institutions of higher education are not always fiscally transparent. Academic leaders must address these issues.

Here, however, academic institutions face a genuine challenge. It is quite clear from parents this Commission talked with, that many members of the general public have little interest in complicated explanations of higher education finance. As important as these matters are for institutional leaders, parents are interested simply in what they will have to pay when their children go to college—indeed if they can afford to send them at all. In responding to public concerns about prices, academic leaders must provide information that is comprehensive, comprehensible, accessible, and persuasive.

Conviction 2: The public and its leaders are concerned about where higher education places its priorities. We have relearned something most academic leaders always knew: higher education costs are driven by people and by how these people spend their time.

But, because academic institutions do not account differently for time spent directly in the classroom and time spent on other scholarly activities, it is almost impossible to explain to the public how individuals employed in higher education use their time. Consequently, the public and public officials find it hard to be confident that academic leaders allocate resources effectively and well. Questions about costs and their allocation to research, service, and teaching are hard to discuss in simple, straightforward ways—and the connection between these activities and student learning is difficult to draw. In responding to this growing concern, academic leaders have been hampered by poor information and sometimes inclined to take issue with those who asked for better data. Academic institutions need much better definitions and measures of how faculty members, administrators, and students use their time.

The skepticism underlying this concern about where higher education places its priorities is a major consequence of higher education's inability to explain its cost and price structure convincingly to the public. Some cost data are unavailable; much of the information that is provided is hard to understand. College finances are far too opaque. Higher education has a major responsibility to make its cost and price structures much more "transparent," i.e., easily understandable to the public and its representatives.

Conviction 3: Confusion about cost and price abounds and the distinction between the two must be recognized and respected. Issues of cost, price, subsidy, and net price have been difficult for the members of this Commission to master. They are equally, if not more confusing to members of the public. These are complex topics, and higher education must strive continuously to clarify and communicate them clearly and candidly.

Beyond that, American families are confused and poorly informed—not only about costs and prices, but also about the entire matter of how to access higher education and its complicated system of financial aid.

The Commission believes that the message about prices (what students and families actually pay) is more encouraging than much of the public dialogue acknowledges, even if it is not entirely comforting. Moreover, the increase in the price students are asked to pay has begun to moderate in recent years. Academic institutions must continue their efforts to control costs—and hence prices—or risk the unpalatable alternative of government intervention.

Conviction 4: Rising costs are just as troubling a policy issue as rising prices. This Commission is concerned because institutional costs (not just prices) are also rising. Unless cost increases are reduced, prices in the long run cannot be contained without undermining quality or limiting access.

Some of the factors behind these cost increases can be understood and explained. As noted previously, tuition tends to go up as public subsidies go down. Administrative costs have increased as a share of total expenditures. The expense of building or renovating facilities and of acquiring and implementing modern technologies has the potential of becoming a significant cost driver. The cost of providing institutional aid (or discounting tuition sticker prices) for needy students increased by nearly 180 percent in the ten years between 1987-88 and 1996-97. Federal, state, and local laws, regulations, and mandates have undoubtedly added to academic costs.

Some policymakers worry that Federal financial aid might have encouraged tuition increases. This Commission is confident that Federal grants have not had such an effect, at either public or private institutions. The Commission believes no conclusive evidence exists with respect to *Federal loans* and believes this issue deserves serious and in-depth additional study.

Aside from such general observations, the Commission does not have solid information to help identify specific factors driving cost and price increases. The simple truth is that no single factor can be identified to explain how and why college costs rise. The Commission suspects that part of the underlying dynamic is the search for academic prestige and the academic reward systems governing higher education. This institutional emphasis on academic status is reinforced by a system of regional and specialized accreditation that often encourages increased expenditures by practically every institution.

The complexity of the interrelationships among these and other factors convinces the Commission that policymakers should avoid simple, one-size-fits-all solutions to the challenge of controlling or reducing college costs. Costs are increasing for a variety of reasons. The response to these mixed and subtle causes, must be similarly mixed and sophisticated.

Conviction 5: The United States has a world-class system of higher education. The United States has a diverse system, one that provides more opportunities to acquire a high-quality education, for citizens of all ages and backgrounds, than any other society. American higher education is a public *and* a private good. American academic institutions represent an investment in the nation's future, one that yields dividends every day, for both individuals and society. It is little wonder that the world has beaten a path to the door of the American university.

Nonetheless, Academic leaders cannot take the continued pre-eminence of their institutions for granted. Although it requires a long time to build an outstanding nationwide system of higher education, such a system can deteriorate very rapidly. In the Commission's judgment, one of the few things capable of precipitating such a decline in the United States would be an erosion of public trust so serious that it undermined ongoing financial support for the nation's academic enterprise. Continued inattention to the imperative to make academic institutions more financially transparent threatens just such an erosion.

RECOMMENDATIONS: AN ACTION AGENDA

The Commission believes its analysis of some of the national data about higher education finance has broken new ground, especially in clarifying the connections between and among cost, price, subsidy, and affordability. Nevertheless, the best national data are insufficient to provide the kind of clear information on these trends that policymakers and the general public need. For example, the terms of analysis used by different parties are not always consistently defined: institutional costs and student costs are two different things; prices and costs are not the same; and prices charged and prices paid often bear little relationship to each other.

The persistent blurring of terms (both within and beyond higher education) contributes to system-wide difficulties in clarifying the relationship between cost and quality; defining the difference between price and cost;

distinguishing between what institutions charge and what students pay; and ultimately to systemic difficulties in controlling costs and prices.

If we are to clarify these relationships and control expenses, several things must happen. Academic institutions should start to use these terms systematically and regularly; policymakers must realize that costs and subsidies need to be better managed if prices are to be controlled; and academic leaders must acknowledge that, before they can manage costs and explain prices to the public, they themselves have to do a better job of measuring and understanding both.

The Commission organizes its recommendations around a five-part action agenda grounded in the concept of shared responsibility. Many different participants have contributed to the academic cost dilemma; all of them must be involved in resolving it. In the Commission's view, these actors have a shared responsibility for achieving five policy goals:

- strengthening institutional cost control;
- improving market information and public accountability;
- deregulating higher education;
- rethinking accreditation; and
- enhancing and simplifying Federal student aid.

Sharing Responsibility. The Commission is convinced that many different stakeholders have contributed to the college cost and price crisis; consequently, all of them will have to contribute to the solution. We believe institutions of higher education, government at all levels—Federal, state and local—the philanthropic community, and families and students have essential and complementary roles to play in maintaining affordable, high-quality education well into the future. Each of these stakeholders in some fashion influences or subsidizes the cost and price of American higher education. They have a common obligation to respond to the issues outlined in this report: Government needs to invest in higher education as a public good; foundations should continue to support policy research and the search for innovation; parents should be prepared to pay their fair share of college expenses; and students should arrive at college prepared for college-level work.

But without doubt, the greatest benefits depend on academic institutions shouldering their responsibility to contain costs, and ultimately prices. Although the responsibility for controlling costs and prices is widely shared, the major onus rests with the higher education community itself.

I. STRENGTHEN INSTITUTIONAL COST CONTROL

THE COMMISSION RECOMMENDS *that academic institutions intensify their efforts to control costs and increase institutional productivity.*

The Commission is convinced that academic institutions have done a lot to control costs but they must achieve more in the way of cost containment and productivity improvement. The drive for greater efficiency, productivity, and fiscal transparency requires an expanded definition of academic citizenship, one that is broadly participatory, involving faculty, administrators, students, staff, and trustees.

The effort the Commission is calling for should challenge the basic assumptions governing how institutions think about quality and costs. This will require a greater willingness to focus institutional resources on a few priority areas where excellence can be sustained. It should include new cost saving partnerships among institutions.

The Commission believes it is impossible to formulate an effective single set of directives on cost control applicable to the diverse institutional settings and missions of American colleges and universities. The responsibility for cost control, like the responsibility for quality improvement, must be shouldered by each institution.

In recent years, American colleges and universities have made major efforts to reduce expenditures and control costs. The Commission applauds this progress; however, it also believes that much more must be accomplished. To do so, the academic community must focus sustained attention on its own internal financial structures, the better to understand and ultimately control costs and prices. To that end, the Commission makes ten implementing recommendations to strengthen cost control and improve institutional productivity.

Implementing Recommendations:

1. Individual institutions, acting with technical support from appropriate higher education associations, should conduct efficiency self-reviews to identify effective cost-saving steps that are relevant to institutional mission and quality improvement.

2. Academic leaders should communicate the results of these self-reviews widely, providing the campus community and institutional constituents with information on issues such as administrative costs, faculty teaching loads, average class size, faculty and student ratios, facilities management, and expenditures on technology.

3. The Commission recommends the creation of a national effort led by institutions of higher education, the philanthropic community, and others to study and consider alternative approaches to collegiate instruction which might improve productivity and efficiency. The Commission believes significant gains in productivity and efficiency can be made through the basic way institutions deliver most instruction, i.e., faculty members meeting with groups of students at regularly scheduled times and places. It also believes that alternative approaches to collegiate instruction deserve further study. Such a study should consider ways to focus on the results of student learning regardless of time spent in the traditional classroom setting.

4. The Commission recommends similar national attention be devoted to developing new alternative approaches to thinking about faculty careers, beginning with graduate school education and extending to tenure and post-tenure review. These should explicitly consider the many ways in which tenure policies vary across institutions.

5. The Commission recommends greater institutional and regional cooperation in using existing facilities at institutions of higher education. Implementation of this recommendation will vary within and across states. Whenever expansion of higher education is contemplated, the existing capacity of all institutions should be considered, including the promotion of greater access through financial aid.

6. The Commission recommends maximizing the opportunity for cost savings through joint campus purchase of goods and services and joint use of facilities, pursuing these opportunities through many different kinds of partnerships. Where necessary, states should consider statutory changes to make such partnerships possible.

7. The Commission recommends greater use of consortia and joint planning to maximize access to expensive academic programs. While acknowledging that some inefficiencies and redundancies are inevitable in America's diverse and decentralized system of higher education, the Commission believes that greater emphasis on consortia and joint planning offers significant opportunities for cost control. In states and regions with large numbers of institutions, creative ways need to be found to make the programmatic variety of each campus available to as many students as possible.

8. The Commission recommends that the philanthropic community, research institutes, and agencies of state and local government adopt the topic of academic cost control as a research area worthy of major financial support. In addition to grants to support efforts to undertake such changes, best-practice and recognition-award programs should be established and supported.

9. As part of the recognition-award effort, the National Association of College and University Business Officers should, in consultation with major higher education associations, develop programs that publicize innovative institutional practices that help control costs. As part of this effort, higher education associations should jointly seek foundation support for annual awards to public and independent colleges and universities that have pioneered cost-management strategies.

10. Finally, we urge Congress to support academic efforts to control costs and improve productivity by:
    a) amending Public Law 100-107 (which created the Malcolm Baldrige Award to recognize continuous quality improvement in the corporate sector) to include education; and
    b) authorizing in the next reauthorization cycle the U.S. Department of Education's Fund for the Improvement of Post Secondary Education (FIPSE) to continue to offer financial support for projects addressing issues of productivity, efficiency, quality improvement, and cost control.

II. IMPROVE MARKET INFORMATION AND PUBLIC ACCOUNTABILITY

THE COMMISSION RECOMMENDS *that the academic community provide the leadership required to develop better consumer information about costs and prices and to improve accountability to the general public.*

The Commission is convinced that both policymakers and the general public need more useful, accurate, timely, and understandable information on college costs, prices, and the different subsidies that benefit all students. Leadership for this effort should come from the academy, from both institutions and higher education associations; but to be really effective, the entire thrust requires a partnership engaging appropriate Federal agencies, states, leaders of the press and electronic media, and the private sector.

For policymakers and the general public to act in a well-informed manner, more timely and reliable data are essential. The Commission was troubled by the sheer amount of incomplete and outdated information available from academic and government sources. Terms of analysis like cost, price, and subsidy are not clearly defined or generally understood. Financial standards, expenditure reports, and cost-recovery principles all rely on different methodologies. There is no common national reporting standard to measure costs or prices.

What is required, first, are comprehensive, easy-to-understand analyses of cost and price issues for different types of institutions by sector (e.g., public and private institutions, two- and four-year, with distinctions between four-year colleges and universities). These analyses should then be transformed into handbooks, available to the public, that provide the following cost and price information:

- the cost of educating students (i.e., the total institutional expenditure—capital costs included—to provide the education);
- actual tuition charges (i.e., sticker prices);
- the general subsidy (i.e., the cost minus the tuition charge);
- instructional costs by level of instruction;
- the total price of attendance (i.e., tuition, fees and other expenses);
- a net price "affordability" measure (i.e., total price minus grants); and
- a net price "accessibility" measure (i.e., total price minus all financial aid).

Although the Commission was not always able to obtain complete data on all these issues, the approach outlined above is consistent with the one used in this report. The Commission is convinced that these materials should also include information on financial-aid availability and options along with information on different types of institutions and their different price structures. To the extent possible, information should also include total and net prices for full- and part-time, dependent and independent students.

Above all, to be useful, these data should be issued annually. The aim is to provide up-to-date information and illustrate how all potential students—but especially those of limited financial means—can gain access to high-quality postsecondary education. The Commission understands that new accounting standards have been developed for private institutions and are currently being developed for public institutions. Further, the Commission is aware of efforts underway to redesign the Department of Education's Integrated Postsecondary Education Data Survey (IPEDS) to make it compatible with such standards. The recommendations below are offered to emphasize the Commission's belief in the importance of these efforts to the Commission's call for institutions of higher education to become more fiscally transparent, that is, more straightforward in describing to the public where they get their money and how they spend it.

To that end, the Commission makes eight implementing recommendations designed to improve market information and public accountability.

Implementing Recommendations:

1. The Commission calls on the higher education community to take the lead in organizing a major public-awareness campaign to inform the public about the actual price of a postsecondary education, the returns on this investment, and family preparation for college.

2. The Commission recommends that individual institutions of higher education annually issue to their constituent families and students information on costs, prices, and subsidies in the way the Commission has approached these issues in this report.

3. The Commission recommends that the U.S. Department of Education collect and make available for analysis not only annual tuition and net price data but also information on the relationship between tuition and institutional expenditures.

4. The Commission strongly encourages multiple agencies in the private sector to use those data for developing college-cost reports or handbooks that are widely disseminated to prospective students, their parents, and the media—in print and over the Internet.

5. The Commission recommends that, where necessary, the format of existing governmental and private higher education data-collection systems and financial reports be modified to allow for collecting and reporting information that calculates costs, prices, and subsidies the way the Commission has approached them in this document.

6. In that regard, IPEDS should be redesigned to collect such information. It can then be made available to any person or institution, in a form that is comparable for public and private institutions. The redesigned survey should include estimates of direct instructional costs by level of instruction, capital expenditures, and the replacement value of capital assets. It should also be expanded to improve data (and data comparability) on faculty compensation and workload as well as on factors related to administrative efficiency.

7. The Commission urges the national accounting standards bodies for institutions of higher education (The Financial Accounting Standards Board for private institutions and the Government Accounting Standards Board for public institutions) take whatever steps are necessary to assure that the financial reports of these institutions offer fiscally transparent information about college finances that allow for valid comparisons between public and private institutions.

8. The Commission recommends the following with respect to the collection and analysis of different kinds of data, particularly financial data:

   a) The National Center for Education Statistics, working with the appropriate organizations, especially higher education associations, should redouble its efforts to ensure that institutions respond in a timely manner to surveys and that survey data are edited and released in a timely manner.

   b) The National Center for Education Statistics should take steps to understand how institutions respond to the IPEDS financial survey, particularly given changes in accounting and reporting standards for private, not-for-profit institutions. This is necessary because there are several acknowledged inconsistencies in the way institutions report the information they are required to submit.

   c) The U.S. Department of Education should undertake a study to gather comprehensive data on the needs of part-time students, including the actual costs to the institutions educating high numbers of such students. This study should be integrated into the Department's higher education data-collection efforts. Given increasing numbers of part-time students and reliance on a formula that equates three part-time students to one full-time student, such a study would provide more accurate and reliable cost measures.

   d) The Commission recommends that the U.S. Department of Education investigate the feasibility of gathering data on proprietary schools and the students who attend them.

III. DEREGULATE HIGHER EDUCATION

THE COMMISSION RECOMMENDS *that governments develop new approaches to academic regulation, approaches that emphasize performance instead of compliance, and differentiation in place of standardization.*

Members of the Commission believe that institutions of higher education have a responsibility to be good public citizens, not just in their teaching, research, and service missions, but also as employers, vendors, and good neighbors in their communities. The Commission is also aware that a variety of regulations, some accompanying public funding and some independent of it, are intended to ensure public health and safety or accountability in the use of tax dollars. The Commission clearly supports these goals.

But the Commission is equally convinced that a fresh approach to academic regulation is required—on the part of government at all levels. This Commission received a lot of testimony about the impact of the regulatory environment on college costs. Academic institutions handling small amounts of toxic substances, for example, are subject to the same regulations as manufacturing enterprises handling the same materials by the ton. Prohibitions against mandatory retirement ages were imposed on academic institutions in recent years (after several decades in which colleges and universities had been legislatively exempt from them) without considering the implications of the change on tenure or maintaining faculty vitality. And regulations regarding such issues as student privacy, the right of students to examine their records, and the incidence of crime on campus are redundant and repetitive.

New approaches need to be developed to ensure public accountability in ways that are less costly and more easily manageable. The Commission believes it is time to replace the current command-and-control approach to academic regulation with an approach that emphasizes performance and accommodates the type and volume of regulation to institutional history, size, and need.

To deal with these issues, the Commission presents nine implementing recommendations

Implementing Recommendations:

1. The Commission recommends the repeal of recently-enacted statutory provisions (from the Tax-payer Relief Act of 1997) requiring that academic institutions provide the Internal Revenue Service with personal financial information on enrolled students and their parents. The Commission believes that the reporting burden this creates for institutions has the potential to add major administrative costs to an institution's budget. While acknowledging the need to ensure reasonable taxpayer compliance with IRS provisions, Congress should work with the appropriate representatives of the higher education community to resolve this issue.

2. The Commission recommends that Congress fund a project by the National Research Council, or some appropriate Federal agency, to develop standards in environmental, health, and safety areas that provide for differential regulation of industrial facilities, on the one hand, and research and teaching laboratories and facilities, on the other. The report should make specific recommendations for statutory and regulatory changes that are needed to develop such a differential approach.

3. The Commission recommends that, where possible, statutes require agencies to adopt performance-based models for monitoring compliance rather than command-and-control regulations that prescribe specific approaches. Likewise, statutes should avoid command-and-control language and move toward performance-based requirements.

4. The Commission recommends that state and county governments undertake a thorough examination of the regulatory requirements they have imposed on academic institutions, particularly those that go beyond or differ from Federal requirements. The purpose would be to determine the cost implications of these requirements and whether their benefits justify the costs they impose. Those deemed to be overly burdensome should be repealed.

5. The Commission recommends that, as Congress and the Executive Branch examine issues related to the electronic production of information, colleges and universities be included in the discussions. As both producers and consumers of electronic information, academic institutions are in a unique central position to provide advice on the complex intellectual property issues involved in this area.

6. The Commission recommends that Congress enact a clarification to the Age Discrimination in Employment Act to assure that institutions offering defined-contribution retirement programs are able to offer early retirement incentives to tenured faculty members. The Commission endorses pending Senate Bill 153, which would accomplish this purpose.

7. The Commission recommends that the Higher Education Act and accompanying regulations be rewritten to consolidate provisions related to the mandated disclosure of information to students and employees under legislation such as the Student Right to Know and Campus Crime and Security Acts.

8. The Commission recommends a change in the refund law and implementing regulations to permit institutions of higher education to require students withdrawing from programs to sign a withdrawal form establishing a firm date of withdrawal for refund purposes.

9. The Commission recommends Congress stipulate that institutions with a demonstrated history of sound financial operations and capable administration be deemed "fiscally responsible and administratively capable" of meeting the eligibility requirements under the Higher Education Act. Evidence of such a sound operation could include a showing that the institution is a public institution (i.e., state controlled); that it has been in continuous existence since November 8, 1965 (the date of enactment of the

Higher Education Act); or that it has participated successfully in Title IV programs for ten years or longer. Congress and the U.S. Department of Education might consider adopting the principles of the Federal Trade Commission's successful voluntary compliance programs.

IV. RETHINK ACCREDITATION

THE COMMISSION RECOMMENDS *that the academic community develop well-coordinated, efficient accrediting processes that relate institutional productivity to effectiveness in improving student learning.*

Accreditation is an honored and essential part of higher education. It assures the education community and the public, as well as funding agencies, that the institutions they are attending or supporting merit their confidence. In addition, it provides a useful tool for institutional self-study and accountability that would be inappropriate to government.

Accreditation strives to assure educational quality and institutional integrity. Basic to the accreditation process are periodic self-studies that evaluate an institution or program in light of publicly-stated objectives—and peer evaluation of those self-studies by a visiting team of academic colleagues. Accreditation seeks not only to judge and assure quality and integrity, but to promote improvement through continuous self-study and evaluation. Regional associations accredit an institution as a whole, while specialized accrediting groups accredit specific educational programs within an institution.

The Commission recognizes and encourages the movement underway at all six regional accrediting associations to focus more on assessing student achievement. Accreditation bodies—both regional and specialized—have been inclined to emphasize traditional resource measures as proxies for quality. Such traditional measures are often difficult to link to demonstrated student achievement. Specialized or professional accreditation has, for the most part, continued to focus on resource measures in making judgments about quality. In fact, to many campus observers, they appear often to be acting more in the economic interest of the professions they represent than in the interest of assuring student achievement.

Moreover, specialized accreditation has, in the eyes of many, taken on a life of its own. It has become too complicated, occurs too often, and makes the case for additional resources to support programs of interest to them without regard to the impact on the welfare of the entire institution.

Today, some 60 specialized accrediting agencies oversee more than 100 different academic programs—ranging from architecture, business, and engineering to journalism, law, medicine, and far beyond. The time-consuming self-study procedures involved with specialized accreditation, the focus on additional resources without regard to their connection to student learning or the welfare of the larger institution, and the expensive duplication involved with different entities, increase red tape and drive up costs.

The Commission believes a great deal of improvement is possible in developing both accrediting standards and evaluation review processes that focus directly on student learning. It believes accreditation should encourage a greater focus at both the program and institutional level on productivity and efficiency. To address these issues, the Commission presents seven implementing recommendations:

Implementing Recommendations:

1. The Commission recommends that accrediting associations reshape existing standards and review processes to include a greater emphasis on measures of effectiveness—especially student achievement—and less emphasis on resources.

2. The Commission also urges accrediting bodies and their member institutions to devise standards and review processes that support greater institutional productivity, efficiency, and cost constraint.

3. The Commission recommends that, with standards and review processes focused more on output and cost efficiency, institutional self-study processes should concentrate on efficiency, productivity, the wise use of resources, and the extent to which the institution is meeting the educational quality goals defined in its mission.

4. The Commission recommends that the Council on Higher Education Accreditation and its member accrediting agencies give high priority to developing a system to coordinate activities (including self-studies and visits) between regional, national, and specialized accreditors in order to minimize costs and recognize the primacy of regional, institution-wide accreditation.

5. The Commission also urges Congress to consider changes in the Secretary of Education's criteria for institutional recognition to encourage voluntary coordination between institutional and specialized accreditors.

6. The Commission recommends that accrediting agencies develop training programs for staff and visiting review-team members that build greater understanding of cost containment and the skills to assist institutions in examining the relationships between and among student achievement, accrediting standards, and costs.

7. Finally, the Commission urges accrediting agencies to emphasize to their member institutions that concentrating on results is not intended to create a single set of standards for higher education but to indicate the importance of performance as a measure of accountability.

V. ENHANCE AND SIMPLIFY FEDERAL STUDENT AID

THE COMMISSION RECOMMENDS *that Congress continue the existing student aid programs and simplify and improve the financial aid delivery system.*

Despite the complexity of the current Federal student-aid system of grants, loans, campus-based aid, and tax benefits, it provides crucial support to students from widely varying personal and financial circumstances. There is value in preserving the current mix of programs that enhance student choice among a variety of institutions. Nevertheless, the manner in which that aid is delivered confuses students and families, and, despite its variety, the aid system struggles to serve the diverse needs of the many different types of students now attending postsecondary institutions. Meanwhile, student aid regulations from the U.S. Department of Education are so extensive, internally inconsistent, and excessive that it is almost impossible for any college, university or other financial aid provider in the country to be sure it is ever in full compliance.

To maintain a strong Federal financial aid system that will improve access to higher education and make it more affordable to students and families, the Commission makes eight implementing recommendations.

Implementing Recommendations:

1. The Commission recommends that Congress continue the existing Federal grant, loan, and campus-based financial aid programs and where possible, strengthen them and provide additional funding.

2. The Commission recommends that Congress simplify and improve the student financial-aid delivery system. This system should have as its primary goals improving the level of service to students and program participants; reducing the costs of administering Federal student-aid programs; increasing accountability; and providing greater flexibility in managing the functions and operations of the grant, loan, and campus-based aid programs.

3. As part of the effort to streamline aid, the Commission supports involvement of the U.S. Department of Education in efforts to develop Electronic Data Interchange (EDI) standards and other experiments in the use of modern technologies for information sharing among institutions.

4. The Commission recommends that Congress monitor the effectiveness of the new higher education and lifelong-learning tax provisions to determine what effect they have on access, the nature of student financial assistance, and institutional decisions about awards of institutional aid and campus-based financial aid.

5. The Commission recommends that Congress investigate the feasibility of broadening eligibility requirements for Federal student aid to include students attending less than half time. Federal aid should also become more flexible to meet a variety of student circumstances, including accelerated degree completion and year-round eligibility for part-time students and lifelong learners.

6. The Commission recommends that the Secretary of Education be required to review and simplify the Department's financial aid regulations, procedures, and forms, especially forms that families must complete to apply for financial aid. Institutional compliance with regulations and procedures is now extraordinarily difficult and expensive because of the inconsistencies and redundancies in statutes and regulations.

7. The Commission recommends that the U.S. Department of Education consider expanding and strengthening the "case management" approach to eligibility and compliance issues associated with the Higher

Education Act. This will allow the Department and institutions of higher education to consider simultaneously issues like institutional audit, program review, and re-certification, thereby allowing both to better coordinate the use of resources and potentially reduce costs.

8. The Commission recommends that Congress require the Program Review branch of the U.S. Department of Education to make available to every institution certified for Title IV participation, a complete, non-redacted copy of its review guidelines and procedures. The Higher Education Act should also be amended to permit institutions to cure inadvertent errors without penalty.

A Word to Students and Families

Finally, this Commission wants to speak directly to students and their families. We realize that decisions about selecting a college and paying for a college education present tough choices to American families. Our system of higher education is big, diverse, and full of opportunity, but making good decisions about college requires information and preparation. Early in the high school years, students and their families need to be asking questions about what they value and want the most from higher education. What type of school are you looking for? What is most important to you? Who has the information you need and where can you find it?

Selecting the right college takes work and the selection process must begin with the family's own assessment of what it wants. Parents and students need to remember that "more expensive" does not always mean "better." And, just because a school ranks high on a "reputational" survey, does not mean your son or daughter will be happy there.

Beyond that, preparation for college starts with families and students working together on the academic preparation necessary for a successful college experience. The first semester of the senior year is too late to begin laying this foundation. Families and students must begin with a solid foundation in elementary school. The next step is taken when they begin to plan for a rigorous course of study in high school, preferably one that involves four years of college-preparatory English and mathematics, and three years each of science, history and social studies, and foreign language. Once the program is defined, success depends on students really concentrating on their schoolwork and getting the support they need from family and teachers.

The members of this Commission also understand the anxiety involved when families face the prospect of paying for a college education. We do not dismiss it; in no way do we minimize it. On the contrary, all the recommendations in this document were developed with one goal in mind: to keep open the door of higher education by maintaining access at prices students and families can afford.

But institutions, governments, and the philanthropic and higher education communities can only do so much. Students and families have a responsibility to do their part as well. Because a major beneficiary of a college education is the individual involved, those with a genuine commitment to their future, should rightfully shoulder part of the load.

The weight of that load can be substantially lessened with careful financial planning. Families obviously need better information in order to plan well; this Commission has laid out an action agenda to provide much of the needed information. A number of states offer widely-publicized tuition pre-payment plans, and financial institutions are eager to encourage regular savings and investment for higher education. Moreover, the 1997 budget agreement incorporated many attractive new tax features to encourage parents to lay aside funds for their children's' education—including permission to establish tax-deferred educational accounts and to withdraw IRA funds for educational purposes. Combined with the widespread availability of grants and loans, the establishment of new Hope Scholarships, and provisions for tax credits for upperclassmen and women, these new provisions promise to bring a baccalaureate education within the grasp of practically everyone.

Most families need to become better informed about these possibilities, and those with the financial means should make an effort to set aside something for their children's future. The Commission encourages them to do so, confident that higher education is not just an expense but also an investment. The long-term financial return on the investment far exceeds the price students and families pay.

NEXT STEPS: PUTTING IT ALL TOGETHER

The Commission's recommendations constitute a framework of shared responsibility to control institutional costs, improve market information and public accountability, deregulate higher education, redesign accreditation, and enhance and simplify Federal financial aid. It is the Commission's strong belief and clear intent that the short- and long-term financial savings realized by implementing its recommendations be used to maintain access at prices students and families can afford.

Developing recommendations is easier than implementing them. Reports do not implement themselves, but must be put into practice by policymakers, members of the academic community, and citizens. Unfortunately, most reports of this nature rest unread on bookshelves. If that becomes the fate of this document and its recommendations, financial support for higher education could erode and others may step in to impose their own regulatory solutions.

The first step to implementing these recommendations is really in the nature of a plea. Everyone must shoulder his or her share of the burden of improving the situation described herein. If academic leaders, policymakers, and the general public satisfy themselves by blaming others, the situation will not change. All of us together must rise above polemics. We must avoid oversimplification. We believe it is time for straight talk about college costs and prices. To maintain access to higher education at a reasonable price, everyone will have to do more, make sacrifices, and work harder. There is ample work ahead for everyone.

The second step is to move forward with the recommendations outlined above. The Commission's charge from Congress was really quite simple: develop a set of recommendations to help keep college education affordable in the United States. No report can guarantee that result. But the steps outlined in this one point the nation, its educational leaders, its citizens, and its public officials in the right direction.

The third step is to continue the research, at both a technical and a policy level, on issues identified in this report and enumerated in Appendix A, *The Unfinished Agenda*. We believe we have made good progress in shedding new light on questions of cost, price and affordability. Yet much more can and needs to be done to continue research before we or others can claim to fully understand our own enterprise.

The entire Commission has learned during this study process that the profile of America's college students is changing profoundly. As noted in the text, more students are older, attending part time while working, first generation college attendees, lower income, and ethnically diverse. At the same time, there is a growing wave of more traditional full time 18-22 year olds headed toward our universities. Therefore, it is essential that the academic and political communities learn a great deal more about these trends, and then adjust major state and Federal programs accordingly.

Commission Vote

Public Law 105-18 creating the National Commission on the Cost of Higher Education requires "any recommendation…made by the Commission to the president and the Congress [be] adopted by a majority of the commission who are present and voting members." The Commission met on January 21, 1998, to vote on this report and the recommendations contained in it. The report was approved by ten of the eleven members of the Commission. Commissioner Frances McMurtray Norris was not present at the January 21st meeting but later submitted the following statement.

I am pleased to have served as a member of the National Commission on the Cost of Higher Education and I have great respect for my fellow members who have put in long hours of hard work at great inconvenience for little reward. However, I am disappointed by the product of our endeavors.

The report which we now release points out some very real concerns and possible answers to specific issues. I find little in the report with which to disagree but, had I been present for the last meeting, I would have been unable to vote for the final report. It is not what is contained in the report that is of concern to me but what is not. Whether it be from a lack of time or interest or the manner in which we approached our task, this report sorely lacks the substance for which many have waited these past five months.

Issues such as tenure, cost and value of research, duplication of facilities, teaching loads, and relationship of student loan programs to rising costs have not been addressed. These key issues have been substantially ignored in deference to ancillary matters of providing better information, reducing government regulation and improving the financial aid distribution system.

The key issues mentioned above require much deeper study. I suggest that any future commissions include business professionals well versed in controlling costs, parents saving for their children's education, and members of the educational community to ensure that a variety of views are heard. And while we have not provided Congress with the information it needs for reauthorization of The Higher Education Act, our report makes it clear that there are real issues yet to be unearthed. I am hopeful that Congress will challenge the higher education community to confront these problems and search for real solutions. The longer we allow the American public to remain ignorant of the facts, the less likely we are to find genuine solutions.

Endnotes

1. U.S. Department of Education, *Digest of Education Statistics 1996,* Table 309.
2. James Harvey and John Immerwahr, *Goodwill and Growing Worry: Public Perceptions of Higher Education.* (Washington: American Council on Education, 1994.)
3. Appendix G, Exhibit 1-1a.
4. These years are examined because our basic financial aid data come from the National Postsecondary Student Aid Study, which was conducted in 1987, 1990, 1993, and 1997.
5. Appendix G, Exhibit 6-1.
6. Appendix G, Exhibit 6-3.
7. Appendix G, Exhibit 6-3.
8. Arthur M. Hauptman and Cathy Krop, *Federal Student Aid and the Growth in College Costs and Tuition: Examining the Relationship.* (Paper prepared for the National Commission on the Cost of Higher Education.)
9. Alan Reynolds, *The Real Cost of Higher Education, Who Should Pay and How?* (Paper prepared for the National Commission on the Cost of Higher Education.)
10. U.S. Department of Education, *Digest of Education Statistics,* 1996.
11. Board of Trustees Report, California State University, January 24-25, 1995.
12. *The New York Times,* February 13, 1996.
13. Association of Higher Education Facilities Officers. 1997. *A Foundation to Uphold.*
14. U.S. Department of Education, *Digest of Education Statistics,* 1996.
15. U.S. Department of Education. National Center for Education Statistics. *1993 National Study of Postsecondary Faculty Instructional Faculty and Staff in Higher Education Institutions: Fall 1987 and Fall 1992.*
16. Association of Higher Education Facilities Officers, *A Foundation to Uphold,* 1997.
17. Kenneth C. Green, *The National Survey of Information Technology in Higher Education,* October 1997.
18. Kenneth C. Green, *The National Survey,* October 1997.
19. Testimony of Gerhard Casper, President, Stanford University. *The Cost of Higher Education: A Discussion with Commission Members,* October 16, 1997.
20. Appendix G, Issue 3, no page.
21. Appendix G, Issue 5, no page.
22. Appendix G, Issue 6, no page.
23. Appendix G, Issue 7, no page.
24. Appendix G, Issue 2, no page.

Appendices

Appendix A: The Unfinished Agenda

Colleges and universities are complex institutions serving millions of students. In the relatively short period of time since the establishment of the National Commission on the Cost of Higher Education, numerous issues have been identified that could contribute to rising college tuitions. Time, as well as the availability of data, did not allow for the thorough review of all of these issues.

- **Graduate Education.** How has the price of graduate education changed over time? What are the relative costs of graduate education as compared to undergraduate education? How can we distinguish these costs? Are undergraduate tuitions paying for graduate programs? Is the time to obtain a Ph.D. increasing?

- **Part-time Students.** How much do part-time students pay to attend a postsecondary institution? What is their price of attendance? How much and what types of financial aid do they receive? How much does it cost institutions to educate part-time students? Do part-time students need special types of services that differ from those of full-time students?

- **Nontraditional Students.** (Often considered to be students over the age of 22 who do not necessarily attend full-time; part-time students can be subsumed under nontraditional students). What types of financial aid do nontraditional students receive? What types of additional supports do they need?

- **Faculty Workload.** How do faculty spend their time? How can we improve upon current methods of obtaining data on faculty work? How much are they asked to teach? How frequently are faculty able to substitute activities for actual classroom teaching? Are there more efficient ways to teach?

- **Persons Who Do Not Attend.** Why do some high school graduates not pursue a college education? To what extent do financial concerns keep persons from enrolling?

- **Proprietary Schools.** How much do proprietary students pay to attend their institutions? What does it cost a proprietary school to educate students? How much and what types of financial aid do proprietary school students receive? Has the availability of Federal aid, both loans and grants, influenced tuition growth in proprietary schools?

- **Costs and Quality.** To what extent are changes in higher education costs related to changes in the quality of higher education? How are higher education products affected by changes in costs? How can quality be improved and costs reduced?

- **Technology.** How can advances in technology change the delivery of higher education? How can technology help colleges and universities to reduce their costs?

- **Saving to Pay for College.** How can students and their families save more efficiently to pay for college? What types of incentives might encourage families to save?

- **Higher Education and the Business Community.** How can businesses become more involved to help reduce some of the costs of higher education? To what extent are businesses currently providing tuition benefits for employees?

- **Remedial Education.** What does it cost colleges and universities to offer remedial education? How can higher education work with elementary and secondary schools to ensure that students are better prepared for college work?

- **Tuition Remission.** Does offering faculty tuition remission for family members drive up institutional costs?

- **Information Needs.** What kinds of information and publications would assist parents and students to make informed decisions about attending college?

Appendix B: Technical Note

Most of the data contained in this report were previously published elsewhere. The reader should consult the original sources for further details concerning cited data. Several of the tables do contain original tabulations of recent college cost and price trends (Issue 1). This technical note provides information concerning how these figures were derived. It describes: the data sources used to produce these estimates; the classification of students; the classification of institutions; the method used to estimate what it costs colleges and universities to provide higher education to students (cost per FTE); and the derivation of "net price" estimates. At the end of this note, several terms that are used throughout the report are defined.

Data Sources

Multiple years of two U.S. Department of Education data sources, the National Postsecondary Student Aid Study (NPSAS) and the Integrated Postsecondary Education Data System (IPEDS) were used to estimate trends in average college costs and prices. NPSAS data were used to estimate student level information (e.g., tuition and total price of attendance) and IPEDS data were used to estimate institutional level figures (e.g., enrollment and cost to institutions of providing higher education).

NPSAS data are not collected annually, but rather every three years: 1986-87, 1989-90, 1992-93, and 1995-96. The Data Analysis Systems (DAS) software and website (http://www.pedar-das.org) maintained by MPR Associates under contract with the National Center for Education Statistics (NCES) were used to generate the NPSAS based estimates.

IPEDS finance and enrollment data were combined to derive estimates of the cost of providing higher education incurred by institutions per full-time-equivalent student. Based on the ongoing work of Gordon Winston[1], information concerning how colleges and universities spend their money as reported on the IPEDS financial form was combined to reflect the fact that these institutions are multi-product entities and produce goods and services beside instruction. The capital costs associated with the value of the land, buildings, and equipment devoted to instruction are also factored into the estimate of the cost of providing higher education. (A more detailed explanation of this calculation is provided under the "Cost per Student" discussion.)

IPEDS finance data are collected every fiscal year. Finance data from fiscal years 1987, 1990, 1993, and 1996 were desired to correspond with the student level information available from the four waves of NPSAS. Final finance data are not, however, available for 1996, so data from 1995 and 1993 were used to estimate 1996 figures. The annual rate of change in the cost of providing instruction observed for each type of institution between 1993 and 1995 was assumed to remain the same through 1996. Comparing the results of this assumption with estimates derived from early release 1996 finance data revealed similar values. Enrollment data from the fall of the academic years in question were used to calculate full-time-equivalent enrollment (FTE). FTE is defined as the number of full-time students plus one third of the number of part-time students attending a given institution.

The first three years of IPEDS finance (1987, 1990, and 1993) and fall enrollment data (1986, 1989, and 1992) were acquired via the CASPAR website (http://caspar.nsf.gov). The 1995 finance and fall 1994 enrollment data were acquired through the NCES website (http://nces.ed.gov).

---

[1]Primarily, in Williams Project Discussion Paper (DP)-32, "Costs, Prices, Subsidies, and Aid in U.S. Higher Education," July, 1995, written with Ivan C. Yen.

Classification of Students

Data presented in this report are for full-time, full-year dependent students attending a single institution only. These students are considered for financial aid reasons to be financially dependent on their parents. Parental as well as the student's own income and assets are considered in the determination of need-based financial aid. Approximately 74 percent of full-time, full-year undergraduates were classified as dependent in 1996. While part-time or part-year students comprise the majority, 62 percent, of all undergraduates, the price paid by full-time, full-year students is more readily interpreted and compared across years.

Classification of Institutions

Institutions were classified based on control, public or private not-for-profit, and level of degree offered. Trends in prices and costs are estimated separately for public four-year, private four-year, and public two-year institutions. In 1996, approximately 78 percent of all undergraduates attended a public institution; 46 percent were in two-year schools, 31 percent attended four-year schools, and the remaining 1 percent were enrolled in institutions offering programs lasting less than two years. Public institutions receive a share of current revenue from state appropriations; therefore tuition charged state residents at these schools is often considerably lower than in the private sector.

Cost per Student

As noted above, the derivation of the cost of instruction per full-time-equivalent student draws heavily from the work of Gordon Winston. Winston's work makes two conceptual improvements over past measures of institutions' cost of providing higher education. First, Winston recognizes that colleges and universities spend money in areas that are clearly related, areas that are partially related, and areas that are completely unrelated to instruction. Second, Winston accounts for the capital costs of the physical resources associated with providing higher education.

Based on Winston's method, instruction costs are the sum of: clearly instructional expenditures; a proportion of the partially related expenditures; and a proportion of the capital costs of all the physical assets used by the institution. The proportion used in these calculations reflects the share instruction holds in the overall operation of the institution. The specific formulation of the cost per student estimation is described below and summarized in Exhibit B-1.

The two IPEDS expenditure categories of instruction and student services were treated as being clearly instructional and all the expenditures in these two categories was included in the instructional cost measure. The three IPEDS expenditure categories of institutional support, academic support, and operation of the physical plant were treated as being partially related to instruction and a proportion of the value of expenditures in these categories was added to the instructional cost measure. This proportion was calculated by dividing the sum of the two clearly instructional expenditure categories (instruction and student services) by the total current fund expenditures less mandatory and non-mandatory transfers, scholarship and fellowship expenditures, and the sum of the three partially instructional expenditure categories (institutional support, academic support, and operation of the physical plant).

EXHIBIT B-1

Annotated Formula for Cost Per Student

Cost =

Clearly Instruction	+	Proportion Partially Instruction	+	Proportion Capital Costs

Current expenditures on: Instruction Student Services	Current expenditures on: Academic Support Institutional Support Operation of Physical Plant	Depreciation (2.5%): Replacement value of Buildings Replacement value of Equipment plus Opportunity Cost (9.12%) : Replacement value of Buildings Replacement value of Equipment Replacement value of Land

Where proportion equals

Current expenditures on instruction and student services
  divided by
Total current fund expenditures less: current expenditures on academic support, institutional support, operation of physical plant, scholarships and fellowships, mandatory and non-mandatory transfers

Cost Per Student =
Cost divided by full-time-equivalent enrollment

Capital costs include both the real depreciation of physical assets and the opportunity costs associated with their use for higher education. IPEDS collects information concerning the replacement and book value of buildings and equipment used by colleges and universities. While the replacement value for land is not collected, book value for land used is. Land book value was converted to replacement or market value by multiplying land book value by 2.138. This correction of land value was based on the relationship observed by Winston and Yen (1995) between the book value and replacement value of buildings. Depreciation was assumed to be 2.5 percent and the opportunity cost was set to equal the average return over the past twenty years of 30 Year Treasury Bills, 9.12 percent. Land values were assumed not to depreciate in value. Hence, the value of all capital resources consumed in the provision of instructional services is computed as follows; 2.5 percent of (Building replacement value + Equipment replacement value) plus 9.12 percent (Building replacement value + Equipment replacement value + 2.138 x Land Book Value).

Due to a high level of missing data in the physical asset information in the IPEDS data, the data imputation techniques discussed in the appendix of Winston and Yen (1995, p.39-40) were adopted. In order to lessen the impact of outlying cases, the highest one percent of estimated values of instructional costs per full-time-equivalent student in each year were deleted from the analysis.

Net Price Calculations

The posted tuition, the "sticker price" is not paid by a substantial portion of undergraduate students due to financial aid. Roughly half of all undergraduates receive some sort of aid. Among dependent students attending a college or university full-time for the entire academic year, the group of students that tables included in Issue 1 focus on, the percentage receiving some type of financial aid is higher still, 64 percent.

Two different definitions of net price are used. In the first version of net price, only grant aid is subtracted from the total price of attendance. In the second version, all financial aid, including loan and work study earnings, is subtracted from the total price. The first definition captures the actual price paid by students and families, regardless of the mechanisms used to finance the purchase of higher education. The second captures the actual cash outlay that students and their families encounter during the year of college attendance.

To maintain a consistent measure of total price of attendance over time, certain adjustments had to be made to the student self-reported total price information available in the NPSAS data for 1987 and 1990. The 1996 NPSAS includes a revised measure of total price, a student budget variable based on the combination of student self-reports and institution provided data. A 1996 comparable version of this student budget variable was added to the 1993 NPSAS data which also contains student self-reports of total price. Using 1993 NPSAS data, which contained both measures, ratios of the revised student budget variable to student self-reports were calculated for each type of institution addressed by the report. The institution specific ratios were then applied to the self-reported total price information available in 1987 and 1990 to make these data comparable to the 1996 student budget estimates.

Definitions

Consumer price index (CPI). This price index measures the average change in the cost of a fixed market basket of goods and services purchased by consumers.

Dependent student. Students who are considered for financial aid reasons to be financially dependent on their parents. Parental as well as the individual student's income and assets are included in the calculation of the expected family contribution and thus financial aid awards.

Independent student. Students who are considered for financial aid reasons to be financially independent from their parents. Parental income and financial assets are not considered when calculating financial aid awards for independent students. Any one of the following criteria is sufficient for defining a student as independent: being 24 years of age or older by December 31 of the academic year in question; past service in the armed forces; being an orphan or ward of the court; being married; having legal dependents other than a spouse; or is a graduate or professional student.

Financial need. The difference between the institution's price of attendance and the student's expected family contribution.

Unmet need. The student's price of attendance at a specific institution less the student's expected family contribution and other financial assistance received.

Full-time-equivalent (FTE) enrollment. For institutions of higher education, enrollment of full-time students plus the full-time equivalent of part-time students. The full-time equivalent of part-time students is calculated in this report as: three part-time students are equivalent to one full-time student. Students are considered *part-time* if their total credit load is less than 75 percent of the normal full-time load.

Income

Median family income. That level of family income that divides the upper from the lower half of all families.

Personal disposable per capita income. The amount of money available per person to spend. The calculation involves subtracting all taxes, depreciation, and corporate reinvestment from the country's Gross National Product, adding transfer payments (e.g., social security payments), and dividing the result by the number of people in the population.

Regulatory Approaches

Performance-based approach. The performance-based regulatory approach fixes a standard of performance but generally leaves to the institution the choice of procedures to meet the standard.

Command and control approach. In the command and control regulatory approach, a government agency fixes both the performance standard and the procedure to meet the standard.

Appendix C: Commissioner Biographies

Martin Anderson

Senior Fellow, Hoover Institution of Stanford University, Stanford, California

Martin Anderson is a Senior Fellow at the Hoover Institution of Stanford University. A former professor at Columbia University, he directed the policy research efforts of three presidential campaigns, and was the domestic and economic policy adviser to President Reagan, 1981-82.

Anderson graduated summa cum laude from Dartmouth College, and received a M.S. from the Thayer School of Engineering and the Amos Tuck School of Business, and his Ph.D. from the Massachusetts Institute of Technology. He is the author of eight books including *Impostors in the Temple: A Blueprint for Improving Higher Education in America.*

Jonathan A. Brown

President, Association of Independent California Colleges and Universities, Sacramento, California

Dr. Brown has been President of the Association of Independent California Colleges and Universities since 1991. Prior to his appointment he was Vice President of the Association. Before that, he served in a variety of political positions including work in the White House, the U.S. Senate, the House of Representatives and the California Legislature. Brown has also served on a variety of boards including the National Association of Independent Colleges and Universities; as founding Chairman of United Educators Risk Retention Group and as a member of the Economics Council for the Universidad Anahuac del Sur in Mexico City.

Brown received his A.B. (Honors) in International Relations from the University of the Pacific. He also studied at George Washington University, Catholic University and the Harvard Institute for Educational Management. He received a D.P.A. from the University of Southern California. His dissertation, on tax simplification, was nominated for dissertation of the year by the American Society of Public Administration. He has been an adjunct professor at USC and Golden Gate University and a visiting professor at Universidad Anahuac del Sur in Mexico City.

"In one sense, the Commission was created as a result of a pervasive syntactic confusion that invades any discussion of higher education. Higher education lives in an environment where an average cost of production of $20,000(COST) is sold for $6,000(PRICE). If we concentrate only on price, we will be unsuccessful in keeping higher education accessible. The balance of our recommendations try to build on the strength of the American system of higher education — one size does not fit all because we have a diverse system. Better focus on and understanding of the costs of higher education among administrators, faculty, students, families and policymakers, will assure a higher educational system that remains able to meet a diverse set of needs, but always in a cost effective manner."

Robert V. Burns

Distinguished Professor and Head of Political Science, South Dakota State University, Brookings, South Dakota

Dr. Robert Burns is Distinguished Professor and Head of Political Science at South Dakota State University in Brookings, South Dakota. He is a Commissioner with the Western Interstate Commission on Higher Education, and former Chairperson of two Governor's Committees focusing on education in the state of South Dakota. He has held teaching positions at the University of Missouri-Columbia and at the University of South Dakota.

He received his B.S. in Political Science from South Dakota State University, and his M.A. and Ph.D. in Political Science from the University of Missouri-Columbia. He is the recipient of several teaching awards, including Teacher of the Year in the College of Arts and Science three separate years, the Burlington Northern Excellence in Teaching Award in 1989, and the 1995 South Dakota Professor of the Year by the Carnegie Foundation for the Advancement of Teaching. He is a former member and president of the Brookings, South Dakota, School Board and candidate for the state legislature. He was awarded the Bronze Star and Air Medal with Oak Leaf Cluster for his duty in Vietnam as a Captain with the United States Army.

"I am convinced that each of the eleven members of the Commission is committed to quality, affordable higher education opportunities for the adult public as a means toward individual and community well being in our nation. The common good and not narrow selfish interests directed the work of the Commission. We were required by law to investigate eleven complex topics in American higher education including costs, prices and subsidies. If our product appears to be overly broad in focus it is because we have sought to be true to our statutory mandate. It is our hope that individuals and communities alike will benefit from our effort to make higher education even more accessible through implementation of our many recommendations."

Clare M. Cotton

President, Association of Independent Colleges and Universities in Massachusetts, Boston, Massachusetts

Clare Cotton has served as the President of the Association of Independent Colleges and Universities of Massachusetts (AICUM) since 1987. AICUM represents 55 independent colleges and universities in Massachusetts. He served as President of the Boston-Fenway Program, Inc., a consortium of 12 non-profit educational, cultural and medical institutions from 1977-1987. Earlier he was Vice President for Government and University Relations at Boston University, Director of European Securities Publications, Inc. in London and a Special Writer for *The Wall Street Journal.*

He received his undergraduate degree from Randolph-Macon College and his masters degree in philosophy from the University of North Carolina, Chapel Hill. He has received honorary doctorate degrees from Randolph-Macon College, Wentworth Institute of Technology, Mount Ida College, Becker College and Northeastern University. He received the Dean College Cameron E. Thompson Medal and the Becker College award for Distinguished Service to Higher Education. He is a member of the Public Education Nominating Council of Massachusetts and a founding member of the Brookline (MA) Chorus.

"The Federal student aid programs, together, represent a kind of policy genius. The variety of the programs combines the Pell national grant system and the national loan systems with campus-based grant, work and loan programs, providing great flexibility in final awards to meet unforeseeable differences in student needs and changing student needs. The principle that <u>need</u> is the basis of awards under-girds these programs. Needs analysis covers the two relevant factors: the resources available to the student/family and the funding needed for the proposed educational program. Basing financial aid solely on income would limit choice and flexibility, and would tend to transform student aid into a part of the welfare system. Support for the Federal system, in my view, entails support for its basic philosophy of needs-based awards."

William D. Hansen

Executive Director, Education Finance Council, Washington, D.C.

Since 1993, Bill Hansen has been the Executive Director of the Education Finance Council (EFC) in Washington, D.C. EFC is a not-for-profit association organized to represent the common interests of state student loan secondary market organizations. Prior to joining EFC, Hansen was the Assistant Secretary of Education for Management and Budget and Chief Financial Officer; the Deputy Under Secretary of Education for Planning, Budget and Evaluation (acting); and Deputy Assistant Secretary of Education for Legislation and Congressional Affairs. He also managed the public affairs office at the U.S. Department of Commerce, directed intergovernmental and industry affairs at the U.S. Department of Energy and served as Deputy Assistant Secretary for Elementary and Secondary Education.

Governor George Allen appointed Mr. Hansen to the Virginia Commission on the Future of Public Education. He also served on the Governor's Commission on Champion Schools in Virginia. He attended Idaho State University and graduated from George Mason University with a B.S. degree in Economics. He lives with his wife and six children in McLean, Virginia.

Walter E. Massey

President, Morehouse College, Atlanta, Georgia

In June of 1995, Dr. Walter Massey was named president of his alma mater, Morehouse College, the nation's only historically black, private, liberal arts college for men. Prior to his appointment at Morehouse, Dr. Massey was a professor of physics and Dean of the College at Brown University, Director of Argonne National Laboratory, Vice President for Research at The University of Chicago, Director of the National Science Foundation and Provost and Senior Vice President for the University of California System.

Dr. Massey received his B.A. in Physics and Mathematics from Morehouse, and his M.S. and Ph.D. in Physics from Washington University. As an expert in the fields of science and technology, Dr. Massey has traveled and consulted around the world for different countries and organizations. He currently serves on the Board of Directors of Rockefeller University and three additional corporate boards. He was previously a trustee for Brown University and the MacArthur Foundation.

"I hope this report becomes a resource for policymakers as they struggle with the critical choices as to how to maintain the excellent system of American higher education. I also hope it will help families and students to prepare early on to finance a college education. We in the education community must do our part by keeping college affordable."

Barry Munitz

President and CEO, The J. Paul Getty Trust, Los Angeles, California

Former Chancellor, The California State University

Vice Chairman, National Commission on the Cost of Higher Education

During the work period of this Commission, Dr. Munitz was Chancellor and Chief Executive Officer of the California State University, a 23-campus system of state universities. He is now the President of the J. Paul Getty Trust, effective January 5, 1998. He is immediate past Chair of the American Council on Education, is a member of the Executive Committee of Los Angeles' KCET Public Television Station, has chaired the Education Round Table in California for the past five years, and is Chairman of the new National Advisory Group for the Ford Foundation-supported Millennium Project on Higher Education Costs, Pricing and Productivity.

He received a B.A. in Classics from Brooklyn College and a M.A. and Ph.D. from Princeton in Comparative Literature. After teaching at Berkeley and serving as Clark Kerr's assistant on the Carnegie Commission on the Future of Higher Education, he worked as the Academic Vice President of the University of Illinois system, as the Chancellor of the University of Houston, and as president of a Fortune 200 corporation. He has written widely on organizational theory, higher education, planning and governance.

"American higher education is the envy of the world, and an absolute requirement for social and economic success. Our colleges and universities must be strongly supported and families must plan to afford them; however, they must make themselves much easier to understand and much easier to afford. This Commission is absolutely and unanimously convinced that America's colleges and universities remain an extraordinary value; but, it is also deeply concerned that most of them obfuscate their current funding patterns and refuse to confront seriously basic strategies for reducing their instructional costs."

Frances McMurtray Norris

Vice President for Congressional Affairs, U.S. West, Inc., Washington, D.C.

Ms. Norris was recently named Vice President of U.S. West, Inc. in Washington, D.C. She is responsible for advocacy before Congress of the company's cable, wireless and telephone strategies. Prior to joining U.S. West, Ms. Norris was the Vice President of the Dutko Group in Washington. Her career in Washington includes a multitude of positions, including Special Assistant to President Bush for Legislative Affairs, Director of Congressional Relations for the Office of National Drug Control Policy, Assistant Secretary of Education, Deputy Assistant Secretary of Education, Assistant to then House Republican Whip, Trent Lott, and Legislative Assistant to Congressman G.V. Montgomery of Mississippi.

She earned her B.S. from the University of Mississippi and her M.S.L.S. from the University of Kentucky. Ms. Norris is listed in *Who's Who in America*, *Who's Who of American Women*, *Who's Who in American Politics*, *Who's Who in Emerging Leaders in America*, *World Who's Who of Women*, and *International Who's Who of Professional and Business Women*.

Blanche M. Touhill

Chancellor, University of Missouri at St. Louis, St. Louis, Missouri

Six years ago, Dr. Blanche M. Touhill became the Chancellor of the University of Missouri at St. Louis. Prior to this, she held numerous other positions at the same university, including Interim Chancellor, Vice Chancellor for Academic Affairs, Associate Vice Chancellor for Academic Affairs, Associate Dean of Faculties, and Professor of History and Education. She has held teaching positions at three other colleges and was also a public school teacher in New York City, St. Louis, and Montgomery County, Maryland. In addition to authoring and editing several books, Dr. Touhill has written over 60 papers on topics ranging from Irish immigration to America, to the issues surrounding campus extension on urban and land grant university campuses. She has also authored numerous articles and book reviews.

Dr. Touhill received all of her degrees from Saint Louis University in St. Louis, Missouri. Her B.S. and Ph.D. are in history and her M.A. is in geography. During her career, she has been on the boards of directors of 29 different organizations. She has devoted much time to the National Association of State Universities and Land-Grant Colleges, the American Association of State Colleges and Universities, the American Council on Education and of the Urban 13 institution group. Dr. Touhill has been honored by many organizations, including a Distinguished Service Award from the Dr. Martin Luther King, Jr. State Celebration Commission and the Humanist of the Year from the James F. Hornback Ethical Society.

"Higher Education is a pathway to opportunity in our country and must provide access and quality offerings to the citizenry through diverse types of institutions. I am pleased that the Commission favors a national data gathering approach focused on part-time students, a constituency which presently makes up 42 percent of all undergraduates enrolled in higher education. Comprehensive study of part-time students must be made in order to understand the complete picture of higher education. Eligibility of these students for Pell grants and other awards addresses one facet of the affordability issue."

William E. Troutt

President, Belmont University, Nashville, Tennessee

Chairman, National Commission on the Cost of Higher Education

Dr. Troutt has been President of Belmont University in Nashville, Tennessee for the last 17 years. During his presidency, Dr. Troutt has helped Belmont increase its enrollment by 75 percent, raise the average ACT score of its incoming students by eight points, and add to the geographic diversity of the student body. He has raised more than $100 million for the endowment and the university gained national recognition when it won the 1995 Innovative Management Achievement Award from the National Association of College and University Business Officers.

He received his B.A. in Philosophy and Religion from Union University, a M.A. in Higher Education and Philosophy from the University of Louisville and a Ph.D. from Vanderbilt University in Higher Education. After working as an admission officer at Union University, he worked as the Assistant Director of the Tennessee Higher Education Commission, as a Senior Associate with McManis Associates of Washington, DC, and then as Executive Vice President at Belmont, prior to becoming President. He was recently named one of the Nation's Most Effective College Presidents by an Exxon Foundation Study and as one of Nashville's Most Influential Citizens.

George W. Waldner

President, York College of Pennsylvania, York, Pennsylvania

Dr. George Waldner has been the President of York College since 1991, leading the institution to attain national recognition for achieving both quality and efficiency in higher education. In addition, he serves as the President of the Board of Directors of the Historical Society of York County and is a member of the board of directors of the Byrnes Health Education Center and South George Street Community Partnership, an urban re-development agency. Dr. Waldner has been active in regional accreditation, serving on evaluation committees for both the Southern Association of Colleges and Schools and the Middle States Association.

Prior to becoming President at York, Dr. Waldner was the Vice President for Academic Affairs at Wilkes University and Provost and Faculty Member at Ogelthorpe University, where he was honored twice as the outstanding classroom teacher. He is the author of numerous publications and papers related to the economics and politics of Japan as well as the economics of higher education. He received his A.B. from Cornell University, his M.A. and Ph.D. from Princeton University, and is a certificate recipient from the Inter-University Center for Japanese Studies in Advanced Written and Spoken Japanese Language.

"Colleges and universities must begin to pursue efficiency with as much fervor as they pursue quality. With creativity and commitment, each institution can find ways to enhance both excellence and value in higher education."

Appendix D: Commission Meetings

COMMISSION MEETING
August 11, 1997
Washington, DC

Presentation:
The Honorable Howard P. McKeon, Member, United States Congress, California

COMMISSION MEETING
September 7-8, 1997
Washington, DC

Presentations:

The Honorable Howard P. McKeon, Member, United States Congress, California
Dr. William F. Massy, The National Center for Postsecondary Improvement, Stanford University, The Jackson Hole Higher Education Group, Inc.

COMMISSION MEETING
October 16, 1997
Hoover Institution of Stanford University, Palo Alto, California

Presentation:
Mr. Gerhard Casper, President, Stanford University

Panel of Presidents
Dr. James L. Doti, President, Chapman University
Dr. Stephen C. Morgan, President, University of LaVerne
Dr. Leo E. Chavez, Chancellor, Foothill-DeAnza Community College District
Dr. Robert L. Caret, President, San Jose State University

PUBLIC HEARING
October 27, 1997
Washington, DC

Presentations:

American Association of Community Colleges
Dr. David R. Pierce, President
Dr. Robert C. Messina, President, Burlington County College

Association of Jesuit Colleges and Universities
Father James C. Carter, S.J., Chancellor, Loyola University New Orleans

Modern Language Association of America
Dr. Herbert S. Lindenberger, President

Urban 13 Institutions
Dr. Gerald L. Bepko, Chancellor, Indiana University-Purdue University
Dr. Patrick M. Rooney, Special Assistant to the Vice President and Associate Professor of Economics, Indiana University-Purdue University
Dr. Gregory M. St. L. O'Brien, Chancellor, University of New Orleans

Association of American Universities
Dr. Cornelius J. Pings, President

State Higher Education Executive Officers
Mr. J. Michael Mullen, Interim Director, State Council of Higher Education of Virginia

United States Congress
The Honorable Michael N. Castle, Delaware

American Association of University Professors
Dr. James E. Perly, President

National Association of College and University Business Officers
Mr. James E. Morley, Jr., President

Committee for Economic Development
Mr. Charles M. Kolb, President

COMMISSION MEETING
November 7, 1997
Northeastern University, Boston, Massachusetts

Presentations:
Dr. Gordon C. Winston, Orrin Sage Professor of Political Economy, Williams College
Dr. Richard M. Freeland, President, Northeastern University
Dr. Neil L. Rudenstine, President, Harvard University

Panel of Faculty Members
Dr. Phyllis W. Barrett, Professor of English, Holyoke Community College
Dr. Robert L. Silbey, Professor of Chemistry, Class of '42 Professor, Massachusetts Institute of Technology
Dr. Jeffrey L. Roberts, Professor of English, Worcester State College
Dr. Raymond J. Starr, Theodora Stone Sutton Professor of Classics, Wellesley College

DISCUSSION GROUP WITH PARENTS
November 10, 1997
Hume Fogg Magnet School
Nashville, Tennessee

COMMISSION MEETING
November 17-18, 1997
Belmont University, Nashville, Tennessee

Presentations:
Dr. Terry W. Hartle, Senior Vice President for Government and Public Affairs, American Council on Education
Mr. Arthur M. Hauptman, Consultant, Arlington, Virginia

COMMISSION MEETING
December 4, 1997
Washington, DC

REPORT RELEASE
January 21, 1998
Washington, DC

Appendix E: Expert Papers

ARE POSTSECONDARY EDUCATION AND TRAINING WORTH IT? HOW DO YOU KNOW?
Educational Testing Service
Anthony P. Carnevale
Donna M. Desrochers
Marlies A. Dunson
Richard A. Fry
Neal C. Johnson

FEDERAL STUDENT AID AND THE GROWTH IN COLLEGE COSTS AND TUITION: EXAMINING THE RELATIONSHIP
Arthur M. Hauptman
Cathy Krop

REMARKS ON RESTRUCTURING HIGHER EDUCATION
William F. Massy

STUDENT AID & TUITION: TOWARD A CAUSAL ANALYSIS
The American Institutes for Research
Roy J. Pearson
Stéphane Baldi

THE REAL COST OF HIGHER EDUCATION, WHO SHOULD PAY AND HOW?
Alan Reynolds

COLLEGE COSTS: SUBSIDIES, INTUITION AND POLICY
Gordon C. Winston

ARE POSTSECONDARY EDUCATION AND TRAINING WORTH IT? HOW DO YOU KNOW?

43

Are Postsecondary Education and Training Worth It? How Do You Know?

Prepared by

Anthony P. Carnevale
Donna M. Desrochers
Marlies A. Dunson
Richard A. Fry
Neal C. Johnson

Commissioned by

National Commission on the Cost of Higher Education

November 1997

The National Commission on the Cost of Higher Education has a broad mandate to review how a variety of factors contribute to the prices paid by families and students for postsecondary education and training.

The purpose of this paper is to step back from some of the specific detailed cost and pricing trend data the Commission is gathering, and to summarize work the Educational Testing Service and others have done to answer questions concerning the impact and value of postsecondary education and training. Specifically, we will provide a snapshot of the costs and benefits of educating and training the diverse wave of postsecondary students that is beginning to arrive on institutions' doorsteps.

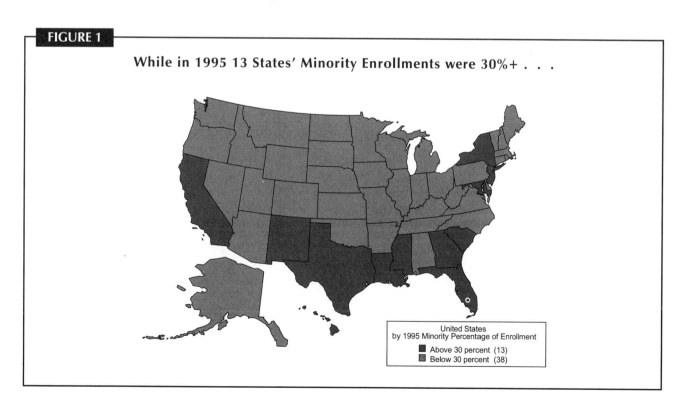

FIGURE 1

While in 1995 13 States' Minority Enrollments were 30%+ . . .

United States
by 1995 Minority Percentage of Enrollment
■ Above 30 percent (13)
■ Below 30 percent (38)

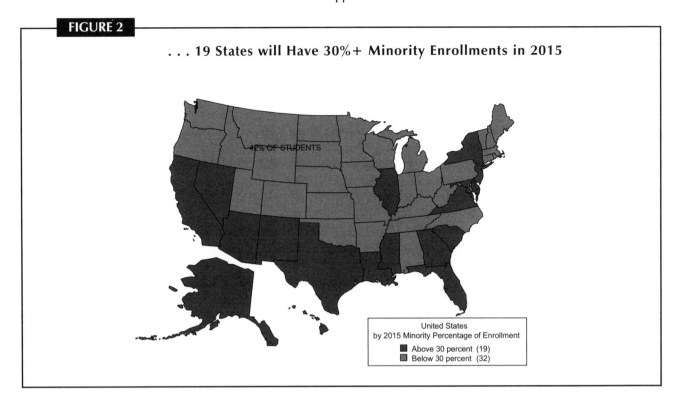

FIGURE 2

. . . 19 States will Have 30%+ Minority Enrollments in 2015

42% OF STUDENTS

United States
by 2015 Minority Percentage of Enrollment
■ Above 30 percent (19)
■ Below 30 percent (32)

Major demographic changes are raising the stakes of the college affordability challenge. Over the next 10 years, college students will be younger and more diverse than today's population. The Census Bureau projects significant growth in the population of traditional college-age students (18-24 years), reversing the past decade's trend toward an older, "non-traditional" population. A growing number of this new, younger college-age population will be from racial and ethnic minority families. By the early 21st century, as many as 20 percent of U.S. children will be first- or second-generation U.S. residents — with much higher concentrations in some regions. (**See Figures 1 and 2.**)

And America's array of postsecondary institutions — including public and private colleges and vocational training institutions — now serve traditional educational goals and a growing number of social, welfare, and job training policy goals. Postsecondary institutions are our primary vehicles for transitioning from school-to-work; are second only to employers in providing lifelong learning; and are the primary and most successful institutions in providing education and long-term employment for disadvantaged youth and adults, welfare mothers, and dislocated workers. For instance, 322,000 welfare mothers or their dependents and 75,000 dislocated workers used Pell grants and 48 percent of dislocated workers used student loans.

The range of institutions that must serve this growing student population — faced with public funding constraints, technological change, and an evolving new economic order — must carefully evaluate the costs and benefits of their institutional practices. The thrust of our argument is that:

- **The earnings returns to postsecondary education and training still justify its cost in general, but there is wide variation in the value of particular kinds of education and training.** Research demonstrates that college has a positive impact on: verbal and quantitative skills; oral and written communication; critical thinking; use of reason and evidence to address real world problems; and intellectual flexibility. Workers who complete college and advanced degrees earn significantly more than workers who do not go to college. These income premiums vary widely by field of study. Measurable (but less substantial) income gains also accrue to persons obtaining associate's degrees and vocational certificates. Even some students who accumulate college credits but do not graduate demonstrate some income benefits. Nontraditional clients such as welfare mothers and dislocated workers who get basic skills training or degrees and certificates from postsecondary institutions are more successful than those who do not.

- **But at present we only have limited information about the performance of postsecondary institutions.** We will review trends in current data such as the Graduate Record Examinations and assessments of literacy. We also will review the most recent findings on after-graduation performance, such as salaries, and the likelihood of graduates to be employed in jobs related to their fields of study.

- **States, systems, and institutions have begun crafting assessments and reporting and funding mechanisms that can support program improvement, increase productivity, and strengthen accountability.** A number of excellent institutional and systemwide, statewide, and regional models are emerging. The best gather and distribute college and university cost and outcome data; provide forums in which students, faculty and administrators, parents, business people, and policy makers can review findings; and provide means of redirecting public higher education resources from low-priority areas to high-productivity uses.

- **In order to simultaneously preserve and expand choice in postsecondary institutions and to encourage efficiency and a consistent quality of offerings,** we will need to continue to expand our ability to measure learning and labor market outcomes relevant to the diverse array of students, institutions, and missions that characterize the American postsecondary education and training system.

We need to encourage innovation and learn from experience. Many colleges and universities have retooled their missions and organizations for market-driven, customer-friendly educational services and economic development opportunities. Entirely new entities such as the Internet-based Western Governors' University and the International Community College are creating new avenues of opportunity and competition.

In this time of economic transition, many colleges and universities are collaborating with their communities to integrate their offerings with those of other employment and training service providers. This is especially important where the traditional educational mission of postsecondary educational institutions overlaps with social welfare policy and job training policy goals such as remediation, positive transitions to work, and work-based learning. We need to resist the temptation to reduce costs by creating more stringent barriers to student aid for those who need remediation and job training. Instead, we should develop more stringent performance standards and measures of ability to benefit that will result in more successful educational experiences for the least advantaged. It is particularly important that higher education continue to expand its role in social welfare and job training at this time. Attempts dating back to the mid-1960s to build a "second chance" education and training system outside the mainstream postsecondary education system have failed. In similar fashion, the attempt to build an employer-based "school-to-work" and job training system have not taken root in America. To the extent that cost and default reduction strategies limit assistance to nontraditional clients, they create a vacuum in the nation's ability to respond to social, welfare, and job training needs.

EARNINGS RETURN TO HIGHER EDUCATION

College graduates earn more than high school graduates, with the wage gains ranging up to 25 percent for associate's degrees and between 31 percent and 40 percent for bachelor's degrees (Jaeger and Page, 1996; Surrette, 1997). Masters and doctorate recipients earn 34-37 percent more than high school graduates, and lawyers and physicians earn as much as 60 percent more (Jaeger and Page, 1996). (**See Figure 3.**)

College graduates' earnings gains vary substantially across their fields of study. College graduates who majored in engineering, health, science and mathematics, and business demonstrate earnings gains between 11 percent and 48 percent — with women gaining even more than men in these fields (Rumberger and Thomas, 1993). (**See Figure 4.**) For community college graduates, a student's field of study is particularly vital to the returns from their community college degree. The earnings returns for community college graduates also depend heavily on whether the students secure a job in their field of study.

Compared to children who don't attend college, children who subsequently graduate from college:

- Come from higher income homes;
- Have better-educated parents; and
- Demonstrate stronger math and verbal skills (NCES, 1995).

Bottom line: does college "pay off"? Specifically, do a person's lifetime earning gains outweigh their initial college investment? Well, yes and no, as we discuss below. (See the box "Why Stay in College?" below.)

FIGURE 3

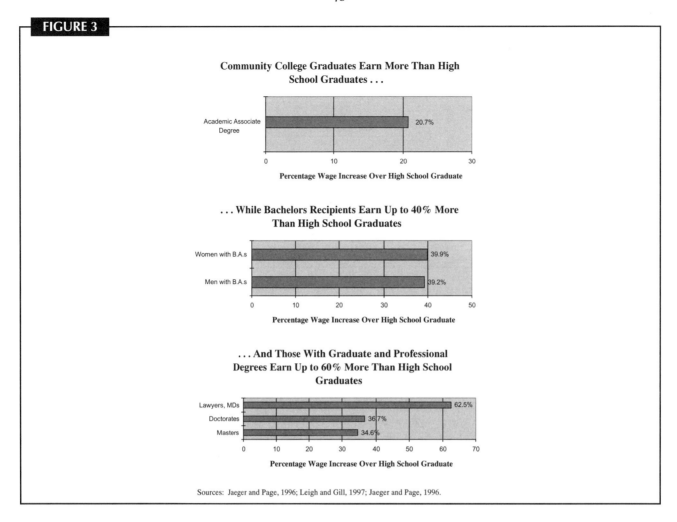

Sources: Jaeger and Page, 1996; Leigh and Gill, 1997; Jaeger and Page, 1996.

LITERACY, EDUCATIONAL ATTAINMENT, AND EARNINGS

The returns to education can be measured by several yardsticks, ranging from increases in cognitive ability to labor market earnings returns for a given level of educational attainment. Comparing the labor market earnings for those who did and did not pursue postsecondary education yields a good gauge of the secondary effects of education. But the earnings returns vary significantly by industry and occupation, generating substantially different outcomes for equally talented students who get different kinds of jobs. Accordingly, the primary measure of the effects of schooling is an increase in cognitive ability. But isolating these cognitive effects and then linking them to labor market outcomes provides a better measure of the earnings returns that results from acquiring increased knowledge.

One measure of cognitive ability that is related to everyday functions at home, in the community, and in the workplace is literacy. Literacy is not a measure of illiteracy—whether a person can read or write. Instead, it measures how a person can use "printed and written information to function in society, to achieve one's goals, and to develop one's knowledge and potential" (Barton and Lapointe, 1995). Literacy is a continuum of knowledge and skills, not a dividing line between the literate and the not literate.

Data from the National Adult Literacy Survey[1] provide a picture of the degree of literacy in America using three proficiency scales — prose, document, and quantitative—on a scale of 0-500 (which is further divided into 5 levels, **see Appendix A**). The three proficiency scales measure three distinct sets of skills.

---

[1] In 1992, the National Adult Literacy Survey was administered by Educational Testing Service (under contract with the National Center on Education Statistics) to nearly 27,000 people and is representative of all adults over age 16 living in households and federal or state prisons. Survey respondents were first asked a series of background questions relating to demographics, education/training experiences, labor force experiences, literacy activities, and political/social activities. The literacy assessment portion of the survey consisted of open-ended simulation tasks that emphasized literacy skills used at home, at work, and in social settings. The proficiency scores in each level indicate that an individual would complete successfully the tasks in that level 80 percent of the time.

ARE POSTSECONDARY EDUCATION AND TRAINING WORTH IT? HOW DO YOU KNOW?

47

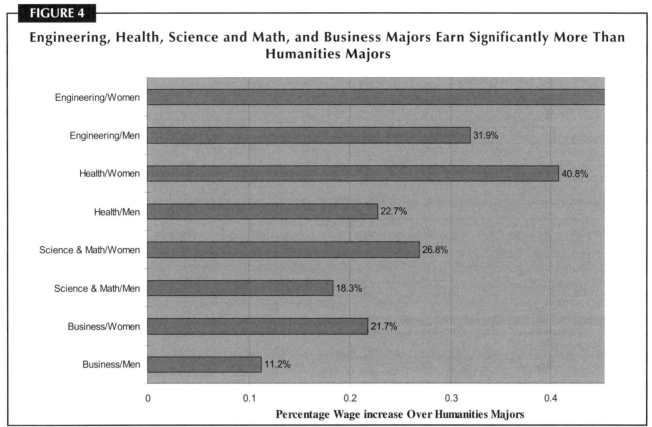

FIGURE 4

Engineering, Health, Science and Math, and Business Majors Earn Significantly More Than Humanities Majors

Source: Rumberger and Thomas, 1993.

- **Prose literacy:** the knowledge and skills needed to understand and use information from texts that include editorials, news stories, poems, and fiction.
- **Document literacy:** the knowledge and skills required to locate and use information contained in materials that include job applications, payroll forms, transportation schedules, maps, tables, and graphs.
- **Quantitative literacy:** the knowledge and skills required to apply arithmetic operations, either alone or sequentially, using number embedded in printed materials (Barton and Lapointe, 1995).

An examination of literacy by level of education yields, as expected, greater levels of literacy as education levels rise. Half of four-year college graduates have prose literacy proficiencies in levels 4 and 5, as do nearly two-thirds of post-graduate students and more than one-third of two-year graduates. (**See Figure 5.**) In contrast, three out of four adults with 0-8 years of education have prose literacy proficiencies in level 1, and 95 percent have literacy scores in the lowest two levels. Nearly three-quarters of all high school graduates have prose proficiencies that fall in either level 2 or 3 (Barton and Lapointe, 1995).

Not only do those with more education tend to have higher literacy proficiencies, but an increase in literacy proficiency increases the probability of an individual attaining an educational credential. If the prose proficiency of an individual increased by 60 points, the likelihood of the individual attaining a high school diploma/GED increases by 17 percentage points. Given that 76 percent of the working-age population already has a high school degree, this 60-point increase in prose proficiency would result in 94 percent of the population attaining a high school diploma/GED — a 22 percent increase (NCES, 1997).

FIGURE 5

Prose proficiency tends to rise with education level.
Three-fourths of adults with between zero and eight years
of school are in Level 1, as are four in 10 high school dropouts.
Over 75 percent of two-year college graduates and
85 percent of four-year college graduates reach at least Level 3.
However, just 4 and 10 percent, respectively, reach Level 5.

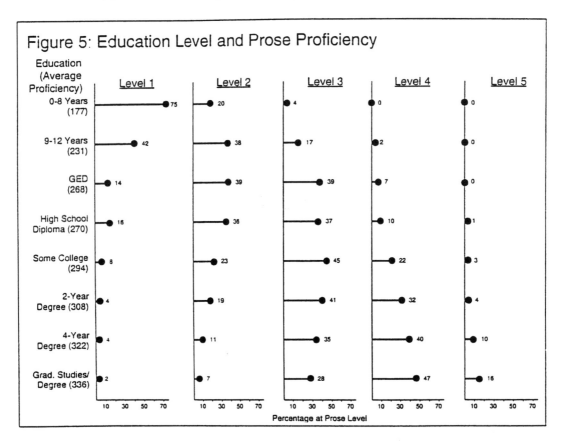

Figure 5: Education Level and Prose Proficiency

Sources: Kirsch et al., 1993; Barton, 1995.

"WHY STAY IN COLLEGE? WHY GO TO NIGHT SCHOOL?"

The economic benefits of some college degrees clearly justify their costs. But other degrees cost more than they pay in income — although such degrees may yield significant intangible benefits.

Take, for example, Marta Gonzalez, a 1990 high school graduate who decided not to go to college, and her classmate, Maria Sanchez, who continued her education, earning an academic associate's degree in April 1992. Marta and Maria had fairly similar childhoods. During the 4th grade, they both read once a week just for fun. And, they both scored around 900 on the college board.

Marta knew that following graduation she could land a job paying about $9.00 per hour. She saw a factoid in *USA Today* that said community college grads earn about 10 percent more than comparable high school grads. Marta figured that the extra 90 cents per hour was not worth it. And the upfront costs intimidated her. She and her parents probably could bankroll four semesters of community college tuition. But that wasn't the big hit. To get that associate's, she could not work for the equivalent of a year, meaning she'd have to forego about $9,000.

Maria reasoned that it might be worth spending ten to fifteen grand for an associate's. Working full-time, an extra 90 cents per hour resulted in about an extra $1,600 in earnings per year. Taxes would eat some of that, but she was young and would probably work at least another forty years. That extra $1,600 a year would be worth about $32,000 today. Maria figured it was a pretty good deal if ten to fifteen thousand spent yielded a gain of thirty or so thousand dollars.

LaTanya and Shawna Petry faced a similar dilemma. Identical twins, they'd both just finished up a master's degree in stats at Virginia State University. LaTanya saw up on the Census Bureau's web site that they were hiring statisticians, and thought the work might be interesting. With only a master's degree, she'd initially come in as GS-8, or making about $27,000 per year. But with Uncle Sam, the pay raises were steady and the job reasonably secure, so she took it.

Shawna considered pursuing a Ph.D. in stats. The university offered to pay her way as long as she stayed in good academic standing and made satisfactory progress toward her degree, so the out-of-pocket costs seemed small. But Shawna realized that unless she could do the extra course work and defend her thesis within a calendar year, she'd give up roughly at least $26,000 getting her Ph.D. A Ph.D. would improve her future earnings, but the boost in earnings over an otherwise similar person with a master's degree tends to be around three percent. Shawna realized that the lifetime earnings gains from an extra $1,200 per year would amount to about $24,000, less than the earnings she was likely to lose pursuing the Ph.D. From a narrow financial standpoint, Shawna could not justify further pursuit of formal education.

Similarly, the probability of an individual attaining a two-year or four-year degree increases by 20 and 17 percentage points, respectively, from a 60-point increase in prose proficiency. Again, given that 29 percent of the working-age population already has a two-year degree and 22 percent already has a four-year degree, the percent of the working-age population that would attain a two- or four-year degree increases to 49 and 39 percent, respective increases of two-thirds and three-quarters over the current mean attainment rates (NCES, 1997).

Although literacy rises with increased education, there is distinct variation in proficiency among people with identical levels of educational attainment. Each year, many students who have the ability to pursue higher education may choose not to do so. Conversely, some who receive a bachelor's degree from an open admissions college would be screened out by a more selective school.

Accordingly, the high school graduates in the top quartile of the prose proficiency distribution demonstrate higher scores than either two-year or four-year graduates in the lowest quartile. Indeed, the top 10 percent of high school graduates score better than half of all college graduates (Barton and Lapointe, 1995). (**See Figure 6.**) In the labor market, the variations in literacy within a given level of educational attainment and the associated return to that level of education can be magnified by occupational choice. A high school graduate who moves into a managerial/professional occupation earns more than a college graduate who does not.

There is a strong link between educational attainment and positive labor market outcomes. The results are higher average earnings, increased labor force participation rates, and lower unemployment rates. The link between literacy and labor market outcomes is equally positive. The average number of weeks worked annually increases as literacy proficiency increases for all adults, regardless of whether they attend college. Similarly, those with higher literacy levels also earn higher weekly wages. (**See Figure 7.**)

FIGURE 6

*Prose proficiency varies significantly at each education level,
although there is a large overlap in the score distributions.
For example, the top 25 percent of high school graduates
score higher than the bottom 25 percent of
four-year college graduates.*

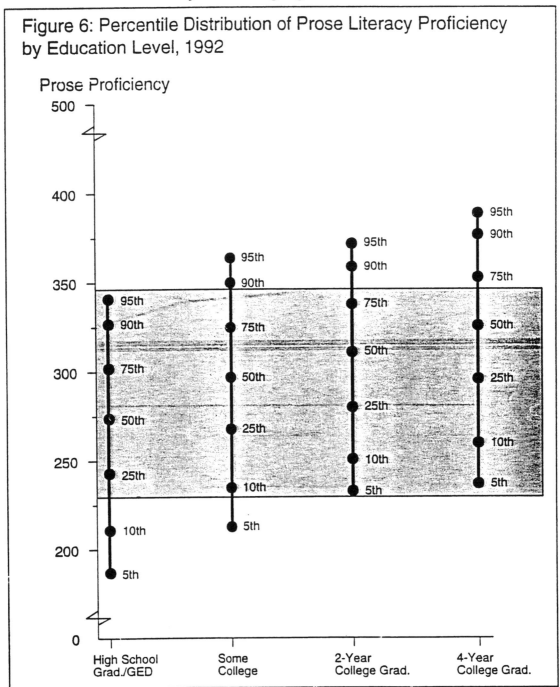

Figure 6: Percentile Distribution of Prose Literacy Proficiency
by Education Level, 1992

Sources: National Adult Literacy Study, 1992; Barton, 1995.

FIGURE 7

College graduates have higher average weekly wages than two-year graduates, who have higher average earnings than high school graduates.
Among college graduates, wages rise with literacy levels.

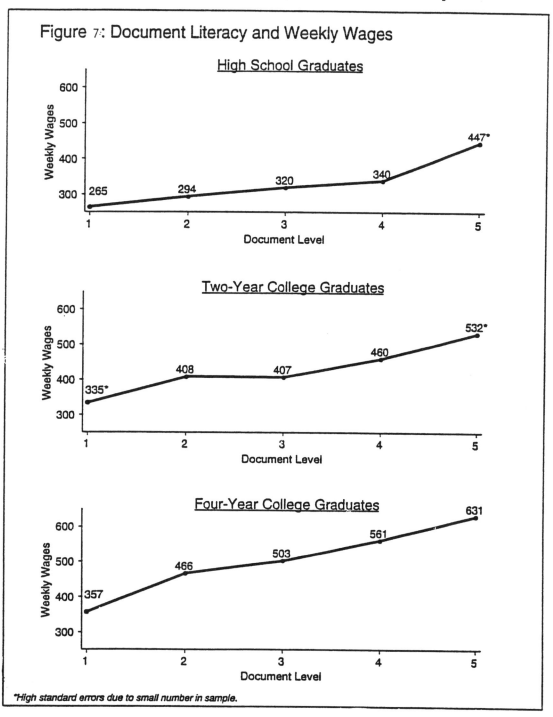

Figure 7: Document Literacy and Weekly Wages

Sources: Kirsch et al., 1993; Barton, 1995.

However, at all literacy levels, baccalaureate degree holders earn higher weekly wages than graduates of two-year institutions in identical levels. And those workers with degrees from two-year programs have higher weekly wages than high school graduates with comparable literacy levels.

But education alone cannot overcome the effect of literacy levels on earnings. Graduates from baccalaureate institutions with document literacy proficiencies in level 1 earn less than graduates from two-year institutions with literacy scores in levels 2 through 4. However, they do earn more on average than a high school graduate with a literacy proficiency in level 4. Interestingly, the weekly wages of baccalaureate graduates with level 2 scores are roughly equal to the earnings of workers with literacy proficiencies in level 4 but have only secured a degree from a two-year program (Barton and Lapointe, 1995). These data suggest that there are real returns to both literacy proficiency and different levels of educational attainment.

Literacy proficiency has a direct impact on earnings. As with educational attainment, suppose the average prose score of the population increased by 60 points, the mean weekly wages of high school graduates would increase by about 11 to 13 percent. The earnings increase for those with at least a two-year degree would increase between 14 and 17 percent. Similarly, annual earnings would also increase. The percent increase in annual earnings for high school graduates is nearly the same as the percent increase in weekly earnings. However, the annual earnings for those with a postsecondary degree are slightly higher — 16 to 19 percent — than the weekly earnings increases (NCES, 1997).

In order to fully explore the impact of literacy on earnings, two impacts must be examined. It was shown previously that increases in literacy proficiency increases educational attainment, which, indirectly, affects earnings. When these indirect effects are combined with the direct effect that literacy has on earnings, the total effect that literacy has on earnings is captured. Given a 60-point increase in the literacy proficiencies of full-time working adults, the combined effects result in weekly earnings increases of 23 to 24 percent, and annual earnings increases of 27 to 31 percent — the combined effects of education and literacy on earnings are nearly double the effects of literacy alone (NCES, 1997).

EARNINGS RETURNS BY OCCUPATION

The evidence clearly suggests that education and literacy are mutually reinforcing — and that both have a positive effect on labor market outcomes. But important questions remain unanswered. Is the economy producing too many college graduates — and not enough jobs that require college credentials? And are the returns increasing for jobs that require college degrees?

By examining the shares of workers in high-paying, moderate-paying, and low-paying occupations over time, we find that the proportion of prime-age male college graduates in high- paying occupations dropped from 83.7 percent in 1969 to 73.4 percent in 1995 — and women baccalaureate holders experienced a similar decline (Carnevale and Rose, forthcoming). This pattern indicates that even though the number of baccalaureate degree holders was increasing, the share of those entering managerial and professional occupations was declining. However, this decrease was offset by an increase in employment in moderate-paying jobs — not in the low-paying jobs.

Overall, the earnings of workers in high-paying occupations have risen considerably since 1959, and although the earnings of workers in moderate- and low-paying occupations rose in the 1960s, what followed was slow growth and then earnings declines in the 1990s. Among prime-age men with a baccalaureate degree, earnings gains from 1979 to 1995 equaled 10 percent, however those gains were generally limited to those in managerial and professional positions. Those with a four-year degree who were not employed as managers or professionals had lower earnings in 1995 than in 1979, and the relative differences increased as well; the earning difference for four-year degree holders in high-paying and moderate-paying jobs was 7 percent in 1959 although it had grown to 29 percent by 1995. Furthermore, even among those in managerial and professional jobs, the earnings increases only accrued to those with at least a baccalaureate degree. These data suggest that it is both educational attainment as well as occupation that drive earnings returns.

Among prime-age men who were high school graduates, there was a pronounced shift from moderate- and high-paying jobs into low-paying jobs. Coupled with within-job earnings losses, this was responsible for one-quarter of the loss in total earnings for this group. The remainder of the loss was from decreased earnings within job titles. Jobs formerly held by high school graduates that paid relatively well — the blue-collar jobs — saw earnings declines of about 18 percent.

ARE POSTSECONDARY EDUCATION AND TRAINING WORTH IT? HOW DO YOU KNOW?

53

Although the earnings of men in high-paying occupations rose significantly while those in moderate-paying occupations rose slightly and those in low-paying occupations declined, the earnings of prime-age women since 1959 have risen for all pay groups. However, as was true for men, the earnings gains were greatest for those women in managerial and professional occupations.

COGNITIVE AND OTHER OUTCOMES

As we have seen, the earnings returns story is complex. The impacts of postsecondary education and training on cognitive, social, and employment outcomes are no less nuanced.

College effects. The most comprehensive research to date on the effects of college (Pascarella and Terenzini, 1991) has found moderate-to-strong evidence that college has a positive effect on:

- Aesthetic, cultural, and intellectual values
- Value placed on liberal education
- Value placed on intrinsic occupational rewards
- Political liberalism
- Gender roles ("towards the 'modern'")
- Academic self-concept
- Social self-concept
- Self-esteem
- Intellectual orientation
- Personal adjustment and psychological well-being
- Use of principled reasoning in judging moral issues

Additionally, after controlling for a variety of other characteristics, such as age and academic ability, they found college to have a positive impact on a variety of skills, including verbal and quantitative skills. Oral and written communication, critical thinking, use or reason and evidence to address real world problems, and intellectual flexibility showed moderate-to-strong evidence of a positive impact. (**See Table 1**.) While this study is the most comprehensive study to date, the authors acknowledge that the evidence is extremely complex, and therefore, the magnitude of the findings is unclear.

Another method of examining the scholastic abilities of college graduates is to compare the standardized test scores of students applying to graduate school. The Graduate Record Examinations (GRE) measures quantitative, analytic, and verbal skills; however, GRE scores are not the best indicator of cognitive learning in college because the examinees are not representative of the majority of college graduates. For instance, in the 1994/1995 school year, only 33 percent of those students graduating with a bachelor's degree took the GRE.

More research on how colleges influence the cognitive abilities of students should be performed. The current data from numerous studies is positive, but inconclusive; and the data collected from GRE scores is imprecise due to the selective sample. (**See Figure 8**.)

After Graduation Measures. The National Center for Education Statistics (NCES) conducts surveys on how well college graduates are doing one year after receiving a Bachelor's degree. These measures include how many graduates — overall and per major — are employed full-time, how many are employed in their area of study, and how many are enrolled in further education. NCES also tracks the wages recent college graduates earn.

While these trends provide an indication of how college graduates have fared over the past several years, they do not take into account the role the economy has played. Graduates leaving school in a recession will not earn as much, regardless of the quality of education they receive. Additionally, the findings should not be viewed in isolation, particularly the data specific to majors. For instance, those students who majored in biology are the graduates least likely to be employed full-time one year after graduation, but they are the most likely to be enrolled in further education.

The first set of figures show that 73.1 percent of bachelor's degree recipients were employed one year after graduation in the 1992-93 school year. Additionally, 4.5 percent of those graduates were unemployed, and 27.3 percent were enrolled in further education. The most notable trend is the sharp decline in graduates enrolled in further education — from 35 percent in 1991 to 27.3 percent in 1994. (**See Figures 9-11**.)

TABLE 1

College has been found to have a positive impact on verbal and quantitative skills, oral and written communication, critical thinking, use or reason and evidence to address ill-structured problems, and intellectual flexibility, after controlling for a variety of other characteristics, and such factors as normal maturation.

Synthesis of Research Studies on the Net[1]
Effects of College on Learning and Cognitive Development

- *General Verbal Skills*

Strong evidence of a positive effect, after controlling for precollege verbal skills, race, and socioeconomic status. Graduates have a 10 to 13 percentile point advantage, over those not going to college.

- *General Quantitative Skills*

Strong evidence of a positive effect, after controlling for precollege quantitative skills, race, and socioeconomic status. Graduates have a 11 to 13 percentile point advantage.

- *Oral Communication Skills*

Moderate evidence of a positive effect, after controlling for age and academic ability. The magnitude of the net effect is unclear.[2]

- *Written Communication Skills*

Moderate evidence of a positive effect, after holding age and academic ability constant. The magnitude of the net effect is unclear.[2]

- *General Intellectual and Analytical Skill Development*

Moderate to strong evidence of a positive effect, after controlling for age, verbal ability, and quantitative ability. Magnitude of the effect is unclear.[2]

- *Critical Thinking*

Strong evidence of a positive effect, after controlling for precollege critical thinking, academic aptitude, socioeconomic status, and educational aspirations. Freshman year net effect was 17 percentile points. Magnitude of the net effect for all four years is unclear.[2]

- *Use of reason and evidence to address ill-structured problems* (reflective judgment, informal reasoning)

Moderate to strong evidence of a positive impact, after controlling for age, intelligence, and academic aptitude. Magnitude unclear.[2]

- *Intellectual flexibility*

Moderate to strong evidence of a positive impact, after controlling for age, intelligence, and academic impact. Magnitude unclear.[2]

---

[1] The college's net or unique impact, "as distinct from normal maturation, mere aging, or other noncollegiate sources of change."

[2] "Unclear," as used by the authors here, means that they acknowledge that the studies do not allow such estimates or that the evidence, though generally consistent, is still sufficiently complex to make an estimate of effect size hazardous.

Sources: Pascarella and Terenzini, 1991; Barton, 1995.

ARE POSTSECONDARY EDUCATION AND TRAINING WORTH IT? HOW DO YOU KNOW?

55

FIGURE 8

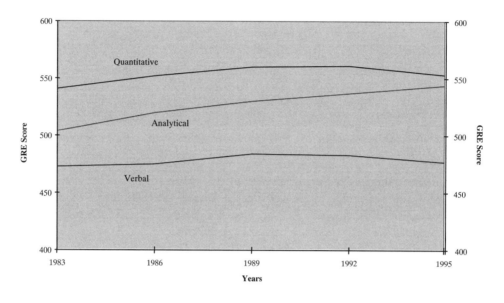

GRE Score Trends, 1983 - 1995

	1983	1986	1989	1992	1995
Volume	263,674	279,428	326,096	411,528	389,539
Verbal Mean	473	475	484	483	477
Quantitative Mean	541	552	560	561	553
Analytical Mean	504	520	530	537	544

Source: Graduate Record Examination Board, National Center for Education Statistics, 1996.

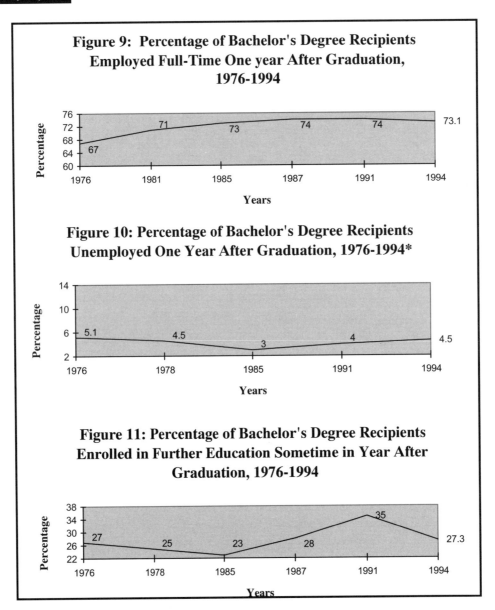

Figure 9: Percentage of Bachelor's Degree Recipients Employed Full-Time One year After Graduation, 1976-1994

Figure 10: Percentage of Bachelor's Degree Recipients Unemployed One Year After Graduation, 1976-1994*

Figure 11: Percentage of Bachelor's Degree Recipients Enrolled in Further Education Sometime in Year After Graduation, 1976-1994

Sources: NCES, 1993; NCES, 1991; NCES, 1996; Barton, 1995.
*Note: Unemployment data exclude those out of labor force.

ARE POSTSECONDARY EDUCATION AND TRAINING WORTH IT? HOW DO YOU KNOW?

57

This decline in enrollment in further education is illustrated by comparing graduates of 1989-90 with graduates of 1992-93 according to specific fields of study. (**See Figure 12.**) But again, it should be noted that business cycles and the economy may play a part in the decisions of graduates to enter into the workforce immediately or to seek further education.

FIGURE 12

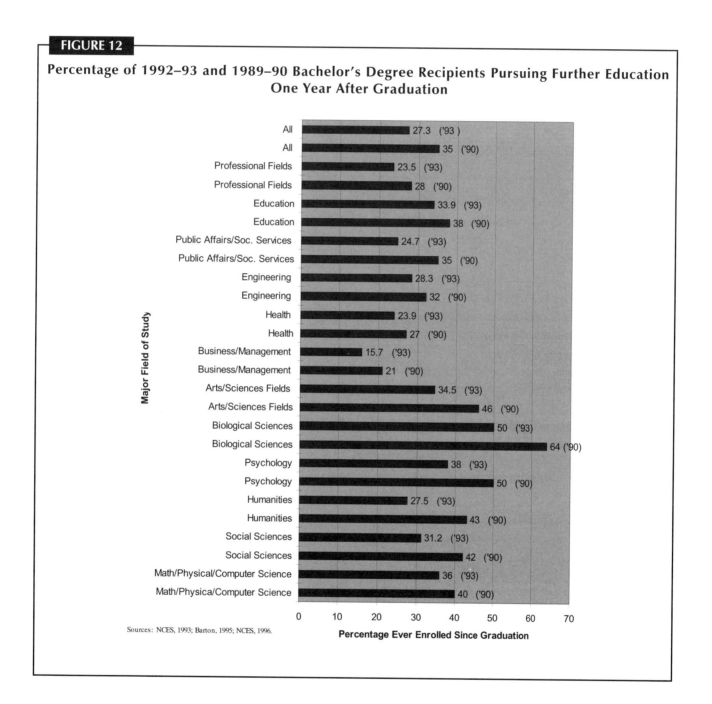

Percentage of 1992–93 and 1989–90 Bachelor's Degree Recipients Pursuing Further Education One Year After Graduation

Sources: NCES, 1993; Barton, 1995; NCES, 1996.

Three-quarters of employed bachelor's degree recipients have jobs related to their field of study one year after graduation. However, 43.2 percent of employed graduates have jobs that do not require a four-year degree. (**See Figures 13-15.**)

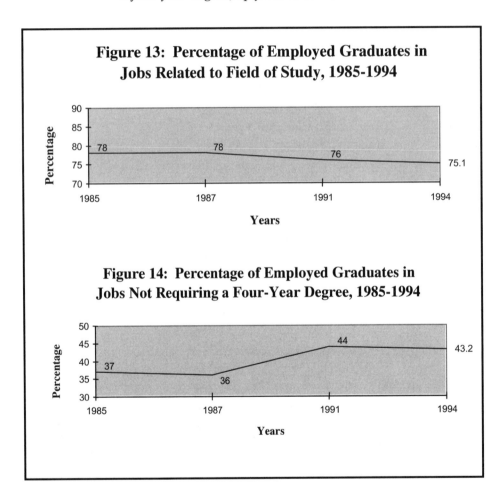

FIGURE 13, 14

About three-fourths of employed Bachelor's degree recipients are in jobs related to their field of study, essentially unchanged from 1985 and 1987. However, 43 percent were in jobs not requiring a four-year degree, up from 1985 and 1987.

Figure 13: Percentage of Employed Graduates in Jobs Related to Field of Study, 1985-1994

Figure 14: Percentage of Employed Graduates in Jobs Not Requiring a Four-Year Degree, 1985-1994

Sources: NCES, 1991; Barton, 1995; NCES, 1996.

ARE POSTSECONDARY EDUCATION AND TRAINING WORTH IT? HOW DO YOU KNOW?

59

FIGURE 15

Figure 15: Percentage of 1992-93 Graduates Employed Full-Time, Who Are Employed in Jobs Related to Field of Study, and Jobs Where a 4-Year Degree Is Not Required.

Employed in Field	Employed in Job Not Requiring Degree
Health Professions (90.5%)	
Engineering (87.4%)	
Business/Management (85.1%)	
PROFESSIONAL FIELDS (83.6%)	
Math, Computer/Physical Science (82.3%)	
Education (78.5%)	
ALL MAJORS (75.1%)	
Other (73.6%)	
Public Affairs/Soc. Serv. (71.6%)	
Biological Sciences (64.3%)	
Arts & Sciences (61.6%)	
Humanities (58.2%)	
Psychology (57.3%)	
Social Sciences (57.2%)	
History (41.6%)	History (57.8%)
	Humanities (55.1%)
	Arts/Sciences, Psychology (49.9%)
	Biological Science (49.6%)
	Business/Management (48.6%)
	Other (48.1%)
	Soc. Science, Pub. Affairs/Soc. Serv. (48%)
	ALL MAJORS (43.2%)
	PROFESSIONAL FIELDS (38.3%)
	Math, Computer/Physical Science (33%)
	Education (32.5%)
	Health Professions (24.7%)
	Engineering (19.7%)

Sources: NCES 1991; Barton, 1995; NCES, 1996.

While annual average salaries of bachelor's degree recipients, adjusted for inflation, dropped from $27,300 in 1991 to $25,600 in 1994, new graduates' salaries have remained relatively constant since 1976. **(See Figure 16.)** The wage difference depends in part on the graduate's field of study. **(See Figure 17.)**

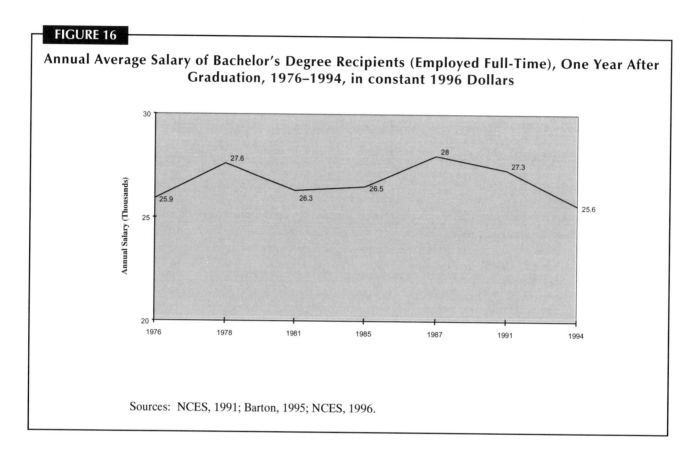

FIGURE 16

Annual Average Salary of Bachelor's Degree Recipients (Employed Full-Time), One Year After Graduation, 1976–1994, in constant 1996 Dollars

Sources: NCES, 1991; Barton, 1995; NCES, 1996.

RECENT DEVELOPMENTS IN HIGHER EDUCATION PERFORMANCE MEASUREMENT AND MANAGEMENT

For almost two decades, the so-called "measurement movement in higher education" has ebbed and flowed. States started getting serious about assessing student learning in the late 1970s — and most states had joined in by the late 1980s. Early assessment efforts were home grown, tailored by individual colleges and universities to their own missions. In the 1980s and 1990s new accountability systems that enabled comparisons between institutions grew from these individual, decentralized approaches (Ruppert, 1994).

As bellwether public colleges and universities and state higher education coordinating boards grew their assessment systems, the array of organizational players involved with them also proliferated. In addition to the federal Office of Postsecondary Education and the National Center for Education Statistics, models and analyses and recommendations flowed from the likes of the Education Commission of the States, the National Governors' Association, the National Education Goals Panel, and the American Association of Higher Education.

Within the National Education Goals Panel alone, a resource group spawned one technical planning subgroup that recommended a sample-based national assessment indicator system — and another technical group that recommended an alternative approach. The National Center for Education Statistics convened workshops in 1992 and commissioned a number of papers (NCES, 1994). In a final assessment flurry, the Department of Education issued a request for proposals to start development of a sample-based system. But the funding cupboard was bare: the RFP was never awarded.

Others have soldiered on. Peter Ewell, Dennis Jones and their colleagues at the National Center for Higher Education Management Systems have done substantial work identifying proxy measures of general educational achievement (Ewell and Jones, 1996). Ranging from institutional requirements to instructional practices and

ARE POSTSECONDARY EDUCATION AND TRAINING WORTH IT? HOW DO YOU KNOW?

61

FIGURE 17

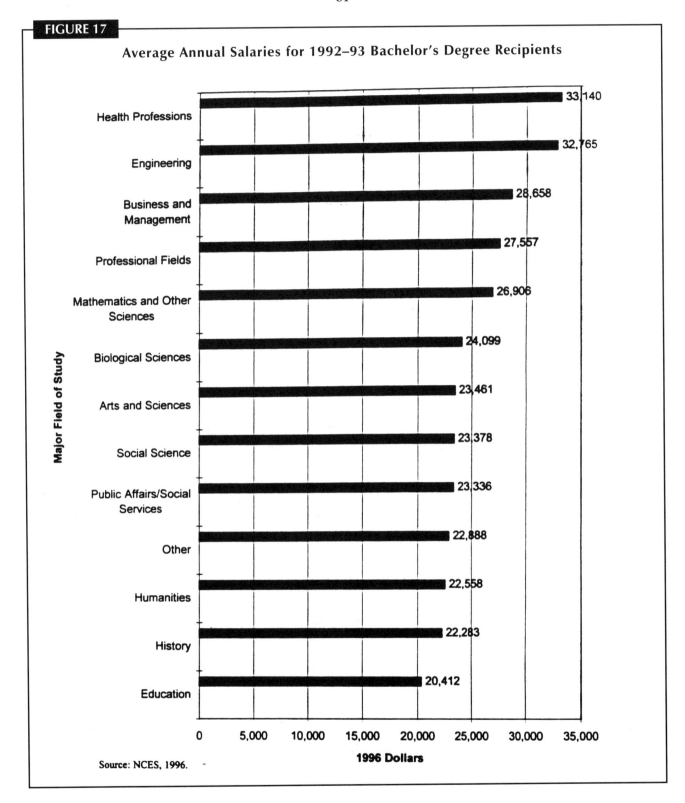

Average Annual Salaries for 1992–93 Bachelor's Degree Recipients

Major Field of Study	
Health Professions	33,140
Engineering	32,765
Business and Management	28,658
Professional Fields	27,557
Mathematics and Other Sciences	26,906
Biological Sciences	24,099
Arts and Sciences	23,461
Social Science	23,378
Public Affairs/Social Services	23,336
Other	22,888
Humanities	22,558
History	22,283
Education	20,412

1996 Dollars

Source: NCES, 1996.

student behaviors, these indicators are being actively analyzed and deployed by a substantial number of colleges and universities. (See Appendix B.)

Institutional performance indicators have been another avenue of research and experimentation in colleges, universities, and systems across the country. An in-depth review of ten states leading the effort to strengthen accountability to the public documented the use of "report cards" on statistics ranging from inputs like faculty/student ratios to outputs such as total degrees awarded and outcomes like student performance on nationally normed tests and alumni satisfaction surveys (Ruppert, 1994). (See Appendix C.)

Most states have signaled that they expect public colleges and universities to measure up if they expect continued support. How? By adopting a variety of performance funding and performance budgeting strategies. (See Figure 18.) "Performance funding ties special sums directly to results on specific indicators. In performance budgeting, governors and legislators consider reports of results on performance indicators as a factor in the total funding of public colleges and universities" (Burke and Serban, 1997).

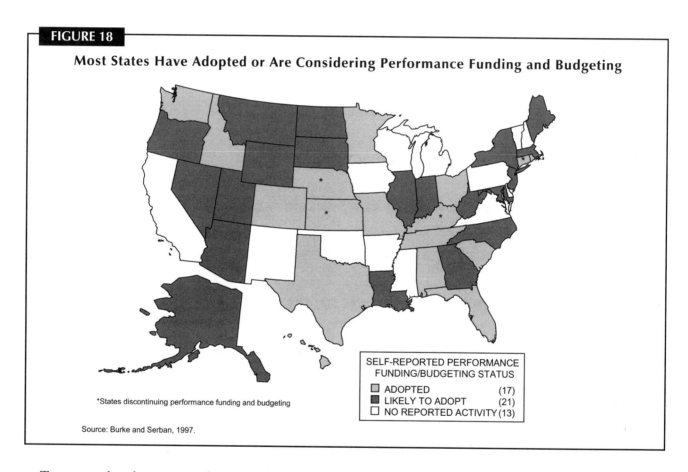

FIGURE 18

Most States Have Adopted or Are Considering Performance Funding and Budgeting

*States discontinuing performance funding and budgeting

SELF-REPORTED PERFORMANCE
FUNDING/BUDGETING STATUS
☐ ADOPTED   (17)
■ LIKELY TO ADOPT   (21)
☐ NO REPORTED ACTIVITY(13)

Source: Burke and Serban, 1997.

Tennessee has been at performance funding the longest. As far back as 1979, the state instituted a performance-based funding system. Now in its fifth incarnation, the system assesses the extent to which the state's two- and four-year colleges meet state-defined goals in general education, major fields, student and alumni satisfaction, and graduate job placement. Roughly five percent of the state's higher education budget is earmarked as incentive bonuses for schools that meet or exceed state goals.

At the University of Tennessee at Martin, for example, departments systematically thought through — some for the first time — precisely what they were trying to accomplish with their students and how to assess those accomplishments. In some cases, degree requirements have been changed as a result. In others, course sequencing has been revised to optimize student learning. In still others, so-called "capstone" courses have been created to integrate what students are learning in other courses. Throughout the university, assessment data is used to design improvements in general education, in major field curricula, even in student counseling services.

Nobody in Tennessee is saying the system is perfect. The available assessment tools still fall short of measuring fully students' general education, for example. And some departments and institutions have been slow to use

ARE POSTSECONDARY EDUCATION AND TRAINING WORTH IT? HOW DO YOU KNOW?

63

assessment information to improve their programs. But over the years, performance funding has boosted the confidence of public and elected officials in the state's institutions of higher education, and the schools — and their students — have benefitted.

If Tennessee's 18-year commitment to performance funding in higher education is evolutionary, South Carolina's is revolutionary. Last year, the state's legislature unveiled some three dozen performance indicators by which public colleges would be judged and announced that the state's higher education system would go to 100 percent performance-based funding — in just three years! Already, South Carolina's Commission on Higher Education is working with legislators, administrators, faculty and higher education management gurus from around the country to apply performance indicators that range from graduation rates and research grants to "employer feedback on graduates" to divvy up new dollars for the next fiscal year. Other states — those already committed to performance funding and those still considering it — are watching closely (Carnevale, Johnson and Edwards, forthcoming).

COSTS AND EFFECTS OF EMPLOYMENT AND TRAINING PROGRAMS

Particularly at the community college level, comprehensively assessing the costs and effects of postsecondary education programs necessitates taking a close look at employment and training programs. Currently 15 federal agencies administer 163 education, employment, and training programs[2]. Typically, those employment and training programs provide similar services such as formal training, on-the-job training, counseling and job-search assistance; however, the recipients originate from diverse populations.

The impacts of public employment and training programs have undergone significant analysis: the results are mixed, varying by population group and type of training. Those programs serving disadvantaged women show modest, although consistent, positive results, at least in the short-term; for men and youth, however, public programs have marginal effects or no effect at all. Among women, JTPA enrollees increased their annual earnings by $735 over 30 months (Bloom et al., 1994). In several different programs, the services that resulted in significant earnings gains were on-the-job training and job-search assistance; more intensive services, such as classroom training, have not had as large an impact on earnings (Grubb, 1995). Adult men who enrolled in JTPA employment and training programs realized annual earnings increases of $640 over 30 months, or 8.6 percent more than men who did not receive similar services (Bloom et al., 1994). In those programs that did affect the earnings of adult men, job-search assistance is the most valuable tool..

There is little evidence of any positive earnings returns for youth who participate in on-the-job training, classroom training, or job-search assistance. The only training program that does appear to have a positive impact, Job Corps, raised the income of participants by $1,600 a year, a gain that persisted for four years after completion of the program. That increase in earnings, however, can be attributed to increased employment rates, not increased wage rates, suggesting that the program does not increase the productivity of its participants (Mallar et al., 1982). Furthermore, Job Corps training costs about $16,400 per participant.

Programs serving dislocated workers also have varying effects, depending on the type of training. Although, there have been no analyses on the effects of JTPA dislocated worker training programs, several demonstration programs targeted toward dislocated workers have been implemented and evaluated. Again, workers benefitted most from job-search assistance, but only in the short run; over time the wages of those who received job-search assistance were no different from those who did not. Although earnings gains accrued to those workers who received classroom training, the benefits did not exceed those realized by participants who received job-search assistance. Even though many displaced workers used Pell grants to continue their education, the cost of training — coupled with foregone earnings — yields benefits that cannot be justified relative to the less costly job-search assistance.[3]

However, there is evidence that classroom training does benefit those who take technical courses, producing positive earnings returns per credit. Conversely, the earnings returns to academic credits are negative (Jacobson and LaLonde, 1997). Furthermore, the length of training affects the earnings gains realized from classroom

[2]Included in this count are those programs that provide financial and other assistance to students attending postsecondary institutions. A discrepancy exists on the number of employment and training programs because of various methods used in determining what qualifies as a separate program. For a comprehensive description of federal job training programs, see: National Commission for Employment Policy, *Understanding Federal Training and Employment Programs*, Washington, DC: January 1995.

[3]For a review of the literature on dislocated worker programs, see: Leigh, Duane E., *Does Training Work for Dislocated Workers?*, Kalamazoo, MI: W.E. Upjohn Institute for Employment Research, 1990.

training. Completing a full year of courses (45 credits) can increase earnings by about $2,800. But on average, displaced workers complete only 17 credits, of which less than half are earned in technical courses (Jacobson and LaLonde, 1997). While the Pell grant opens the classroom door for those workers who need skill improvement, many workers already have the skills they need to secure employment. They just need help finding a job.

Welfare-to-work programs, unique to each state, were designed to provide job training and job assistance services that would move AFDC recipients into jobs. On balance, those programs have had marginal positive effects. Although the likelihood of being on welfare was not reduced, several programs increased annual earnings, but most by less than $500.[4] It is estimated that a welfare recipient would need an additional $5,000 in annual earnings to escape poverty, and even with a 10 percent earnings return to training, that translates into a $50,000 human capital investment just to bring about that increase (Heckman, 1996). Thus earning increases realized from training programs are unlikely to raise women from poverty.

WORLD CLASS POSTSECONDARY EDUCATION AND TRAINING FOR A WORLD CLASS WORKFORCE

We know that the earnings returns to postsecondary education and training still justify its cost in general. The demographic wave of younger, more diverse students faced with decisions about pursuing further studies should — and will — continue to say "yes" to building their knowledge base.

The key to developing a world class, cost-effective education and training system with a distinctively American signature is better information on education and training service performance — the kind of information that informs and strengthens the decisions of students, parents, faculty and administrators, public managers and policymakers and creates positive incentives for providers of education and training services to meet their customers' needs.

Three sets of reform movements — in higher education, employment and training, and welfare — are already in motion on these issues.

Tennessee and other states have blazed the trail on making assessments matter — and on supporting policy, funding, and management that enable institutions to improve student outcomes. South Carolina is testing the proposition that its public colleges and universities can attain broad, statewide educational outcome and efficiency goals through full-scale performance-based funding. Federal policy should heed the lessons being learned from these important initiatives.

Similarly, more sophisticated accountability mechanisms are critical at the juncture between welfare, employment, and student aid. The current education and training system provides numerous choices. But those choices would be more effective if they could be based on information that tells clients what works and want doesn't. Fortunately, Oregon, Florida and other states and communities are crafting workforce development strategies that recognize the critical value of performance information and consumer choice.

And elements of the two workforce bills that the U.S. House and Senate recently passed would provide important building blocks for a more rational system: streamlining the current snarl of job training programs; requiring stronger performance measurement and accountability systems; and creating more one-stop employment centers.

With performance information-driven, market-oriented reforms like those being tested by these pioneering states and communities, we will know at last how our postsecondary education and training investments are performing — and so will the customer. What could be more American?

BIBLIOGRAPHY

Barton, Paul E. and Lapointe, Archie, *Learning by Degrees, Indicators of Performance in Higher Education*, Princeton, NJ: Policy Information Center, Educational Testing Service, 1995.

Bloom, H. S., Orr, L. L., Cave, G., Bell, S. H., Doolittle, F., and Lin, W., *The National JTPA Study: Overview: Impacts, Benefits, and Costs of Title II-A*, Bethesda, MD: ABT Associates, March 1994

Burd, Stephen, "Congressional Panel on Education Costs Is Urged to View Colleges Skeptically," *Academe Today*, October 28, 1997.

Burke, Joseph C., *Performance Funding Indicators: Concerns, Values, and Models for Two- and Four-Year Colleges and Universities*, Albany, NY: Nelson A. Rockefeller Institute of Government, 1997.

---

[4]For a review of the literature on welfare-to-work programs, see: Grubb, W. Norton, *Evaluating Job Training Programs in the United States; Evidence and Explanations*, Berkeley, CA: National Center for Research in Vocational Education, May 1995.

ARE POSTSECONDARY EDUCATION AND TRAINING WORTH IT? HOW DO YOU KNOW?

65

Burke, Joseph C. and Serban, Andreea M., *Performance Funding and Budgeting for Public Higher Education: Current Status and Future Prospects*, Albany, NY: Nelson A. Rockefeller Institute of Government, 1997.

Burke, Joseph C. and Serban, Andreea M., "Performance Funding of Public Higher Education: Results Should Count," *Rockefeller Reports*, September 25, 1997.

Carnevale, Anthony P., Johnson, Neal C. and Edwards, Anne. "Making Performance Count," forthcoming.

Carnevale, Anthony P. and Rose, Stephen. "Education for What? The New Office Economy," forthcoming.

Christal, Melodie, "Preliminary Results from the SHEEO State Survey on Performance

Measures," Education Commission of the States/State Higher Education Executive Officers, 1997.

Cole, John J. K., Nettles, Michael T., and Sharp, Sally, *Assessment of Teaching and Learning for Improvement and Public Accountability: State Governing, Coordinating Board and Regional Accreditation Association Policies and Practices*, Ann Arbor, MI: University of Michigan Center for Study of Higher and Postsecondary Education, June 2, 1997 draft.

Ewell, Peter T. and Jones, Dennis P., *Indicators of "Good Practice" in Undergraduate Education: A Handbook for Development and Implementation*, Boulder, CO: National Center for Higher Education Management Systems, 1996, p. 27.

Graduate Record Examination Board, *Examinee and Score Trends for the GRE General Test*, various years.

Grubb, W. Norton, *Evaluating Job Training Programs in the United States: Evidence and Explanations*, National Center for Research in Vocational Education, May 1995.

Heckman, James J., "What Should Our Human Capital Investment Policy Be?" *Jobs & Capital*, Milken Institute for Job and Capital Formation, Vol. 5, Spring 1996.

Jacobson, Louis and LaLonde, Robert, *Net Impact Evaluation of Retraining Under ESHB 1988*, Rockville, MD: Westat, Inc., January 1997.

Jaeger, David A. and Page, Marianne, "Degrees Matter: New Evidence on Sheepskin Effects in the Returns to Education," *Review of Economics and Statistics*, November 1996, pp. 733-40.

Jordan, Stephen M., "The Challenge of Keeping College Affordable: A Response to the National Commission on the Cost of Higher Education," an unpublished paper submitted by State Higher Education Executive Officers to the National Commission on the Cost of Higher Education for a hearing on October 27, 1997.

Kirsch et al., *Adult Literacy in America*, Princeton, NJ: Educational Testing Service, under contract with the National Center for Education Statistics, 1993.

Leigh, Duane E. and Gill, Andrew M., "Labor Market Returns to Community Colleges: Evidence for Returning Adults," *The Journal of Human Resources*, Vol. XXII, No. 2, Spring 1997, pp. 334-53.

Mallar, Charles, et. al., *Evaluation of the Economic Impact of the Job Corps Program: Third Follow-Up Report*, Princeton, NJ: Mathematica Policy, Inc., September 1982.

Morley, James E. Jr., unpublished letter submitted by the National Association of College and University Business Officers to the National Commission on the Cost of Higher Education for a hearing on October 27, 1997.

Nettles, Michael T., Cole, John J. K., and Sharp, Sally, "A Comparative Analysis of Trends and Patterns in State Assessment Policy," paper to be presented at the Association for the Study of Higher Education, November 8, 1997.

Pascarella, Ernest T. and Terenzini, Patrick T., *How College Affects Students*, San Francisco, CA and Oxford: Jossey-Bass, 1991.

Progress and Freedom Foundation, *The Digital State: How Governments are Using Digital Technology*, Washington, DC, 1997.

Rumberger, Russell W. and Thomas, Scott L., "The Economic Returns to College Major, Quality and Performance: A Multilevel Analysis of Recent Graduates," *Economics of Education Review*, Vol. 12, No. 1, 1993, pp. 1-19.

Ruppert, Sandra S., *Charting Higher Education Accountability, A Sourcebook on State-Level Performance Indicators*, Denver, CO: Education Commission of the States, June 1994, pp. 156-157.

Surette, Brian J., *The Impacts of Two-Year College on the Labor Market and Schooling Experiences of Young Men*, Washington, DC: Federal Reserve Board, June, 1997.

U.S. Department of Education, National Center for Education Statistics, *A Descriptive Summary of 1992-93 Bachelor's Degree Recipients: 1 Year Later*, NCES 96-158, Washington, DC: U.S. Government Printing Office, 1996.

U.S. Department of Education, National Center for Education Statistics, *Digest of Education Statistics 1996*, NCES 96-133, Washington, DC: U.S. Government Printing Office, 1996.

U.S. Department of Education, National Center for Education Statistics, *Digest of Education Statistics 1993*, NCES 93-292, Washington, DC: U.S. Government Printing Office, 1993.

U.S. Department of Education, National Center for Education Statistics, *High School and Beyond: 1992 Descriptive Summary of 1980 High School Sophomores 12 Years Later*, NCES 97-269, Washington, DC: U.S. Government Printing Office, 1995.

U.S. Department of Education, National Center for Education Statistics, *Literacy in the Labor Force*, NCES 94-277, Washington, DC: U.S. Government Printing Office, 1997.

U.S. Department of Education, National Center for Education Statistics, *National Assessment of College Student Learning: Identification of the Skills to be Taught, Learned, and Assessed*, NCES 94-286, Washington, DC: U.S. Government Printing Office, August 1994.

U.S. Department of Education, National Center for Education Statistics, *Survey of Recent College Graduates*, report for 1991 survey, NCES 94-391, Washington, DC: U.S. Government Printing Office, 1994.

ACKNOWLEDGMENTS

The authors are grateful to the many colleagues, scholars and practitioners who helped us assemble these data in a very short period of time.

Peter Ewell of the National Center for Higher Education Management Systems, Joseph Burke and Andreea M. Serban of the Nelson A. Rockefeller Institute of Government Public Higher Education Program, and Michael Nettles and John Cole of the University of Michigan Center for the Study of Higher and Postsecondary Education rapidly provided us with their most recent work on issues of assessment and accountability. Any errors of interpretation are certainly our own.

Much of the outcome information discussion built on the solid foundation provided by our colleagues Paul Barton and Archie Lapointe in their 1995 ETS report, *Learning By Degrees:Indicators of Performance in Higher Education*. And our ETS colleague June Elmore artfully crafted the report's graphic elements.

Appendix A

Table 1: Measures of Literacy in the National Adult Literacy Survey, 1992			
	Prose	**Document**	**Quantitative**
Level 1 (0-225)	Can read short text to locate a single piece of information that is identical to the question. Distracting information is minimal.	Can locate a piece of information based on a literal match between the task and the document or enter personal knowledge onto a document. There is little distracting information.	Can perform a single, simple arithmetic operation such as addition. The numbers used are provided and the operation to be performed is specified.
Level 1 examples	- Identify a country in a short article - Locate 1 piece of information in a sports article	*- Locate the time of a meeting on a form* *- Use a pie graph to locate the type of vehicle having specific sales*	- Total a bank deposit entry
Level 2 (226-275)	Can locate a single piece of information when there is distracting information, and can contrast or compare 2 or more pieces of information.	Can match a single piece of information, with distracting information present, requiring little inference, and can integrate information from several parts of the document.	Can perform a single arithmetic operation using number that are given in the task or easily located in the material. The arithmetic operation is either described or easily determined from the format of the materials.
Level 2 examples	- Underline the meaning of a term in a government brochure - Interpret instructions from an appliance warranty	*- Locate an intersection on a street map* *- Enter background information on a social security card application*	*- Calculate postage and fees for certified mail* *- Determine the difference in price between tickets for two shows*
Level 3 (276-325)	Can match information in the text and in the task when low level inferences are required, integrate information from dense or lengthy text, and generate a response based on information easily identifible in the text.	Can integrate several pieces of information from one or several documents and deal with complex tables or graphs containing information that is irrelevant to the task.	Can perform tasks where two or more numbers are needed to solve the problem and they must be found in the material. The operation(s) needed can be determined from the arithmetic relation terms used in the question or directive.
Level 3 examples	- Write a letter explaining an error on a credit card bill - Read a news article and identify a sentence that provides interpretation of a situation	*- Enter information into an automobile maintenance form* *- Identify information from a bar graph depicting source of energy and year*	*- Use a calculator to calculate the difference between the regular and sale price* *- Calculate miles per gallon from information given on a mileage record chart*
Level 4 (326-375)	Can match text with multiple features, integrate or synthesize information from complex/lengthy passages and make more complex inferences.	Can perform tasks that require them to draw higher level inferences and numerous responses with being told how many, and can perform tasks that contain conditional information.	Can perform two or more operations in sequence or a single operation in which the quantities are found in different types of displays, or the operations must be inferred from the information given or from prior knowledge.
Level 4 examples	- State in writing an argument made in a lengthy newspaper article - Contrast views expressed in two editorials	*- Use a bus schedule to determine the appropriate bus for a given destination and time* *- Use a table of information to determine the pattern of oil exports across years*	*- Determine the correct change using information in a menu* *- Using an eligibility pamphlet, calculate the amount a couple would receive from basic Supplemental Security Income*
Level 5 (376-500)	Can find information in a dense text that has considerable distracting information and can make high-level inferences or use specialized background Level 5 knowledge.	Can search complex displays that contain several pieces of distracting information, make high level inferences, and make use of specialized knowledge.	Can perform multiple operations sequentially, and can also find problems embedded in text or rely on background knowledge to determine the quantities or operations needed.
Level 5 examples	- Compare the approaches stated in a narrative - Summarize two ways lawyers may challenge prospective jurors	*- Use a table to complete a graph, including labeling axes* *- Use a table to compare credit cards and write about the differences between them*	*- Use a calculator to determine the total cost of carpet to cover a room* *- Use information in a news article to calculate the difference in time for completing a race*

Source: Adapted from Barton, Paul E. and Archie Lapointe, *Learning by Degrees*, Princeton, NJ: Policy Information Center, Educational Testing Service, 1995.

ARE POSTSECONDARY EDUCATION AND TRAINING WORTH IT? HOW DO YOU KNOW?

67

Appendix B

Summary Chart of Potential "Good Practice" Indicators

Indicator Domain/Dimension	Relative Strength of Association with Goal 5.5 Outcomes	Available Methods for Collective Indicators Data	Relative Ease of Data-Gathering	Policy Relevance	Overall Potential
A. Institutional Requirements:					
Broad General Education Curriculum/Requirements	Weak/Moderate	- Catalogue Review - Institutional Questionnaires/ Inventories (e.g., Peterson 1987)	Difficult	High	Low
Breadth of Coursetaking/ Types of Coursetaking	Moderate	- "Breadth" and "Depth" of Courses Taken (Zemsky 1989) - "Differential Coursework Methodology" (Ratcliff & Associates 1988)	Moderately Difficult	Moderate	Moderate
Special Courses/ Instructional Designs	Moderate (but likely derivative)	- Catalogue Review - Institutional Questionnaires/ Inventories (e.g., Gamson & Poulsen 1989)	Difficult	Low	Low
Levels of Expectation	Moderate/Strong (via association with "Small Liberal Arts College" effect)	- Rating Examinations and Course Materials by Level of Difficulty (e.g., Braxton & Nordvall 1985)	Difficult	Moderate	Moderate
B. Instructional "Good Practice":					
Class Size and Structure	Low/Moderate (but likely derivative)	- Institutional Surveys/ Statistics	Moderately Difficult	High	Moderate
"Active Learning" Practices in Class		- Faculty Surveys (e.g., 7 Principles Surveys, Gamson & Poulsen 1989)	Not Difficult	Moderate	High
- Practice of Skills	Strong	- UCLA Faculty Survey			
- Frequent Feedback	Strong	(Astin 1992)			
- Peer Interaction	Strong	- Student Surveys (e.g., CSEQ - Pace 1987, CIRP - Astin & Associates 1992)			
Wider Institutional Environment					
- Involvement	Strong/Moderate (Complex Interaction of Factors)	- CSEQ (Pace 1987) - CIRP (Astin & Associates 1992)	Not Difficult	Moderate	High
- Student/Faculty Contact	Strong/Moderate (but also may require data on nature of interaction)		Not Difficult	Moderate	High
C. Student Behavior:					
Time on Task	Strong/Moderate (but also requires quality of investment measures)	- CSEQ (Pace 1987) - CIRP (Astin & Associates 1992)	Not Difficult	Moderate	High
"Quality of Effort"/ Involvement and Investment	Strong	- CSEQ (Pace 1987)	Not Difficult	Moderate	High
D. Self-Reported Cognitive Development:					
	Moderate/Strong	- CSEQ (Pace 1987) - CIRP (Astin & Associates 1992) - ACT-ESS (ACT 1982) - NCHEMS SOIS (NCHEMS 1983)	Not Difficult	N/A	Moderate

Source: Ewell and Jones, 1996.

Appendix C

Analysis of State-Level Indicators in the Case-Study States

	INSTRUCTIONAL INPUTS	INSTRUCTIONAL PROCESSES/ USE OF RESOURCES	INSTRUCTIONAL OUTCOMES
COLORADO	o ACT/SAT scores of entering freshmen	o Availability of academic programs o Sustained financial commitment to instruction o Student/faculty ratios	o Graduation rates by ethnicity o Performance of graduates on licensure exams
FLORIDA	o Mandated basic skills testing	o Total credits produced by discipline o Total contact hours by faculty rank/level o Time to degree and number of credits required o Course demand analysis o Classroom utilization	o CLAST examination on basic skills o Total degrees awarded by discipline o Performance of graduates on licensure exams o Alumni/employer follow-up responses o Retention/graduation rates by ethnicity o Job placement rates for vocational students
ILLINOIS	o Student demand (PQP)	o Centrality of programs to mission (PQP) o Faculty workload o Time to degree	o Persistence and graduation rates o Follow-up of graduates o Success of graduates (PQP)
KENTUCKY	o Number of students in remediation	o Total credits produced by discipline o Total contact hours by faculty rank/level o Specific faculty workload measures o Time to degree and number of credits to complete o Course demand analysis o Classroom utilization	o Total degrees awarded by discipline o Graduate performance on licensure exams o Graduate/employer satisfaction o Persistence and graduation rates by ethnicity
NEW YORK	o Trends in admissions data, high school graduates, etc.	o Time to degree completion o Freshman-to-sophomore persistence o Percentage resources for undergraduate instruction o Class size by level	o Graduation/persistence rates o Graduate performance on licensing exams o Student perceptions of quality
S. CAROLINA	o Number and performance of remedial students	o Lower-division courses taught by faculty type o Upper-division students in sponsored research o Graduate students drawn from in-state	o Graduation/completion rates o Placement of graduates o Grad. performance on licensing exams
TENNESSEE	o Remedial students and effectiveness of remediation o ACT scores of entering students	o Graduation/completion rates o Lower-division courses taught by faculty type	o Grad. performance on licensing exams o ACT-COMP scores o Major field test scores o Student satisfaction ratings o Job placement rates for graduates
TEXAS	o TASP examination results	o Within-term persistence rates o First-year retention rates o Classroom utilization	o Graduation/completion within 6 years o Grad. performance on licensing exams
VIRGINIA	o Admissions standards and requirements o Number of students meeting admissions standards o High school courses taken o Levels of remediation required	o Average class sizes o Percent undergraduates taught by senior faculty o Small class/seminar experiences o "Capstone"/integrative experiences	o Graduation/completion rates o Employment/graduate school placement rates
WISCONSIN	o ACT/SAT Scores o Resident Students Accepted * o WI high school graduates enrolled *	o Average time to completion o Courses taught by faculty type/level o Average class size o Percent classes of 100 or more	o Numbers of degrees granted o Graduation/completion rates o Graduate satisfaction/outcomes * o ACT-CAAP Results *

* Indicators from the Governor's Task Force on UW Accountability Measures.

ARE POSTSECONDARY EDUCATION AND TRAINING WORTH IT? HOW DO YOU KNOW?

69

EFFICIENCY/ PRODUCTIVITY	CONDITION OF THE ASSET	DIVERSITY/ACCESS/EQUITY	ARTICULATION/ K-12 LINKAGES	RELATION TO STATE NEEDS
o Student/faculty ratios	o Total revenues per student o Alumni and private contributions o State approp. per resident student o State approp. per capita o Grant and contract dollars per FTE o Average faculty salary	o Graduation rates by ethnicity o Availability of student financial aid o Faculty diversity o College participation rate		
		o Retention/graduation rates by ethnicity	o Performance of transfers at senior institution	
o Program costs (PQP) o Faculty workload		o Various measures in individual reports	o Feedback on performance to high schools o Performance of transfers at senior institution	o Relation of program to employment needs (PQP)
	o Number/proportion of accredited programs	o Persistence and graduation rates by ethnicity	o Research and service in support of K-12 o Number and performance of two-year transfers	
o Credits per faculty produced o Student/faculty ratios	o Graduate program and faculty "quality" measures o Condition of campus facilities o External fundraising success	o Student demographics o Persistence/graduation by ethnicity o Ethnicity of faculty o Trends in "costs to attend"		o Graduates in science, engineering, etc. o Economic impact on state
	o Number/proportion of programs accredited	o Number and trends in minority enrollment	o Transfer rates and transfer performance	
	o Number/proportion of programs accredited	o Minority enrollments o Completion/graduation rates for minorities	o Two-year college transfer rates and performance	
	o Value of externally-sponsored research	o Minority first-year persistence o Minority performance on TASP	o Mandated feedback on peformance to high schools o Mandated feedback on performance to two-year colleges	
	o Quality of institutional assessment program o Level of sponsored research activity	o Graduation/completion rates by ethinicity		
o Sponsored resarch levels *	o Faculty recruitment/retention * o Faculty development resources * o Maintenance investments * o Accidents/injuries *	o Progress in affirmative action * o Minority graduation rates * o Sexual harrassment incidents *		o Employer ratings of "responsiveness" * o Continuing education activities *

Source: Ruppert, 1994

Federal Student Aid and the Growth in College Costs and Tuitions: Examining the Relationship

Arthur M. Hauptman & Cathy Krop
Prepared for the National Commission on the Cost of Higher Education by the
Council for Aid to Education (CAE), An Independent Subsidiary of RAND
December 1997

SUMMARY OF FINDINGS AND RECOMMENDATIONS

The question of whether federal student aid has fueled the growth in tuitions and other charges has been the subject of heated debate at least since William Bennett raised the issue when he served as Secretary of Education during the mid-1980s. Bennett's argument then was that colleges and universities were chasing their own tail by relying on federal student aid to raise their tuitions and other charges at a rate much greater than the general rate of inflation. An alternative view advanced by most higher education officials has been that critics who accuse them of gouging the consumer and the taxpayer are wrong. They argue that there is no correlation between increases in federal student aid and the rapid growth in tuitions and other charges.

As is often the case in public policy debates, both positions probably have been overstated. The purposes of this paper are: 1) to identify possible ways in which federal student aid policies over time may have affected the growth in college costs and tuitions, and 2) to make recommendations for how the possible inflationary effects of federal student aid policies might be ameliorated.

To assess the possible effects of federal student aid policies on the growth in college tuitions, this paper examines the extent to which the different federal student aid programs covered the total costs of attendance (defined as tuition, fees, and room and board) in 1975, 1985, and 1995.

Federal student aid — grants, loans, and work-study — paid more than two-fifths of the total costs of attendance faced by college students in 1995. Federal aid covered nearly one-half of the total costs of attendance for public college students and nearly two-fifths of the costs for private college students.

The proportion of total costs of attendance met through federal student aid has increased dramatically over the past two decades. Federal student aid in 1975 represented less than one-tenth of the total costs of attendance in the public sector and less than one-fifth in the private sector. In 1985, those proportions had grown to about one-third for the public sector and about one-quarter for the private sector.

Federal loans have become a particularly important source of funding for college students and their families.[1] Federal loans accounted for more than one-third of total costs of attendance in 1995, compared to less than one-tenth in 1975. Given the growing importance of federal loans in paying for college, it is increasingly difficult to argue that they have had no effect on tuition-setting at many institutions. This is not to say that college officials stay up nights figuring out how they can set tuition and other charges to maximize the federal aid eligibility of their students. Many other factors probably play a more important role in tuition pricing decisions, including the availability of state funding for public institutions, the demands on all institutions for greater quality in the services they offer, the limited possibilities for offsetting efficiencies and economies of scale, and students' continued willingness to pay higher prices as demonstrated by application patterns at many public and private institutions.

At the very least, however, the tremendous growth in the availability of federal loans has facilitated the ability of both public and private colleges to raise their tuitions at twice the rate of inflation for nearly two decades without experiencing decreases in enrollment or other clear signs of consumer resistance. In particular, it seems evident that private colleges could not have stabilized their share of total enrollments over the past two decades without the tremendous expansion in federal loan availability.

---

[1] In this paper, the term *federal loans* refers to the various federally sponsored loan programs, including those financed with federal capital as well as privately financed loans that are either subsidized or guaranteed by the federal government or its agents. The term *subsidized loans* refers to loans for which the federal government pays the interest while the borrower is in school; *unsubsidized loans* are federally guaranteed but provide no federal in-school interest payment. All federal loans are subsidized, however, in that the effective rate of interest, which is set by law, is well below what the private sector charges in the absence of a federal guarantee.

The potential effect of federal loans on college tuition levels is magnified by the fact that, since 1981, student eligibility for the federal in-school interest subsidy has been determined by subtracting family resources and grant aid from the student's total costs of attendance. As a result, eligibility for loans and loan subsidies grows as tuitions and other charges increase, constrained by the amount of annual and cumulative loan limits. Thus, whenever federal loan limits increase, the potential link between tuitions and loans strengthens.

By using total costs of attendance, the federal aid formulas also ignore the growing use of discounting at many institutions. While more and more students and families do not pay the full sticker price for tuitions, fees, and room and board, the current aid system continues to calculate federal aid eligibility as though the stated costs are what people actually pay.

Both public and private institutions have greatly increased the discounts they provide in the form of grant aid from their own resources. The aid private institutions provided from their own resources in 1995 equaled one-fifth of the total costs of attendance—triple what it was in 1975. Compared to private institutions, public institutions provide far less aid from their own resources—one-twentieth of total costs of attendance— but the proportion they do provide grew fivefold from 1975 to 1995. When the discounts provided by institutions are subtracted from the total costs of attendance, federal student aid in 1995 covered more than half of public sector costs of attendance minus institutional aid and nearly half of the "net" private sector costs of attendance. Federal loans financed more than two-fifths of the net costs of attendance at both public and private institutions in 1995.

The 1981 decision to use total costs of attendance in determining eligibility for the in-school interest subsidy has had another important effect: a student's qualification for the subsidy now varies depending on where he or she goes to school. Middle income students who are ineligible for loan subsidies if they attend institutions that charge $10,000 may be eligible at institutions that charge $20,000 or more. That is why federal loan subsidies stretch much further up the income scale than do federal grants or the new tuition tax credits, which address this issue by limiting benefits to families with incomes below $100,000.

Federal grants probably have had less impact on college pricing decisions than loans have. Compared to loans, federal grants cover a much smaller share of total costs of attendance. A smaller proportion of students receive grants than borrow, meaning that federal grants insulate a smaller proportion of students from the effects of higher prices than loans do. Perhaps most important, in the largest grant program—Pell Grants—costs of attendance are effectively no longer a factor in award calculation, thereby reducing the potential link between aid and charges.

This paper suggests that although federal policies have not been the principal factor in the growth of college costs and tuitions, the federal government should consider taking two steps to reduce the potential impact of federal student aid on college costs:

- First, the federal government should no longer recognize total costs of attendance in determining eligibility for federal loan subsidies. Instead, only a portion of tuition (say, 50 percent) over some base level (e.g., $3,000, average public sector tuition) and a standard amount of living expenses should be used in determining eligibility for federal loan subsidies. In addition, there should be an overall limit on the amount of federal aid that a student may receive, including unsubsidized loans, with the limit being lower for undergraduates than for graduate and professional school students.

There are precedents for allowing only a portion of costs to be used in federal aid calculations. Since 1992, a standard amount for living expenses has been used in the Pell Grant program. In addition, the two new tuition tax credits only recognize a portion of tuition costs. Partial cost reimbursement for determining eligibility for loan subsidies could have several distinct benefits over the traditional practice of using full costs of attendance. It could: 1) better target low and middle income students for loan subsidies; 2) reduce the government's role in subsidizing student lifestyle choices; and 3) recognize the growing use of discounting by many colleges in the federal student aid equation.

While some will argue that the proposal for partial cost reimbursement is a form of price control, it is not. Institutions would not have to charge below a specified limit in order for their students to be eligible for federal student aid; nor would the federal government need to monitor what institutions charge. This paper makes it clear that federal price controls and federal monitoring of college charges are inappropriate mechanisms for dealing with the issue of college costs. But this paper also makes it clear that the federal government has a right and a responsibility to the taxpayer to make a policy determination about how much of tuitions and other charges it is willing to subsidize.

One purpose of imposing an overall annual limit on federal aid is to ensure that students can still borrow adequate sums through various federal loan programs while minimizing the potential link between college costs and unsubsidized loans, including in the federal Parent Loans (PLUS) program, in which no annual dollar limit currently exists. Another purpose of an overall federal aid limit, however, is to better target the types of aid that various groups of students receive. With an overall limit on federal aid, students from low income families would receive more of their aid package in the form of grants, while upper income students would mostly borrow in the unsubsidized loan programs up to some overall limit.

Some will argue that if federal loan policies in the future meet only a portion of charges and the annual amount of federal aid students may receive is limited, institutions will respond as they have in the past to cutbacks in federal student aid—i.e., they will raise their prices still further to generate more discounts for students whose aid has been reduced. But past declines in the real value of federal grants could not have been offset through higher tuitions if more loans had not been available to pick up some of the newly created need. If eligibility for loans and loan subsidies is what is being reduced in this case, institutions would be hard pressed to raise their prices to pay for even more discounting. Moreover, many institutions are reaching or have exceeded the limits of the discounting strategy, because each increase in tuitions and other charges now nets fewer and fewer dollars for non-student-aid purposes.

- Second, the federal government should reduce the regulatory and reporting requirements for institutions that demonstrate they are doing a good job in administering the federal student aid programs through low default rates and other measures of performance in the federal aid programs.

Many college officials argue that the costs of complying with a wide range of federal laws, regulations, and reporting requirements have been an important factor in the overall growth of college costs and tuitions. In the federal student aid programs, the prevailing philosophy in both statute and regulations has been to impose the same rules and reporting requirements on all institutions regardless of how well they administer the federal aid programs. Thus, an institution with a student loan default rate of two percent must comply with the same set of requirements as an institution with a 20 percent default rate.

A system of performance-based deregulation could be designed to make distinctions among institutions as to the types and amounts of regulations and reporting requirements that would be required of them, based on a series of readily available program performance indicators. Such a shift in regulatory philosophy in the federal student aid programs not only would reduce the costs of high performing institutions, it also would allow federal officials to focus their limited resources on institutions that demonstrably are not performing at a minimum level.

THE PARAMETERS OF THE DEBATE

The question of whether federal student aid has fueled tuition growth has been the source of heated debate at least since William Bennett raised the issue when he served as Secretary of Education during the mid-1980s. Bennett's argument then was that colleges and universities were chasing their own tail by relying on federal student aid to raise their tuitions and other charges at a rate much greater than the general rate of inflation. Further assertions by Bennett and others making this argument were that college officials explicitly took federal aid into account in setting their prices and that many students spent the federal aid they received frivolously, buying stereos or taking trips.

An alternative view advanced by most higher education officials has been that critics who accuse them of gouging the consumer and the taxpayer are wrong. They argue that there is no correlation between increases in federal student aid and the rapid growth in tuitions and other charges. They further point to the evidence that *decreases* in federal aid may have led to higher tuitions as institutions attempted to make up for federal aid cutbacks by providing more aid from their own resources, paid for by higher tuitions charged to students judged able to pay the full sticker price. Many college officials also believe that the costs of complying with federal student aid and many other federal as well as state regulations has further contributed to inflated cost structures at many institutions.

As is often the case in public policy debates, both positions in this debate probably have been overstated. By and large, the critics are wrong to argue that colleges and universities are setting their prices largely on the basis of the availability of federal aid. Many other factors probably have contributed more to the rapid growth in college costs and tuitions over the past two decades. Expanding demands on both public and private institutions to provide more and better services have contributed greatly to the cost spiral. Students and parents have indicated through their actions that they are willing to pay a higher price to have good professors, a wide range of programs, more student services, up-to-date facilities, and pleasant surroundings.

Many officials and analysts also point to the growing gap in lifetime earnings between college graduates and those who do not complete college as being a critical factor in allowing institutions to charge higher prices. Under this view, students and their families have been willing to pay higher tuitions because they recognize that the value of a college education is growing commensurably in terms of labor market differentials.

On the other hand, defenders of the current structure are being unrealistic when they argue that federal aid plays no role at all in tuition pricing decisions. Most observers agree, for example, that many proprietary schools price themselves according to how much federal aid is available. One strong indication of this is that when eligibility for federal unsubsidized student loans was restricted for students attending proprietary schools in the late 1980s, tuitions at many of these schools dropped accordingly. But the potential link between college costs and federal student aid is not limited to the proprietary sector.

Perhaps the most compelling evidence that federal aid has had an impact on tuitions at public and private nonprofit institutions comes from examining the extent to which federal aid now covers total costs of attendance. As shown in Table 1, federal aid in 1995 constituted roughly two-fifths of the total costs of attendance—i.e., the total amount that college students pay for tuition, fees, and room and board.[2] Federal loans alone covered more than one-third of the total costs of attendance in 1995. By contrast, in 1975, federal aid paid only one-eighth of the total costs of attendance, and loans paid for less than one-tenth of the total bill.

These figures underscore why it is important to differentiate between grants and loans in assessing the possible significance of federal student aid in the college cost equation. Throughout the twenty year period from 1975 to 1995, federal grants paid for less than one-tenth of the total costs of attendance and were awarded to less than one-third of all students. This relatively stable proportion of funding, combined with the fact that costs of

Table 1: Federal Aid, Federal Loans, Federal Grants, and Institutional Aid
as a Percentage of the Costs of Attendance

	Percentage of costs of attendance						
	Federal loans	Federal loans less institutional aid	Federal grants	Federal grants less institutional aid	Total federal aid	Total federal aid less institutional aid	Total institutional aid
Public Institutions							
1975	3%	3%	6%	6%	9%	9%	1%
1985	25%	25%	9%	10%	34%	35%	3%
1995	41%	44%	7%	7%	48%	51%	6%
Private Institutions							
1975	13%	14%	4%	4%	17%	18%	6%
1985	22%	25%	6%	6%	27%	31%	11%
1995	34%	42%	3%	4%	38%	46%	19%
Total, Public and Private Institutions							
1975	8%	9%	5%	5%	13%	14%	3%
1985	23%	25%	7%	8%	31%	33%	7%
1995	38%	43%	5%	6%	43%	49%	12%

SOURCE: NCES, *Digest of Education Statistics*, various years; and College Board, *Trends in Student Aid*, various years.

attendance effectively no longer determine the size of the Pell Grant a student receives, suggests that Pell and other forms of federal grant aid have not played a major role in most colleges' pricing decisions.

The growth in the share of the total bill financed by federal loans, by contrast, suggests that increased reliance on borrowing has played a significant role in allowing the rapid growth of college tuitions and other charges over the past two decades. Federal loans have grown tremendously as a proportion of costs of attendance, from less than one-tenth of total costs of attendance in 1975 to nearly two-fifths in 1995. The potential importance of federal loans is reinforced by the fact that one out of every two college students who are eligible to borrow now do so. With so many students borrowing such a high proportion of costs of attendance, it seems that loans must be providing some degree of insulation to institutions when they raise their prices. In the face of these figures, to argue that student loans are not a factor in college tuition patterns is akin to arguing that the ready availability of mortgages has no impact on the price of housing in this country, or that car manufacturers could maintain their prices even if loans and leases were not available to finance automobiles.

---

[2]Figures for federal student aid provided in this analysis come from College Board, *Trends in Student Aid*, various years. Figures for institutionally funded student aid, costs of attendance, and full-time equivalent student enrollments are as reported in the *Digest of Education Statistics*. Costs of attendance estimates do not include books, supplies, transportation, and other expenses. While the methodology used in this paper differs from one used by Jerry Davis in his recent analysis, *College Affordability*, the results are strikingly similar.

Another striking trend in the financing of higher education over the past two decades is the rapid growth in the grant aid institutions provide in the form of discounts from their sticker price of tuitions, fees, and room and board. As seen in Table 1, institutional aid quadrupled as a proportion of total costs of attendance, from three percent in 1975 to 12 percent in 1995. For a variety of reasons, higher education traditionally has accounted for the student aid institutions provide from their own resources as an expenditure item along with faculty salaries and heating bills. But in recent years, a growing number of higher education officials and analysts have recognized that institutionally funded student aid more properly should be accounted for as a discount from revenues, and that the price students pay minus the financial aid they receive is a more appropriate measure of the costs students face than is the sticker prices published in the college catalogue.

There are a number of important differences in the trends in how students in public and private institutions finance their education, as indicated in Charts 1 through 5. As Chart 1 shows, federal aid in 1995, for example, financed nearly one-half the costs of attendance for public sector students, compared to about one-third those for

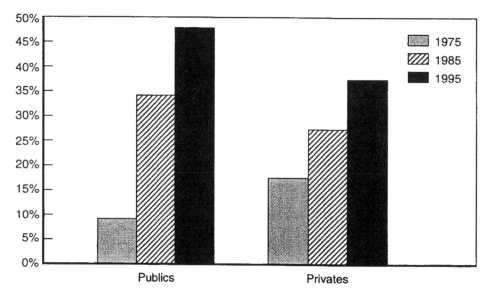

Chart 1: Federal Aid as a Percentage of Costs of Attendance

private sector students. Both public and private institutions have seen the share of costs of attendance met by federal aid increase rapidly between 1975 and 1995. But, whereas federal aid covered a larger portion of costs of attendance in private institutions than in public institutions in 1975, this was no longer the case by 1985.

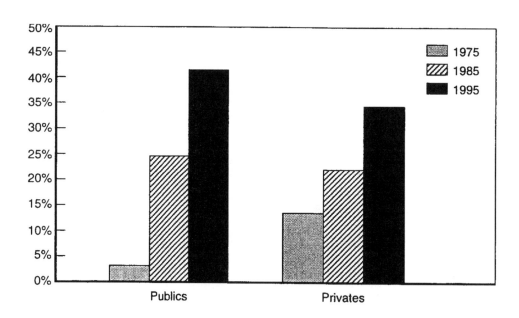

Chart 2: Federal Loans as a Percentage of Costs of Attendance

Most of this growth in the share of costs of attendance covered by federal aid was due to the growth in federal loans (Chart 2). Federal loans accounted for about two-fifths of total costs of attendance in the public sector in 1995, up from less than one-twentieth in 1975. For private sector students, federal loans in 1995 paid for about one-third of costs of attendance, up from one-seventh in 1975 and one-fifth in 1985.

Both public and private institutions have greatly increased the discounts they provide in the form of grant aid from their own resources (Chart 3). The use of discounts has traditionally been far more prominent in the private sector. There, discounts represented nearly one-fifth of the total costs of attendance in 1995, up from one-

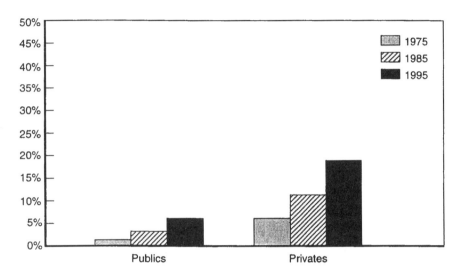

Chart 3: Institutional Aid as a Percentage of Costs of Attendance

twentieth in 1975. Discounting is less prominent at public institutions, representing just one-twentieth of costs of attendance in 1995. But the growth in this sector has been rapid—student aid funded by public institutions as a proportion of costs of attendance grew fivefold from 1975 to 1995.

As shown in Chart 4, when these discounts are subtracted from the sticker price, federal aid covered just over one-half of the amount students actually paid on a net basis in 1995 in public institutions and almost one-half in private institutions.

In addition, as Chart 5 shows, federal loans financed more than two-fifths of the net bill for both public and private sector students in 1995.

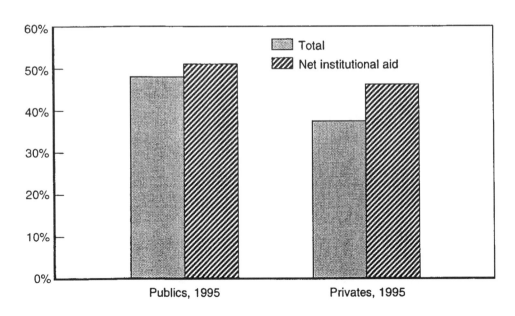

Chart 4: Federal Aid as a Percentage of Costs of Attendance

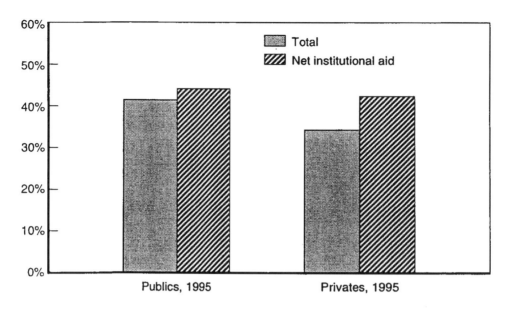

Chart 5: Federal Loans as a Percentage of Costs of Attendance

Loans have traditionally been a particularly important source of financing for students attending private colleges. In this regard, it is hard to imagine that private colleges could have stabilized their share of college enrollments over the past two decades—which they have, at around 20 to 25 percent of all students—without a healthy growth in student loan availability (chart 6). This is not to say that federal loan availability has caused private institutions to raise their tuitions or that private college officials spend all their waking hours trying to set tuitions and other charges to maximize the federal aid eligibility of their students. Many other factors can be given greater weight in explaining the growth in tuitions in recent decades, including the pressures to improve programs, facilities, and services to compete for the declining numbers of traditional college age students.

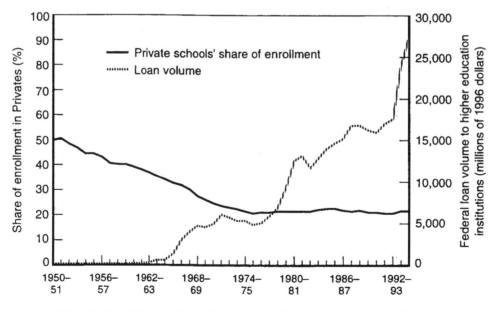

Chart 6: Total Federal Loan Volume and Share of Enrollment in Private Higher Education Institutions

But it is also no doubt the case that the growing availability of federal loans has facilitated the execution of the "high tuition/high aid" strategy that so many private colleges pursued in the 1980s. An integral component of that strategy was to provide financial aid to those students who become "needy" by virtue of the higher prices that are being charged. And as we have shown, loans represent a large share of the aid that was used to fill this need gap.

Loans traditionally have been far more critical in the financing of private institutions than they have been in the public sector, where tuitions are much lower and the need for loans has been less pressing. And it is clear that loans are not the principal reason public sector tuitions have grown so rapidly in the 1980s and 1990s—that starring role belongs to the slowdown in growth of state support for higher education and the use of tuition to make up for the shortfall in state funding. But the fact that two-fifths of public sector costs of attendance in 1995 were met through loans—up from one-twentieth in 1975—suggests that borrowing must have helped public college students pay the higher tuitions and other charges of the 1980s and 1990s.

RECENT ANALYSES OF THE IMPACT OF LOANS ON COSTS

At least two recent analyses have examined whether a correlation exists between federal loans and the rapid growth in tuitions. Using different methodologies, both studies found no correlation and thus concluded that the growing availability of federal loans has not influenced tuition patterns. Both of these studies, however, present an incomplete picture of the issue, and neither addresses the question of whether a correlation between tuition growth and federal loan availability or the lack thereof is an adequate measure of the possible relationship between tuitions and federal loans.

One of these analyses appears in a memorandum prepared by Jamie Merisotis, of the Institute for Higher Education Policy, for Senator James Jeffords, chairman of the U.S. Senate Committee on Labor and Human Resources. The memorandum to Senator Jeffords presents graphs comparing the annual percentage increases in loan volume and tuitions at public institutions on both a concurrent and lagged basis. The graphs indicate there is no correlation between the annual increases in college tuitions and federal loan volume.

However, studies of year-to-year changes, by their nature, fail to take into account longer term trends and patterns. If the same data in the memorandum to Senator Jeffords are presented on a cumulative basis over time and compared to the growth in the general rate of inflation, there is a much more striking correlation between the

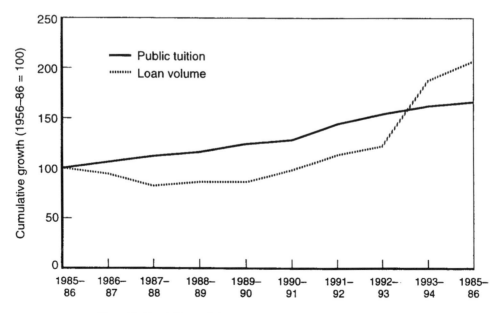

Chart 7: Real Growth in Aggregate Tuition and Total Loan
Volume at Public Institutions

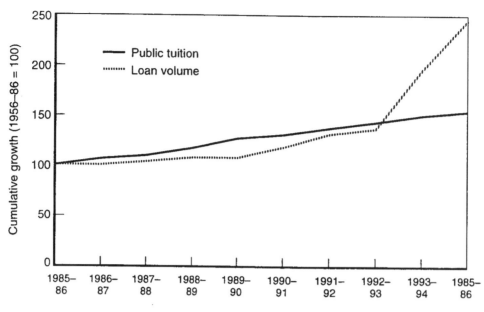

Chart 8: Real Growth in Aggregate Tuition and Total Loan Volume at Private Institutions

growth in loans and tuitions relative to the growth in inflation in both public and private institutions, as Charts 7 and 8 indicate.

This longer term connection between tuition growth and federal loans seems far more relevant than what happens from year to year. The thrust of our argument in this paper is that college officials set their tuitions each year and then gauge whether students and their families are willing and able to pay the higher prices. In those instances where demand slackens, colleges then either reduce the rate of increase in tuition and other charges in the next year or become even more aggressive with their student aid strategies. In this kind of scenario, growing loan availability over time is a much more important factor in determining students' ability to pay than are annual changes in eligibility rules and limits for federal loan programs.

The other recent analysis of this issue was done by the Coopers and Lybrand consulting group on contract with the American Council on Education. This study used multiple regression techniques to conclude there is no correlation between loan subsidies and the growth in tuitions over the past five years. But for this type of analysis, loan subsidies are an inappropriate measure of the impact of federal loans. The dollar amount that students and their families have borrowed is a much better measure than loan subsidies of the effect of federal loans on college costs, because the amount borrowed represents how much students and their parents do not have to pay out of their own pocket while the students are enrolled. Loan subsidies are also the wrong measure in this case because unsubsidized loans have accounted for most of the increase in federal loan volume since 1992. Unsubsidized loans now represent one-third of all federal loan volume. By looking only at the loan subsidy value, the Coopers and Lybrand study ignored the most significant aspects of recent federal student loan trends.

IS THERE A FEDERAL ROLE IN CONTAINING COLLEGE TUITIONS AND COSTS?

As with assertions about the role of federal aid in the tuition-setting process, proposals about what, if anything, the federal government should do about rising tuitions have been stated in extremes. On the one hand, some would have the federal government limit what institutions can charge or how fast they can increase their tuitions in order to have their students qualify for federal student aid. On the other hand, for those who believe there is no relationship between federal aid policies and tuition inflation, the federal government should play no role in the tuition-setting process.

Both of these extreme responses ignore key historical evidence. Proposals that would allow the federal government to control what institutions can charge seem unwarranted. Past federal efforts at wage and price controls in other industries have been unable to offset much stronger market pressures. But those who advocate no change in the federal student aid programs to address college cost concerns are refusing to recognize the growing role of federal aid, particularly loans, in financing higher education in this country.

The traditional federal policy response to growing college costs and tuitions has been to seek ways to increase aid to keep college affordable. Another way to keep college affordable, however, is to try to keep tuitions and other charges down. The 105th Congress, as evidenced by creation of the National Commission on the Cost of Higher Education, seems prepared to devote considerable time to the question of what, if anything, the federal government might do to encourage institutions to lower the rate of growth in college costs and tuitions.

Some Members of Congress have suggested that the federal government should limit how much institutions can charge in order for their students to remain eligible for federal student aid. Another legislative suggestion has been to limit aid for students attending institutions where tuitions and other charges increase more rapidly than inflation. Both of these approaches, however, would involve the federal government in the process of setting tuitions and other charges, a process in which many would argue it simply does not belong. Either of these approaches also would entail a massive effort on the part of the federal government to monitor how much institutions charge. In the absence of more constructive suggestions for dealing with college costs and tuitions, however, these kinds of federal limits on tuitions and other charges could possibly emerge in the reauthorization process.

The approach of limiting what institutions may charge in order for their students to be eligible for federal aid would be counterproductive, just as past efforts at wage and price controls have failed for other industries. The proposal to limit aid for students attending institutions where tuitions have increased too rapidly would create perverse incentives or lead to accounting tricks. For example, one decision an institution could make to conform its tuition increases to this kind of federal rule would be to cut back on the aid it provides from its own resources. This is certainly not the intention of those who propose such a limit. Another way institutions might react to such a rule would be to restrict tuition growth by shifting to fees or to other charges that would not be subject to the federal limitation. Again, this would not be a particularly desirable or useful result.

TWO PROPOSALS FOR REFORM

This paper proposes that the federal government could address the issue of rising college costs and tuitions in two ways without imposing on institutional autonomy. By making these proposals, we do not mean to imply that federal policies have caused the explosion in college costs and tuitions. As we have already indicated, a number of factors other than federal student aid probably have contributed more to the patterns of tuition inflation in this country. It is worthwhile, nonetheless, to consider whether there are actions the federal government could take to reduce inflationary pressures or incentives that exist in current procedures and rules.

One approach is for the federal government to use only a portion of costs of attendance in determining students' eligibility for loan subsidies and to limit the amount of federal aid students can receive annually, including unsubsidized student and parent loans. The other is to reduce regulatory and reporting requirements for institutions that are judged to be doing a good job in administering the federal student aid programs, thereby reducing their costs of compliance.

PARTIAL COST REIMBURSEMENT AND AN ANNUAL LIMIT ON FEDERAL AID

The federal Guaranteed Student Loan (GSL) program was established in 1965 to ensure that college students would have access to private financed loans that, in the absence of a federal guarantee against default, either would not have been available or would have charged prohibitive interest rates. The program was a federal entitlement in that lenders were insured against default as long as they exhibited "due diligence" in servicing the loan. The federal government was obligated to pay the statutorily set interest rate for borrowers as long as they were in school. In addition, lenders were eligible to receive federal "special allowance" payments to compensate them for the difference between market interest rates and the student interest rate.

To the extent that there may be a policy connection between federal loans and tuition escalation, it can be traced to the decision in 1981 to tie eligibility for federal in-school interest subsidies to a student's need. Prior to passage of the Middle Income Student Assistance Act (MISAA) in 1978, eligibility for the federal in-school interest payment was limited to students with family incomes of $25,000 or less. With the passage of MISAA, which, incidentally, was partially a response to efforts at the time to pass tuition tax credits, the income cap on in-school interest subsidies was removed entirely. In addition, in 1979 the limit on federal special allowance payments was removed so they could float with then volatile market conditions.

These two legislative changes led to the first of several explosions in loan volume in the late 1970s and early 1980s. (Since the mid-1970s, total volume in the federal student loan programs has grown fivefold in real terms.) In response to this boom in student loans, budget reconciliation legislation in 1981 reimposed a cap on which students could receive the federal in-school interest subsidy. But instead of being based solely on family income, the limit imposed in 1981 was based on a student's need—costs of attendance minus expected family contribution and other aid received.

Having a subsidy cap based on need rather than income has changed the dynamics of the federally subsidized student loan programs. With a need-based cap, any increase in student charges potentially translates into greater eligibility for the in-school interest subsidy. The annual and cumulative dollar limits on how much students can borrow become the only thing standing in the way of tuition increases resulting in even more borrowing. As long as loan limits are relatively low, as they were when the need-based cap on the in-school interest subsidy was imposed in 1981 and as they continue to be for certain groups of students, the connection between loan policy and college charges is tenuous.[3] But when loan limits are increased, the threat of loans spurring further tuition inflation also increases. This is now most obviously the case with the Parent Loans (PLUS) program where there are no dollar limits and a student's costs of attendance are the only limit on how much parents can borrow.

The 1981 policy shift to a need-based subsidy cap also created issues of equity and effectiveness because borrowers' eligibility for the in-school interest subsidy now varies depending on the costs of the institution they attend. A student from a family with $80,000 in family income is now ineligible for federal in-school interest payments if he or she goes to a public institution where the total costs of attendance, including room, board, and other expenses, in addition to tuition and fees, may be $10,000. But if that same student goes to a private institution where the average costs of attendance exceed $20,000, he or she may well be eligible for federal in-school interest payments. At current tuition levels, students with family incomes in excess of $100,000 can qualify for the in-school interest subsidy at the highest-priced institutions. Moreover, eligibility for this interest subsidy continues if the borrower goes to graduate school, thus adding substantially to the long-term federal taxpayer cost.

A need-based subsidy cap can also lead to a situation where the federal government is subsidizing students' lifestyles. For example, if an institution decides to upgrade its dormitories and increases its room fees to pay for the renovations, the federal government could become a partner in this decision by subsidizing loans that reflect the higher cost. Similarly, a student may choose to live in a single dorm room rather than double up, and the government could end up subsidizing this choice. Again, as in the case of higher income students attending higher priced institutions, this subsidy lasts through graduate or professional school and so can be quite expensive to the taxpayer.

Partial Cost Reimbursement. One means for the federal government to address the question of college costs and student aid without intruding on institutional autonomy would be to consider only a portion of a student's total costs of attendance in calculating his or her eligibility for federal loan subsidies. This partial cost reimbursement model would represent a shift from the traditional federal aid practice of recognizing a student's total costs of attendance in determining eligibility for federal student loans. Such a change in policy could have the beneficial effect of decoupling or at least reducing whatever link may now exist between federal aid and tuition setting, since the federal government no longer would match every increase in student charges on a dollar-for-dollar basis.

The federal government could move in the direction of partial cost reimbursement by recognizing a portion of tuition costs (say, 50 percent) above some base level of tuition (say, $3,000, to reflect average tuition and fees at public institutions) and a standard amount of nontuition expenses to determine a student's eligibility for federal loan programs. This proposed change would have no effect on determining eligibility for Pell Grants, which should be allowed to continue to serve as the foundation aid program. In addition, under this proposal, institutions could continue to use the total costs of attendance in determining an individual student's eligibility for the federal campus-based programs.

It also is important to understand that the federal government under the partial cost reimbursement plan described here would not tell institutions how much they could charge. Nor would there be any need to monitor how fast their charges increase. Instead, the federal government would be limiting how much of a student's total

---

[3]Michael McPherson and Morton Schapiro in Chapter 8 of their new book, *The Student Aid Game*, reject the notion that federal loans have contributed to tuition inflation largely on the basis that there are limits on how much students can borrow.

costs of attendance can be subsidized through the federal loan programs. In operational terms, what the family is expected to contribute and whatever federal grant aid the student receives would be subtracted from the partial costs of attendance, rather than the current practice of using whatever the institution charges as the upward bound of federal subsidies.

There are precedents for this kind of partial cost reimbursement approach. The Pell Grant program, for example, since 1992 has only recognized a standard living expense in its award formula. And the two newly enacted tuition tax credits—the HOPE and Lifetime Learning tax credits—recognize only a portion of tuitions, precisely to discourage institutions from raising their tuitions in order to capture more federal tax benefits for their students. Interestingly enough, neither of these precedents was criticized as being an example of federal price controls.

A primary argument against partial cost reimbursement will be that students will no longer be able to go to the school of their choice if they are no longer eligible for subsidized loans. There are at least two counter arguments to this contention. First, students and their parents could still borrow in the unsubsidized loan programs. Second, by not using total costs of attendance as a benchmark, federal policies would finally recognize the growing role of states and institutions in the provision of student aid, unlike the traditional practice where the federal government acts as though it is the only source of funds in the student aid process. Thus, partial cost reimbursement could help to address the growing concern in the Congress that institutions use their sticker price to determine federal aid eligibility for all students, even those who do not pay the full sticker price because of institutional discounts.

Partial cost reimbursement also represents a way to limit how much in the way of family resources students may have and still qualify for the federal in-school interest subsidy. In the current federal student loan structure, the higher the costs of attendance, the higher the income that students can have and still qualify for the in-school interest subsidy. If the federal government were to set limits on how much it would reimburse through subsidized borrowing, the in-school interest subsidy would be better targeted than is currently the case. In addition, if nontuition expenses were limited to a standard amount, the federal government could get out of the business of subsidizing student lifestyle choices.

In effect, partial cost reimbursement is a way to reestablish an income limit on subsidies in the federal student loan programs while improving upon a simple income cap. Unlike a cap on income, subtracting expected family contribution from the partial costs of attendance would have different effects on students whose family incomes are similar but whose other circumstances differ. For example, students from families with two children in college might still be eligible for the subsidy, while another family with similar income but only one child in college would be ineligible. In addition, subtracting a student's family contribution from partial costs to determine eligibility for subsidized loans reduces the "notch effect" that simple income limits can create. With an income cap, students with one dollar less than the limit may participate fully in the program, while those with one dollar more would not be eligible at all, i.e., a notch effect exists at the dollar limit. Under the approach suggested here, one more dollar in family contribution simply would mean the student is eligible for a dollar less in subsidized loans.

Students whose family contribution and other aid are less than their partial costs of attendance would still be eligible for the in-school interest subsidy. Students whose family contribution exceeded the partial cost calculation would be ineligible for subsidized loans, but could still borrow in the federal unsubsidized loan programs. In a time of more limited federal resources, targeting subsidies to those students with lower family incomes regardless of where they go to school and providing unsubsidized loans to meet the cash flow needs of students from families of more substantial means seems far more appropriate than the current policy of providing better-off students with expensive federal subsidies throughout their educational careers.

The important point here is that policymakers ought to decide how far up the income scale they want to provide subsidies, rather than have the limit on who receives the subsidy be a consequence of how much an institution charges, as is currently the case in the federal loan programs. If properly structured, partial cost reimbursement could reduce whatever incentive exists for higher-priced institutions to increase their tuitions, since students with family incomes above the cap would no longer find their eligibility for subsidized loans increase as tuitions rise.

A partial cost approach could lead to lower federal subsidy costs, but that need not be its underlying purpose. Limits on the amount of subsidy that higher income students receive also could be used to increase subsidized loan limits for students from lower income families. If that were the case, the result of adopting a partial cost approach would be a redistribution of subsidies rather than an overall reduction in federal expenditures for student loans.

Some will argue that if federal loan policies in the future meet only a proportion of tuitions and other charges, many institutions could respond by raising their prices still further to generate more discounts for students whose eligibility to borrow had been reduced. But most institutions in the past could not have offset federal grant decreases through higher discounts if federal loans had not been available to pick up much of the newly created need. If loan eligibility is what is being reduced in this case, institutions would be hard pressed to raise their prices to pay for more aid discounting.

We want to emphasize again that under partial cost reimbursement, institutions could charge whatever they want and there would be no federal role in monitoring their tuitions and other charges. The federal government simply would stop providing subsidized loans to students with family contributions above a certain level.

Imposing an Annual Limit on Federal Aid. The preceding discussion does not address the question of whether students who become ineligible for federal in-school interest subsidies under a partial cost reimbursement approach should be able to participate fully in the federal unsubsidized loan programs, and whether parents should continue to be able to borrow up to the full costs of attendance in the PLUS program.

The dilemma here is as follows: If what students and parents may borrow in the unsubsidized programs is limited to the partial costs of attendance, then many current students and their families will simply not be able to borrow enough through the federal loan programs to attend the institution of their choice. On the other hand, if students can borrow unsubsidized loans up to the total costs of attendance, then nothing will have been done about the issue of college costs and federal loans. Whatever link between college tuitions and federal loans may now exist will simply shift over to the unsubsidized federal loan programs, with lower federal expenditures for student loans but higher borrowing costs for many students.

One solution to this dilemma would be for the federal government to limit how much federal aid students can receive annually, including through the various unsubsidized programs. Each of the federal student aid programs has limits on how much students can receive, but there is no limit on the total amount of federal aid they can receive, either annually or over the course of their education. As a result, rising college tuitions and other charges often are financed through a progression of federal student aid programs. Campus-based aid is added to Pell Grants, subsidized loans are added to the campus-based programs, unsubsidized student loans and PLUS loans are added to the subsidized loan amounts. The total amount of federal aid through the Title IV programs sums up to well in excess of $15,000 for undergraduates and more than $20,000 for students in graduate and professional school fields of study.[4] While few students receive this much in federal aid, adding one federal program on top of another with no sense of an overall limit increases the potential link between college costs and federal aid.

The lack of an overall annual limit on federal aid also contributes to concerns about the fragmentation of the student aid delivery system and an overall lack of coherence in federal policies. If one were to ask how much federal aid a student can receive, few people could answer that question, because an overall figure never appears in the legislation or in federal student aid documentation. Students and their families do not know how much federal aid is available, because the information is never provided. In addition, the absence of an overall limit means no tradeoff exists among federal aid programs. What students receive in grants typically does not affect how much they or their parents can borrow.

Placing a limit on total annual federal aid would build on the proposal for a Student Total Education Package (STEP), the keystone of the 1993 report of the National Commission on Responsibilities for Financing Postsecondary Education. The STEP proposal principally was made to increase awareness about the availability of federal aid and to generate support for more funding of federal aid. But such an approach also could help to reduce the potential link between college tuition costs and federal student aid programs by removing total costs of attendance from of the student aid equation. Imposing an overall limit on how much federal aid students may receive would have another important favorable consequence. It would introduce greater policy coherence into the federal student aid structure by establishing a relationship among the various federal programs.

---

[4]These figures do not include veterans' education benefits and other specialized forms of aid, such as scholarships and fellowship programs provided under Title IX of the Higher Education Act. Nor do they include health professional loans and other specialized loan programs not authorized by the Higher Education Act.

PERFORMANCE-BASED REGULATORY RELIEF

Colleges and universities, like any other organizations in our society, are obligated to comply with a broad range of federal and state laws and regulations. As issues in our society have become increasingly complex, the breadth of laws and regulations with which higher education institutions must comply has similarly grown.

For colleges and universities, these laws and regulations govern the safety of their workers, the security of their students, and the environmental hazards created in their laboratories. Many higher education officials believe that compliance with federal and state laws and regulations has contributed greatly to increased costs and consequently to the tuitions charged. Some have estimated that as much as ten percent or more of total expenditures at their institutions go toward providing the necessary information to dozens of federal and state agencies.

These concerns are not new, however. The American Council on Education, for example, issued a report in 1976 on the costs of federally mandated social programs at colleges and universities. That report suggested that while the compliance costs to individual institutions were small—less than 5 percent of operating budgets—they were growing much faster than instructional costs or total revenues. Interestingly, the highest cost item identified in the 1976 report was the payment of social security taxes. The belief that federal laws and regulations are adding to the costs of higher education has not abated in the intervening two decades, although environmental regulations are now a more likely target of criticism of excess regulations. Few college officials would now mention social security taxes as a burdensome regulation.

With regard to the federal student aid programs, the prevailing philosophy in both statute and regulation has been to have all institutions comply with the same set of rules and reporting requirements. To participate, all institutions must comply with uniform requirements, including maintaining a default rate in the student loan programs below certain specified levels, meeting certain minimum financial requirements, being accredited by a recognized accrediting agency, and providing annual audits and other information as required by the Higher Education Act and related regulations. In the existing regulatory structure, little or no distinction is made based on how well institutions administer the federal aid programs. Institutions with low default rates and well-run aid offices are subject to the same reporting requirements as institutions with high default rates and understaffed or nonexistent financial aid offices.

The Clinton Administration has proposed moving away from this traditional philosophy. It advocates instead the development of a system in which institutions determined to have done a good job in administering the federal student aid programs would be subject to less intensive regulatory and reporting requirements than those institutions that have not performed as well. The Administration's proposal was prompted in part by comments it had received from a number of college officials who argue that their institutions are doing a good job administering the programs and that they should not be subject to the same rules and regulations as institutions with an inferior track record.

The Administration sponsored a set of discussions in 1995 and 1996 on a preliminary proposal of performance-based deregulation and invited formal written responses from interested parties. While there was considerable interest on the part of many college and university officials in pursuing the notion of performance-based deregulation, the response from much of the higher education community, as represented by their associations, was lukewarm at best. Representatives of at least several of the associations suggested instead that broad-based deregulation was a more appropriate approach to the issue of overregulation in higher education than deregulation based on the performance of institutions. In the heated environment preceding the 1996 presidential campaign and election, the Administration chose to postpone deliberations on its proposal.

The notion of differentiating regulatory and reporting requirements on the basis of how well institutions are administering the federal student aid programs remains a good idea, however, and one worth further exploration and debate. A performance-based deregulation approach would appropriately reward institutions that demonstrate they are doing a good job administering the federal student aid programs. It also would allow federal regulators to target their limited resources for enforcement on those institutions that are not meeting minimal standards in administering the federal student aid programs.

Remarks on Restructuring Higher Education

Remarks by William F. Massy [*]

National Center for Postsecondary Improvement (NCPI), and

The Jackson Hole Higher Education Group, Inc.

Stanford University

September 7—8, 1997

U.S. higher education may be the envy of the world, but, as for many industries before it, the time has come for restructuring.

TOPICS TO BE COVERED

1. Institutional market segments and competition
2. Educational quality (root cause of the cost problem; hopefully part of the solution)
3. Price in relation to cost (the demand side of the cost equation)
4. Cost drivers (the supply side)
5. Policy implications

SEGMENTATION AND COMPETITION

1. Carnegie classifications: oriented toward mission and resources: may encourage mission creep; becoming obsolete.
2. Two new schemes are being developed, both market oriented. (The following represents my own characterization of materials not yet published.)
3. NCPI (Zemsky): <u>brand name, mass providers, convenience</u> (defined statistically using publicly available data; correlates with popular indices):
   - *brand name* (includes medallion and super-medallion as subsegments): institutions whose selectivity gives them market power; they cater mostly to traditional students and have high graduation rates, traditional academic values;
   - *center of the market:* non-selective institutions that cater to a mix of traditional and non-traditional students; they have much less market power, but fairly traditional academic values;
   - *convenience/user friendly* (includes super convenience): non-selective institutions that cater mostly to non-traditional and part-time students; their values may be more in line with the business "quality culture" than academe; emergent segment with growing market power as evidenced by recent price increases.

---

[*]These remarks are the sole responsibility of the author. They do not necessarily represent the views of NCPI, its sponsor (the Department of Education's Office of Education Research and Improvement), or Stanford University. These speaking notes have been edited slightly after the session to incorporate new information and respond to certain points made at the meeting.

4. Rand (Goldman): <u>prestige, prestige-seeking, [educational] reputation</u> (based on case studies):
   - *prestige:* institutions that compete on the basis of visibility and image, usually based on faculty research; durable market power rooted in traditional academic values;
   - *prestige-seeking:* institutions that aspire to prestige-based market power and that are pursuing a strategy for achieving it; traditional academic values but less market power;
   - *[educational] reputation:* institutions that are attempting to build a market franchise by catering to student needs; market power depends on continuing to deliver quality that can be identified by customers; "quality culture" rather than traditional academic values.

5. The NCPI and Rand segments are similar at the extremes. The common points are:
   - Prestige (brand name, especially medallion) confers the greatest market power and attendant benefits for pricing and institutional autonomy—though recent data shows some restraint in their exercise of pricing power.
     - The prestige system stems partly from centuries of academic history and partly from the difficulty of measuring educational as opposed to research quality (research is used as a surrogate for educational quality).
     - Prestige also confers credentialing and networking benefits; though not necessarily related to delivered educational quality, they do provide tangible advantages (for example, medallion graduates are much more likely to go to graduate and professional schools).
     - This is an elite system: the benefits of prestige for both institutions and students depend on its scarcity value.
   - It would be a mistake to restructure policy solely in response to the image presented by the prestige schools.
     - They represent only a small fraction of institutional and student numbers.
     - They rely heavily on gifts, endowments, and grants and contracts.
     - They are the most impervious to change.
     - It's not obvious that they should in fact change dramatically.
       They safeguard an important academic, cultural, and artistic heritage that should be preserved.
       Most have done a good job in using financial aid and outreach mechanisms to achieve diversity.
       They represent the largest and best part of the nation's academic research capacity.
   - The prestige-seeking schools represent a much larger and a more problematic segment.
     - Rand concludes that prestige-seeking behavior represents a high-risk institutional strategy and that it may not further national goals.
     - My research on the academic ratchet (see below) shows that prestige-seeking is both dysfunctional and widespread.
     - One can view prestige-seeking behavior either as an effort to force-fit elite academic values to a massified system or to escape from massification.
     - Converting the pursuit of traditional prestige measures (by schools not now in the high-prestige category) to pursuit of well-grounded educational-delivery reputations should become a public policy goal.
     - This will require changing the "winning conditions" for both institutions and students: from "have versus have-not" to "have this or have that."

QUALITY

1. The traditional model of educational quality (based on centuries of experience, mostly in elite systems):
   - For students, education is a "journey of inquiry," aided by faculty content experts and mentors but fundamentally the student's responsibility.
   - The process of teaching and learning is a "black box": effective teaching is an art and not a very fruitful subject for inquiry, training, or systematic improvement.

- Good teaching depends on research and scholarship: in fact, improvements in research and scholarship will improve teaching more or less automatically.

2. Massification of education and growth of research funding have undermined the traditional model:
   - Student bodies are less homogeneous, less like faculty; traditional academic values are less relevant to these students.
   - Faculty seek leverage to spend time on research; they want doctoral students who can help in research and teaching.
   - Sponsored *research amplifies the need for leverage.*

3. An alternative, emergent, view of higher education is rooted in the kinds of quality principles that have been applied by business in response to foreign competition.
   - Education should be *customer (client) oriented, process focused, and data driven.*
   - Quality should be defined empirically as *fitness for use,* not in terms of academic disciplines or abstract principles.
   - Education should be viewed as an *end-to-end process,* encompassing all parts of the curriculum plus support services, not as a series of unconnected courses and experiences ("silos").
   - The result should *respond to individual needs* more effectively than the traditional model as currently applied in most institutions ("mass customization").
   - Implementation should be subject to strong *quality assurance* processes which operate at both the design and delivery stages of education.
   - *Continuous improvement* should be an overriding priority for all educational processes ("good enough isn't").

4. The U. S. lags the international community in the development and deployment of   m o d e r n educational quality assurance and improvement methods.
   - Though the problems are difficult and the methods controversial, significant progress is being made in the UK, The Netherlands, Denmark, Sweden, Hong Kong, Australia, New Zealand, and other countries.
   - These initiatives are hardly known in the U.S.
   - Few U.S. entities take part in the International Network of Quality Assurance Agencies in Higher Education (INQAAHE), for example.

COST AND PRICE

1. Bowen's law: "universities will raise all the money they can and spend all the money they raise" ("raising money" means generating funds from all possible sources, not just from   gifts). Bowen's law follows directly from the economic theory of non-profit entities.
   - Bowen's law is reinforced by the accreditation agencies, especially when they focus on inputs rather than outputs or process. (The subject-specific agencies tend to apply the strongest spending pressure.)
   - There is no mystery about how institutions can contain or even cut costs: the job is painful but it can be done. The real question is whether, and how, costs can be cut of contained without sacrificing quality.

2. All institutions are constrained by markets (and political/PR factors); the stronger the market forces the less the effect of cost-rise pressure (see below).
   - Many private institutions are discounting tuition heavily through financial aid ("dialing for dollars"): for many, the marginal net revenue achieved from tuition increases is less than 50% or even one-third; the situation is similar to hospital pricing and net revenue during the 1980s.
   - Financial aid expenditures surely help drive tuition increases, though the relationship is difficult to prove statistically (institutional resource allocation is a zero-sum game).
   - Medallion institutions are less constrained; tuition's continue rise because of these schools' market power.

- Endowment and gift support don't seem to make much of a difference in tuition levels for individual institutions:
  - institutions price according to the market and use endowment payout and gifts as discretionary revenue;
  - the impact of endowment and gifts on the overall tuition market is not known.
- Convenience institutions tend to price their services as commodities, depending on marginal cost and competition; financial aid discounting isn't much of a factor.

3. Cross-subsidies are a way of life in colleges and universities.
   - Cross subsidies represent the ascendancy of institutional values over market forces
     - for example, in the relative importance of different fields, of different student groups, of teaching versus research—and sometimes in the support of internal stakeholders.
   - They are a necessary and desirable attribute of not-for-profit organizations—entities that reinvest to further their mission rather than distributing profits to external stakeholders.

     I may disagree with your choices but I will defend your right to make them.
   - Eliminate cross subsidies and one has the equivalent of a profit-making enterprise (this is a provable theorem in economics).

4. Price and cost are often used as surrogates for quality.
   - Quality is hard to measure; price and cost are easy are well known.
   - *Given conventional approaches to education, there* is *a positive correlation between cost and quality.*
   - However, the correlation breaks down at high expenditure levels—the question becomes, "what do institutions do with the money they collect?"
   - Because the conventional approaches to education are giving way to new processes and technologies, the correlation between cost an quality will be even smaller in the future than today.

5. What do institution do with "excess revenue"? According to the Rand study and my own research:
   - *Prestige institutions* spend the money on salaries and perquisites (especially for faculty), faculty research, and lavish campuses and amenities.
     - Many of these expenditures are driven by external market factors—they are seen as required in order to maintain prestige status.
     - These market forces are especially powerful for faculty salaries and research support ("it takes a generation to build a great department but you can destroy one in a year or two").
     - Because support levels are seen as "property rights" by faculty, restructurings and reallocations are especially difficult for these institutions—hence improvements are achieved mostly by adding cost to the existing base.
     - However, administrative salaries and perquisites (including those of presidents and chancellors) usually are scrutinized and disciplined by the faculty as well as be external stakeholders.

     On balance, the pursuit of prestige for its own sake produces a vicious circle of cost escalation.
   - *Prestige-seeking institutions* invest in infrastructure and activities aimed at improving prestige.
     - Research usually is the operative investment goal.
     - Salaries and perquisites are selective, not as property rights.
     - The investments are increasingly at high risk—there is no guarantee that they will produce the market power associated with prestige.
   - *[Educational] reputation* institutions invest in activities that enhance educational quality.
     - They spend heavily on quality assurance and improvement processes, for example.
     - They support research mainly when it offers an identifiable educational payoff.

     The pursuit of demonstrable educational process and outcome quality produces a virtuous circle which tends to generate better value for money.

6. Up to now I've dealt mainly with the demand side of the pricing equation. Because the cost side also exerts a strong effect, we turn now to the matter of *cost drivers*.

- The cost drivers affect all institutions, but the effects are larger for institutions with greater pricing discretion.
- There are important interactions between the cost drivers and the aforementioned demand-side effects.

COST DRIVERS

1. The *cost disease* (Baumol): what happens to labor intensive industries with stagnant productivity.
   - Unit labor costs rise faster than inflation because of economy-wide productivity gains.
   - This translates to higher prices unless output per hour can be increased ("the live string quartet, the barber").
2. The *administrative lattice:* the tendency for administrative and support structures to replicate themselves because of their own internal dynamics.
   - Why the lattice replicates:
     - "needs" that are perceived as unbounded
     - function lust
     - risk aversion
     - organizational incentive structures (e.g., power, promotion)
   - Institutions should place strict limits on the growth of administrative and support cost or on such cost as a percentage of total expenditures. These limits:
     - force tradeoffs that halt growth of the lattice;
     - trigger major reengineering that can roll back the lattice without loss of quality.
3. *Regulation and litigation:* the effect of external legal forces.
   - Anecdotal evidence demonstrates that responding to regulation and the threat of litigation can drive up costs—especially when such responses interact with the lattice forces;
   - Because of confounding with the lattice forces, it appears impossible to identify the full cost of regulation and litigation statistically.
   - The combined effect can be documented.
   - Case studies might disentangle the causality to some extent.
   - Devolving authority while improving after-the-fact accountability for processes and outcomes usually represents the best policy strategy.
     - Examples include outcomes sampling and process review.
     - NACUBO can provide good examples on the business side; foreign experience can provide them on the academic side.
4. *The academic ratchet:* the process by which institutionally funded faculty research grows over time, often at the expense of educational quality. This surely the largest driver of costs in many institutions.
   - Intrinsic and extrinsic incentives drive faculty toward research, away from teaching.
     - The faculty marketplace pays off on research, not teaching.
     - Promotion, salaries, and internal prestige favor research.
     - PhDs are trained and socialized for research, not teaching.
     - Faculty receive big "bonuses" (summer salary support) and perquisites by winning sponsored research awards.
   - Therefore, faculty tend to "satisfice" their teaching, maximize their research.
     - The standard for teaching quality may be quite high, but research becomes dominant once the threshold is reached.
     - The pressures for research erode teaching quality standards over time; this reduces the satisficing threshold.

- Research pressures also reduce teaching load norms and increase the demand for support services to leverage faculty time—both add cost and reduce quality;
  - The satisficing process also applies to collegial processes ("hollowed collegiality"); this undermines the institution's adaptive ability.
  - These processes work only one way—hence the "ratchet" metaphor.
- The unrelenting pressure to do research also:
  - produces, in many fields, a glut of work that has little real value despite the fact of publication ("papers no one reads", "journals created to serve the needs of authors rather than readers");
  - drives institutions to over-produce PhDs;
  - makes it more difficult for institutions to mount effective educational quality improvement and assurance processes based on modern quality principles.
- Research can be a mixed blessing, especially for institutions outside the top tier of research quality.
  - Research can shift large amounts of faculty time and attention away from educationally-related tasks;
  - The reduction in time on task can more than offset the gains provided by research (Nerlov's complementarily-substitution model).
  - The costs of research may well be passed on to students, especially if the bid for prestige is less than fully successful.

5. Information technology
   - IT will revolutionize post-secondary education, although it may take some time to overcome cultural barriers.
   - Information technology is driving up costs at the present time.
     - Institutions are investing heavily in IT infrastructure and running conventional teaching and learning processes in parallel with new ones ("institutions are becoming labor *and* capital intensive").
   - IT innovation proceeds in three phases:
     - personal productivity aids;
     - enrichment add-ins;
     - paradigm shifts.

     Only the last can save money. (The first two enhance quality but cost more.)
   - In the long run, IT will move postsecondary education from a handicraft industry to a process-oriented and more capital intensive one.
   - IT will offer economies of scale and increase the ratio of fixed to variable cost, and these will change the nature of competition.
   - IT will broaden faculty responsibilities to include process design and management as well as content expertise.
   - IT, and the competitive changes that will come with it, will break down traditional academic viewpoints and stimulate the adoption of modern quality principles.

POLICY IMPLICATIONS

1. Regulation can't solve either the cost problem or the quality problem.
   - To regulate price, one would have to have widely applicable quality norms and also regulate financial aid.
     - No such are available or likely to become available.
     - Price regulation is a blunt instrument in any case; the market can be more effective.

- To regulate cross subsidies would be bad in principle and impossible in practice.
  - Not-for-profit entities should be allowed to balance values and market forces.
  - The data needed to track the cost of individual activities aren't available or likely to become available.
- Some states have tried to regulate teaching loads, but this is a poor solution because:
  - there are too many legitimate reasons for exceptions and ways to recast the data;
  - information technology is making conventional contact hour measures irrelevant.
- Requiring detailed teaching quality assessment reports hasn't worked at the state level or abroad, and it would be a disaster at the federal level.
  - Efforts to produce valid and universally applicable quality measures have not succeeded.
  - Complexity and the need for judgment require that, to be effective, assessment must be done locally as part of an improvement culture—not a compliance culture. However, assessment *is* possible at the local level for local purposes.
  - Requiring detailed regulatory reports and second-guessing institutional quality judgments would destroy the conditions necessary for effective assessment at the local level.
  - Experience shows that institutions can and do spin the data anyway.

"Quality has to be built from the ground up, you can't inspect it in at the end."

2. In my view, the best hope for containing cost while maintaining or enhancing quality is to discredit the idea that classical prestige is the highest and best goal for most colleges and universities. Instead, the goal should be to provide the best possible educational value for money.
   - Changing the goal structure will require provision of an attractive alternative aspiration set while making pursuit of the traditional set more costly and problematic.
   - The limited experience to date suggests that institutions and faculty who learn to apply modern quality principles and paradigm-changing technology enjoy high demand for their services and high intrinsic satisfaction.
     - Such work requires strong disciplinary or similar content knowledge as well as process knowledge—it is not "AV 101."
     - Results can be reviewed for quality and disseminated via publication or other media.
   - The federal government has limited power to affect such changes. However, we should not underestimate the influence of government—and this Commission—in framing the terms of the public dialog, providing information, and promulgating incentives.
   - These are long-term solutions. Given the strength of the demand- and supply-side cost drivers, and the entrenched interests that support them, it may be impossible to find a quick-acting solution. So far there seems to be no magic bullet.

3. More specifically, the federal government might adopt the following strategy.
   - Encourage institutions in the middle segments to compete on the basis of educational quality reputation.
     - These are the prestige-seekers, the non-medallion name brand and mass- provider institutions.
     - Their efforts to gain the market power that goes with conventional measures of prestige are socially dysfunctional and not likely to succeed in any case.
   - Provide incentives and, where possible, infrastructure for developing and disclosing meaningful education-quality data—a "truth in education" program.

- Where possible, reduce the rewards associated with the conventional prestige measures and increase those associated with educational value for money.
- Let the market operate.

4. A program to implement the strategy might include these elements. *

- Use federal influence to make *educational quality assurance and improvement processes* a central theme of:
  - accreditation—institutions without effective processes should be denied full accreditation and the reasons for this should be made public;
  - state oversight of public institutions—states should take the lead in developing effective review processes and the results of these reviews should inform their institutional funding decisions.
- Task the Department of Education and other appropriate federal agencies to:
  - embed the development and dissemination of educational quality assurance and improvement methods as a major priority;
  - encourage benchmarking by individual institutions of process improvement and output-quality assessments in both the educational and support areas (the American Productivity and Quality Center is working with a number of entities to further this goal);
  - develop and disseminate survey information about the utilization of these methods by individual institutions and groups of institutions;
  - extend the Baldrige awards to colleges and universities on a permanent basis.

  Progress in these areas will enhance the market's ability to detect and reward educational value for money, and thus drive institutions toward containing costs while improving quality.
- In addition, the federal government should:
  - limit the rewards of prestige-seekers by strengthening barriers to entry into the sponsored research "market;
  - encourage concentration and size-limitation of research-oriented doctoral programs in most fields;
  - stimulate the development of new educational-process oriented doctoral programs that would combine disciplinary training with work on quality processes and technology applications;
  - support the use of paradigm-shifting educational information technology applications, on-campus as well as for distance learning, wherever possible.

---

*NCPI currently is doing research on educational quality assurance and improvement.

Student Aid and Tuition: Toward A Causal Analysis

Roy J. Pearson & Stephane Baldi
American Institutes for Research, Pelvin Research Center
December, 1997

INTRODUCTION

Two of the issues being addressed by the Commission involve assessing the impact of institutional aid and discounting on tuition and the impact of student financial aid programs on tuition. These issues are conceptually linked and we treat them in this manner in this paper.

Even though increases in tuition are caused by numerous factors, one "prime suspect" is the growth in student financial aid. The argument is sometimes made that the additional resources made available by these programs are "appropriated" by universities and colleges in the form of higher tuition. Another "prime suspect" is institutional aid, most frequently offered in the form of tuition discounts and fee waivers. It is sometimes argued that tuition is increased to help fund this internal source of student financial assistance.

After briefly reviewing what the literature says about these two issues, we examine the role of internal and external sources of student financial aid in the wider context of the cost of higher education cost and its affordability, as well as the narrower context of what impact they have on tuition. A rigorous analysis of these issues must be guided by a proper understanding of the underlying processes and causal mechanisms. For this reason, we first present and describe, at a conceptual level, a simplified view of the social determination of higher education cost and its affordability. Also, we examine recent empirically based analyses of these issues and conclude that the technical methods used to assess them seem inappropriate. Consequently, their findings may be unreliable. We end by discussing some alternative approaches to analyzing these issues, and sketch out a research design that uses one of them.

TUITION AND AID

Various theories have been used as a basic framework for analyzing trends in the cost of higher education. In 1980, Bowen promulgated what became known as the revenue theory of higher education cost.[1] Briefly stated, this theory contends the dominant goals of an institution consist of seeking excellence, prestige, and influence, in a quest to attract students, research dollars, grants, gifts, and faculty. In seeking to reach these goals, it is argued that there is no limit on the amount of money instutions could spend. Hence, each institution will try to raise all the money it can, and will spend all it can raise. According to this theory, institutions raise tuition to support their spending habits, which are conditioned by the goals they seek. In the market theory, expounded by Getz and Siegfried, the intensely competitive nature of the market for higher education explains why expenditures increase.[2] According to this theory, market conditions influence tuition to rise.

Observers of the higher education sector offer many arguments to explain the substantial increase in tuition that has been occurring. Generally, these arguments fall inside one of these frameworks. Hauptman, for example, argues that the increased availability of student aid, particularly federal student loans, makes it easier for institutions to raise tuition charges and other costs of attendance.[3] St. John, on the other hand, contends that competitive pressures have produced incremental increases in educational expenditures and this has convinced many institutions to raise tuition.[4] Others, such as Reynolds, note that private universities and colleges, and

---

[1] Bowen, H.R. "The Cost of Higher Education." Jossey-Bass. 1980.

[2] Getz, M. & Siegfried, J.J. "Cost and Productivity in American Colleges and Universities." In, Economic Challenges in Higher Education, edited by Charles T. Clotfelter, et. al. University of Chicago Press. Chicago. 1991.

[3] Hauptman, A.M. "The College Tuition Spiral." Report to the College Board and the American Council on Education. Washington, D.C. 1990.

[4] St. John, E.P. "Prices, Productivity, and Investment." The George Washington University. Washington, D.C. 1994.

public institutions more recently, have increased tuition and reallocated tuition revenue to maintain enrollment and maximize their overall tuition revenue base.[5]

The literature articulates many potential reasons for the increasing cost of higher education—changes in federal financial aid and institutional aid being among them. However, the literature has failed in one important way—many of the perceived linkages are suspect, including the effect of expenditures on tuition, the effect of revenue on expenditure, the effect of institutional aid on tuition, and the effect of federal student aid on tuition. Without doubt, correlations appear to exist; but probably not the direct causal links claimed in much of the literature. However, merely demonstrating that a correlation exists provides a fragile basis on which to formulate policy.

The issue of increasing tuition invariably gets analyzed as an economic issue, even though it probably should be addressed as much in sociological terms as economic ones. Consequently, empirical studies of tuition changes adopt a rather limited view or treatment of the subject. Also, economists tend to focus on only one set of behaviors at a time. Most of the literature deals predominately with the effects of tuition increases on changes in enrollments only in the context of student behavior. A smaller part deals with changes in tuition in the context of institutional behavior (e.g., price setting).

EMPIRICAL ASSESSMENTS OF THE IMPACT OF FINANCIAL AID ON TUITION

In their studies, McPherson and Shapiro used econometric regression models to examine the interactions among federal assistance, tuition, institutional aid and other key variables.[6] A Coopers & Lybrand, *LLP* report, relying on the McPherson and Shapiro analytical framework, but using more recent data, re-examined these interactions in a study sponsored by the American Council on Education.[7]

The main findings of the McPherson and Shapiro studies were that:

- Increases in federal student assistance did not have an impact on tuition levels at private four-year colleges and universities.

- Institutional aid appeared to increase as a consequence of greater federal assistance for students enrolled at these colleges.

- Tuition at public four-year institutions did appear to increase as a result of increased federal assistance for students (but not at public two-year institutions).

Using only the subsidy element of the federal loan programs,[8] the Coopers & Lybrand, *LLP* report examined the effect of changes in these programs on tuition changes and changes in institutional aid among higher education institutions. Their key findings (based on 90 percent level of significance) related to private four-year institutions only were that:

- Federal grant aid has the effect of reducing tuition levels.[9]

- Increases in institutional aid accompanied substantial increases in tuition.[10]

- Federal aid is not treated as a substitute for institutional aid.[11]

- Increases in state and local appropriations were associated with increases in institutional aid.

- A proportion (15 percent) of tuition increases are earmarked for student assistance.

- Colleges with large endowments provide very slightly more institutional aid than those with modest endowments.

- Rapid enrollment growth was associated with raising tuition more and smaller increases in institutional aid.

---

[5] Reynolds, A. "The Real Cost of Higher Education, Who Should Pay It and How." Paper submitted to the National Commission on the Cost of Higher Education. Washington, D.C. 1997.

[6] See for example, *Keeping College Affordable*, Brooking Institution, 1992; *Paying the Piper: Productivity, Incentives, and Financing U.S. Higher Education*, University of Michigan, 1993; and *Does Student Aid Affect College Enrollment? New Evidence on a Persistent Controversy*, American Economic Review, March 1991.

[7] Coopers & Lybrand, LLP. *The Impact of Federal Student Assistance on College Tuition Levels.* September 1997, Washington, D.C.

[8] Assumed to be 28 percent of aggregate volume.

[9] **However, in real terms, grants barely increased in the period analyzed (1989-90 to 1994-95), therefore, the effect on reduced tuition was minimal.**

[10] The authors of the report hypothesized that colleges were compensating for the lack of growth in federal grant aid.

[11] In fact the opposite occurred. Every dollar increase in federal grant aid appeared to induce an 18 cents increase in institutional aid.

CRITIQUE OF REGRESSION BASED STUDIES

McPherson and Shapiro hypothesized the effects that various factors would have on tuition based on an articulation of the underlying theory of the causal mechanisms. However, all the effects hypothesized were tested in a single equation regression model. Moreover, the same model was applied to both public and private institutions despite the strong possibility that their institutional behaviors are different, not least because these two groups deal with different constraints.

Despite some similarities, the findings of the McPherson and Shapiro and the Coopers & Lybrand, *LLP* studies are sometimes inconsistent and contradictory. For example, McPherson and Shapiro found that federal student assistance failed to have an impact on tuition at private four-year institutions, but did have an impact at public four-year institutions (but not public two-year institutions). Using more recent data, the Coopers and Lybrand *LLP* report could not find evidence to support McPherson's and Shapiro's finding that federal student assistance resulted in tuition increases at public four-year institutions. In a more recent publication, McPherson and Shapiro argue that the substantial increases in tuition at public four-year institutions since the mid 1980s will mean far fewer of them can gain federal student aid revenue by increasing tuition and, therefore, the effect of federal student aid on public tuition may have been substantially reduced.[12]

With regard to the effect of changes in tuition and changes in institutional aid, the Coopers & Lybrand, *LLP* model projected that for every dollar increase in tuition at private four-year institutions, 15 cents goes toward institutional aid compared to 25 cents at public four-year institutions. This finding is contrary to expectation and what the actual data shows. Tuition discounting and institutional aid availability is greater at private institutions, and their net retention rate (i.e., gross tuition minus all discounts divided by gross revenue) is about 80 percent, compared to an average of 85 percent at public institutions.

In both studies, changes in tuition were hypothesized to be a function of changes in federal grant aid, federal student loans, federal and state grants and contracts, state and local appropriations, and institutional scholarships and fellowships. Formulated in this way, the models are probably not well specified. For example, while revenue streams are well represented in the model, cost pressures are entirely ignored. The availability of state student financial aid programs is ignored also. The model also fails to account for family resources or ability to pay and the inter-relationship between tuition, student need, and internal and external sources of aid. Finally, the models specify changes in tuition as a function of changes in federal and institutional aid, but institutional aid itself may be influenced by the availability of federal aid.

In reality, the cost of higher education and its affordability is determined by the concerted actions or behavior of several key actors – institutions, families and students, governments (federal, state, local), as well as the general condition of the economy. Moreover, each actor's behavior often affects the others. Thus, many of the relationships observed are two-way. Findings obtained by analytical methods that fail to recognize all the actors involved, and the simultaneity of some of the relationships, are likely to be unreliable or misleading.

A SOCIAL DETERMINATION OF THE COST OF HIGHER EDUCATION

To help analyze the issue of tuition and aid, we have developed a simplified diagram to illustrate, at a conceptual level, the social determination of the cost of higher education and its affordability (exhibit 1). The complex set of relationships depicted in this exhibit are generated by four actors – the external economy, institutions, families and students, and public administrators who guide the external student financial aid programs. Initially, the diagram can be explained in terms of the relationships involving each actor, and then by the key linkages that exist between the different actors.

One set of relationships involves the economic circumstances that result in the severe cost pressures with which universities and colleges are contending, including the rapidity of technological progress and the surging demand for highly trained workers. A second set of relationships delineates institutional behavior. For example, the relative growth in expenditures and revenues will govern the financial condition of higher education institutions. Another important aspect of institutional behavior concerns the relationships between gross tuition, net tuition, and institutional aid. The third set of relationships involves students and families. By relating the cost of college attendance to families' ability to pay these costs, and the availability of financial aid, these relationships

---

[12] McPherson, M.S. & Schapiro, M.O. "The Student Aid Game." Princeton University Press, Princeton. 1998.

delineate the issue of college affordability. The final set of relationships involves the public administration of the external financial aid programs. They relate the growth in student need to the availability of student financial assistance.

There are several key relationships shown in exhibit 1 that directly or (more usually) indirectly establish the linkages between tuition and aid. These include the effect of:

The economy (or market conditions) on institutional costs;

The economy on family resources;

Changes in family resources on tuition;

Changes in family resources on need;

Changes in institutional costs on revenue sources, including tuition;

Changes in revenue sources on tuition;

Federal and state aid on institutional aid;

Changes in tuition on student need;

Changes in student need on external on external financial aid;

Changes in student need on internal financial aid;

Institutional aid on tuition;

Tuition on institutional aid; and

Federal and state aid on tuition.

Clearly, any attempt to analyze the effects of changes in financial assistance (whether provided from external or institutional sources) on tuition must fully recognize that several other important factors influence the level of tuition, and that this level is not determined solely on the basis of institutional behavior. Below, we embellish our conceptual understanding of the forces involved by describing in more detail the anticipated relationships and the key linkages that are postulated.

Exhibit 1: The Social Determination of the Cost of Higher Education and Its Affordability

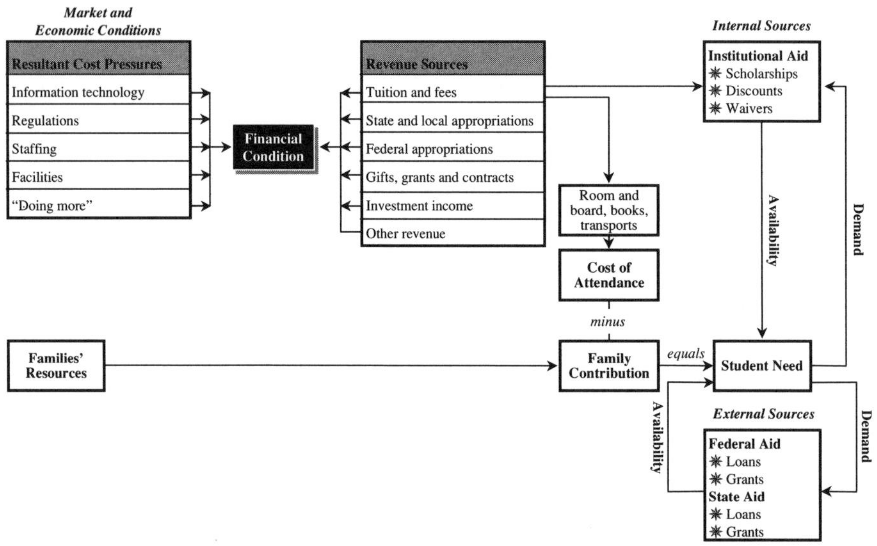

Institutional Behavior

To at least improve its financial condition, an institution must grow revenues at least as fast as the growth in expenditures. Historically, institutional expenditures per student have increased not only faster than the general level of inflation (as measured by the Consumer Price Index) but also faster than even the Higher Education Price Index (HEPI). To survive and prosper, institutions must respond to market conditions, such as rapid technological progress, rapid scientific advancement, increased demand for highly trained and specialized workers, rising student expectations, maintenance and enhancement of reputation to attract students and staff, etc. As a result, many institutions constantly are undertaking more activities, improving services, and striving to increase the quality of students' educational experiences.

The resources needed to respond to market conditions come from both public and private sources. Particularly at public institutions, the share of revenue from state and local appropriations has been diminishing. If one source of revenue fails to grow as fast as is needed to keep pace with rising expenditures, the institution can either decline to respond to market conditions (with all the risks that entails) or turn its attention to increase some other revenue source – particularly one that has "soft," rather than "hard," constraints.[13] Generally, institutions have responded to the need for revenues to keep pace with expenditures by increasing tuition and fees. The end result is that tuition is increasing faster than per student expenditures. More importantly, at least from the consumer's standpoint, tuition is rising substantially faster than the general level of inflation or the rate of growth in family incomes.

Family/Borrower Behavior

The disparity between growth in tuition and family income is raising concerns about the affordability of college. If tuition (and other components of cost of attendance) rise faster than families' ability to pay for college, greater student need will be created. As a result of expanded need, students will require more financial assistance. Student need is normally met by a combination of internal (i.e., institutional) and external (i.e., federal and state) financial aid. Historically, this need has been fulfilled largely through external sources (mostly federal aid) but, more recently, institutional aid has increased substantially in relative importance.

Financial Assistance – External (Public) Sources

Whenever cost of attendance increases faster than the growth in family resources, student need (and, therefore, the demand for financial aid) will increase. However, some part of this demand may go unsatisfied by external student aid sources because the flow of financial resources from this source is constrained by program policy— particularly those governing program eligibility and maximum borrowing limits. Program policies sometimes are changed to increase or decrease the rate of flow of financial aid, rather like adjusting a spigot. However, if the spigot stays in the same position, in order to maintain the affordability of college, increasing need must be met by other means. One of these means relies on the institution providing financial assistance from its own resources. If the institution fails to respond in this way student need will go unmet, with the accompanying danger that enrollments may decline or stagnate or prospective students may seek more affordable alternatives.

Financial Assistance – Internal (Institutional) Sources

The spigot on Federal student aid programs gets adjusted infrequently. Largely because of this, external financial aid has failed to keep pace with the growth in student need. In these circumstances, a substantial demand for institutionally funded financial aid is created. Institutions may meet this demand for financial assistance by using their own resources to offer aid to students, either by direct expenditures (e.g., using income from endowments to fund scholarships) or through tuition discounts, fee waivers, etc.

McPherson hypotheses that institutions cut back their aid when federal aid programs expand.[14] He further suggests that when federal aid is falling (in real terms), institutions will increase tuition to provide greater financial assistance from institutional revenues. Conversely, when federal aid is increasing, the rate of increase in tuition may slow because expanded student need will be absorbed by government sources of finance. However, to complicate the issue, greater federal assistance may create the need for *additional* institutional aid if expanded federal aid induces more low-income students to enroll. A priori, the direct net effect of increased federal aid on institutional aid, and its indirect effect on tuition, is uncertain.

The growth in institutional aid that has taken place in recent years appears to have been funded largely through increases in gross tuition. Nationally, the percentage of gross tuition retained (i.e., tuition retention)[15] has been falling at private and public universities and colleges since the mid 1980s.[16] Currently, the tuition retention rate is about 80-85 percent of gross tuition revenue. If tuition discounting grows to provide even more institutional

---

[13] In the case of a revenue source such as tuition and fees income, in relation to further tuition increases, the "soft" constraint is "what the market will bear." The ability to obtain increased revenue from this revenue source is under the institution's direct control and the results are returned quickly. (However, for public institutions, state legislatures may impose constraints on tuition increases.) For other revenue sources, such as federal grants and contracts, institutions face "hard" constraints. That is to say, their ability to obtain increased revenue from such sources lies mainly outside the organization's direct control and results are less immediate.

[14] McPherson, M.S. *On Assessing the Impact of Federal Student Aid.* Education Review, Vol. 7, No. 1, p.82. 1988.

[15] The rate of tuition retention is defined as gross revenue from tuition and fees less institutionally funded aid as a percent of gross tuition revenue.

[16] National Association of College and University Business Officers. *Tuition Discounting: The Impact of Institutionally Funded Financial Aid*, p. 18. Washington, D.C., 1992.

financial aid, gross tuition must increase at a faster rate than net tuition to avoid reductions in total tuition revenue.

ALTERNATIVE ANALYTICAL APPROACHES

As was argued earlier, single equation estimation methods are simply not capable of adequately representing the complex way tuition levels or changes are determined. To properly portray all the paths involved, a system of interdependent structural equations is needed. In econometric terms, accurate estimates of the determinants of tuition levels or changes requires a system of simultaneous equations. In simultaneous systems of equations, variables that are endogenous to the system are determined jointly (as in the real world) rather than sequentially. Unlike single equation regression models, path models can reveal the different *causal* relationships within the system. In addition, this modeling technique can detect both the direct and indirect impact of changes in the variables being studied and assess the total impact on the system. Path models also are excellent for addressing "what-if" questions, such as:

- What will happen to tuition if there is no further growth in student financial aid?
- What will happen to tuition if cost per FTE student is contained?
- What will happen if institutions did not offer tuition discounts?
- What will happen to tuition if inflation increased more than family incomes?

Proposal for a Causal Analysis

The impact of institutional aid and discounting on tuition costs, and federal student financial aid programs on tuition costs, has become the focus of much interest in policy circles. Therefore, when trying to model the relationship between institutional aid, financial aid programs, and tuition costs, a primary concern is the ability of the model to capture the causal ordering of the process that we are trying to explain. Furthermore, institutional-level aid and discounting, as well as amounts of state and federal student aid, are themselves responsive to other factors such as the amount of government appropriations (e.g., state, federal, local) or non-governmental subsidies received by an institution, in addition to changes in the level of family resources (i.e., students' and families' ability to pay for college).

Because of the specific *causal* relationships among the various actors involved in setting tuition costs, we need to develop a model that not only can make use of the information we have about the existing causal processes, but also allow us to disentangle any unclear or reciprocal causal effects. Given this goal, we propose using a structural equation model (SEM). An explanation follows of why we believe SEM is the most appropriate model for the task at hand.

Advantages of a Structural Equation Model

Traditional single-equation multivariate regression techniques require that the dependent variable of interest be caused by the independent variables attempting to explain it, but do not ask the researcher to make any assumptions regarding the causal relationships among the *independent* variables in the model. While single-equation techniques are perfectly appropriate when the researcher has no knowledge of the causal interworkings of his or her independent variables, when something is known about the causal relationships among these variables, single-equation techniques do not make use of this information during estimation. In other words, single-equation techniques assume that all of the covariates in a model *directly* influence the dependent variable. Yet, in the empirical world, it is more likely that some–if not most–of the independent variables in a model are themselves partly caused by others in the same model. When this is the case, structural equation models are better suited to estimating the effects of given covariates because they make use of all of the causal information provided by the researcher, allowing the decomposition of a variable's total effect into direct and indirect effects.

The decomposition of effects is not possible when one uses a single-equation model. Therefore, when using this technique, the researcher is unable to assess the relative role of each actor within a larger system. Overall, structural equation models allow a *systemic* representation of phenomena in which various actors influence a given outcome through various other actors. Specifically, a central purpose of SEM is to assess the extent to which the *direct* effect of a given independent variable on a dependent variable disappears when that variable's effect is specified as operating *indirectly* through other independent variables.

While structural equation models using a cross-sectional design require the researcher to have a well formulated idea of causal processes before specifying the model, by adopting a longitudinal/panel design, SEM will allow the exploration of reciprocal causal directions. For example, in a situation in which we are interested not only in determining whether institutional aid and discounting affects tuition but also whether tuition, in turn, affects institutional aid, by having data on two time points (i.e., panel data) for each of these variables, we can model the reciprocal effect by:

- Regressing tuition at time 1 on institutional aid at time 1.
  (This will provide an estimated effect of institutional aid on tuition.)
- Regressing institutional aid at time 2 on both tuition and institutional aid at time 1.
  (This will provide an estimated effect of changes in tuition on changes in institutional aid.)

This brief example illustrates how, from a longitudinal structural equation model, we can determine not only the effect of institutional aid and discounting on tuition, but also the effect of changes in tuition on institutional aid and discounting.

The Causal Model

As explained previously, various actors interact in a web of causal relationships that help determine the cost of higher education. In this section, we describe the specific causal model that we propose to use to estimate each actor's relative role in affecting the amount of institutional aid and discounting available, as well as tuition costs.

Exhibits 2 and 3 present the conceptual causal model of the relationship between institutional aid, student financial programs, and tuition costs. Exhibit 2 is a cross-sectional model in which tuition is being determined by all of the actors preceding it. Exhibit 3 represents the longitudinal model that will estimate the effect of change in tuition on subsequent institutional aid and discounting.

Starting to the left of the models, each conceptual variable—indicated by a box with a one-way arrow coming into it—is assumed to be caused by the variable from which the arrow originated. Each set of connected arrows constitutes a path, hence the name "path model" for some structural equations model.

As mentioned earlier, a major advantage of structural equation models is the ability to decompose the total effect of a given variable, with the underlying theory being that the effect of a variable that is causally prior to another one on a given dependent variable should be largely explained through its *indirect* rather than *direct* effect. Thus a major goal of our model will be to test the extent to which the direct effect of a given variable becomes statistically insignificant as a result of operating through another variable. To illustrate, looking at Exhibit A, we can see that we hypothesize a direct relationship between family resources and tuition (indicated by an arrow directly linking these two variables). Yet, we also specify that the effect of family resources on tuition works

Exhibit 2: Cross-Sectional Causal Model of The Cost of Higher Education

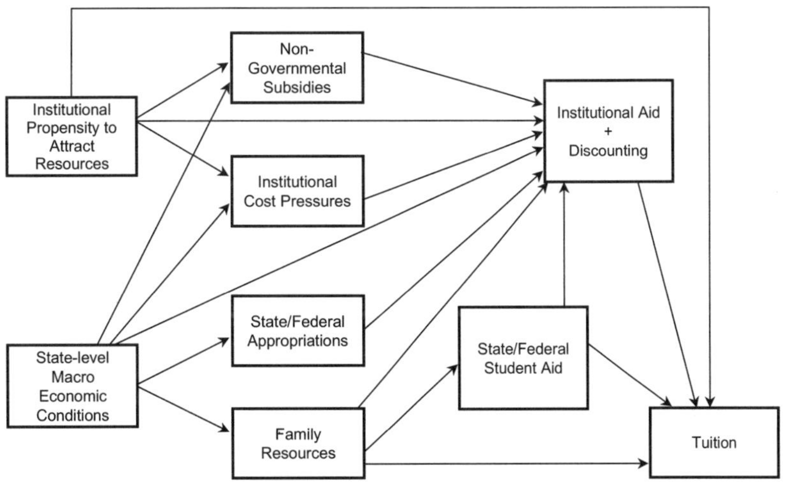

Exhibit 3: Longitudinal Causal Model of The Cost of Higher Education

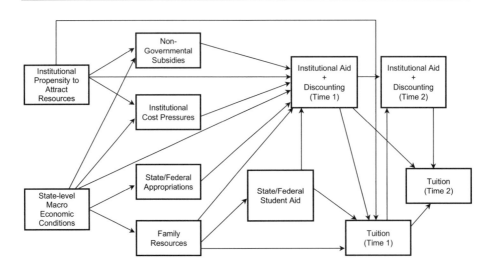

indirectly through institutional aid and discounting, as well as through state and federal student aid. In other words, our model hypothesizes that the amount of family resources available will affect the amount of state and federal student aid required by students, which in turn will affect tuition. We also hypothesize that family resources will affect the amount of institutional aid and discounting available, which in turn will affect tuition. Finally, we also hypothesize that family resources will have an additional *direct* effect on tuition costs that is not explained through state and federal student aid or through institutional aid and discounting.

A structural equation model will estimate the extent to which the hypothesized direct effect between family resources and tuition disappears as a result of operating through the other two paths (i.e., through state and federal student aid and through institutional aid and discounting). Furthermore, a structural equation model will estimate whether the effect of family resources on tuition is stronger through state and federal student aid than through institutional aid and discounting, or vice versa. Overall, a structural equation model is a powerful tool to assess the relative direct and indirect effects of various actors on the cost of higher education.

Exhibit 3 illustrates another advantage of our proposed model, namely, sorting out the hypothesized reciprocal causal relationship between institutional aid and discounting and tuition. By adopting a longitudinal model, we can readily assess the relationship between institutional aid and discounting and tuition costs as a reciprocal causal relationship in which institutional aid affects tuition at time 1, and whether this change in tuition in turn affects institutional aid at time 2. Our model will estimate the magnitude of the effects of institutional aid on tuition, and tuition on subsequent institutional aid; thus allowing us to gauge which relationship is stronger.

Modeling Different Groups of Institutions

Because past research suggests that different types of institutions react to actors' inputs differently (e.g., market forces do not affect public and private institutional cost pressures in the same way), we will estimate our proposed model of the cost of higher education separately for institutions we believe are substantially different. For example, it will make little sense to estimate the cost of higher education by including two-year colleges and Research I universities in the same model. Of specific interest for our purposes are the differences among public and private institutions, as well as differences among types of institutions as indicated by Carnegie classification (e.g., Research, Doctorate, Masters, and Baccalaureate). Unfortunately, our ability to carry out analyses on separate groups will be limited by the number of degrees of freedom available to carry out robust statistical analyses. For example, since there are only about 100 or so Research I institutions, we do not expect to be able to carry out analyses on that subgroup given the proposed number of independent variables in the model.

A Note on Model Estimation

Exhibits 2 and 3 are simply conceptual representations of the actual causal model. In fact, most of the variables identified by a box represent *concepts* that are indicated by several indicators (i.e., factors). For example, the concept of "non-governmental subsidies" is actually a latent factor that is made up of several measured variables such as the alumni or corporate giving rate. In other words, most concepts in our model are actually common factors or latent variables captured by multiple indicators. This means that the structural equation model that will be used to estimate the cost of higher education will be what is known as a *latent variables model* in which factors (i.e., the boxed "concepts" in Exhibits 2 and 3) are made up of multiple indicators.

CONCLUSION

Stemming from dissatisfaction with extant technical approaches, this paper has presented a proposal for a causal model of the cost of higher education that will be better able to answer two central questions of interest to policy makers:

- To what extent increases in institutional aid and discounting have affected tuition increases; and
- To what extent student financial aid programs have contributed to changes in tuition.

We argued above that these questions couldn't be properly answered without developing an overall causal model of the cost of higher education and without properly identifying all of the crucial actors involved in influencing this cost. Because we are interested in explaining and illuminating causal processes and have a strong theoretically based belief that the various actors operate within a larger system of interdependent relationships, we believe that the most appropriate way to model these systemic relationships is by estimating a latent variables structural equation model. This type of model will allow us to decompose each actor's relative influence on the overall cost of higher education. Not only will a structural equation model allow us to identify the extent to which an actor's influence is mitigated through another actor but, by adopting a longitudinal approach, we should be able to clarify the causal relationship between institutional aid and discounting and tuition costs.

The Real Cost of Higher Education, Who Should Pay It and How?

Alan Reynolds

Director of Economic Research, Hudson Institute

Widely repeated generalizations about the cost of higher education have already provoked hasty enactment of a federal tax credit, as well as congressional suggestions that the federal government ought to regulate tuition.[1] Before rushing to solve a problem, however, it is usually prudent to define and identify that problem with as much precision as possible.

It has become commonplace to begin any investigation of the "soaring" cost of higher education by observing that the institutional expense of providing higher education, or average tuition, has been rising faster than the consumer price index (CPI). Two quite separate issues of *costs* (for the institution) and *tuition* (for students not offered financial aid) are too often lumped together by an implicit "cost-plus" assumption — namely, the belief that the measured increases in gross tuition must be virtually synonymous with increases in the cost of providing instruction.

The assumption that instructional costs are the main force driving tuition higher leads down blind alleys. The *Chronicle of Higher Education* thus notes that "college officials often say . . . that many core expenses, such as libraries, computers and salaries, especially for faculty members, rise faster than the rate of inflation."[2] That cannot explain why tuition has increased far more rapidly than costs of instruction. Neither can Hoxby's theory that "changes in tuition correspond to commensurate changes in college quality."[3] Even if increased competition had caused costs of producing higher education to accelerate, as Hoxby contends, that would not explain why competition was only in quality rather than price, nor why there has been no discernible upward trend in instructional costs (relative to past trends or to costs in other service industries), nor why tuition has increased more rapidly than instructional costs.

In reality, the most interesting questions have to do with the fact that *gross* tuition costs (aside from financial aid) *appear* to have increased much more rapidly than costs of providing instruction. And what is even more intriguing is the proliferation of selective discounts from tuitions involves a rapid expansion of cross-subsidies from some students (and taxpayers) to others.

When it comes to institutional expenses alone, it is not at all surprising that such educational costs have increased more rapidly than the consumer price index. Education is a service industry. Half of the consumer price index consists of *goods*, the prices of which tend to decline with cost-reducing technological progress. Most services, on the other hand, are dominated by labor costs.

A very large share of the costs of the educational service industry (including the often neglected costs of providing room and board) consists of wages and benefits. *If employee compensation did not increase more rapidly than prices in general, on average, then real incomes of the employees would never rise.* This is why rices of labor-intensive services almost always increase more rapidly than prices of goods, *except during periods of very high inflation (such as 1973-82).* And that fact, in turn, ensures that tuition costs are almost certain to rise more rapidly than any price index, such as the CPI, that combines both goods and services, unless there is an unusual increase in productivity.

Aside from possibilities of using interactive computers and video tapes to increase the ratio of students to teachers, productivity gains in higher education are difficult to achieve except by reducing the ratio of nonteaching personnel (such as administration and research) to students. Even that may not be feasible in the case of research, to the extent that research employees are fully funded from nontuition sources, such as federal grants.

The most rapid increases in costs of higher education occurred at the same time that inflation in general was very high. Research Associates' cost index for higher education increased by 8.4% a year from 1970 to 75, and 10.2% from 1980 to 1982. *Because overall inflation also averaged 10% a year from 1980 to 1982, college costs did not rise faster than the CPI.* Was that something to admire or emulate? How anyone can now look back with admiration at the fact that inflation was about equally nasty in both services and goods is a mystery.

Figure 1 shows that an index of the *costs* of higher education has *not* increased more rapidly than the consumer price index for all services. Those who complain that costs of higher education have increased more rapidly than the CPI are (without knowing it) actually complaining about the dramatic disinflation in prices of *goods* since 1982, such as energy, food, shoes and electronic gadgets. Since 1982, inflation in higher education and other services has slowed dramatically, even though that disinflation has not been quite as subdued as the nearly unchanged prices of goods. This is the normal pattern in periods of relative price stability — prices of labor rise more than goods, so real wages and salaries increase. Far from being a crisis, this is a fair definition of prosperity.

It might be objected that leaving medical costs out of the CPI for services would make recent increases in education costs look *slightly* faster than for nonmedical services. The difference is barely discernible in a graph. But it would be bad economics to arbitrarily exclude medical services from the averages. Institutions of higher education have to compete with medical institutions, Wall Street and other service industries for highly educated employees. Although the Labor Department had expected the

Figure 1

PRICE INDEXES FOR HIGHER EDUCATION, GOODS & SERVICES

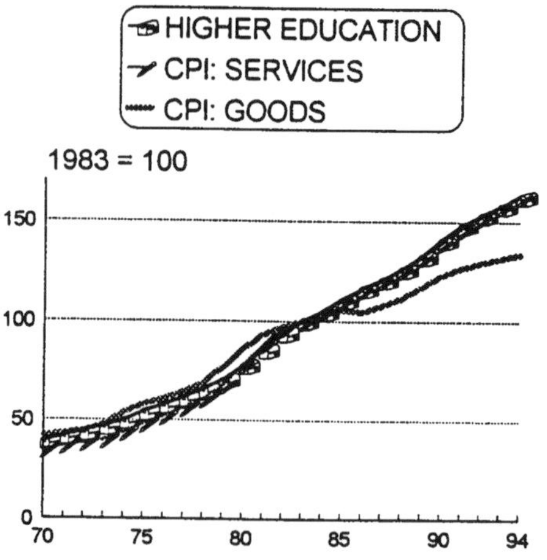

- HIGHER EDUCATION
- CPI: SERVICES
- CPI: GOODS

Index for higher education from Research Associates, D.C.

number of college and university faculty to drop by 13.8% from 1984 to 1995, it actually increased by 11.8%, to 848,000.[4] This has required competitive salaries, to minimize "brain drain" from American universities. Returns on a college education increased in the eighties, and college faculty members are among the college educated.

MEAN TUITION VS. MEDIAN INCOME

Even though the costs of providing higher education and other services (such as research) have *not* increased more rapidly than costs of any other service industries, it is nevertheless true that measured tuition does *appear* to have increased much more rapidly than can be explained by cost increases. A common, but highly misleading, way of making this point is to compare average (mean) tuition per full-time equivalent (FTE) student with *median* household or family income.

Comparisons of tuition with median family income may *appear* more rigorous than comparisons of educational costs with the consumer price index. But this measure too has serious problems.

Attempts to measure "average" tuition are inherently distorted, because the distribution of students by tuition levels is highly skewed. At four-year institutions, only 28.9% percent of students face tuition and fees that exceed $6,000, while 55.8% pay less than $4,000.[5] In the usual comparison, a *mean* average of gross tuition is contrasted with a *median* average of household or family income. This is comparing apples and oranges. *Median tuition and fees are below $4,000.* But *mean* tuition and fees appear nearly twice that high because a few elite schools that charge more than $20,000 can drive that type of average up. Mean family income is likewise much higher than median income, because a small number of people with high incomes drive the mean average up. It is careless to compare different types of averages, such as mean tuition and median income. But that is only the beginning of the statistical confusion.

Relatively few families with college-age children earn as little as the median family (or household) income, and those who do earn only that much or less rarely pay much tuition. Most are eligible for financial aid from the college or university, for grants or subsidized loans from the federal government, and often for a combination of several forms of private and public aid.

The income of the median family is *not* representative of typical income of parents of college-aid students, because family income (and household income even more so) includes many young people and retired couples. Family income also includes a rapidly increasing percentage of single moms, making comparisons over time misleading (the meaning of "family" has changed). Most people earn much less when they are very young or old than when they are in their forties. *Parents of college-aid students are usually middle-aged, which is when earnings are typically near a lifetime peak — clearly higher than the median for families of all ages.* Among male full-time workers, for example, median income in 1993 was $26,087 at age 25-34, but $39,685 at age 45-54. In the same year, median income was only $36,959 for *all* families, but $60,711 for married couples in which both the husband and wife worked full time.

A recent College Board press release noted that, "half of all students enrolled in postsecondary education receive some financial aid, *often a combination of grants or scholarships, loans, and work-study* from federal, state, and private programs [emphasis added]."[6] The half of all students who are receiving one or more forms of aid (averaging $4,926) do *not* come from the half of all families below median family income. On the contrary, many have incomes much higher than that. A widely publicized 1996 GAO study compared tuition with median *household* income, which is even lower than family income because it includes singles.[7] That is even more inexcusable, and further removed from typical income of parents of college-age children. Indeed, *median household income even includes the incomes of students*, if they are not living at home. The use of median household income as a benchmark is presumably intended to imply that half the parents of college-age students earn less than median household income. That is false.

In the absence of a relevant sample of actual incomes among parents of college-age students, perhaps the best available income measure to use for comparisons is personal disposable (after-tax) income *per capita*.

Whatever income measure is used, if the figures are adjusted for inflation then the same price index should be used for both income and college expenses, rather than using a special index for college expenses alone. Unfortunately, *most published figures from the Department of Education adjust for inflation by using an index of costs paid by colleges and universities*. To see what is wrong with that, imagine adjusting faculty salaries by a price index consisting entirely of faculty salaries. By definition, such an index could never show *any* real increase in salaries. A correct definition of "real" faculty income actually depends on what the salary and benefit package buys, in terms of an index such as the CPI or the GDP deflator for personal consumption expenditures. Similarly, the real cost of tuition to parents cannot logically be deflated by index of how *colleges* spend their money, but must instead be deflated by an index of how parents would have spent their money.

Scary projections of what a college education will cost in the future are usually based on a doubtful rule of thumb provided by the College Board — namely, that tuition will increase at a rate of 7% a year indefinitely (faster than the Board's own figure of 5% for the past four years).[8] Such pessimistic projections can certainly give parents a bad case of sticker shock, but budget constraints ensure that unsustainable trends will not be sustained. It would take a high rate of inflation to push tuition costs up that quickly, and in that case parents' income would usually be inflated too. Besides sticker prices are not what most people pay.

Using a better measure of real income than median household income would soften but not totally change the conclusion that tuition and fees *have* increased more rapidly than typical incomes. As it happens, this does not matter as much as it may appear to. The usual "average" of tuition per student is *not* a valid measure of what *any* parent or student actually pays, much less what most pay.

Figure 2

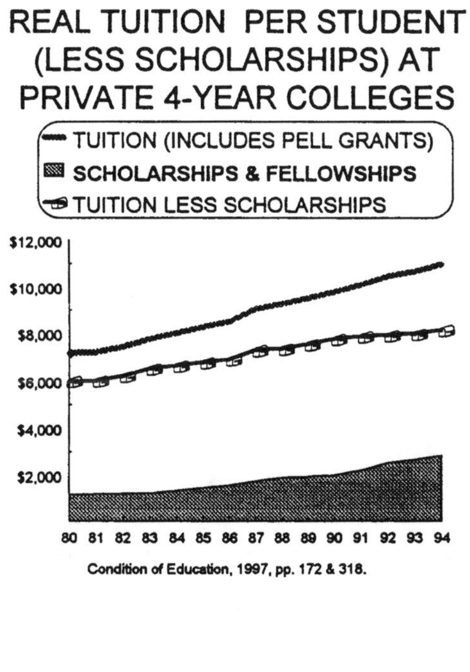

REAL TUITION PER STUDENT (LESS SCHOLARSHIPS) AT PRIVATE 4-YEAR COLLEGES

- TUITION (INCLUDES PELL GRANTS)
- SCHOLARSHIPS & FELLOWSHIPS
- TUITION LESS SCHOLARSHIPS

Condition of Education, 1997, pp. 172 & 318.

IT ONLY LOOKS LIKE TUITION

Tuition and fees per "full-time equivalent" or FTE student (hereafter called "tuition") is a measure of what institutions *receive* from this source, per student, not a measure of what students pay. Tuition includes, for example, Pell grants, and any other tuition paid by third parties. Those who see the rise in tuition as an argument for larger Pell grants are apparently unaware that *if tuition remained unchanged and Pell grants were increased, then measured tuition per student must rise* (even though taxpayers would then be paying more tuition, not students or parents). Conversely, eliminating Pell grants would make measured tuition fall, if colleges and universities did not change their pricing at all. This is merely one illustration of the fact that *statistics on gross tuition grossly exaggerate actual costs to most students or parents*.

Unlike Pell grants, scholarships and fellowships (hereafter called "scholarships"), are *not* included in the usual tuition figures. Yet scholarships need to be subtracted from the gross tuition figures in order to get a rough idea of average net cost to students. **Figure 2** (in which costs are in 1996 dollars), shows that even though some major grants are already included in "tuition," removing scholarships nevertheless results in a much more moderate increase in net tuition in recent years. Subtracting *both* Pell grants and scholarships from the "list prices" of tuition and fees would further reduce the apparent level of tuition, and possibly its growth.

Subtracting all of the various grants and scholarships (and using a consumer-relevant price index to adjust for inflation) might even leave *net* tuition more-or-less unchanged in real terms over the past decade or so, on average. But such an average would be nearly as misleading as ignoring grants and scholarships. The reason is that not everyone gets grants or scholarships, and for those that do not the gross tuition figures *do* matter.

Federal, state, and institutional aid amounted to $55.7 billion in 1996-97, according to the College Board (although much of that was loans). Private charitable aid added another $28 billion.[9] These sums are too large to simply ignore. On the other hand, *gross tuition figures are quite relevant for those who are compelled to pay full tuition* so that others can pay less.

Table 1 shows some information about financial aid for a dozen institutions selected by *Money* as providing the best value, once financial assistance is taken into account (the "discounted" price). This sample is by no means extreme (an extreme example would be Manhattanville College, where tuition and fees are $16,910 and institutional aid averages $12,197). On the contrary, since the schools in this table have a superior reputation of providing good educations at a reasonable cost, they have less incentive than others to use financial aid as a *selective* device to recruit freshmen.

TABLE 1: MONEY'S LIST OF BEST COLLEGE VALUES

	Tuition and Fees	Average Institutional Aid	% of Freshman (Students) Receiving Aid	% of Need Met
Calif. Inst. of Technology	18,816	6,667	74 (67)	100
Elizabethtown College	16,230	6,459	94 (92)	95
Notre Dame College of Ohio	12,150	1,549	96 (63)	100
Spelman College	9,421	7,968	na (81)	85
Millikin University	14,079	5,634	94 (93)	100
Wabash College	15,700	7,968	96 (92)	100
Grove City College	6,576	535	63 (55)	78
New College, U. of S. Florida	9,342	730	65 (47)	85
University of Dallas	12,885	3,955	96 (89)	91
DePaul	13,490	1,747	70 (65)	70
Muskingum College	10,885	6,937	89 (94)	91
Monmouth College	14,442	2,945	93 (93)	80

Tuition for public institutions is for out-of-state.

Several generalizations are readily apparent from **Table 1** (or any other sample):

- Schools with the highest tuition usually offer the most generous "institutional aid" — 35-85% of tuition and fees. This does not include loans, nor federal, state or charitable aid, which often make up the balance (indicated by the fact that 100% of needs were met). Institutional aid is essentially a discount that varies in amount from zero to much more than the averages shown in the table.
- About 65-95% of freshmen typically receive some sort of financial aid (including loans). Institutional aid, averaging $5,150, goes to 43% of all undergraduates at 4-year private, nonprofit schools (and to a substantially larger share of full-time freshmen).[10]

- Financial aid — for those who get it — usually covers 80-100% of the cost of tuition, fees, room and board. Relatively few students or parents pay more than a small fraction of these expenses while in college, although many pay later (because of loans). A small minority pays the entire bill out of current income or assets.

- Schools with the highest tuition provide aid to the largest percentage of freshmen.

- A larger percentage of freshmen typically receive aid than do all students (which, since it includes freshmen, overstates the percentage of upperclassmen receiving aid).

Note that it cannot possibly be the case that financial aid in general is targeted toward the poor, unless we are to believe that 65-95% of students are poor. Nor can it be the case that schools actually allocate *institutional* aid on the basis of "need," unless we are to believe that freshmen have more need than sophomores, juniors and seniors, or that 43% of all students are needy. The seemingly curious combination of raising tuition and financial aid is not consistent with institutional altruism, but it is quite consistent with revenue-maximization through price discrimination.[11]

Schwartz and Baum found that "the distribution of total educational subsidies is clearly more pro-poor in the private sector than in the public sector."[12]   Lee and Carroll found the exact opposite:

> Undergraduates in the lowest income quartile attending public 4-year institutions were more likely to receive institutional aid than those in higher income group. Undergraduates in the lowest income quartile who attended private 4-year institutions were not significantly more or less likely to receive institutional aid than undergraduates in any but the highest income quartile.[13]

Actually, neither study can tell us who benefits from financial aid, on balance, without understanding how increased aid is *combined with increased tuition* in order to charge each student as much as possible.   Even if institutional aid was *only* used for price discrimination, it would nevertheless tend to appear to be more-or-less based on "need" (albeit with plenty of elbow room for negotiation). That is because information about a family's income and assets provides admissions officers with a strong clue about how much they can get away with charging in each case, without causing too many students to apply elsewhere.   Means-testing for federal, state and charitable financial aid may be well intentioned, but the fact that price discriminating admissions officers can easily incorporate that aid into their "net" pricing is likely to thwart the intent.   The net effect is likely to result in increased aid being offset by increased tuition in many cases.

In 1995-96, 30% of all undergraduates received Pell grants.[14] As Turner suggests, "institutional adjustments to the Pell program, particularly in the allocation of discretionary aid and the determination of tuition, may have undone or offset much of the intended targeting of the federal Pell initiative."[15]   If so, then increasing the size of Pell grants to keep pace with increased tuition will not fix this problem. It merely frees up more institutional aid to be used for selective discounts, allowing even higher "sticker prices" for those not receiving discounts.

Federal and state grants are increasingly targeted toward students whose parents' income is below some cutoff point (albeit far above any poverty level). Most private scholarships, from sources other than the educational institutions themselves, are also means-tested. By one estimate, "only 10% of the 28 billion available in private scholarships — those not granted by the government or the schools — are awarded for academic achievement."[16]

With Pell grants picking up a greater share of the cost for students from low-income families, thus allowing more institutional aid to be used for recruiting students from families which are far from poor, only that small fraction of students who do not get aid are left to pay full tuition with cash or unsubsidized loans. And that fraction seems destined to decline in the most aggressive price-discriminating institutions as students from "rich" families, who may be unwilling to pay more and more for less and less, either avoid college or gravitate to elite schools at home and abroad.

Successful or not, the attempt to shift more and more of the full tuition charges to a small fraction of students from relatively affluent families raises two troublesome *economic* issues. One is the "moral hazard" associated with means testing (such as discouraging saving for college because accumulated savings will result in denial of aid). The other is the inefficiency and inequity of price discrimination itself — trying to charge much different prices for the same educational service.

THE MORAL HAZARD OF MEANS TESTING

To ensure the widest practical access to higher education, the ideal would be to have admission depend entirely on the aptitude and motivation of potential students, *not* on the income of their parents. Yet policies of educational institutions, charities and the federal government continue to move toward making all financial assistance, even loans, almost totally dependent on the current annual income and/or assets of parents. "Means testing" is becoming more pervasive. Merit scholarships are becoming relatively rare.

Conflicting studies complaining that a surprisingly small fraction of financial aid at public schools (Schwartz and Baum) or private schools (Lee and Carroll) goes to students with low-income parents are nonetheless in agreement about goals. That is, they assume that (1) redistribution rather than price discrimination is the real motive for institutional aid, and that (2) success of such aid is thus properly measured by the extent to which it is actually means-tested in practice. But it is by no means clear that helping the ill-defined "needy" is the primary purpose of institutional aid, nor that it should be the primary purpose of other aid.

Basing access to higher education on the current income of parents (rather than on the potential future income of students) may not always turn out to be as "fair" as is commonly assumed. For one thing, annual income is a notoriously poor measure of lifetime income. Medical students may be annually poor but lifetime rich. Gamblers and musicians may be annually rich but lifetime poor. To tax gamblers and musicians in order to subsidize medical students is a popular but indefensible definition of "fairness."

Another, less important problem is that intergenerational altruism varies. The fact that a student's parents have a relatively high income does not necessarily mean they will be willing to devote a large share of that income to their child's college education. Some affluent parents act on the belief that college should be a struggle or children will be spoiled. Other parents are simply not very generous. Besides, students with high income parents can often make themselves eligible for means-tested aid by simply becoming classified as "independent" — getting married, for example.

Means-testing grants and scholarships according to recent annual income also introduces a "moral hazard" that affects families unevenly. Some parents have more capacity than others to lower their income temporarily in order to qualify for student aid. Professionals, investors, the self-employed, and two-earner couples have considerable latitude about varying the *timing* of their income. Families with one salaried worker have far less flexibility.

Means-testing on the basis of eligible *assets* presents a more obvious moral hazard. If parents or grandparents save in order to establish a fund to finance a young person's college education, such admirable sacrifices will render the student ineligible for financial aid from institutions, governments and private charities. Means-testing of such valuable benefits is a powerful disincentive to saving.

Some people have low incomes but ample wealth (e.g., at retirement), while others have fairly high incomes but no cushion of savings (e.g., young professionals). Efforts to include parental *wealth* in the means-testing formulae, however, turn out to be quite ineffective. Wealth is defined to exclude the largest, most tax-advantage assets — houses and pension funds. The rationale that houses and pension funds are not "liquid" is not persuasive, since it is easy to borrow against them. Even with these gigantic exclusions, parents are not expected to use more than 5.6% of their savings for college expenses. In short, the emphasis is put on recent *reported* income, rather than net worth, although current income is an arbitrary and incomplete measure of ability to pay.

Most importantly, both income-based and asset-based criteria for financial aid exclude the largest, most relevant asset of all — namely, the "human capital" of the student (i.e., a lifetime of higher earnings). We return to that issue later, when we discuss who should pay and how. For now, we focus on the issue of price discrimination.

PRICE-DISCRIMINATION

Increases in gross tuition costs (aside from grants and scholarships) have far exceeded increases in spending on instruction. But only those students whose parents have relatively high incomes and/or savings, and/or those who are not clever at negotiating discounts from admissions officers, actually face these higher tuitions. A huge share of the increases in tuitions has been used to provide more institutional aid. The actual basis on which this sort of financial aid is granted appears more closely related to maximizing the school's revenues rather than to any believable criteria of "need." Only price discrimination, not need, could explain why freshmen get more aid than others, early decision students get less, and nearly everyone gets something.

Publications offering advice on how to get financial aid are quite revealing about how the game is really played. *Money* advises "play hard to get" and "you may be able to negotiate a great deal."[17] The *Time/Princeton Review* guide says, "Some desirable students will win a 'full ride' as a result of bidding wars that use sweetened financial-aid packages as a weapon."[18]

The economic incentive for institutions to simultaneously increase tuition and aid was explained by Rothchild and White. If a college increased *both* tuition and scholarships by $10,000, it "could *selectively* offer scholarship increments that were *less* than $10,000 to *some* students and still not lose those students, then the university's net revenues would increase [emphasis added]."[19]

This method of charging "what the traffic will bear" provides a more plausible explanation of why *both* tuition and scholarships have increased than, say, explanations based on some newfound quest for "diversity" in the student body. And that is why the Justice Department, in a 1991 antitrust case against the Ivy League elite, focused on institutional financial assistance rather than tuition *per se*. It is the universality of institutional assistance that makes uniform tuition hikes feasible, without losing too many students or revenue.

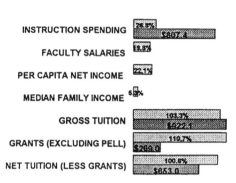

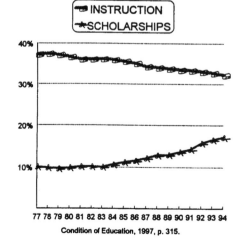

A 1996 GAO study of *public* colleges and universities found that costs of instruction had increased by 108% from 1980-81 to 1993-94, while gross tuition increased by 234%. "Expenditures by public colleges for scholarship and fellowships experienced the fastest rate of growth of all . . . [247%]."[20] **Figure 3** puts some of the GAO figures in constant dollars, showing the "real" increase over the same period of time. It also contrasts per capita disposable income (up 22.1%) with median family income (up only 5.1%) to illustrate our earlier point about median family income being a low estimate of mean income gains.

Note that the absolute, inflation-adjusted increase in gross tuition was larger ($922 per student) than the increase in instruction costs ($807). In this important respect, *investigations into what made institutional costs increase are clearly insufficient to explain why tuitions increased.* A major reason why tuitions increased is that rising tuitions from some students had to cover rising discounts to others.

Figure 4 makes a very similar point about *private* colleges. It shows the percentage of total expenditures accounted for by only two items. Instruction has accounted for a falling share of expenses while scholarships have accounted for a larger share. Once again, it appears clear that the relatively small percentage of students who are actually being asked to pay rising tuitions are *not* buying more or better education, but are paying for increasing discounts for other students (and for added research in the case of *public* colleges and universities, as we show later).

The leading institutions of higher education appear to be acting as if they formed a price discriminating cartel, adjusting prices in order to extract the most they can from each separate customer. Local general stores used to do that before James Cash Penny (and, later, the Sears Roebuck catalog) introduced the novelty of charging the same price to everyone.

True, the nominal tuition remains the same for everyone. But the actual transaction price is varied by prying into each customer's financial affairs, then giving highly selective and variable discounts (more than $10 billion of institutional aid) to those who seem most likely to be deterred by overt price gouging.

As was always true of previous price-discriminating industries, such as the airlines and telephone company before deregulation (or the U.S. Postal Service today), the rationale is that the industry is acting as a self-appointed welfare state. Industry spokesmen can be expected to argue that they have to overcharge some customers in order to cross-subsidize other, more needy customers.[21]

To the extent that an institution is heavily subsidized from nontuition sources — a category that includes *all* state colleges and universities, and private institutions with large endowments — charging full tuition to a select minority of students is feasible only because even the highest price charged to a few students may still be below the expected market value of the education. This does not, however, justify charging widely different prices to different students. Such discriminatory pricing is inherently *inefficient*. It artificially recruits subsidized students who have relatively little motivation or ability, while artificially repelling more able students who (because of their parents' income) are asked to pay a much higher price. This inefficiency is often rationalized as promoting "diversity," but that convenient argument deserves more skepticism than it usually gets. As noted earlier, *the evidence that price discrimination actually favors students from low-income families is weak and ambiguous.* And to the extent that favoritism really might exist toward those who keep reported income and savings low, then that would foster socially dangerous moral hazards.

When AT&T was a monopoly, its officers (and those of the Communications Workers of America) argued that it was necessary to rent phones and overcharge for long distance calls in order to subsidize local services in remote rural areas. When price competition and new entrants were banned in the airline industry, officers of the airlines (and of the Airline Pilots' Association) argued that it was necessary to keep prices sky high for long distance business travelers in order to fly half-empty planes in every little congressional district. The idea that price discrimination and cross subsidies are a form of charity, conducted at the whim of unelected and unaccountable managers, is nothing new. There is little reason to find this argument more credible in the case of educational officials than it was in other cases.

The Department of Education recently released a study of institutional aid which says, "Every time an institution raises tuition, a larger share of their increased income must be dedicated to institutional aid to help the expanding number of students who otherwise could not afford to enroll."[22] It would be more candid to turn that around: *Every time an institution expands institutional aid to recruit students who might not otherwise enroll, it must raise tuition.* In his case study of elite institutions, for instance, Clotfelter found that *financial aid spending was the single largest cost increase,* amounting to as much as 31-34% of all cost increases.[23]

Once price discrimination is recognized, supposed mysteries are easily solved. Coopers & Lybrand note that "institutions experiencing significant student enrollment increases appeared less likely to increase aid." The explanation (ours not theirs) is that *institutions with plenty of applicants have no need to offer deep discounts.* Coopers & Lybrand also note that "those with large endowments were likely to provide only slightly more in aid than schools with modest endowments."[24] The explanation (ours not theirs) is that the amount of aid does not depend on how much money a school has, because *tuition can always be increased to pay for transfers from secure to reluctant applicants.* The size and breadth of institutional aid is a measure of how much *price discrimination* is going on, not of how well endowed the institution is.

Aside from all these troublesome signs of price discrimination, Hoxby has good reasons for viewing the market for higher education as becoming more competitive. However, her claim that "tuition is rising because the open market has ignited quality competition" implies that quality is improving at nearly all institutions, particularly those with the fastest tuition hikes. Are no schools getting *worse,* and therefore cutting prices? She infers quality from price, rather than presenting any evidence that the most rapidly improving schools are those with the fastest (gross?) tuition hikes. Most importantly, Hoxby completely ignores (or denies) price discrimination, and also fails to adequately explain why nonprice competition is the norm. In any other case study of industrial organization, such as the previously regulated airlines, prevalence of nonprice competition and price discrimination has always been considered more than enough evidence of insufficient competition.

Markets are normally far more effective than antitrust lawyers in fostering competition that ensures the most value for the lowest possible consumer outlay (in economic jargon, competition maximizes "consumer surplus" while price discrimination minimizes it). In theory, the apparent increase in the use of price discrimination by public and private institutions should provide more incentive for *some* institutions to eschew cross subsidies and compete on *price* — that is, to charge a much lower tuition and simultaneously eliminate *institutional* aid (there are, after all, many other sources of scholarships, grants and loans). In that case, we would expect to see a growing number of institutions (probably starting with small, private liberal arts colleges) expanding enrollment by offering relatively low tuition for *all* students and little or no use of selective institutional discounts. While it would require a detailed look at many colleges over time to find out if this has been happening, a casual review of institutional aid does not look too encouraging. Of the 12 schools in Table 1, for example, only Grove City College and New College combine low tuition with low institutional aid. That could change. Hoxby is surely right that costs of transportation (air fare) and communication (e-mail) are rapidly eroding the ability of institutions to more-or-less collude on a regional basis by keeping tuition and aid packages similar. And the cost of acquiring nationwide comparisons of pricing and quality is also coming down, thanks to innovative magazines and online sources, although *actual* costs are more difficult for consumers to discover because of whimsical variation in discounts.

Ironically, a major obstacle to *competitive, uniform pricing* may be public attitudes. It is common to consider institutional financial assistance an unambiguous sign of virtue, because it is not perceived to be linked to revenue-maximizing price discrimination and therefore increased tuition. Still, if a few bold institutions were to experiment with a nondiscriminatory, uniform low tuition policy, they stand a good chance of capturing a growing market share at the expense of institutions that attempt to gouge a few students in order to negotiate variable discounts for others.

RESEARCH VS. TEACHING?

It has been suggested that one reason for rising tuitions is that undergraduates may be subsidizing lavish research facilities and salaries (it must be poor sportsmanship to mention the analogous connection between rising student fees and athletic entertainment).

Figure 4 already showed that instruction has been accounting for a shrinking share of expenses for *private* universities, while scholarships have accounted for a rising share. Instruction has also accounted for a shrinking share of expenses among state-subsidized ("public") institutions, but mainly for a different reason. **Figure 5** shows that *it is mainly in the public institutions rather than private that research expenses have been rising relative to total expenses.*

The relative increase in research costs at public institutions could be part of the explanation for the slightly more rapid increase in tuitions and fees at those schools, but it would be rash to leap to that conclusion. If it were as simple as that, then we would expect to see enrollment shift out of public research universities toward those that did little or no research, because the research-oriented universities would be charging more and more for less and less instruction. An exodus from such universities does not appear to have been happening, at least in absolute terms (a market share analysis would be useful). To Rothchild and White, this suggests that the advantages of enrollment in a research-related institution must be rising as quickly as the costs. But it might also mean that the rising costs of research have been largely or entirely covered by nontuition source — most likely by federal grants.

Federal spending on "research at educational institutions" is where the money is. Measured in constant 1997, such research grants increased from $9.8 billion in 1975 to $16.2 billion in 1996, while all other direct federal support for *institutions* of postsecondary education (excluding aid to students) dropped to the same amount ($16.2 billion) from $22 billion in 1975.[25]

Not surprisingly, public (subsidized) institutions have an advantage in attracting "public" research funds from government agencies. Between the 1989-90 and 1994-95 school years, federal grants and contracts per FTE student increased by 37.6% for public 4-year institutions, compared with 13.2% for private 4-year institutions.[26]

Even aside from the impact on tuition, it would be a matter of some concern if the federal shift toward aiding public institutions through research grants has diverted educational resources away from teaching and toward

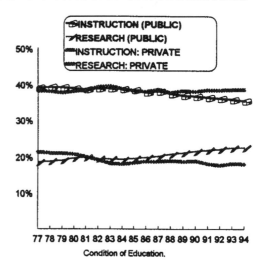

Figure 5

PERCENTAGE OF EXPENDITURES AT PUBLIC AND PRIVATE UNIVERSITIES

INSTRUCTION (PUBLIC)
RESEARCH (PUBLIC)
INSTRUCTION: PRIVATE
RESEARCH: PRIVATE

77 78 79 80 81 82 83 84 85 86 87 88 89 90 91 92 93 94
Condition of Education.

research. As St. John remarks, "Faculty are rewarded for their productivity in research rather than in teaching. And administrators are rewarded based on their portfolios — the number of programs they manage — rather than for their efficiency."[27]

Coopers & Lybrand updated an analysis by McPherson and Schapiro which had estimated that among public 4-year colleges, "an increase in federal financed aid of one dollar [led] . . . to an increase in tuition and fees of 50 cents."[28] That study found no effect on *private* college tuition, however, which could only be literally true if there was no competition at all between public and private institutions.

By contrast, Coopers & Lybrand claim to be "unable to detect any relationship at all between federal student aid and tuition charged for *public* institutions." However, they *did* find an interesting relationship between federal research grants and contracts and tuition charged: "Increases in federal grants appeared to be related to tuition increases in public 4-year colleges." That result was relegated to a footnote because "the model could not accurately predict tuition changes at public 4-year colleges." But that means the study cannot "detect any relationship at all between federal student aid and tuition charged for public institutions" only because the model *fails. A mysterious statistical black box that has no predictive value cannot be used to prove or disprove anything.*

For private colleges, Coopers & Lybrand also find little net effect. But that is only because one type of spending supposedly lowers private tuition while most others raise it. An additional dollar of Pell grants and scholarships is said to reduce tuition by 34 cents. But an extra dollar of federal grants and contracts *raises* tuition by 27 cents, state and local grants and contracts raise tuition by 19 cents, federal loans raise tuition by 16 cents, and another dollar of state and local appropriations raises tuition by 46 cents. To the extent that one has confidence in the model producing these results, they suggest that aid to students (with the notable exception of loans) does not raise *private* tuition, but all federal or state funding of private institutions *does* raise tuition.

Indeed, the single most consistent finding in Coopers & Lybrand is that federal or state research contracts and grants *to institutions* result in higher tuition at both public and private institutions. One possible explanation is that increased research grants raise tuition *per student* because the emphasis on federally-funded research tends to hold down the number of students, thus requiring additional rationing of one sort or another.

Start with the reasonable assumption that states try to keep public colleges and universities under some budgetary limits. As these institutions become more and more geared toward research, because they are bribed to do so by large and expanding federal grants, then constraints on the total budget would *require* a cut in the share of resources devoted to instruction (which is evident in **Figure 5**). One way to accomplish a relative reduction in the share of the budget going to education would be to severely ration entry. The usual ways of rationing entry to the best public universities are by raising academic standards and/or by raising tuition and fees. Since the restricted enrollment at research universities would leave many aspiring students with little option but to enroll in lesser state colleges, those colleges could safely raise their tuitions too.

While this scenario is not conclusive proof that rising research outlays are contributing to rising tuitions at public colleges and universities, the facts in **Figure 5**, and in Coopers & Lybrand, are certainly consistent with that possibility. The Coopers & Lybrand sample of 394 *public 4-year colleges experienced only a 0.7% increase in enrollment over five years.* Enrollment among private 4-year colleges — which experienced much smaller increase in federal grants — increased by 2.2% over the same period.

THE BENNETT HYPOTHESIS

The theory and evidence that federal spending on research may drive up tuitions is just one example of a broader charge that *all* sorts of governmental spending, including aid to students, might inflate educational costs. This is called the "Bennett hypothesis" in honor (or otherwise) of former Education Secretary Bill Bennett.

It must first be conceded that the impact of increased student aid is likely to be *relatively* small, because most federal "support" of higher education consists of sending checks to (mostly public) colleges and universities, not grants or loans to students. In constant 1997 dollars, federal aid to students increased from $17.7 billion in 1980 to 19.5 billion in 1997, but federal funding of institutions of higher education increased from $21.8 billion to $31.3 billion over the same period.[29] Proponents of additional federal funding often refer to this trend as a "decline," claiming that "reduced" federal support has forced institutions to raise tuitions, while higher tuitions have supposedly forced them to increase institutional aid.[30] This reverse alchemy, turning increases into declines, results from counting only federal programs that declined and ignoring those (notably research) that increased.

Coopers & Lybrand contend that aid to students (quite unlike their finding for research grants or student loans) actually lowers tuition at *private* institutions. Pell grants, they argue, result in more students from low-income students attending private colleges, thus making a larger percentage of students eligible for institutional assistance as well. We have previously argued otherwise — that Pell grants free-up institutional money for the less-poor. But even if the Coopers & Lybrand interpretation was correct, it would just mean that *net* tuition is not increased *for those students who receive federal and/or institutional aid*. Additional *institutional* assistance for one group of students, whether caused by Pell grants or not, implies higher tuition for the rest.

Once again, it is important to distinguish between inflating costs to the institutions, and inflating costs to students. Recall that **Figure 1** demonstrated that the costs that institutions pay, even including research, have *not* risen faster than those of other service industries. In this limited sense, increased federal outlays of any sort do not appear to have had much effect.

The effect on the gross "sticker price" of tuition is quite a different matter. If it were true that government grants *to students* do not tend to drive tuition charges up, then that could only be because (1) student aid has been ineffective in raising the demand for higher education, or (2) the increased demand has been fully met by increased supply, or (3) the increase in demand relative to supply has resulted in more nonprice rationing rather than higher prices.

If larger federal aid to students resulted in smaller state, institutional and private aid to students, for example, then it would have zero effect on demand and therefore no effect on prices. But in that case, all federal student aid programs could be eliminated with no effect on access to education.

If federal programs are effective in increasing the number of applicants at any given price, which is their stated intent, then they *must* result in an increase in rationing — either by higher prices or more restrictive admission standards.

In the unlikely event that the supply of educational facilities was quite responsive ("elastic") to price, then the added number of institutions and classrooms might eventually bring tuition back down. But it is surely much easier to throw dollars at colleges than to build more classrooms, so the Bennett effect seems plausible.

Hoxby, on the other hand, says Clotfelter's "assumption" that "the supply of college is inelastic . . . seems unlikely." But Clotfelter was making a factual *observation*, not an assumption: "Applications to Ivy League and other selective institutions rose steadily at the same time that their enrollments remained virtually constant."[31] With more applicants for the same number of spaces, entry clearly had to be rationed either by price or by some less efficient mechanism (alternatives to the price system include the queue, the lottery, bureaucratic favoritism, and influence-peddling). We have likewise noted Coopers & Lybrand's finding that enrollments in public 4-year institutions have also grown slowly in recent years, although that could conceivably have resulted from relatively weak demand rather than restricted supply. In any case, facts are neither likely nor unlikely, they are just facts. The burden of proof is on those who would even dare to imply that the supply of higher educational services has kept pace with demand. If it has not, the supply of college is "likely" to be inelastic.

Hoxby also says, "The primary problem with [Bennett's] theory is that federal moneys account for a much smaller share of payments in college tuition than in medical bills." The primary problem with Hoxby's argument is that it does not say that Bennett is wrong, only that the impact of third party payments is probably *smaller* than the effect of Medicare and Medicaid in bidding-up prices of medical services. Since costs of producing higher education *have* increased less rapidly than costs of medical services, this is not a serious challenge. To say that the effect of third party tuition payments is relatively small, when compared with the notorious explosion of medical costs, is no excuse for ignoring it.

Hoxby also asserts, without explanation, that the Bennett hypothesis requires "captive consumers" or a "very poor consumer information." Apparently, mobile and well-informed consumers could shop around for a school that would not hike tuition by enough to wipe-out any federal grant or loan. But if the net cost to the student is zero anyway (because federal grants and tax breaks cover, say, the entire cost of community college), why shop around?

She argues (plausibly) that consumers are less captive than they used to be, because states are providing smaller subsidies to in state students. However, since most Pell grant students go to community or home-state colleges, they are more captive than other students. She also says information about tuition is more available than ever before, but that is not entirely relevant. The true cost, net of financial aid, is extremely variable on a case-by-case basis, so the only way to determine the price is pay several application fees and go through the process of negotiating aid packages by trial and error.

Those who say that federal money has had no effect on prices (or on nonprice rationing) are simply arguing, in a roundabout way, that federal aid to students has had no effect at all, but has merely crowded out other varieties of financing. For at least some types of federal aid, the assumption of no net increase in funding is about as plausible as the Bennett hypothesis, as we mentioned above in the context of Pell grants substituting for institutional aid. Indeed, the best possible argument against the Bennett hypothesis may be that the reason federal student aid does not increase demand and prices is that it merely substitutes for aid that would otherwise have been provided by states, charities and institutions.

Note that both arguments point to the same policy conclusion. Additional federal aid is either ineffective because it is dissipated in higher fees, or because it crowds out other varieties of aid. The actual impact might be somewhere in between, of course, with tuition being bid up a bit and state and private efforts also being scaled back. In any case, it is hard imagine any federal financing scheme that involves neither of these self-defeating effects. Would building a bigger pipeline to the U.S. Treasury foster cost-conscious management of institutions of higher learning? Would it encourage states and charities to expand scholarships? To ask such questions is to answer them.

GET SOMEONE ELSE TO PAY

Alarming articles about the supposedly high and rising cost of higher education often make no suggestions at all about ways to curb those costs. Instead, the usual complaint is that grants make up "only" 42% of financial aid, and that loans create onerous debts. The alleged solution is to have the federal and state governments pick up a large share of the tab. Coopers & Lybrand thus figure that government was paying "only" 47% of the total bill for higher education in 1993-94, down from 51% in 1989-90 (although the federal bill remained the same, at 13%).[32] But governments have no "resources" except what they take from taxpayers.

Taxpayers have been recruited to subsidize community college and state colleges and universities.

Despite this enormous advantage for so-called "public" institutions, many *private* colleges and universities have to turn away an excess of applicants who have shunned the heavily-subsidized "public" alternatives. If the objective is to offer the highest quality education to the largest number who are willing and able to take advantage of it, then the whole idea of state-subsidized higher education is flawed. If private schools are better than public schools, on average, then higher subsidies to public schools must depress the average quality of U.S. education by luring students into inferior institutions (if public institutions were not inferior, why would they need a subsidy?).[33]

There is no reason to expect something as valuable as a good college education to be cheap. An investment in college is expected to yield a very valuable return to the student — a lifetime of higher earnings — while the "social benefit" is far more nebulous. In 1975, Gary Becker's classic work on *Human Capital* promised a "social gain from college education as measured by its effects on national productivity."[34] Yet productivity gains *slowed* as more Americans acquired college degrees. If the largest and most measurable benefits of a college education accrue to the individual recipient, why should other people subsidize this particular investment as much as they do, much less even more?

The *personal* value of a higher education, in terms of higher lifetime income, means the most equitable and efficient method of finance is not taxpayer subsidies to either students or institutions, but intelligent use of capital markets. At present, that means student loans, although equity claims are certainly feasible.

In 1995-96, 22% of all undergraduates received a federally subsidized loan, averaging $3,114. About 10% received an unsubsidized Stafford loan, averaging $2,925.[35] Clearly, it would not take many years of higher earnings to more than compensate for borrowing of about $3000 a year. There is no viable argument for such loans to be subsidized. Although part of the subsidy (deferral of payment until after graduation) makes practical sense, the interest rate should be a bit higher to compensate.

Only 29% of 1992-93 bachelor's degree recipients were repaying student loans in 1994. For them, "the average payment was $135, which averaged 9 percent of their April 1994 salary."[36] Of course, every rational student would prefer a tax-financed tuition subsidy or federal grant to either equity or debt financing, in which those financing the cost of education have to be repaid out of the economic return. And there is no shortage of researchers (at subsidized institutions) who seem eager to make an emotional case against loans and in favor of expanded state and federal funding.

There are only a few minor legal obstacles to creating an effective equity market to finance education, in which mutual funds could offer shares in securitized bundles of promises to share a fraction of future incomes, similar to mortgage-backed securities.[37] If loans were no longer subsidized, the many advantages of equity finance would probably dominate the market before long.

SUMMARY

The fact that cost of providing educational services has increased faster than inflation merely reflects the slowdown in inflation in prices of goods since 1981. The only time tuition and the CPI rose at the same pace was 1980-82, when both rose by 10% a year.

It is statistical gibberish to compare mean gross tuition with median income of all families, regardless of family age or composition. Tuition is widely discounted in any case, through the device of institutional aid. And tuition figures include tuition paid by governments, such as Pell grants (which are received by 30% of undergraduates).

There are many signs that institutions which combine high tuition with high institutional aid are attempting to maximize revenues through price discrimination — charging all the traffic will bear.

Public institutions have benefited most from rapid growth of federal research grants, and appear to have devoted fewer resources to instruction as a result. With very little expansion of enrollment, and tuition heavily subsidized by state taxpayers, this tilt of expenditures toward research would be expected to result in more stringent rationing of admission into public institutions, through higher tuition or otherwise. Higher tuition is a more efficient rationing device than alternatives.

Federal grants to students have been smaller and grown more slowly than federal grants to institutions, including research. To the extent that federal aid to students displaced or "crowded out" state, private and/or institutional aid, it has not been effective. To the extent that it may have been effective, it would have aggravated the rationing problem, most likely resulting in higher tuition.

Education is a valuable investment. Investments are properly financed by tapping the future earnings they produce, through debt or equity.

[1] Alan Reynolds, "Extra Credit" *National Review* September 15, 1997. The proposal for federal price controls was made by Sen. Christopher Dodd and Rep. Howard McKeon ("Congress, Educational Officials at odds on college cost control," *USA Today*, May 29, 1997). Price controls invariably stimulate demand and retard supply, creating "shortages" until the controls collapse. Artificial limits on one part of the price (tuition) would result in faster increases in other parts of price (higher fees, room and board, smaller financial aid). To the extent that controls cannot be evaded in this way or others (such as "key money" and subleasing in the case of rent control), quality deteriorates rapidly.

[2] Kit Lively, "An Inside Look at How a Private Research University Sets Tuition Rates and Spends the Money," *Chronicle of Higher Education*, May 30, 1997, p. A12.

[3] Caroline M. Hoxby, "How the Changing Market Structure of U.S. Higher Education Explains College Tuition," NBER draft, 1997, p. 40.

[4] *Monthly Labor Review*, September 1997, p. 21.

[5] College Entrance Examination Board.

[6] A 1997 press release from the College Board (www.collegeboard.org).

[7] GAO/HEHS-96-154, "Rising College Tuitions and Costs."

[8] David Elbert, "By 2015, education may cost $100,000," *Des Moines Register*, October 15, 1997.

[9] "College Guide," *Money*, September 1997, pp. 122 & 129.

[10] NCES, "Student Financial Aid Estimates for 1995-96," August 1997.

[11] Hoxby, *op. cit.*, argues that because most institutions are either state-subsidized or tax-exempt they are therefore not motivated to maximize "profits." But agents within government bureaucracies, foundations and other "nonprofit" organizations *are* motivated to maximize *revenues*, because doing so expands their power and perks. To say that they are relatively unconcerned about profits is merely to say that they are not very cost-conscious.

[12] Saul Schwartz and Sandy Baum, "Education," in Charles T. Clotfelter, ed., *Who Benefits From the Nonprofit Sector?* University of Chicago, 1992, p. 87.

[13] John B. Lee & C. Dennis Carroll, "Institutional Aid 1992-93," National Center for Education Statistics, 98-104, September 1997, p. 16.

[14] "Student Financial Aid Estimates for 1995-96," NCES 97-570, "Highlights," August 1997.

[15] Sarah Turner, "Does Federal Aid Affect College Costs? Evidence From The Pell Program," University of Virginia draft, August 20, 1997, pp. 5-6.

[16] *Money, op.cit*, p. 122.

[17] "College Guide," *Money*, September 1997, p. 130.

[18] Time/ Princeton Review, "The Best College For You and How to Get In," 1998 edition, p. 60.

[19] Michael Rothchild & Lawrence J. White, "The University in the Marketplace: Some Insights and Some Puzzles," National Bureau of Economic Research *Working Paper* No. 3853, 1991.

[20] GAO, *op. cit.*, p. 33.

[21] Alan Reynolds, "A Kind Word For Cream-Skimming," *Harvard Business Review*, Nov/Dec 1974.

[22] Lee & Carroll, *op. cit.*, p. 3.

[23] Charles T. Clotfelter, "Higher Education," NBER Reporter, Spring 1996.

[24] Coopers & Lybrand, "The Impact of Federal Student Assistance on College Tuition Levels,"
D.C., September 1997, p. 16.

[25] Charlene M. Hoffman, "Federal Support for Education: Fiscal Years 1980 to 1997," NCES 97-383, September 1997, Appendix Table A, p. 33. The largest sources of research dollars, by federal department, are HHS $7.1 billion, Energy $2.6 billion, NSF $2 billion, NASA $1.5 billion, and Defense $1.5 billion (*Ibid.*, p. 10). Defense research has gone down sharply, of course, but the others have more than taken up the slack.

[26] *Ibid.*, p. 13.

[27] Edward P. St. John, "Why Are College Costs Controversial?" ERIC Clearinghouse on Higher Education (Internet), George Washington University, D.C.

[28] Hoffman, *op. cit.*, p. 8.

[29] *Ibid.*, p. 17.

[30] Association of Governing Boards, "The Tuition Booklet," D.C., 1986.

[31] Clotfelter, *op. cit.*, p. 7.

[32] *Ibid.*, p. 3.

[33] See Gary Wolfram, "The Threat to Independent Education: Public Subsidies and Private Colleges," Cato Institute *Policy Analysis*, August 15, 1997.

[34] Gary Becker, Human Capital, Columbia U.P., 1975, p. 233.

[35] "Student Financial Aid . . ." *op. cit.*

[36] "Early Labor Force Experiences and Debt Burden," NCES 97-286, "Highlights," September 1997.

[37] Randall Lane, "Colsobs" *Forbes*, November 4, 1996; Chris Middleton, "Market Approach to Education," *Washington Times*, December 5, 1995; Charles E.M. Kolb, Testimony before the National Commission on the Cost of Higher Education, October 27, 1997.

Prepared for:
The National Commission on
The Cost of Higher Education
November, 1997

College Costs: Subsidies, Intuition, and Policy

Gordon C. Winston [*]

Williams College

Williams Project on the Economics of Higher Education

I. INTRODUCTION

Until recently, we've had an oddly fragmented picture of the economic workings of colleges and universities, mainly because of a long tradition of college "fund accounting." It had its virtues, but clarity about economic structure wasn't one of them. That's changing.

One of the first fruits of better economic information has been a clear picture of a college's "sources and uses of funds" — where the money comes from and where it goes. And one of the first fruits of that information is a better picture of their economic structure and with it the key role played by student subsidies. Most important is the deep difference now revealed between colleges and the ordinary business firms we're familiar with.

So this paper will do three things, broadly. It will describe the economic structure of the typical college or university, it will show, as matter of some pretty straightforward arithmetic, how that differs from the structure of a business firm, and it will suggest why that fact matters so much in a world where business intuition — reinforced by economics courses — is the foundation for common sense. Business intuition doesn't just make it hard to see what's going on in higher education, where price doesn't cover production costs, it distorts our understanding by making us see the wrong thing: we search for rising educational costs when they're falling and we don't look for evidence of falling subsidies because business firms don't pay subsidies.

II. PRICES, COSTS, SUBSIDIES AND STRATEGIES: THE ECONOMIC STRUCTURE OF A COLLEGE

The most fundamental anomaly in the economics of higher education is the fact that virtually all US colleges and universities sell their primary product — education — at a price that is far less than the average cost of its production. The subsidy that that gives to nearly every college student in the country is neither temporary nor small nor granted only by government institutions: student subsidies are a permanent feature of the economics of higher education; they represent a large part of total costs; and they are only slightly smaller in private than in public institutions. In total, student subsidies exceeded $82 billion in 1995.

Subsidies involve a unique set of strategic decisions for colleges and universities and unique circumstances for public policy that are familiar neither to for-profit firms nor to the economic theories designed to understand them. In 1995, the average American college produced an $11,967 education that it sold to its students for $3,770, giving them a subsidy of $8,197 a year: it's as if cars that cost the dealer $20,000 to put on the showroom floor were routinely sold for $6,300. We expect normal, for-profit firms to grant *negative* subsidies — to earn a profit — by selling at a price greater than the costs of production. Non-profit firms don't do that.[1]

It's not that student subsidies have been ignored in the analysis of higher education; they have, indeed, attracted a great deal of attention ever since the 1969 Hansen-Weisbrod study showed that the university system in California subsidized higher income students at the expense of lower income taxpayers. But that study also established what has become the conventional framing of the issue of subsidies as a matter of *student* characteristics — Which students with what characteristics get how much subsidy? In the recent work reported on here, the focus is shifted to *institutions* — Which colleges grant how much subsidy to their students and how do they choose to do it? Subsidies are a central part of the admissions-quality-pricing policies of colleges and universities.[2]

The Economic Structure of a College

Since the structure of costs, prices, subsidies, and aid in colleges and universities is not part of the familiar logic and vocabulary of for-profit economics or accounting—or the intuition it supports—it is worth a few paragraphs to spell it out.

Figure 1 provides a useful if stylized description of that economic structure in a typical college or university. In the first two columns, the stuff of a school's yearly accounts is pictured as (a) the *sources* of its income and (b) the *uses* of that income. By definition, they are equal. The height of the bars and segments represents dollars per student per year and the scale is roughly appropriate to the average student at the average college in 1995. Income is inclusive, global, income — the value of *all* the resources that accrue to the institution in the course of the year —rather than a sub-component of that income like the operating budget or current fund revenues that has dominated attention until recently.[3] For present purposes, not a lot of detail about the sources of income is needed —how much of it comes separately from government appropriations, gifts and grants, asset income, auxiliary and other income, etc.—so only tuition and auxiliary[4] income components are identified in column (a). The rest, non-tuition income, comes from what Hansmann called "donative resources"—from gifts, grants, appropriations, and asset earnings. And in column (b), the uses of income can similarly be simplified, described as auxiliary expenditures, educational and general spending (including capital costs),[5] and saving. Finally, since auxiliary activities are usually expected to break even, we can simplify things at the outset by setting auxiliary revenues equal to auxiliary expenditures and ignoring them in what follows.

The sources, then, are tuition and non-tuition income. That income is used to cover the costs of production. What's left over is saving. Sources equal uses in any period.

Figure 1

Global Income, Costs, Prices, Subsidies, & Aid

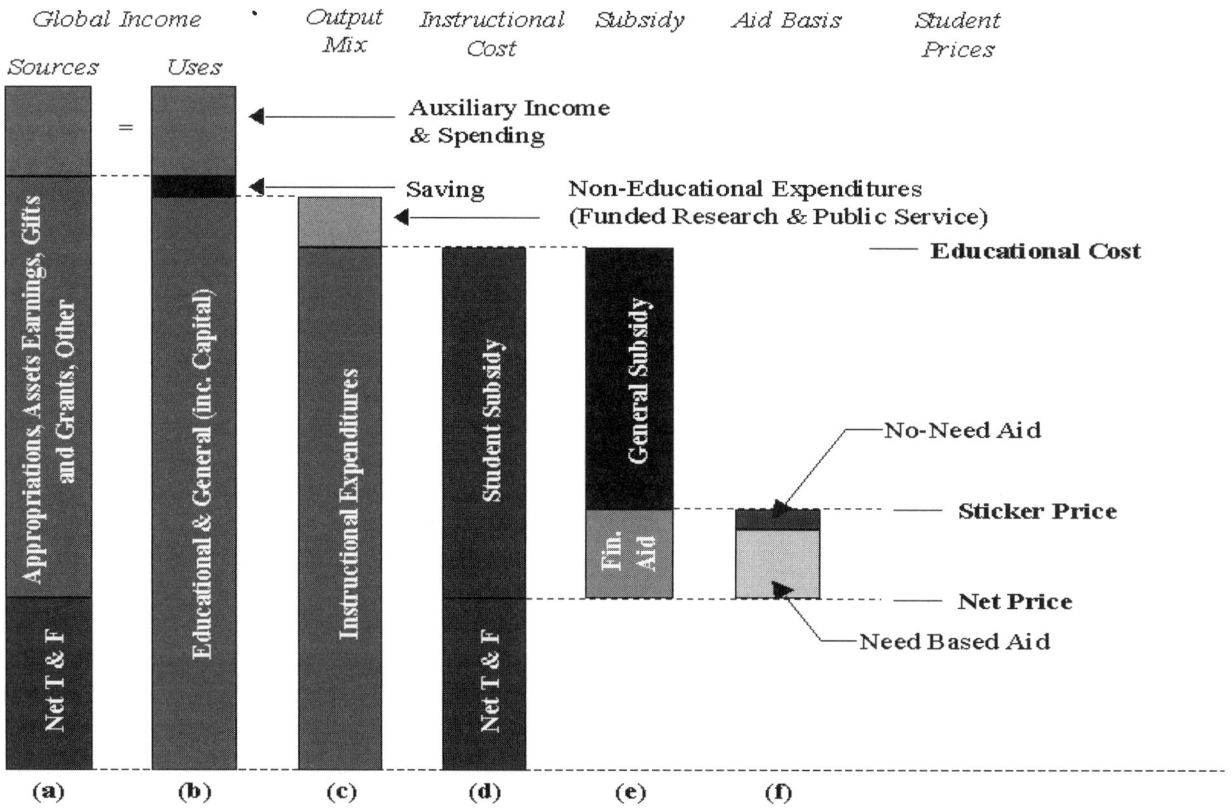

These two broad categories, sources and uses, fully encompass yearly flows in the accounts of a for-profit firm. More details would, of course, be needed to answer important questions, but they would simply come from disaggregating columns (a) and (b) to tell where, more specifically, the money came from and where it went. In the typical for-profit firm, income would come largely from the sale of its product. When that income was larger than production costs, the firm would show a profit (positive saving); when income was smaller than costs, it would show a loss.

So a whole additional set of questions, embedded in columns (c) through (f), is introduced by the fact that for a college, only a fraction of its total income is generated by sales proceeds — by the tuition and fees paid by its student-customers. In Figure 1, the *sources* column, (a), appropriately shows income from sources other than the sale of educational services — non-tuition income —- to be a lot

greater than tuition income. The uses column, (b), is more conventional in showing that total income can be used for production costs or, if it's big enough, that some can be left over as saving.

Together, columns (a) and (b) illustrate the fact that all those who buy the product in higher education are getting something that costs a lot more to produce than they're paying for it —- net tuition and fee income is a good deal less than the average cost of producing the services that the student gets.

The next four columns, then, frame the key question of how that subsidy is divided up among students: the institution's decisions on the sticker price that determines the general subsidy, and on individually targeted financial aid, need-based or merit.

Column (c) recognizes that higher education is "a multi-product industry" that makes a lot of things beside instruction. The college's sale of (largely) hotel and restaurant services in the form of its auxiliary income was just noted. Other major products of the university that don't have a lot to do directly with its instructional functions are recognized by subtracting off its funded research, public service, and a share of joint costs to leave instructional costs. These are identifiable in the data.[6]

Column (d) shows how that instructional cost per student is divided between the part the average student pays in net tuition and fees — his price — and the part that represents a subsidy. Column (e) describes how that subsidy portion is divided, in turn, between general subsidy and individual student aid. A "general subsidy" is given equally to each student at a college whenever its sticker price is set below production cost while financial aid[7] is a further price reduction based on individual student characteristics. Finally, column (f) divides that financial aid between the part that is awarded on the basis of an individual student's economic *need* and the part that's based on *"merit"* — his other characteristics like athletic or academic abilities or race. Since the height of these columns represents dollars per student, we can indicate, at the far right of Figure 1, the sticker price and net price levels consistent with the breakdowns shown in the columns (d) through (f).[8]

Strategic Decisions

The schema of Figure 1 highlights the most important strategic economic decisions facing a college or university.[9] Given its total non-tuition income, the school must make (implicitly, explicitly, historically...) the following choices:

A decision on size—total enrollment—that will influence[10] non-tuition income <u>per student</u>. So, for instance, by restricting its student body to 1,300, Swarthmore has protected its per-student endowment income; if it had twice as many students, other things being equal, it would have half as much endowment income per student.[11]

A decision on cost per student, and hence on net tuition and fees, given its non-tuition income. A school's per student non-tuition income fixes the <u>difference </u>between costs and price — its maximum subsidy — but it supports <u>any</u> combination of costs and price that maintains that difference. So the school must determine, simultaneously, the nature of its educational product[12] and how much students will have to pay for it. With, say, $10,000 of non-tuition income per student to support the subsidy, one school could produce a $15,000 a year education to be sold at a $5,000 average net tuition while another produced a $35,000 a year education to sell at a $25,000 net tuition. Subsidy resources (S), costs (C), and price (P) are locked together, arithmetically and relentlessly, by $S = C - P$.

A decision on mission—output mix—determines how much of the school's total spending will go to education. At the highly stylized level of Figure 1, that's about all that can be said, but at the finer grained level on which colleges actually function, this decision involves urgent questions of identifying an institution's core activities, setting priorities, and increasing the efficiency with which those activities are done. The higher the share of instructional costs, the more the student is subsidized, other things being equal.

A decision on sticker price divides the subsidy into the *general* subsidy that goes to all students, undifferentiated (74% on 1995 average), and financial aid that goes to those who have specific, desirable characteristics (the remaining 26%). The same $10,000 average yearly subsidy can be given in equal amounts to all enrolled students through a sticker price set just $10,000 below instructional costs or — at the other extreme — it can be given through a sticker price set equal to costs, then offset selectively by individually targeted financial aid that averaged $10,000 per student. Finally,

A decision on merit-based and need-based aid — the division of any individually differentiated subsidies — student aid — according to student characteristics, whether it is to be based on the student's economic circumstances or on other characteristics, academic or athletic or artistic merit or race or whatever.

These are strategic choices that all colleges and universities have to make about output, quality, and pricing. And they simply have no parallel in for-profit firms. In any school, history will matter a whole lot — resources can be highly "illiquid" and traditions, cultures, alumni, and faculties resistant to change. And some public institutions will have been given limited discretion by legislatures. But Figure 1 pictures the underlying economic relationships, in their barest structural form, that define possibilities and set constraints on a college's costs, prices, subsidies, and aid. The magnitude of a school's subsidies is determined by its access to non-tuition resources and its size and any student subsidy is exhaustively divided between general subsidies and financial aid based on need or on merit.

III. THE FACTS: SUBSIDIES AND STRUCTURE IN U.S. HIGHER EDUCATION

The purpose of this paper is not to analyze what we've discovered about the role of subsidies, costs, prices, and aid in the structure of U.S. higher education — that's been done at some length elsewhere (see note 2). But it will be useful, nonetheless, to look briefly at the facts of Table 1 with its summary data for 2,739 degree granting schools in 1995.[13]

Subsidies (Col. 3) are simply educational costs per student (Col. 4) *less* what he or she paid the school in net tuition (Col. 5). So, as noted in the introduction, averaged over all schools, an $11,967 education was sold in 1995 for a price of $3,770, giving the student an $8,197 subsidy. That, of course, is given in part as a *general* subsidy to all students (Col.8), got by setting the sticker price (Col. 6) less than educational costs, and in part as additional *financial aid* to some students (Col. 9), got by charging them less than the sticker price. The "Net Price of Education" of Col. 7 is especially useful — it describes what the average student pays for a dollar's worth of higher education. Finally, the last two columns show how any given subsidy is distributed between general subsidy and financial aid.

While resisting the temptation to say much about the rich information in Table 1, the most important facts, I think, are (a) the sheer size of student subsidies (b) the fact that they are both (c) ubiquitous and (d) about the same in public and private sectors (e) distributed to students largely in the general form of sticker prices set well under costs so that little of the subsidy is left over to be given as financial aid (f) that there's a high degree of variety among schools and (g) the difference between those giving large subsidies and those giving small ones is very great. These characteristics and differences describe, I think, the core economic structure of US higher education.

IV. SO WHAT? IMPLICATIONS

There are three kinds of answers to the ever-important question, "So What?"

Our Mental Model of Higher Education

Most basically, understanding the structure of costs, prices, subsidies, and aid in and among colleges and universities is essential to understanding the "industry" and what it's like. If our shared conception of higher education isn't reasonably accurate, we'll look for the wrong things and fail to see the importance of the right things. A model built on the facts of Table 1 can illuminate the roles of competition, collegiate wealth, student quality and selectivity, faculty tenure, and institutional saving. And the facts of Table 1 are crucial to assessing the likely impact of new technology and the inroads that privatization can make into college and university activities. So, broadly, improved understanding — a better "mental model" — has to be the primary implication of the facts. But not here — other papers have developed that. (Again, see note 2. above.)

Table 1

Subsidies, Costs, Prices, and Aid
by Control, Subsidy Size & Carnegie Classification
in Dollars Per Student [FTE]
1994 - 1995

	Number of Institutions	Enrollments Average	Subsidy	Educational Spending	Net Tuition and Fees	Sticker Price	Net Price of Education	General Subsidy	Financial Aid	General as Percent Subsidy	Aid as Percent Subsidy
	(1)	(2)	(3)	(4)	(5)	(6)	(7)	(8)	(9)	(10)	(11)
All Institutions	**2,739**	**3,493**	**8,197**	**11,967**	**3,770**	**5,919**	**31.5%**	**6,048**	**2,149**	**73.8%**	**26.2%**
Public	**1,420**	**5,140**	**8,686**	**9,919**	**1,233**	**2,272**	**12.4%**	**7,648**	**1,038**	**88.0%**	**12.0%**
Private	**1,319**	**1,721**	**7,670**	**14,172**	**6,502**	**9,846**	**45.9%**	**4,326**	**3,344**	**56.4%**	**43.6%**
Public Institutions by Subsidy Size											
Decile 1	142	5,316	22,915	24,551	1,636	3,257	6.7%	21,295	1,621	92.9%	7.1%
Decile 2	142	5,695	10,516	11,680	1,163	2,471	10.0%	9,208	1,308	87.6%	12.4%
Decile 3	142	6,060	9,082	10,311	1,229	2,405	11.9%	7,906	1,176	87.0%	13.0%
Decile 4	142	5,310	8,260	9,567	1,307	2,394	13.7%	7,173	1,087	86.8%	13.2%
Decile 5	142	5,294	7,592	8,738	1,145	2,165	13.1%	6,573	1,020	86.6%	13.4%
Decile 6	142	4,816	6,931	8,031	1,101	2,057	13.7%	5,974	956	86.2%	13.8%
Decile 7	142	4,867	6,364	7,448	1,084	1,976	14.6%	5,472	892	86.0%	14.0%
Decile 8	142	4,224	5,810	6,981	1,171	2,032	16.8%	4,950	861	85.2%	14.8%
Decile 9	142	5,304	5,215	6,330	1,115	1,907	17.6%	4,424	792	84.8%	15.2%
Decile 10	142	4,511	4,174	5,555	1,381	2,053	24.9%	3,502	672	83.9%	16.1%
Public Institutions by Carnegie Type											
Research	83	21,399	10,298	13,448	3,150	4,571	23.4%	8,877	1,421	86.2%	13.8%
Doctoral	63	11,363	8,499	11,155	2,656	3,776	23.8%	7,378	1,121	86.8%	13.2%
Comprehensive	271	6,428	8,117	9,933	1,816	2,907	18.3%	7,026	1,091	86.6%	13.4%
Liberal Arts	80	2,477	7,809	9,389	1,580	2,857	16.8%	6,532	1,277	83.7%	16.3%
Two-Year	874	3,186	7,309	8,022	714	1,623	8.9%	6,399	910	87.6%	12.4%
Specialized	49	1,672	35,338	36,978	1,640	3,537	4.4%	33,442	1,896	94.6%	5.4%
Private Institutions by Subsidy Size											
Decile 1	132	2,780	22,235	30,325	8,089	13,353	26.7%	16,971	5,264	76.3%	23.7%
Decile 2	132	1,228	12,050	19,095	7,045	11,782	36.9%	7,313	4,737	60.7%	39.3%
Decile 3	132	1,506	9,594	15,961	6,368	10,357	39.9%	5,605	3,989	58.4%	41.6%
Decile 4	132	1,716	7,953	13,824	5,871	9,523	42.5%	4,301	3,652	54.1%	45.9%
Decile 5	132	1,757	6,726	13,094	6,368	9,944	48.6%	3,150	3,576	46.8%	53.2%
Decile 6	132	1,710	5,725	11,758	6,033	9,339	51.3%	2,419	3,307	42.2%	57.8%
Decile 7	132	1,594	4,900	10,946	6,046	9,067	55.2%	1,879	3,021	38.3%	61.7%
Decile 8	132	1,906	3,941	10,466	6,525	9,078	62.3%	1,388	2,553	35.2%	64.8%
Decile 9	132	1,403	2,723	8,835	6,112	8,097	69.2%	737	1,986	27.1%	72.9%
Decile 10	132	1,606	801	7,363	6,562	7,907	89.1%	-544	1,345	-67.9%	167.9%
Private Institutions by Carnegie Type											
Research	39	11,821	20,369	32,014	11,646	16,975	36.4%	15,039	5,329	73.8%	26.2%
Doctoral	43	5,800	7,720	18,736	11,016	14,417	58.8%	4,320	3,400	56.0%	44.0%
Comprehensive	245	2,460	5,504	12,903	7,399	10,484	57.3%	2,420	3,084	44.0%	56.0%
Liberal Arts	526	1,228	9,064	15,425	6,361	10,505	41.2%	4,920	4,144	54.3%	45.7%
Two-Year	243	572	5,164	10,227	5,063	7,565	49.5%	2,662	2,502	51.5%	48.5%
Specialized	223	771	7,261	12,906	5,646	7,949	43.7%	4,958	2,303	68.3%	31.7%

Understanding Trends and Changes

The facts of Table 1 provide a structure with which to monitor changes in higher education — changing circumstances and strategies like those associated with the tax revolt and increased private competition.[14] Those facts, over time, describe patterns of change in colleges and universities in response to circumstances, opportunities, and pressures. And they make it clear that, among colleges and universities, circumstances and strategies are so very different that adaptation to change will be very different, too — we think of "higher education" as a single, monolithic entity, only at risk of considerable error. Recognizing the fundamental differences among colleges and universities is central to understanding what's happening and why.

Public Policy and Common Sense

The third implication is the one I want to concentrate on for the rest of this paper — large and ubiquitous student subsidies in higher education mean a very great deal for public understanding and public policy. It is there that the most serious — and most dangerous — implications lie, because it is there that the disjunction between the facts and what people "know" to be the facts is the greatest and likely to be most influential.

V. PUBLIC POLICY, ECONOMICS, AND BUSINESS INTUITION

Paradoxically, the single most serious problem facing the understanding of higher education — and hence public attitudes and public policies — may well be common sense. Very persuasive and appealing common sense. We have, collectively, a well-schooled intuition that's based on a whole lot of experience with business firms. We've lived with ordinary business firms all our lives and from them we've absorbed a strong feeling for what makes economic sense and what doesn't. And anyone who's taken Econ 101 will have had that common sense reinforced by graphs and lectures and quizzes and a final grade. But unfortunately, what's happening in colleges and universities — their economics — is counter-intuitive in these terms; what's accurate is unfamiliar and what's obvious is often just plain wrong. So it's worth the risk of belaboring what's basically different about a college and a business firm.

I want to use two simple pictures to describe two key facts — arithmetic facts – about businesses and colleges and universities. The pictures and the facts are highly stylized, but aside from neglected details, correct. Colleagues who have looked at these graphs have accused me of working on an Economics Coloring Book and it's at about the coloring book level that things start going wrong.

Figure 2 shows a business firm on the left and a college or university on the right. Like Figure 1, it describes sources and uses of funds for those organizations. The left hand bar describes the firm's yearly income and what it does with that money — where it comes from and where it goes. Income derives from the sale of the things the firm produces — their price. That income goes to pay the costs of production and — if costs are less than sales income — what's left over is profit. So a car dealer earns money from the cars he sells and pays that money out as costs — the wholesale cost of the car, salaries, commissions, building, heating oil… —- and keeps what's left as profit. A car sold for $25,000 that costs $23,000 to deliver to the customer means $2,000 as the dealer's profit. Pretty routine stuff that my granddaughter has started to learn with a lemon-aid stand at the age of seven.

The right hand bar shows the same basic facts for a college or university. But, of course, only a fraction of its income comes from the sale of its product, from the price or net tuition its student-customers pay for the educational services it sells them. Most, has to come from somewhere else, from those donative resources from alumni and taxpayers and earnings from endowments and the services of expensive buildings and equipment that support that student subsidy. Of course, the reason society makes donations to colleges and universities — and doesn't make them to the local Ford dealer — is that higher education is considered to be socially A Good Thing so we encourage people to buy more of it by offering generous subsidies on its purchase.[15]

From this, two crucial facts emerge:

*For a __business firm__, price is always __greater__ than production costs and the difference is **profits**. So*

$$Price \equiv Cost + Profits, \qquad or\ P \equiv C + P.$$

Sell the product for $5 and if it costs $4 to make, $1 is left as profit.

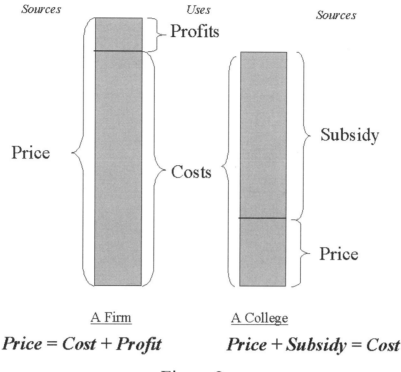

Figure 2

*For a <u>college</u>, price is always <u>less</u> than production costs **and any difference is student** subsidy.* **So**

Price + Subsidy ≡ Cost,   *or*   P + S ≡ C.

Sell the product for $1 and if it costs $4 to make, a $3 subsidy will have to come from donative resources.

This simple, essentially arithmetic, difference has profound consequences. And more so the less clearly it is recognized.

VI. THROUGH THE LOOKING GLASS

Let me illustrate the dangerous role of business intuition and its accompanying common sense with four examples: the confusion of "costs" and "prices" and "net prices" that enters most discussions of college costs; the difficult task of the Cost Commission if they're armed only with the business model and its intuition; the popular tuition-relief policies modeled on Georgia's Hope Scholarship program; and the strange threat posed by increased "sales" in higher education. I'll end with a comment on "cross-subsidies" in colleges and universities.

Costs and Prices and Net Prices

A major semantic problem with our national talk about "college costs" should be clear from what's been said so far, but the role of business intuition may not be so apparent. We use "college costs" to mean three very different things: (1) *production costs*, the cost of delivering a year of education to a student, (2) *sticker price*, the posted, nominal (and maximum) price any student pays, and (3) *net price*, what the average student actually pays, after financial aid grants. But we give them all the same name and don't often notice. It's not just carelessness. Economics 101 goes to great pains in describing competitive for-profit businesses to argue that in the long run, any business' economic profits will disappear so price will just cover costs and price and cost can be treated as the same thing. And intuition and common sense confirms the idea that production costs and prices are, if not exactly the same thing, pretty close. In business, they usually are. In higher education, they usually aren't. And in the long run, persistent price discounting will become well known and routine. So even basic economics tells us there should only be a single price and it will come to be the same thing as costs.

The Cost Commission's Task

The Commission is to figure out why a typical family's costs of higher education (read "net tuition" or "price," of course) have risen so much in the recent past.

From the perspective of the business intuition embedded in P º C + P, that most of us share, the answer looks pretty simple. Since the price (P) has gone up, it has to be because costs (C) went up or because profits (P) went up. Colleges are non-profit firms, so the place to look is at costs; they must have gone up. And that leads directly to questions about increased waste, about rising administrative costs, a less productive faculty, elaborate buildings and equipment, a too-exuberant embrace of expensive technologies or the costs of increased regulation. This is an agenda right out of Price º Cost + Profit and the solid business intuition it describes. Sensible, from that perspective, but guaranteed to obscure the facts.

What has been happening in public higher education (where 80% of the students go) shows up only when we look at Price + Subsidy º Cost, that describes a college or university.

There it's clear that tuition (P) *might* have gone up because costs (C) went up, but it might also have gone up because subsidies (S) went *down*. And that's what appears to have happened. The taxpayers' revolt that restricted state appropriations (donative resources) has met an increase in enrollments and together these have reduced student subsidies in public higher education. That, of course, is a very different picture from the one that comes from business intuition. And if subsidies go down at a college, it means either of two things. Prices *have to* go up or educational spending and quality *have to* go down, or both. We've seen both. Students in public colleges are paying a higher price in 1995 than in 1987 to get a less costly, lower quality education with fewer and larger classes and more TAs and TVs.

So, sensible business intuition doesn't just obscure what's been going on in higher education — making it harder to see — it misleads, distorting our understanding of what's been happening by making us focus on the wrong thing. We search for rising educational costs though they're falling. And we don't look for evidence of falling subsidies because business firms don't have subsidies. And, I say with the regret of a long-time Economics teacher, the more we rely on Econ 101, the more we'll miss what's going on.

The Promise of Government Tuition Support

A rash of appealing proposals have offered direct government support of family tuition costs in the hope of easing the burden and increasing college enrollments – from President Clinton's national tax relief to the Zero Tuition plan proposed for Massachusetts' two-year colleges and, of course, the original Hope Scholarship Plan in Georgia. Business intuition and its Price º Cost + Profit logic says those measures make good sense — like food stamps, the government will pick up part of the price, allowing people who can't afford higher education to buy it anyway.

But the reality of higher education, where Price + Subsidy º Cost leads to a very different picture — one of declining quality and rising tuition.

The table above showed that over all institutions, students' tuition payments cover only 32 cents of each dollar of their costs. In the public colleges where most students go, tuition pays 12 cents on the dollar. So if a new student is induced by these policies to go to the average public college, for every dollar he brings with him in new tuition revenues, he'll give rise to <u>nine</u> dollars in additional costs. The question, then, is, "Who's going to pay the rest?"[16]

The most realistic answer sees two unhappy outcomes. One is that spending per student — and hence educational quality — falls. The other is that, trying to protect educational quality,[17] colleges and universities will raise tuition so it covers more of the cost. That, of course, revives the old familiar charge that government efforts to help students always induce colleges to jack up their prices.

Since these plans are based on Georgia's Hope Scholarship program, it's instructive to look at what happened there. Between 1986 and 1994, a panel of 2,300 colleges and universities from our data shows that those in Georgia increased enrollments by 33% while the average increase for the US was 14% and for the Southeast states, 23%. So the Hope program does appear to have encouraged more people to go to college. And Georgia disproportionately increased appropriations to their public colleges — by 17%, against a more modest increase in the Southeast (5%) and a decrease (-2.3%) in the US. But because their appropriations increased less than enrollment, even Georgia's appropriations *per student* went down by 12% and so did its spending per student. So as a result of the Hope plan, more students got less education. Georgia's two-year colleges, seen alone, tell the same story even more dramatically: enrollment went up by 51% while appropriations rose 40% so expenditures per student fell by 17%.

The Hope Scholarships, then, created more students who brought more tuition revenues to the colleges but because they cover only part of the cost and weren't fully matched by more money in appropriations, the quality of education fell.

(Are any colleges and universities winners under these tuition-support policies? Yes, ironically. The very wealthy and selective schools that restrict enrollments in face of long queues of would-be students — Harvard and Stanford and Swarthmore — won't be induced to expand so they won't need extra resources. For them and their students, tuition-relief policies will only help pay their often-considerable tuitions.)

The Worrisome Prospect of Increased Sales

We're facing an increase in enrollments over the next decade estimated at 10% to 30%. That kind of demand increase would be cause for dancing in the streets in any for-profit industry. But for higher education, it is cause, instead, for genuine panic. If it comes to pass that 3 million more students enter US colleges and universities, they will bring with them an additional $11.3 billion in net tuition revenues, but they will also bring an additional $35.9 billion in costs — if quality is to be maintained at 1995 levels — and that will require $24.6 billion of additional non-tuition resources. From somewhere. Our for-profit intuition doesn't prepare us for a dilemma like that.

Cross-Subsidies

In business firms, a product is cross-subsidized if profits from another product or activity are used to offset losses on that one. So new car sales are cross-subsidized if profits from the service department are needed to offset losses on new cars. But in a college or university, things are more complicated. That's frustrating because we'd like very much to understand cross-subsidies in higher education — to find out if the rich students subsidize the poor ones or undergraduate education subsidizes faculty research or PhD programs or if football subsidizes Classics courses.

But cross-subsidies are much harder to measure in a university than in a business firm. Because *all* activities taken together are heavily subsidized, it's difficult to tell the difference between a genuine cross-subsidy — where one activity supports another (football supports women's ice hockey) — and simple differences in the amount of subsidy given to two well-subsidized activities. "Robinhooding" is a popular case in point where it is sometimes asserted (most recently in a *Time* article last March) that colleges make a profit by charging high prices of their rich students in order to subsidize their poor students. But we've seen in Table 1 that except at the very bottom of the pecking order (in the bottom decile of private colleges) the fact is that the rich kids get a smaller subsidy than the poor kids, but they all are subsidized, even those who pay the full sticker price.

More basic is the fact that nobody knows how much a college's activities actually cost since there's only the vaguest recognition of the costs of the capital services they use — the services of the buildings and computers and libraries and stadiums used in those activities. Yet we do know that facilities account for 20% to 30% of the total cost of educational production.[18] Those large and important cost elements can be estimated for a single school with a great deal of work and a great deal of cooperation from their accountants and facilities managers. But they haven't been and until they are, any guess at the magnitudes of cross-subsidies can only be a guess.

VII. CONCLUSION

Colleges and universities are very different, in fundamental *economic* ways, from the for-profit businesses on which our intuitions and economic theories are based. Sometimes those differences don't much matter. But too often they matter very fundamentally and policies based on common sense can produce results that are puzzling, unintended, and damaging. No task is more difficult than convincing people that what makes good common sense is likely to be wrong and what's right is flatly counter-intuitive. But that's the challenge facing those who would make effective policy for higher education. "Mosquitoes," it was said with confidence in 1904, "couldn't possibly cause malaria and yellow fever." The idea that they could was implausible, counterintuitive, and, of course, entirely correct.

NOTES

*This paper relies heavily on Williams Project Discussion Paper (DP)-32, "Costs, Prices, Subsidies, and Aid in U.S. Higher Education," July, 1995, written with Ivan C. Yen. The Andrew W. Mellon Foundation has generously supported the ongoing research that informs this paper. It has benefited a great deal from the comments of Henry Bruton, Jared Carbone, Clare Cotton, Stuart Crampton, Al Goethals, Jim Kolesar, Mike McPherson, Hank Payne, and the Commission members during its discussion on November 6, 1997.

[1]The fundamental legal and economic characteristic of nonprofit firms is that any profits they earn cannot be distributed. See the seminal paper by Henry Hansmann, "The Role of Nonprofit Enterprise," 89 *Yale Law Journal* 835 (1980).

[2]The core studies are reported in a series of Discussion Papers from the Williams Project on the Economics of Higher Education: DP-23, "A Note on the Logic and Structure of Global Accounting," on colleges' economic information; DP-32, "Costs, Prices, Subsidies, and Aid in U.S. Higher Education," on the structural economic facts summarized here; DP-35, "Physical Capital and Capital Service Costs in U.S. Colleges and Universities, 1993," on the large role of capital services in college costs; DP-40, "The Economic Structure of Higher Education: Subsidies, Customer-Inputs, and Hierarchy," on the model of higher education implied by these facts; and DP-41, "Subsidies, Costs, Tuition and Aid in U.S. Higher Education, 1986-87 to 1993-94," on changes in these circumstances, strategy, and performance over time. All are available from wpehe@williams.edu.

[3]See, for more details on global accounting, Winston, "Global Accounting," in Massy, William F., *Resource Allocation in Higher Education*, Ann Arbor: The University of Michigan Press; 1996. The new FASB 117 accounting standards required last year go a good distance toward an economically coherent description of a college or university [DP-23].

[4]Including Hospitals and Unrelated Enterprises.

[5]Note that current spending is *net* of institutional grant aid, so financial aid is treated as a price discount rather than a cost of education. See Winston, "Notes on the Costs of Delivering a Year of Undergraduate Education," draft, October 21, 1997.

[6]It would be useful, too, to pull out all the other primary non-instructional products of the university and their costs — like television programming through athletics — but these can't always be disentangled from strictly instructional costs for many schools, so they aren't segregated. Fortunately, some of the largest, like Hospitals and Independent Operations, can be identified and are removed from the subsidy calculation. More subtle judgments about the "necessity" or "appropriateness" of particular components of spending are beyond the scope of this paper: while there is undoubtedly some gilding of the lily, not only are data unavailable, but it would be hard to get agreement on which spending is "too much," an issue made even more complicated by the role of subsidies in increasing student demand and selectivity [DP-40].

[7]Lee calls these "institutional subsidies" and "student subsidies." [Lee and Sango-Jordan]

1) Income Sources = Net Tuition and Fees + Non-tuition Income + Auxiliary Income

2) Income Uses = Auxiliary Expenditures + Saving + Educational and General Spending (E&G&K)

3) E&G&K = Instructional E&G&K + Research + Service

4) Instructional E&G&K = Net Tuition & Fees + Subsidy

5) Subsidy = General Aid + Individual Aid

6) Individual Aid = Need-based Aid + No-need Aid

So

7) Income = Net Tuition and Fees + Auxiliary Expenditures + Saving + Need-based Aid + No- need Aid + General Aid + Research + Service.

[9]Were data available, we would have to include a decision on how much of total income to save each year.

[10]For a private institution with subsidy resources that are fixed without regard to enrollment — like endowment — size *determines* per student resources.

[11]Size enters importantly, too, as a determinant of student selectivity, but that is a subject of other papers, namely, DP-40 and "Why Can't a College Be More Like a Firm?" *Change*, September/October, 1997.

[12]It is quite inaccurate to suggest that resources translate simply into educational quality since that ignores institutional differences in mission, care, attention to students, ideology, location, and all the rest that distinguishes individual schools and it neglects the opportunities that surely exist to produce education more efficiently. Yet, the magnitude of the differences in resources per student in US data appear to justify a rough association of quality and costs, other things being equal, and the temptation to see costless elimination of waste-abuse-and-corruption as a silver bullet that avoids hard choices should certainly be resisted. Fewer dollars — given a college's mission — usually mean a lower quality education.

[13]Based on 1995 IPEDS (Integrated Postsecondary Educational Data System, published yearly by the Department of Education's National Center for Educational Statistics) data for the colleges and universities in the fifty states that reported positive expenditures, FTE enrollments of more than 100 students, of whom 20% or more were undergraduates.

[14]See DP-41, "Subsidies, Costs, Tuition, and Aid in US Higher Education: 1986-87 to 1993-94" with Ethan Lewis.

[15]The past decade (sadly) has seen this emphasis on the economic and civic virtues of an educated citizenry largely replaced by attention to "human capital investment" and individuals' gains from higher education. But even that narrow view still supports the ideals of distributional equity and access.

[16]The GI Bill, too, channeled funds to the student, rather than the college, but that was in a climate where expansion of public sector schools was supported with increased appropriations (donative resources) and private schools, with their limited non-tuition resources, resisted expansion. So the answer to "who's going to pay the rest?" was "society," willingly.

[17]It is devoutly to be wished that cost savings could make it unnecessary to choose between higher prices and lower quality with expanded enrollments — that colleges and universities could simply produce the same education at lower costs through new technology and belt-tightening. But (a) it's not clear that there's that much room for belt-tightening — there's no firm evidence that even for-profit firms

operate with a great deal more efficiency than nonprofit firms in producing "products" with complicated characteristics (see Pauly, Mark, "Nonprofit Firms in Medical Markets," *American Economic Review* 77:257-62 (1987) and Oster, Sharon, "An Analytical Framework for Thinking About the Use of For-Profit Structures for University Services and Activities," Paper presented at the Forum for the Future of Higher Education, The Aspen Institute, September 22, 1997) — (b) new learning technologies appear able to reduce the cost of some of what colleges and universities do, but their impact on quality is still unknown, and (c) the magnitudes involved make it unrealistic to hope that efficiencies in production could offset the increases in costs that come with increased enrollments. Finally, for Economics majors, the well-learned idea that marginal cost is less than average cost and marginal cost is what really counts, runs into a difficult problem of quality — those neat diagrams on the blackboard always assumed that output of the product could be expanded, moving out the Q axis, without affecting its quality. But that's simply wrong for higher education where adding more students with the same faculty and facilities inevitably degrades quality unless schools are operating initially with excess capacity.

[18]Winston and Lewis, "Physical Capital and Capital Service Costs in U.S. Colleges and Universities: 1993," *Eastern Economic Journal*, v.23, No. 2, Spring, 1997.

Appendix F: Consultants

AMERICAN INSTITUTES FOR RESEARCH
Rita J. Kirshstein, Project Director
Amy Smith O'Malley
Roy J. Pearson
David A. Rhodes

JAMES HARVEY AND ASSOCIATES
James Harvey
Roger M. Williams

THE INGRAM GROUP
Lewis Lavine
Joe Hall
Chris Jewell

THE INSTITUTE FOR HIGHER EDUCATION POLICY
Jane V. Wellman

Archives

Commissioner briefing books, the original transcripts from each of the meetings, press releases and correspondence have been sent to the United States National Archives and Record Administration, 8601 Adelphi Road, College Park, Maryland, 20740-6001. Telephone: 301-737-7110.

Transcripts and Commissioner briefing books have also been sent to the archives of the American Council on Education located at the Hoover Institution of Stanford University, Stanford, California, 94305. Telephone: 650-723-3563.

Appendix G
Supplementary Research Material

Prepared by The American Institutes for Research
Pelavin Research Center
1000 Thomas Jefferson Street, N.W.
Washington, D.C. 20007

List of Contents and Exhibits

Technical Note

Issue 2:   Innovative methods for reducing or stabilizing tuition

Issue 3:   Trends in college and university administrative costs, including administrative staffing, ratio of administrative staff to instructors, ratio of administrative staff to students, remuneration of administrative staff, and remuneration of college and university presidents or chancellors.

Issue 4:   Trends of (a) faculty workload and remuneration (including the use of adjunct faculty), (b) faculty-to-student ratios, (c) number of hours spent in the classroom by faculty, and (d) tenure practices, and the impact of such trends on tuition.

Issue 5:   Trends in (a) the construction and renovation of academic and other collegiate facilities, and (b) the modernization of facilities to access and utilize new technologies, and the impact of such trends on tuition.

Issue 6:   The extent to which increases in institutional aid and discounting have affected tuition increases, including the demographics of students receiving such aid, the extent to which such aid is provided to students with limited need in order to attract such students to particular institutions or major fields of study, and the extent to which Federal financial aid, including loan aid, has been used to offset such increases.

Issue 7:   The extent to which Federal, state, and local laws, regulations, or other mandates contribute to increasing tuition, and recommendations on reducing those mandates.

Introduction

Fueled by concerns that attending college was rapidly becoming unaffordable for large segments of the American population, Congress created the National Commission on the Cost of Higher Education in June 1997. Its mandate included examining 11 specific topics:

- The increase in tuition compared to other commodities and services
- Innovative methods for reducing or stabilizing tuition
- Trends in college and university administrative costs, including administrative staffing, ratio of administrative staff to instructors, ratio of administrative staff to students, remuneration of administrative staff, and remuneration of college and university presidents
- Trends in (a) faculty workload and remuneration (including the use of adjunct faculty), (b) faculty-to-student ratios, (c) number of hours spent in the classroom by faculty, and (d) tenure practices, and the impact of such trends on tuition
- Trends in (a) the construction and renovation of academic and other collegiate facilities, and (b) the modernization of facilities to access and utilize new technologies, and the impact of such trends on tuition
- The extent to which increases in institutional aid and discounting have affected tuition increases, (including the demographics of students receiving such aid, the extent to which such aid is provided to students with limited need in order to attract such students to particular institutions or major fields of study, and the extent to which Federal financial aid, including loan aid, has been used to offset such increases
- The extent to which Federal, State, and local laws, regulations, and mandates contribute to increasing tuition, and recommendations on reducing those mandates
- The establishment of a mechanism for a more timely and widespread distribution of data on tuition trends and other costs of operating colleges and universities
- The extent to which student financial aid programs have contributed to changes in tuition
- Trends in State fiscal policies that have affected college costs
- The adequacy of existing Federal and State financial aid programs in meeting the costs of attending colleges and universities

In addition, the Congress asked the Commission to consider other topics that might illuminate rising costs and prices.

This appendix of supporting materials supplements the Commission's report to Congress. It includes previously published data that relate to each of the 11 issues as well as original data analysis. In addition, this appendix contains selected testimony presented before the Commission by the three University Presidents who hosted meetings of the Commission, and five papers written for the Commission.

Preface: Setting the Stage for Understanding Rising College Costs and Prices

Understanding college costs and prices requires understanding the diversity of American higher education. The approximately 3,700 not-for-profit colleges and universities vary in terms of size, geography, sector, selectivity, and mission, to name but a few factors that distinguish institutions from one another. The students who attend these institutions in the late 1990s are also diverse and attend college for many different reasons.

Some Characteristics of American Higher Education

- 73 percent of all four-year institutions of higher education are private; 72 percent of all two-year institutions are public. (Exhibit i-1)
- 78 percent of all students and 81 percent of all undergraduates enrolled in institutions of higher education in the fall of 1994 were enrolled in public colleges and universities. (Exhibit i-2)
- 70 percent of all students enrolled in public four-year institutions in the fall of 1994 were enrolled full-time, while 64 percent of all students enrolled in public two-year institutions that same year were enrolled part-time. (Exhibit i-3)
- The percentage of undergraduates enrolled part-time increased from 28 percent of all enrollments in 1980 to 42 percent in 1994.
- Over 70 percent of all part-time undergraduate students were over the age of 21 in the fall of 1995. The percentage of full-time undergraduates over the age of 21 ranged from 27 percent in private four-year institutions to 62 percent in private two-year colleges. (Exhibit i-4)
- The percentage of full-time undergraduates receiving any financial aid in the fall of 1995 ranged from 53 percent of those attending public two-year institutions to 82 percent of those in private two-year colleges. (Exhibit i-5)
- The percentage of part-time undergraduates receiving any financial aid in 1995 ranged from 36 percent in public two-year institutions to 60 percent in private four-year institutions. (Exhibit i-6)

EXHIBIT i-1					
Number of Higher Education Institutions by Sector and Type: 1995-96					
	Public		**Private**		
	Four-year	**Two-year**	**Four-year**	**Two-year**	
	608	1,047	1,636	415	
Source: *Digest of Education Statistics* 1996, Table 237.					

- 73 percent of all four-year institutions of higher education are private.
- 72 percent of all two-year institutions of higher education are public.

EXHIBIT i-2

Enrollment in Higher Education by Sector and Type: Fall 1994

	Public		Private	
	Four-year	Two-year	Four-year	Two-year
Total Enrollment	5,825,213	5,308,467	2,923,867	221,243
Undergraduates	4,636,762	5,308,366	2,096,237	221,243

Source: *Digest of Education Statistics* 1996, Tables 192 and 194.

- 78 percent of all students enrolled in institutions of higher education in the fall of 1994 were enrolled in public colleges and universities.

- 81 percent of undergraduates enrolled in institutions of higher education in the fall of 1994 were enrolled in public colleges and universities.

EXHIBIT i-3

Enrollment in Institutions of Higher Education by Type and Sector of Institution and Attendance Status: Fall 1994

	Public		Private	
	Four-year	Two-year	Four-year	Two-year
Total Enrollment				
Full-time	4,065,067	1,885,753	2,040,995	145,961
Part-time	1,760,146	3,422,714	882,872	75,282
Undergraduates				
Full-time	3,520,989	1,885,752	1,616,004	145,961
Part-time	1,115,773	3,422,614	480,233	75,282

Source: *Digest of Education Statistics* 1996, Table 174.

- 70 percent of all students enrolled in public four-year institutions are enrolled full-time.

- 64 percent of all students enrolled in public two-year institutions are enrolled part-time.

- 76 percent of all undergraduates enrolled in public four-year institutions are enrolled full-time.

- 70 percent of all students enrolled in private four-year institutions are enrolled full-time.

- 66 percent of all students enrolled in private two-year institutions are enrolled part-time.

- 77 percent of all undergraduates enrolled in private four-year institutions are enrolled full-time.

EXHIBIT i-4

Percent of Undergraduates Over the Age of 21 by Type and Sector of Institution and Attendance Status: Fall 1995

	Public		Private	
	Four-year	Two-year	Four-year	Two-year
Full-time	34.5%	41.5%	27.1%	61.5%
Part-time	71.2	73.8	76.0	77.1

Source: *National Postsecondary Student Aid Study* 1995; run by AIR.

EXHIBIT i-5

Percent of Undergraduates Receiving Any Financial Aid by Type and Sector of Institution and Attendance Status: Fall 1995

	Public		Private	
	Four-year	Two-year	Four-year	Two-year
Full-time	66.3%	52.6%	80.4%	81.8%
Part-time	48.2%	36.1%	59.7%	48.5%

Source: *National Postsecondary Student Aid Study* 1996.

EXHIBIT i-6

Percentage of Undergraduates Receiving Loans, Grants and Work Study by Type and Sector of Institution and Attendance Status: 1995-96

	Grants	Loans	Work Study
Full-time Students			
Public four-year	49.4%	45.2%	8.2%
Public two-year	44.6%	15.8%	5.7%
Private four-year	71.9%	57.2%	26.1%
Private two-year	63.3%	55.6%	5.8%
Part-time Students			
Public four-year	34.2%	29.6%	3.5%
Public two-year	30.9%	7.7%	1.3%
Private four-year	47.1%	28.9%	4.3%
Private two-year	33.7%	30.2%	0.0%

Source: *National Postsecondary Student Aid Study* 1996.

Glossary of Terms

Cost and Price. This report distinguishes between costs and prices. Although often used interchangeably in discussions of higher education finance issues, our use of these terms follows the guidelines below:

Costs. What institutions spend to provide education and related educational services to students.

- **Cost per student.** The average amount of resources that institutions expend annually to provide education and education-related services to each full-time equivalent student. The measure adapted is based on a series of papers by Gordon Winston.[1]

Prices. What students and their families are charged and what they pay.

- **Sticker price.** The tuition and fees that institutions charge students.
- **Total price of attendance.** The tuition and fees that institutions charge students as well as all other expenses related to obtaining a higher education: housing expenses (room and board if the student lives on campus; rent or related housing costs if the student does not live on campus); books, transportation, etc.
- **Net price.** What students end up paying to attend a higher education institution after financial aid is subtracted from the total price of attendance. NOTE: This report uses two different concepts of net price: one that only subtracts the value of grants from the total price and one that subtracts all financial aid awards—grants, loans, and work study—from the total price of attendance.

General subsidy. The difference between the cost to the institution of providing an education ("cost per student") and the tuition and fees charged to students ("sticker price"). All students who attend institutions of higher education, regardless of whether they receive financial aid, benefit from this general subsidy.

Consumer price index (CPI). This price index measures the average change in the cost of a fixed market basket of goods and services purchased by consumers.

Dependent student. Students who are considered for financial aid reasons to be financially dependent on their parents. Parental as well as the individual student's income and assets are included in the calculation of the expected family contribution and thus financial aid awards.

Independent student. Students who are considered for financial aid reasons to be financially independent from their parents. Parental income and financial assets are not considered when calculating financial aid awards for independent students. Any one of the following criteria is sufficient for defining a student as independent: being 24 years of age or older by December 31 of the academic year in question; past service in the armed forces; being an orphan or ward of the court; being married; having legal dependents other than a spouse; or is a graduate or professional student.

Financial need. The difference between the institution's price of attendance and the student's expected family contribution.

Unmet need. The student's price of attendance at a specific institution less the student's expected family contribution and other financial assistance received.

Full-time-equivalent (FTE) enrollment. For institutions of higher education, enrollment of full-time students plus the full-time equivalent of part-time students. The full-time equivalent of part-time students is calculated in this report as: three part-time students are equivalent to one full-time student. Students are considered part-time if their total credit load is less than 75 percent of the normal full-time load.

---

[1]See Gordon C. Winston and Ivan C. Yen, "Costs, Prices, Subsidies, and Aid in U.S. Higher Education." Williams Project on the Economics of Higher Education, Discussion Paper No. 32, 1995. Ethan G. Lewis and Gordon C. Winston, "Subsidies, Costs, Tuition, and Aid in U.S. Higher Education: 1986-87 to 1993-94." Williams Project on the Economics of Higher Education, Discussion Paper No. 41r, 1997. Gordon C. Winston, "College Costs: Subsidies, Intuition, and Policy." Paper prepared for The National Commission on the Cost of Higher Education, 1997.

Income

Median family income. That level of family income that divides the upper from the lower half of all families.

Personal disposable per capita income. The amount of money available per person to spend. The calculation involves subtracting all taxes, depreciation, and corporate reinvestment from the country's Gross National Product, adding transfer payments (e.g., social security payments), and dividing the result by the number of people in the population.

Selected Testimony

In addition to the testimony presented at the October 27, 1997, Public Hearing, the Commission heard testimony from a number of individuals at its meetings. This section includes the text of three such testimonies:

The Cost of Higher Education: A Discussion with Commission Members
Gerhard Casper
President, Stanford University
October 16, 1997

Remarks Before the National Commission on the Cost of Higher Education
Richard M. Freeland
President, Northeastern University
November 7, 1997

Testimony to the National Commission on the Cost of Higher Education
Neil L. Rudenstine
President, Harvard University
November 7, 1997

National Commission on the Cost of Higher Education
College Cost Working Group/Monday Group

Stauffer Auditorium, Herbert Hoover Memorial Building, 11:00 a.m.

**The Cost of Higher Education: A Discussion with Commission Members
Gerhard Casper, President, Stanford University**

Three major points:

1. The importance of undergraduate education in a research-intensive university.
2. The costs of research that universities bear.
3. The high-cost/low-benefit ratio of excessive government regulation.

Introduction

As we begin, let me offer a bit of context on the cost of college. As Derek Bok, the former president of Harvard, pointed out in 1989, most of the public attention focuses on tuitions at institutions that are attended by a tiny percentage of all undergraduates. In a more recent study the Sallie Mae Education Institute suggests that about 5% of all undergraduates are concerned. At least half of this population receives financial aid.

Nonetheless, as one of this small cluster of institutions, Stanford is greatly concerned about tuition, as are most research-intensive universities. And Stanford has been working on the problem. Since 1989, we have cut expenses in the budget supported by unrestricted funds by approximately $60 million, allowing us to hold down our tuition-rate increases—not to as low as we would like but lower than any time in the last two decades.

Why can we not restrain tuition as much as we would like — say, to no more than the rise in Consumer Price Index? There are many reasons, such as the labor-intensive nature of education or the fact, that over the last 15 years, on the average, domestic book prices increased at the rate of 2 times the CPI, foreign titles at 4 times the CPI. However, two seldom examined reasons are the cost of excessive government regulation and the disproportionate cost of government research borne by the universities. To cover those costs, Stanford must use the very same sources—unrestricted gifts, endowment, investment earnings—that otherwise might be applied to further restraining tuition.

Reimbursement for research costs and excessive government regulation are the second and third major points I wish to discuss with you today. The first is the importance of undergraduate education in a research-intensive university.

1. *The importance of undergraduate education in a research-intensive university.*

Contrary to the belief of some, tuition does not subsidize research. Indeed, our calculations indicate that undergraduate tuition covers only about 2/3 of the true cost of attending Stanford. Undergraduate education and every student—even those paying full tuition—are highly subsidized by gifts, our endowment and our other investment earnings.

Stanford also directly subsidizes the tuition costs of many of our students through some of the most generous financial aid policies in the nation. For over a generation, we have been committed to admitting the most talented students who apply, without considering whether they can afford to pay. Once a student is admitted, Stanford will meet that student's demonstrated financial need through a combination of scholarship grants, loans, and job opportunities. More than 60% of our students get some form of financial aid, and, last year alone, Stanford committed $38 million of its own funds to undergraduate scholarships.

And let me briefly point out how the research enterprise actually enriches undergraduate education. Many undergraduates specifically choose a research-intensive university because of the opportunity to interact with faculty members who are at the frontier of their field. Students who seize the initiative, and seek out the incredible range of opportunities offered at Stanford and other research-intensive universities are rewarded in ways that cannot be matched in other settings.

Let me offer some examples of the opportunities available to our undergraduates:

- Each year, between 1/3 and 1/2 of our graduating seniors will have worked closely with a senior faculty member on an honors thesis or research project.
- Last year, our Undergraduate Research Opportunities program awarded $610,00 in grants to cover the expense of 410 student research projects. The money came from private donations, and each of the students worked with a Stanford faculty member.

However, federal reimbursement for such overhead is continually dropping, a particular problem at private universities, which cannot rely on state subsidies to make up the difference. Overhead reimbursement for general administrative and student service costs is capped at 26 points. This policy has the effect, at Stanford, of forcing about $10.6 million of legitimate costs of government research to be absorbed by university funds—funds thus not available for academic purposes.

The contrast with government treatment of other research sources is rather stark. In most industrial research, overhead rates are roughly twice those of private research universities, and there are no arbitrary caps. And the federal Small Business Innovation Research Program gives small businesses an automatic 100% overhead rate.

Yet, university research not only is cheaper for the government, it provides an important side benefit for the nation: the training of graduate students to become the next generation of researchers. And, as any faculty member working on a sponsored agreement will quickly confirm, graduate students are essential contributors to the process of research and creation of knowledge.

2. *The cost of research overhead that universities must disproportionately bear.*

The inability of the federal government to pay the full costs of sponsored research is forcing those costs back on universities, thus absorbing funds that otherwise might relieve pressure on tuition.

Let me remind everyone of the rationale for government reimbursement of overhead costs. Were the federal government to directly conduct all its research, rather than have it done at universities, it would have to set up labs with all the overhead costs they would involve, such as buildings, utility bills, salaries and benefits for researchers and staff. Instead, this nation chose a system of university-based research, with the universities reimbursed for the overhead costs they incur and the government escapes. This system has served the nation well. At Stanford alone, research results range from new cures for disease, to insights about life on Mars, to breakthroughs in technology.

However, federal reimbursement for such overhead is continually dropping, a particular problem at private universities, which cannot rely on state subsidies to make up the difference. Overhead reimbursement for general administrative and student service costs is capped at 26 points. This policy has the effect, at Stanford, of forcing about $10.6 million of legitimate costs of government research to be absorbed by university funds—funds thus not available for academic purposes.

The contrast with government treatment of other research sources is rather stark. In most industrial research, overhead rates are roughly twice those of private research universities, and there are not arbitrary caps. And the federal Small Business Innovation Research Program gives small businesses an automatic 100% overhead rate.

Yet, university research not only is cheaper for the government, it provides an important side benefit for the nation: the training of graduate students to become the next generation of researchers. And, as any faculty member working on a sponsored agreement will quickly confirm, graduate students are essential contributors to the process of research and creation of knowledge.

3. *The high-cost/low-benefit ratio of excessive government regulation.*

I now turn to the costs of excessive government regulation. The costs of complying with federal, state, and local regulations are considerable at almost any organization in American society. Research universities, such as Stanford, however, bear some particularly irrational costs. Let me give you two examples.

Our Dean of Research, Charles Kruger, was working with a new faculty member to put in place some combustibles for a lab. It is important to note that these were non-toxic fuels and no unusual gases were being used. Meeting the various requirements cost $600,000. Dean Kruger asked how many kilowatts of combustion were being produced and, when he got home, looked at the amount of combustion produced by his own home's furnace and water heater. He found they were roughly the same. Now, housing in California is expensive, but no one would dream of paying $600,000 to set up a furnace and water heater in their home.

The second example is a pending regulation from the federal EPA. As a result of an inspector general's interpretation of one line of the 1990 Clean Air Act, the EPA has proposed a new regulation that would require application of Maximum Achievable Control Technology to all air emissions from research and development facilities. This could mean that every single fume hood—and at Stanford we have more than 1,000 of them—would need to be retrofitted with a $10,000-to-$20,000 filtration unit, for a total of $10-to-$20 million, plus annual operating and maintenance costs of $1/2 to 1 million. The issue is not whether we should be concerned about air emissions; we long have been. It is about whether the cost and benefits are rational.

By a very conservative accounting, Stanford already incurs about $20 million per year in on-going costs related to compliance with regulations. It is important to emphasize that this figure does not include any capital costs. A portion of these costs are recovered through outside overhead payments. However, $7.8 million of the $20 million in such costs are not recovered by outside sources of funds and bear directly on tuition and other sources of unrestricted income.

In addition to the on-going operating costs of compliance, we are also forced to absorb costs that in other organizations would have been picked up by the research sponsor. This amounts to approximately $21 million.

When we take the $7.8 million in on-going operating costs for compliance and the $21 million I just mentioned, we calculate that approximately 7 1/2 cents on every tuition dollar goes toward supporting these costs.

I must point out that this does not even count the value of the considerable amount of time spent by Stanford faculty and staff time in compliance related meetings, on panels, doing paperwork, meeting with compliance officials, and performing other tasks. These kinds of activities are simply absorbed into the days and nights of our people, and reduce the amount of time available for teaching and research. I have to believe that these hidden costs amount to at least another 5 cents of each tuition dollar.

And, I repeat, these examples do not include any capital costs, of which there clearly have been many as we have struggled to meet our obligations under government regulation.

When I say "government" regulation, I do not wish to imply one, uniform set of regulations. Take a one-pint bottle of alcohol, which could be found in most of our bathroom medicine chests. If found in a university laboratory, it falls under the regulation and scrutiny of at least six different regulatory agencies, all of whom have varying administrative requirements for that same container. These include:

- The air quality management district, which regulates the use of material to minimize air releases.
- The sewer district, which regulates the use, storage and disposal of material to minimize inadvertent releases to drain.
- OSHA, which regulates the use, handling and storage of the material.
- The local fire department, which regulates the amount, use and storage of the material.
- The county environmental health department, which regulates the use, handling, storage and disposal of the material.
- The state hazardous waste agency, which regulates the handling and storage of material when no longer wanted in the laboratory.

Even when dealing with a single agency, we too often are confronted by regulations intended for an entirely different setting. Let me offer a quick case study of such an agency—the California EPA—and how such regulatory processes have begun to interfere seriously with the very nature of the academic enterprise.

At Stanford, more than 4,000 faculty, staff, and students work with chemicals and the resulting waste, in one way or another. Research involving usually small amounts of thousands of chemicals is conducted in roughly 700 locations in schools and departments throughout the campus.

California has promulgated hazardous waste regulations to protect human health and safety, preserve the environment, minimize waste, and prevent pollution. These rules, however, were developed with large-scale manufacturing processes and industrial settings in mind. And that was a wise decision by the state because 99.99% of all hazardous chemical waste comes from manufacturing and industrial processes; less than one one-hundredth of a percent (0.01%) comes from university laboratories.

State officials freely admit that the development of the regulations did not take into account the nature and organization of universities. The result is agreement between the university and the state on objectives and outcomes – safe practices, sound management of waste, environmental protection – and sharp disagreements on paperwork, administration, and organizational requirements.

Take, for example, labeling. Research and teaching at Stanford produce about 25,000 small containers of chemical waste annually – most of them smaller than a glass of water. State regulators require that each of those containers be labeled with a special label itemizing six specific pieces of information, even if the chemical is in its originally labeled container provided by the manufacturer. An error on any one of these items is a violation. Furthermore, if a state inspector finds a container mislabeled in laboratory A on the west side of the campus and on a subsequent visit finds that another container is so mislabeled in laboratory B on the east side of the campus, Stanford can be considered "recalcitrant" because "repeat" violations have occurred. Labeling fines range from $100 to $10,000 per violation. A 1% error rate, therefore, could result in annual fines of $25,000 to $2.5 million.

In one actual incident, a conscientious graduate student at Stanford put the wrong date on a bottle because his calendar watch was off by a single day, and by chance a state inspector that day noted the resulting labeling violation. The student's supervising professor, a distinguished member of our chemistry department, wrote a memorandum on the incident to our Environmental Safety Office. The professor commented:

> *I would invite … the inspector to meet with this individual and better understand how serious he and others are about compliance and how inspections that focus on such human errors and not on more pressing issues of safety serve only a destructive purpose…. We have very little time these days to do much science because it seems that every week there is a new issue, many of a reasonable nature but far too many of which simply do not address safety…. If we continue to focus on non-problems, we will not achieve what should be the objective of our safety programs and legislation, i.e., to create a safer environment. Instead we will discourage compliance and drive our educational and research system into the ground.*

This illustrates the regulatory attitude we are dealing with. Nevertheless, we could live with labeling – if that were our only problem. But it is not.

Far more important to us are complicated issues of authority over laboratory practices, the definition of laboratory and associated work spaces, the requirements for supervision and storage of chemicals, the length of time substances can remain in a laboratory, when a substance becomes a waste, when containers can be reused, what training documentation is required for different job classifications and for students, and other important issues.

In the end, the California EPA chose to interpret existing regulations in ways that bore no rational relationship to the reality of the university setting, and imposed $460,000 in fines, $235,00 in state administrative costs and $300,000 in contributions to private environmental groups. Perhaps worse, it imposed expensive and unnecessary bureaucratic requirements on us for the future. Real environmental protection was not at issue, nor was compliance with the law. The dispute was not about whether these activities should be regulated; it was over the state's rigid interpretation of regulations designed for industrial processes and its insistence on applying those to university laboratories.

It is the country that will suffer if the research enterprise is smothered by red tape. And, I will add, it is students and families who suffer as funds that could go to academic purposes and perhaps greater tuition relief are eaten up excessive regulation and the shifting of legitimate expenses from the government to universities.

With that, I conclude and welcome your questions.

REMARKS BY
PRESIDENT RICHARD M. FREELAND
BEFORE THE
NATIONAL COMMISSION ON THE COST OF HIGHER EDUCATION
NOVEMBER 7, 1997

INTRODUCTION

Welcome to Northeastern University. You are visiting us as we celebrate our centennial year, and you are addressing a subject that has been close to our hearts for the entire century of our existence. We were founded during the Progressive era as a place of opportunity for urban, working class, and immigrant students who found themselves unable to afford or attend the fine, traditional private colleges of the region. Despite many changes since our founding, the goals of access and affordability for young men and women from modest backgrounds have remained central to our identity.

The last eight years have been particularly challenging for Northeastern. During this period we have undertaken a major transformation in our character, shifting from a large, locally oriented, no frills, commuter school to a smaller institution serving an expanded geographic area with programs of heightened academic quality. Ours is just one story, but I believe it illuminates the socially constructive dynamics of the academic marketplace while exemplifying the challenges facing many mainstream colleges and universities today. It is a story, I believe, that says more about the recent history of colleges attended by significant numbers of Americans than headline grabbing articles about skyrocketing costs at a handful of Ivy League schools.

This morning I want to emphasize three points:

- First, while higher education has been criticized for failing to respond to the needs of undergraduates, our transformation suggests the opposite. Some eight years ago the market spoke. Prospective students and their families made it clear that if we did not change, our future was very much in doubt. We heard the message, and we are acting on it.

- Second, while our transformation is incomplete, we have been able to significantly increase the value of a Northeastern education with only modest increases in real tuition charges to our students and even more modest increases in total tuition revenues from undergraduates.

- Third, our efforts at institutional adaptation are greatly affected by federal and state higher education policies. We strongly support the availability of low-cost, state-sponsored, higher education in Massachusetts, but it is also evident that our ability to serve the students we most want most to enroll— talented, ambitious sons and daughters from modest backgrounds—is greatly affected by state and federal action with respect to financial aid.

BOSTON'S URBAN UNIVERSITY

As background to the case I wish to put before you, let me provide some additional detail about the transformation to which I referred a moment ago. In the years before World War II and well into the postwar period, Northeastern functioned as a kind of quasi public institution in a state that lacked a well developed system of state- supported higher education. We kept our costs down by providing a bare-bones campus and keeping faculty salaries low. Despite minimal charges to students, we survived almost entirely on tuition revenues.

Our distinguishing feature throughout these years was—and remains today—cooperative education. Under this program, students alternate terms of full-time, paid employment with periods of full-time classroom study. The money students earn helps pay the next term's tuition bills while the practical experience they gain reinforces learning in the practical fields that we have historically emphasized. Functioning in this way we grew by the 1970s into the largest private university in the United States.

Beginning in the 1960s, however, our circumstances began to be affected by the long delayed growth of public higher education in Massachusetts. A new system of community colleges was developed. The existing teachers' colleges were transformed into full four-year and masters institutions. Most important of all, in 1964 the state established a comprehensive campus of the University of Massachusetts in the heart of urban Boston.

By the 1980s it was becoming increasingly clear that the growth of the public sector was seriously eroding Northeastern's ability to serve our traditional constituency. As our costs crept upward in these years a larger and larger tuition gap developed between ourselves and the state supported schools. Then, suddenly, in 1990, accumulating changes coalesced into genuine crisis. That fall we missed our freshman enrollment goal by 28 percent, or about 1,000 students. For a tuition-driven institution like Northeastern, this precipitated a financial free fall of major proportions. The next year was equally disastrous.

In assessing our situation we confronted a stark dilemma. On one side, many students who historically might have attended Northeastern now had respectable low cost options in the public sector. On the other side, many who had the means to pay private tuition did not see sufficient qualitative differences from the state's public campuses to justify our higher costs. The conclusion was unavoidable: we could no longer attract students based on accessibility and low prices; our only choice was to improve our offerings and attract students because of the quality of our programs.

1990-1997: RECASTING NORTHEASTERN AS A SMALLER, BETTER INSTITUTION

Spurred by the crisis of the early 1990s, Northeastern set out to systematically recast ourselves as a smaller and better institution. Between the fall of 1990 and the fall of 1997 we reduced undergraduate enrollments by 20 percent from about 15,000 to about 12,000 today. During this same eight-year period, we pared staff by 18 percent—from about 2,800 full-time faculty, administrators and support staff to 2,300.

While absorbing these painful reductions, we began to systematically improve quality. First and foremost, this meant improving our long neglected physical facilities. So, despite the severe financial pressures of those years, we embarked on a $100 million building program supported by a newly aggressive effort to raise private support from our alumni combined with heavy borrowing. We built a new classroom building and an engineering and science research center; we renovated our student center, rehabilitated several older classroom facilities, upgraded campus housing and opened a student recreation complex. We also put $20 million into computing infrastructure and wired the campus to hook up students, faculty, and staff to both the University computer system and the Internet.

While we were improving our facilities, we launched a multifaceted effort to improve the quality of our programs. We eliminated 13 majors that were weak or outdated, approved 32 new programs and degrees, strengthened general education, and undertook a comprehensive review of our graduate offerings. We also initiated a major effort to increase the scholarly qualifications of our faculty through both hiring and promotion, and in the process increased our level of extramural funding for research and education while remaining a student-centered university primarily focused on undergraduate teaching.

Moreover, we have worked hard to leverage more value for students in our cooperative education program. This year we will spend approximately $6 million on a co-operative education infrastructure that will place nearly 6,000 students with some 1,400 employers. We are aggressively developing placements in technically oriented, high-demand labor market segments populated by corporate customers willing to pay for the talent and skills of our students on co-op. Our goal is to establish Northeastern as an educational destination of choice for students across the region and nation attracted to our distinctive form of practice-oriented education.

While our transformation is a work in progress, early results are promising. At the beginning end of the continuum, our applications are up 52.6 percent from a low of about 9,100 in 1991. At the same time, our selectivity has increased markedly. Mean combined S.A.T scores have risen 105 points in eight years, including 33 points between the fall of 1996 and the fall of 1997. Freshman enrollment has stabilized and retention rates have risen steadily. The results for those who have completed our programs are equally encouraging. A careful study of the class of 1996 six months after graduation revealed that 83% were employed full-time in a field related to their studies and half the remainder were not interested in full-time jobs at that point. Moreover, during years when real wages for most Americans have declined, average salaries for our graduates have risen 6.6 percent in real dollars since 1991 and in 1996 exceeded $33,000.

1990–1997: A LOOK AT THE BUDGET

Against the background of Northeastern's recent strategic restructuring, let me address more directly the issue with which this commission is most concerned: the impact of the changes I have described on our budget and particularly on tuition charges to our undergraduates.

Let us first consider revenues. In recent years, we have worked aggressively to develop non-tuition sources of funding. I have already alluded to the growth of extramural funding for research and education. We are also setting institutional records in private giving. We will intensify these efforts because we know our future depends on them, but we also recognize that in the near term we will remain largely dependent of student payments. The heart of our financial story is an account of tuition policy.

Since the fall of 1990, the sticker price of tuition for full-time undergraduates at Northeastern has increased at an annual rate of about 8 percent—from $9,300 to $14,600. But the sticker price is not what we actually charge to many students. We have, in fact, offset a substantial proportion of these apparent increases by dramatically raising institutional financial aid. In fact, per student aid from institutional sources increased from about $700 per year in 1990 to almost $3,200 this year, chiefly through reductions in actual tuition charges to individual students. If nominal tuition increases are reduced by the average amount we returned to students in financial aid, the result is a net or actual tuition increase of only 4.9 percent per year over the eight-year period I have reviewed. During these same years, the annual increase in the CPI averaged 3.3 percent.

As for our overall revenue picture, gross tuition revenues from full-time undergraduate students—that is nominal revenue growth prior to the distribution of financial aid—rose by 29 percent—from $131 million to $169 million—between FY 1991 and FY 1998. Yet, institutional financial aid for undergraduates grew more than 278%, from $9.8 million to $37.6 million. The result was that our net tuition revenue—that is, gross tuition less institutional financial aid—has increased only $10.7 million or just 9 percent—which is 1.3 percent per year over eight years. During these same years, the CPI rose 23 percent.

Thus, at a time when were putting in place a new strategy of qualitative improvements, we had to figure out a way to make progress with only modest revenue growth.

How was this accomplished?

I have already mentioned our faculty and staff reductions. We combined our reduced payroll with painful restraint on salary increases throughout this period. In three of these eight years our employees had no increases at all. We also sought new efficiencies in our benefits programs, and were able to reduce these costs by nearly nine percent. The story is similar for most non-personnel costs: we have essentially frozen real dollar non-salary expenditures throughout this period. Adjusted for inflation, between FY1991 and FY1998 total university expenditures have increased by only four percent.

While we worked to restrain expenditures in most categories, we did make critical investments in key areas. We increased our debt to fund the capital projects that were central to our new strategy. And we invested heavily in computer and telecommunications technologies that are indispensable to quality education in the 1990s. Over the past seven years we have spent an average in real terms of nearly $17 million per year on debt service and maintenance.

In summary, we been able to recast ourselves as a smaller, better university that preserves our distinctive approach to practice-oriented education and at the same time keep our tuition in check primarily by becoming more efficient, by cutting back on operational costs, by increasing our debt, and by rapidly expanding our financial aid expenditures.

PROSPECTS FOR THE FUTURE

Let me now turn briefly to the third of the three points I mentioned at the outset—the impact of governmental policies on Northeastern.

We are determined, as I have indicated, to continue enrolling students from modest backgrounds. But it has become harder and harder to do so in the recent context of rising institutional costs and declining state and federal student aid. In spite of our growing financial aid expenditures, debt incurred by our students has risen alarmingly. Moreover, the average income of our entering students is edging upward. In this connection, we are grateful for current government aid programs for students, and we especially appreciate recent tax incentives to support college attendance. We hope the government will continue to make enrollment at independent colleges possible through portable aid programs.

Public policies on student aid affect institutions like Northeastern as much as they affect individual students. Our need to forego much of the tuition income we might have received between 1991 and 1998 in order to expand financial aid has prevented us from making many investments that are critical to our overall goal of raising the quality of our programs. As my account of our expenditure budgets indicates, we have been forced to skimp on faculty and staff salaries and neglect expenditures in most non-personnel accounts for too many years in a row.

Without new support for students from outside sources, this tension between financial aid and institutional investment will only mount. We would respectfully urge the commission to consider the social value of enabling talented and ambitious students from modest backgrounds to attend private institutions like Northeastern that are attempting to stay affordable.

Given our defining characteristic, we have, of course, a particular interest in how federal policy impacts cooperative education. Throughout Northeastern's history, our students have depended upon earnings from co-op assignments to help pay for college. Today, a Northeastern student can earn as much as $10,000 for a six month assignment, although many earn significantly less than this. While co-op thus remains an important source of support for many students, living expenses during co-op terms can consume a sizable portion of these funds. Moreover, under federal law, co-op earnings are taken into account when determining a student's financial need under federal financial aid guidelines.

I would like to take this opportunity to endorse a proposal made by the National Commission for Cooperative Education to exempt some or all co-operative wages from the financial aid formula. As it is, federal law is in the peculiar position of treating students more favorably if they avoid cooperative education. We are working hard to infuse new quality into our co-op program so that it might better serve students. A supportive federal policy in this regard would be tremendously beneficial to our efforts to continue enrolling students of limited means. A similarly helpful proposal would be a federal tax credit for employers that participate in workforce development by employing co-op students.

CONCLUSION

Let me return at the end to a point I emphasized at the beginning. Northeastern's recent history is a story of working hard to survive in a competitive academic marketplace. Facing our crisis at the beginning of this decade was not easy. But competition has made us a better institution and enhanced our ability to contribute to our students and to the economy of the region. I have little doubt that many other institutions have found new strength and have crafted their own unique ways of meeting the educational needs of our citizenry.

I am by no means a myopic apologist for higher education. I believe, in fact, that many of the current criticisms of the nation's colleges and universities, including those that brought this commission into being, are well founded. But I also believe that competition among academic institutions remains a powerful guarantor that, over time, our campuses will seek out strategies of price and program that best meet the needs of the public. I believe that the Northeastern story is an excellent illustration of how well this dynamic can work. From my perspective, that is a critical part of the recent history of American higher education that is too often lost in public discussions of the shortcomings of our academic institutions.

Testimony to the National Commission
On the Cost of Higher Education

Neil L. Rudenstine
President, Harvard University
November 7, 1997

I appreciate the opportunity to meet with you to discuss the important subject of the cost of higher education. Our time is limited, so I will not try to cover a number of topics addressed by others with whom you have already met. Instead, I will concentrate on a few points related to universities that have a strong commitment to undergraduate education, as well as to graduate and professional education, and to excellent research. I will use Harvard as my main example, primarily because I can offer you more detailed (and current) information about it.

Let me begin with a brief sketch of the university. At its heart is our undergraduate college, which is fully residential, and is home to nearly 6,600 students. They come from across the United States and beyond, and they bring with them an immense diversity of backgrounds and perspectives. Harvard College is now 361 years old, and its approach to education has long reflected a belief that undergraduates stand to benefit greatly from the opportunity to be part of a larger community — of faculty, graduate students, and others — all engaged in the process of advanced learning and
discovery.

In addition to the college, Harvard has ten graduate and professional schools, which enroll some 12,000 full-time degree candidates from across this country and more than 100 other countries around the world. The operating budget for the entire university is about $1.6 billion this year. Our endowment is large, but the "payout" from endowment covers less than one-quarter of our annual operating expenses — a percentage that has been remarkably constant for half a century. So we must make up the other 75 to 80 percent of our $1.6 billion in expenditures from other sources of income — annual gifts, sponsored research funds, tuition and other student fees, and other miscellaneous sources, ranging
from technology licensing to Harvard T-shirts to parking fees.

Finally, we have a longstanding commitment to offering educational programs for working adults and other "nontraditional" students who cannot study full-time. Harvard's Extension School, founded in 1909, now offers more than 550 courses a year, at relatively modest cost, to some 13,000
local students. Last June, we were proud to graduate the oldest person ever to earn a liberal arts degree from Harvard — Mary Fasano, ALB '97, age 89.

Access and Affordability: A Commitment to Need-Based Aid

With this as background, let me try to address, head on, the question that led to the convening of this Commission: how do we ensure that college education remains accessible and affordable to students from across the economic spectrum?

I want to talk about Harvard's approach, not because it represents some sort of platonic ideal, or a model that is workable for all institutions of higher education. Still, it is a powerful model, and one
that illustrates a systematic effort to address a serious problem.

Let me begin with the number that all too often serves as not just the beginning, but the end, of discussions about college access. What might be called our comprehensive fee — the total of tuition, room, board, and other charges — is now around $30,000 a year. It is not quite the highest in the nation, but it is still very steep. Yet, based on our estimates, it is still only about two-thirds of what it actually costs to provide our students with an undergraduate education in a residential setting. The remaining third is underwritten largely by endowment and annual gifts. In this sense, all of our undergraduates — even those who pay the full comprehensive fee — receive a significant subsidy or implicit
scholarship.

As a private college and university committed to a very broad set of programs in education and research, Harvard has for many decades had high fees which — if viewed in isolation — would place a Harvard education well beyond the reach of the great majority of students and families in the United States. But there is, of course, more to the story. Back in 1854, Harvard's President Walker summarized the problem and the solution very succinctly: "There is no objection," he said, "which weighs so heavily

against an education in Cambridge as the expense; and the only practicable way of reducing it would seem to be by the institution of scholarships."

As this suggests, Harvard's approach to college access has long been rooted in a simple insight: given that it is inherently expensive to provide an excellent residential college education, and given that a great many families are not able to afford the full price, financial aid based on need is the most direct, effective, cost-effective, and economically practicable way to reduce the net cost of college for many students — while also maintaining a steady flow of tuition revenue from those students whose

families can afford to pay the total sum.

The modern version of this philosophy has been with us for several decades now. We have made it a cardinal principle that students should be considered for admission without regard to their financial need. We want our doors to be open to the most able and promising students — rich, poor, or in between.

That's only half the principle. The other half — the one that converts ideal into reality — is that students who are admitted, and who choose to come to Harvard, are provided with a package of financial aid that is sufficient to enable them to attend.

We advertise the nature of this program widely, and we recruit students vigorously. As a result, we are able to attract a wide range of applicants from literally all income groups, and from an enormous variety of backgrounds. The number of applicants to our first-year class has grown, over the past five or six years, from 12,000 to more than 16,500 —essentially 10 applicants for every place in the class — and over three-quarters of the students who are offered admission choose to enroll.

Our commitment to need-based aid is expensive. Two-thirds of our undergraduates receive some form of financial aid, and they will together receive some $80 million in aid this year — in the form of scholarships, loans, and work-study jobs. More than half of that aid — $42 million — takes the form of scholarships; and nearly nine out of every ten of those scholarship dollars come from our institutional funds.

Almost half of all our undergraduates qualify for scholarship grants, averaging $14,000. Added to that are a loan and a job that cover another $6,500. That combined total — around $20,500 — is roughly two-thirds of our full comprehensive fee. In other words, for about half of our students, the average amount remaining to be paid, on a current basis, for a year at Harvard College is roughly $9,500.

I want to emphasize that the figures I've given are averages: some students receive well more than $20,500; others receive less, depending on their own level of need. And the aid reaches students from a very broad band of family incomes. Our scholarship students include, for example, some 375 students whose family incomes are less than $20,000 a year — as well as some 250 students whose family incomes are greater than $120,000 a year — with all of the many more falling in between.

Over time, as our comprehensive fee has steadily increased, we have tried to make sure that the families of our scholarship students not be asked to bear an increasing share of the students' budgets. In 1980-81, for instance, the typical parental contribution for students on scholarship was 26 percent of the total student budget. Seventeen years later, the figure is still 26 percent. Meanwhile, the portion of the total student budget covered by scholarship funds has grown, on average, from 43 percent to 49 percent.

We have also tried, by investing heavily in need-based scholarships, to avoid leaving our students with huge debts when they graduate. In our most recent graduating class, almost half our seniors managed to leave Harvard without any outstanding student loan debt at all. And only 8 percent of all our seniors graduated with debt burdens of more than $20,000.

In fact, as the real value of federal scholarship grants has eroded in recent years, and as the balance of federal aid has shifted strongly in the direction of loans, colleges and universities have reached deeper into their own funds to provide scholarship aid. At Harvard, while tuitions have continued to rise faster than inflation, our own undergraduate scholarship budget has risen at a significantly faster rate than tuitions: more than twice as fast, when measured in constant 1997 dollars over the last decade.

Having said all this, I do not at all underestimate the severe problems and real anxieties faced by many students and families struggling to pay for college. And I do not propose that strong need-based aid is the be-all and end-all of an effective approach. We need to keep up the effort to moderate the growth of tuition and fees, as we have been doing. At Harvard, we have lowered the rate of tuition growth each of the last five years. The increase from last year to this — 4.1 percent — was the lowest in percentage terms since 1969. Our intention is to continue this trend — although it will require even more intensive efforts to raise endowment and other sources of revenue, to budget systematically, to control our expense growth, and to make sensible cuts and economies that do not compromise the

fundamental quality of our academic programs. It will also require some help from the national economy.

All in all, however, we need to be realistic in our expectations. Whatever the exact percentage increase in next year's tuition and fees, the full price of attending Harvard will still be high — higher than a great many students and families can reach on their own. We will be left to do what I believe it is absolutely essential for us to do: reaffirm and redouble our commitment to a program of need-blind admissions and strong need-based student aid.

A Broader Perspective: Curriculum, Libraries, Information Technology

To this point, I have focused on how we try to keep our doors open to talented students, whatever their economic means. Let me now broaden the angle of vision a bit, to consider just a few of the forces that shape the economy of a major private residential university, some of the ways in which undergraduates benefit from being at such a university, and some of what we do — along with our financial aid program — to minimize the economic impact on students and their families. I know that you have already heard from others about some of these matters, so let me try to be selective and illustrative, rather than comprehensive. I want to touch upon each of three areas: the undergraduate curriculum; the function and cost of research libraries; and, finally, modern information technology.

We should take a moment to remember how our universities are structured, because the American university model is significantly different from others, and it did not come about by accident. Those who created it consciously set out to integrate undergraduate education, graduate and professional education, and advanced research — all within the same environment.

For faculty members, that means a commitment to constant learning through research and the discovery of new knowledge and ideas. It also means a continual importation of new knowledge and ideas from the laboratory or library directly into the lecture hall or the seminar room — where the discussion can then lead to further insights, inquiry, and discovery.

For students, meanwhile, the basic goal is to bring them, as quickly as possible, to the point where they become researchers and discoverers in their own right, while also absorbing a good deal of

established knowledge. We want them to confront real problems — whether in physics or history or contemporary politics — where most of the answers are in doubt, and it is a challenge even to formulate the key questions.

Curriculum: Breadth and Depth

With this in mind, let me turn more specifically to the curriculum. At Harvard, the undergraduate curriculum aims to balance breadth and depth. The breadth is represented, in part, by our Core Curriculum, which requires our undergraduates to devote a quarter of their studies to courses in each of several areas: foreign cultures, historical study, literature and arts, moral reasoning, science, and social analysis. The Core, alone, encompasses some 85 to 100 different courses in a given year, ranging from "Matter in the Universe" to "Justice" to "Children in Their Social World." At last count, some 92 percent of the Core courses were offered by senior, tenured members of our faculty.

In addition to fulfilling their Core requirements, undergraduates are expected to devote another substantial part of their coursework to a field of concentration, or major. There are forty such fields — Anthropology, Biology, Classics, East Asian Studies, Economics, Philosophy, and so on. In all, there are more than 2,000 departmental courses that occupy more than 600 pages of our catalogue. Together, they represent an incredible invitation to explore a vast universe of knowledge and ideas.

Some people may wonder whether this is all an exercise in excess. Is it really cost-effective to teach the Classics — or offer courses in Sanskrit — when relatively few students choose either as a concentration? In response, we have to ask ourselves whether we would really want to abandon, now and for generations to come, the effort to understand the major writers and thinkers of ancient Greece and Rome, whose works have been so integral to the shaping of our culture. We have to ask whether an

important piece of civilization would be lost if none of our students (and perhaps no student in the nation) were able to read and study Sanskrit — one of the world's greatest languages, one that contains some of the most important sacred texts ever composed. If we were to let the study of Classics wither away, or the study of Sanskrit fade into oblivion, what would be next? Archaeology? The Renaissance? Buddhism? Or perhaps the Industrial Revolution, which in today's high-tech information age might

strike some people as something close to ancient history?

My point is not only that some of our universities have an obligation to sustain important fields of learning, even if the student demand for courses is not and may never be overwhelming. It's also that, over time, fields or subjects which in one era may seem obscure and "irrelevant" can quite suddenly, in another era, assume much greater significance. A century ago, or even fifty or sixty years ago, some people wondered why Harvard was investing significantly in the study of China, Japan, and the rest of East Asia. After all, as late as the 1930s, only a very few Harvard students were studying Chinese language, history, and culture. Now, the world has turned, and East Asian Studies is one of our

highly subscribed concentrations. Enrollments in introductory Chinese have tripled over the last fifteen years, to the point that Chinese is now one of the three most studied languages at Harvard. Few people, if anyone, would now pause to question the level of our commitment to understanding East Asia.

We could make much the same observations about the study of the Islamic world, where enrollments have risen markedly, and the so-called "relevance" of the subject — which some may have doubted not so many decades ago — is now scarcely open to question. Needless to say, developing real strength in such fields — fields that are not available for extensive study in many institutions of higher education — is not something that can happen quickly. It takes a sustained, farsighted commitment, over long periods, to seek very substantial resources, persuade donors, stare down skeptics, acquire the right books and manuscripts, train the right graduate students, and build not simply a faculty, but a genuine program.

Meanwhile, new fields also emerge. The newest field of concentration at Harvard College is environmental Science and Public Policy. It is about five years old, and its number of undergraduate

concentrators has already surpassed 100. It draws on faculty from many schools and departments, and it represents a consciously interdisciplinary approach to learning: the kind of approach that is next to impossible if an institution hasn't made the efforts and the investments needed, over the years, to build real academic strength in each of the many fields and subfields — including those in our professional schools — that contribute to the whole.

Maintaining this sort of curricular breadth and depth is expensive. And so, for more than a century, we have made special efforts to cover a very significant fraction of the associated costs through endowment, so that the added pressure on tuition would be as little as possible. Even in the 1870s at Harvard, people were wondering about the need for Sanskrit, but President Eliot did not view the program as though it were a production plant generating insufficient revenues. Rather, recognizing that "the number of students in the department is inevitably small," he set out to endow a professorship in Sanskrit — and succeeded.

This simple example suggests why Harvard has worked so hard, for so long, to endow many of its professorships — to the point where 46 percent (almost half) of our budget for faculty salaries in the Arts and Sciences is today supported by endowment. We hope to press ahead still further.

Meanwhile, our undergraduates are more and more involved in advanced study and original research. It's worth noting that, of the 1,600-plus undergraduates who enter Harvard from year to year, there are now typically more than 600 who qualify, on the basis of their academic records before college, for what we call advanced standing: the opportunity to graduate, with a regular bachelor's degree, in three years — and thereby save the cost of a fourth year. In our most recent graduating class, only 30 students (some five percent of the roughly 600 eligible) actually exercised that option and left after three years — a strong indication, to my mind, that they are both interested in pursuing advanced coursework, and that they (and their families) consider the quality of their actual educational experience worth the very substantial cost.

Last year, a quarter of our seniors took graduate-level courses. Undergraduate science concentrators work in laboratories side by side with graduate students and faculty. Other students are doing fieldwork and archival research that, years ago, would have been hard to imagine at the

undergraduate level. The list of examples could go on and on. But the basic point is simply this: our undergraduates benefit in significant, powerful ways from the opportunity to be part of a major university that is devoted to learning in its largest sense — where faculty, graduate students, and undergraduates are all engaged in a continuous process of research, exploration, and discovery.

The Library: New Challenges, New Approaches

Let me turn now to the library, where we see a somewhat different picture: a major resource for students and faculty, but one that is in a state of exceptionally rapid change, driven by new technologies, and that at the same time faces intense rises in cost. The special challenges here are how to stay abreast of these changes; how to assure access by faculty and students alike to the greatly expanded range of materials now becoming available; and how to achieve all of this in a way that is institutionally

affordable. While increased endowment and gifts are part of the answer, an equally — if not more — significant part lies in our ability to bring about major fundamental changes in the nature of the library itself. In other words, this is an example of — to use the current jargon — reengineering,

restructuring, and increased productivity.

The Harvard University Library operates on a massive scale. Its collections are housed in more than 90 different libraries, containing over 13 million volumes, as well as manuscripts, microforms, maps, slides, photographs, databases, and other materials, tangible and virtual. Harvard's is the largest university library in the world, and it is among the largest libraries of any kind, anywhere. Its total annual budget for this year is some $80 million, and the staff numbers more than 1,100 people, roughly 400 of whom are library professionals.

Like other colleges and universities, Harvard faces relentless annual increases in basic library costs, and a recent explosion in the demand for services from users who are now becoming accustomed to instant information retrieval. These forces have combined to erode the purchasing power of all academic libraries. In the fifteen years from 1980 to 1995, for example, Harvard's library expenditures grew at an average annual rate of 8.5 percent. During the same period, however, our staff grew by only

1.2 percent per year; we acquired additional volumes at a rate of only 1.8 percent per year; and we added new serials at only 0.2 percent per year.

The dramatic disparity between the large growth in expenditures and the very modest growth in staff and acquisitions can be accounted for largely by the steep continuing rise in the cost of journal subscriptions, led by scientific and technical journals that we simply must continue to buy. Chemistry and physics journals, for example almost tripled in price from 1977 to 1987, and then tripled again during the last decade. In 1997, the average annual journal subscription in three scientific disciplines

cost over $1,000 a year, with journals in physics leading the way at $1,494, chemistry journals close behind at $1,359, and astronomy journals at $1,084. In an additional 10 of the 31 Library of Congress categories, journal subscription costs now average between $500 and $1,000 a year.

At the same time we face these spiraling costs, the library is obviously entering a period of profound transformation, driven by the rise of new information technologies and by the increasing availability of information in digital form. We can hope, over time, that these developments will help us contain at least some costs. But for the foreseeable future, we are faced with the prospect of maintaining and building our invaluable historical collection of books, journals, and other documents, while also creating a new electronic, digital library of the future. We are, in other words, confronted with a situation in which we need to conceive of the library both as a vitally important physical location for the collection and preservation of tangible documents and materials — and as a gateway to a vast universe of information and knowledge that exists beyond the library's walls, in a huge multiplicity of

digital formats and forms.

The new information technologies are already doing much to extend the library's traditional capacities. But the incremental costs are considerable. Harvard, for example, spent over $13 million between 1984-85 and 1995-96 on developing a massive, on-line library information system that is still evolving. What began as a back-room system for making acquisitions more efficient has, ten years later, become a comprehensive on-line catalogue containing millions of titles, searchable in any number of ways by anyone with a link to the Internet. A companion system provides network connections far beyond the Harvard library, to a vast array of government documents, electronic databases, and bibliographic materials. Meanwhile, the annual operating costs of maintaining (and inevitably upgrading) these systems already requires several million dollars each year.

Faced for now with the escalating costs of books and journals on the one hand, and the advent of the digital library on the other, how have we tried to tackle the problem in a cost-effective way, while maintaining quality and ensuring access for students and faculty to an ever-increasing range of

materials?

First, we have slowed the growth rate of our acquisitions. We pay the steeply rising prices for the books and journals we do acquire. But at a time when the number of new publications continues to grow at an accelerating rate, we have felt compelled to limit our own growth, to the quite modest rates I mentioned earlier.

Next, while we have undertaken major renovations of existing libraries, we have essentially stopped building new on-campus space to accommodate our collections. Instead, we recently made a genuinely historic decision — in the face of considerable opposition — to create something called the Harvard Depository, a library facility that already houses some 2.5 million of our volumes in highly economical space about 30 miles away from Cambridge. There is some loss of convenience to users, who have to wait (up to 24 hours) to have books delivered, and who cannot browse through the volumes in storage. But the cost savings are dramatic — and, as an added benefit, the Depository's climate-control system does a better job than our traditional libraries of preserving documentary materials, many of which are increasingly at risk of deterioration. As we buy new books and periodicals each year, a roughly equivalent number are now shipped out to the Depository.

Next, we are sharing materials with other libraries, and cooperating with other institutions to address preservation problems and expand access. For instance, we have always had some cooperative library arrangements with MIT, but in the past two years we have moved to an essentially "open" system, with members of each institution having full and free access to the other's collections.

Next, as suggested by some of the data I mentioned earlier, we are tightly controlling the growth of our library staff, even as the demand for their services continues to grow — because of higher circulation levels, the need of users to be guided in the use of new technologies, and other factors. In short, we have been working to realize steady gains in productivity — and are achieving them.

Finally, we are seeking to strengthen, by nearly $80 million, the endowment funds that support our library system — so that rising costs have the smallest possible impact on tuition and other elements of our internal economy.

All the while, we are working to integrate the total resources of our traditional library and our emerging digital library even more fully into the academic life of our undergraduates. We track the patterns quite closely. For example, our college students are borrowing more books from Widener — our main research library — than ever before. In fact, undergraduate borrowing from Widener increased by 11 percent in the last academic year alone — with our students checking out more than 80,000 books and other items. In contrast to an earlier era, when our college students tended to confine themselves much more to libraries with limited collections created specifically for undergraduate use, our undergraduates now borrow more books from Widener than our faculty or our graduate students. And, with the guidance of our library professionals, our college students are not just traversing the stacks of Widener, but following the seemingly endless strands of the World Wide Web into realms that many of us, who attended college in an earlier day, could hardly have imagined.

New Information Technologies: A Stimulus to Learning

That leads me to my final point. I have touched on only a few of the major factors that drive expenses within the modern university. But if we want to focus especially on new developments, it is hard not to say a few words about information technology in the larger sense — including but also transcending its impact on the finances of our libraries.

What distinguishes the Internet and related new technologies from many of their predecessors is their extraordinary versatility and their interactive quality — features that set them decisively apart from media such as television, radio, or film. In my view, the arrival of the Internet and the World Wide Web — along with the inevitable evolution of their successor technologies — represents the most far-reaching development in the capacity of our universities to seek, find, analyze, and synthesize information and knowledge since the creation of our major research libraries roughly a century ago.

We are dealing here not merely with a change in the amount of readily accessible information, but with a clear transformation in significant aspects of teaching and learning — one that is already upon us. The new technologies strongly reinforce the student's ability to explore and discover, and to interact with both faculty members and other students, in an energetic and effective way. They put the student in the driver's seat, so to speak, and help strengthen the kind of environment I referred to earlier — an environment in which students are challenged, with faculty as their guides, not just to absorb established knowledge and ideas, but to search for relevant and reliable evidence, to frame and reframe significant questions, to test hypotheses, and to pursue convincing answers and solutions.

Of course, creating the infrastructure to support these elaborate new networks carries a large price tag. At Harvard, over the past five years we have already invested at least $50 million in this effort — wiring dormitories, offices, and various other facilities, including a growing number of classrooms. We have had to engage a new cadre of professional staff — who are very much in demand — and to keep pace as best we can with rapid changes in technologies that sometimes seem on the verge of

obsolescence as soon as they are put in place.

In the coming years, we will have to invest more than $100 million more in this effort throughout the university, because it is increasingly central to programs across Harvard. Within our Faculty of Arts and Sciences, we estimate that expenditures related to information technology now account for something in the range of 15 percent of the annual operating budget, and are growing at a rate of roughly 20 percent a year.

Already, more than 200 courses in the Arts and Sciences have Web pages, with faculty using the network to organize discussion groups, to distribute assignments, and to create links to special teaching and research materials on-line. Faculty in science courses are beginning to simulate complex experiments on-line — experiments that it would be impractical or too expensive to perform in the classroom or laboratory, but which students can now study in detail — over and again, if they wish to —

on their computer screens. Students in social sciences courses now regularly work with vast on-line databases — such as census materials or voting records — to expand the scope of their research. Increasingly, music students can read scores on-line — and hear performances of selected works, in order to compare interpretations.

As with any medium — certainly as with the books in our research libraries — it is possible to spin one's wheels, waste time, or simply procrastinate while roaming or surfing the Net. But I believe that the upside potential of these new technologies is very high, and that they represent a relentless and irreversible development, not a mere fad or distraction. At the same time, in the context of a residential college devoted to humane learning, there is ultimately no substitute for the kind of exchange that takes place through sustained, face-to-face human contact. In this sense, the new technologies expand our capacities for teaching and learning, but do not supplant the traditional ones. They represent a

significant new area of investment with real educational dividends — but not a substitute for the seminars, tutorials, discussion groups, or even lectures that are at the core of our college programs. And so, we will have to invest, carefully yet actively, in these important new components of the educational process. And, as we do, we will have to seek gifts, endowment, and other forms of support to absorb much of the costs.

Were there time, I would be happy to speak with you about other major aspects of education and economics in our private research universities. For now, let me stop here and invite your questions — on areas I have covered, or those I have not. Let me mention, in particular, that I know at least some members of the Commission have an interest in graduate education in relation to the undergraduate enterprise. While this is a large subject in itself, I would be glad to be helpful to the extent I can. The task before this Commission is an extraordinarily important one — for students, for colleges and universities, and for society — and I believe you have an unusual opportunity to clarify many issues, correct some misperceptions, and advance our collective understanding of a complicated but very significant set of issues. Thank you again for inviting me to be with you.

Issue 1: The increase in tuition compared to other commodities and services

Comparing tuition increases to trends in the prices of other goods and services provides a context for evaluating the escalating price of attending college. Because a large proportion of college students receive financial aid and therefore do not pay the full "sticker price," trends in "net price" (college expenses minus financial aid) need to be examined. Further, because colleges and universities typically spend more money to provide undergraduate instruction than is recouped through tuition revenue, it is important to distinguish between the cost to provide higher education and the price paid to acquire it. The distinction this report makes between "cost" and "price" is spelled out in further detail in the provided Glossary of Terms. The details of the empirical estimation of these concepts is provided in a Technical Note section.

Findings

- Since 1980, tuition at all types of institutions has approximately tripled. (Exhibit 1-1)
- Even after controlling for inflation, tuition at each type of institution has roughly doubled since 1980. (Exhibit 1-2)
- The similar percentage increases across sectors have widened the tuition gap between public and private schools. In 1980, attending a private rather than public university meant $2,971 more in tuition. By 1996, the difference between private and public universities had increased to $12,430. (Exhibit 1-1)
- Between 1987 and 1996, tuition (what students and their families pay for higher education) increased substantially more than the average cost per student (what colleges and universities spend to provide higher education) at all types of institutions. (Exhibits 1-3, 1-5, and 1-7)
- The proportion of cost per student covered by tuition has increased over time at all types of institutions. (Exhibits 1-3a, 1-5a, and 1-7a)
- Total price (tuition, room, board, and other education-related expenses) has increased substantially since 1987. However, between 1993 and 1996, the rate of increase in total price has declined relative to earlier time periods. In fact, when all forms of financial aid (grants, loans, work study and other) are subtracted from total price, there is not a statistically significant increase in this type of "net price" measure between 1993 and 1996. (Exhibits 1-4, 1-6, and 1-8)
- Increases in household income have not kept pace with tuition increases and have varied substantially for different segments of the income distribution. Since 1980, the bottom 60 percent of all households have experienced 5 percent or less increase in income, after controlling for inflation. In comparison, the top fifth experienced a 32 percent real increase. (Exhibit 1-21)
- Ratios of tuition to household income have approximately doubled for the bottom fifth of the income distribution, while remaining virtually the same for the top fifth. (Exhibit 1-22)
- Despite the media attention given to tuition at expensive colleges and universities, 56 percent of four-year, full-time students attend colleges that charge less than $4,000 in tuition. (Exhibit 1-24)
- The earning differentials enjoyed by workers holding a bachelor's degree compared to workers having only a high school diploma has increased substantially and fairly consistently over the last twenty years for both men and women. (Exhibits 1-26 and 1-27)

Conclusions

Has tuition increased faster than other goods and service?

Yes, in some cases. Tuitions charged by all types of colleges and universities have typically increased faster than many other goods and services over the past decade. In comparison to other professional services, such as medical care, tuition price increases seem more in line. When tuition rates are compared to the costs institutions incur to provide education (cost per full-time-equivalent student), tuitions appear to have increased faster than costs.

However, the price institutions charge (tuition) is often not the price students pay. Financial aid helps to offset the tuition and other education charges (e.g., room, board, transportation, etc.). If all forms of aid — grants, loans, and work study — are subtracted from the price of attendance, the "net price" full-time, dependent students paid did not increase between 1993 and 1996. The increased availability of loans probably accounts for this finding.

EXHIBIT 1-1
Average Tuition and Fees (Sticker Price) by Type of Institution: 1975-1996
(in Current Dollars)

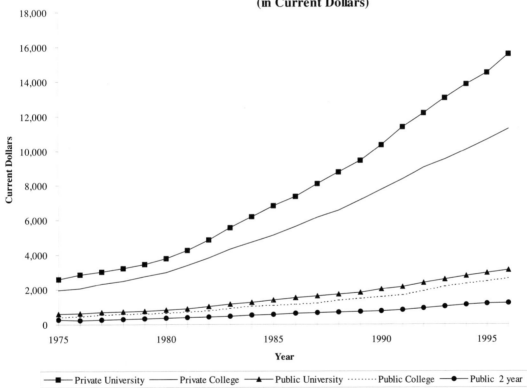

Source: *Digest of Education Statistics* 1996, Table 309.

EXHIBIT 1-1a

Average Tuition and Fees (Sticker Price) by Type of Institution: 1975-1996
(in Current Dollars)

Year	Public			Private	
	University	College	Two-year	University	College
1975	$599	$448	$277	$2,614	$1,954
1976	642	469	245	2,881	2,084
1977	689	564	283	3,051	2,351
1978	736	596	306	3,240	2,520
1979	777	622	327	3,487	2,771
1980	840	662	355	3,811	3,020
1981	915	722	391	4,275	3,390
1982	1,042	813	434	4,887	3,853
1983	1,164	936	473	5,583	4,329
1984	1,284	1,052	528	6,217	4,726
1985	1,386	1,117	584	6,843	5,135
1986	1,536	1,157	641	7,374	5,641
1987	1,651	1,248	660	8,118	6,171
1988	1,726	1,407	706	8,771	6,574
1989	1,846	1,515	730	9,451	7,172
1990	2,035	1,608	756	10,348	7,778
1991	2,159	1,707	824	11,379	8,389
1992	2,410	1,933	937	12,192	9,053
1993	2,604	2,192	1,025	13,055	9,533
1994	2,820	2,360	1,125	13,874	10,100
1995	2,977	2,499	1,192	14,537	10,653
1996	3,151	2,661	1,245	15,581	11,294

Source: *Digest of Education Statistics* 1996, Table 309.

EXHIBIT 1-2
Average Tuition and Fees (Sticker Price) by Type of Institution: 1975-1996
(in Constant 1996 Dollars)

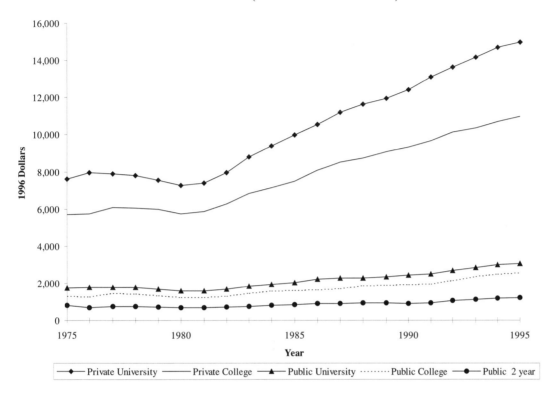

EXHIBIT 1-2a

Average Tuition and Fees (Sticker Price) by Type of Institution: 1975-1996
(in Constant 1996 Dollars)

Year	Public			Private	
	University	College	Two-year	University	College
1975	$1,747	$1,307	$808	$7,623	$5,699
1976	1,770	1,293	676	7,944	5,747
1977	1,784	1,459	734	7,898	6,088
1978	1,771	1,434	737	7,797	6,063
1979	1,679	1,345	707	7,537	5,990
1980	1,599	1,261	676	7,256	5,751
1981	1,579	1,246	675	7,379	5,852
1982	1,684	1,322	706	7,946	6,264
1983	1,834	1,474	745	8,795	6,819
1984	1,939	1,589	797	9,388	7,137
1985	2,021	1,629	852	9,978	7,488
1986	2,199	1,656	918	10,556	8,075
1987	2,280	1,724	912	11,212	8,523
1988	2,290	1,866	936	11,633	8,719
1989	2,335	1,917	924	11,959	9,075
1990	2,442	1,930	908	12,423	9,337
1991	2,488	1,967	949	13,109	9,664
1992	2,695	2,161	1,047	13,635	10,124
1993	2,828	2,380	1,113	14,175	10,351
1994	2,985	2,498	1,191	14,688	10,693
1995	3,065	2,573	1,228	14,966	10,968
1996	3,151	2,661	1,245	15,581	11,294

Source: *Digest of Education Statistics* 1996, Table 309.
CPI is from Bureau of Labor Statistics.

EXHIBIT 1-3
Percent Change in Cost, Sticker Price, and Subsidy 1987 to 1996
Public Four-Year Colleges and Universities

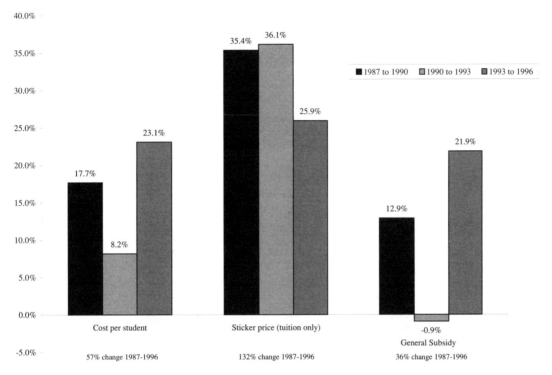

Source: National Center for Education Statistics, *National Postsecondary Student Aid Study,* 1987, 1990, 1993, and 1996.

Note: Cost per student estimates are derived from IPEDS financial and enrollment data. The cost per student figures for 1996 are imputed based on the rate of change observed between 1993 and 1995 data.

EXHIBIT 1-3a
Cost per Student, 1987 to 1996
Public Four-Year Colleges and Universities

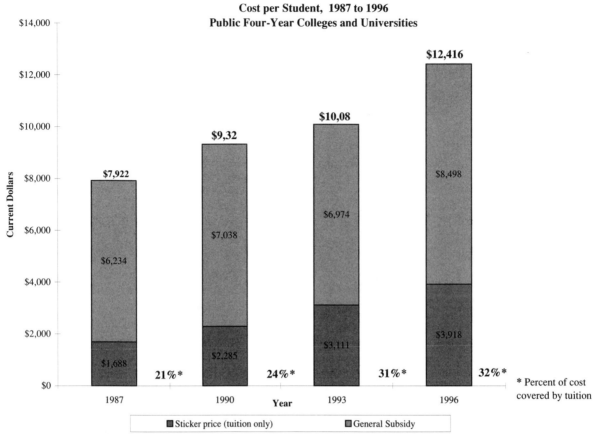

Source: National Center for Education Statistics, *National Postsecondary Student Aid Study*, 1987, 1990, 1993, and 1996.

Note: Cost per student estimates are derived from IPEDS financial and enrollment data. The cost per student figures for 1996 are imputed based on the rate of change observed between 1993 and 1995 data.

EXHIBIT 1-4
Percent Change in Total and Net Prices, 1987 to 1996
Public Four-Year Colleges and Universities

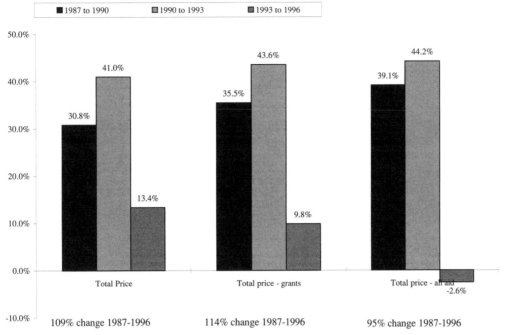

109% change 1987-1996   114% change 1987-1996   95% change 1987-1996

"Total price" includes tuition, room, board, books, transportation, and other expenses.
"Total price - all aid" equals total price minus grants, loans, work study, and other aid.

Source: National Center for Education Statistics, *National Postsecondary Student Aid Study,* 1987, 1990, 1993, and 1996.
Note: Total and net price estimates from NPSAS data were adjusted in order to be comparable with the 1996 "Budget" variable.

EXHIBIT 1-4a
Total and Net Prices, 1987 to 1996
Public Four-Year Colleges and Universities

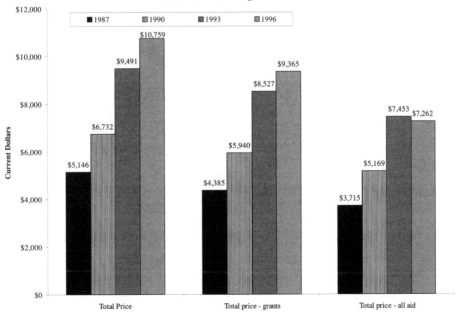

"Total Price" includes tuition, room, board, books, transportation and other expenses.
"Total price - all aid" equals total price minus grants, loans, work study, and other aid.

Source: National Center for Education Statistics, *National Postsecondary Student Aid Study,* 1987, 1990, 1993, and 1996.
Note: Total and net price estimates from NPSAS data were adjusted in order to be comparable with the 1996 "Budget" variable.

EXHIBIT 1-5
Percent Change in Cost, Sticker Price, and Subsidy 1987 to 1996
Private Four-Year Colleges and Universities

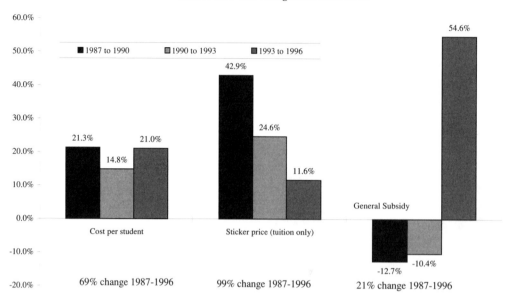

Source: National Center for Education Statistics, *National Postsecondary Student Aid Study,* 1987, 1990, 1993, and 1996.

Note: Cost per student estimates are derived from IPEDS financial and enrollment data. The cost per student figures for 1996 are imputed based on the rate of change observed between 1993 and 1995 data.

EXHIBIT 1-5a
Cost per Student, 1987 to 1996
Private Four-Year Colleges and Universities

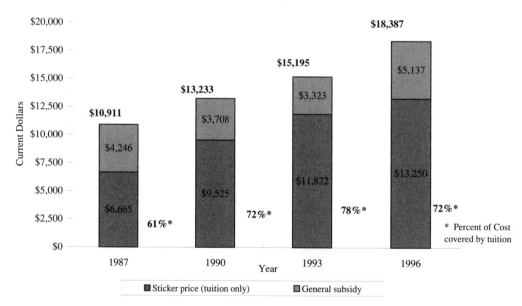

Source: National Center for Education Statistics, *National Postsecondary Student Aid Study,* 1987, 1990, 1993, and 1996.

Note: Cost per student estimates are derived from IPEDS financial and enrollment data. The cost per student figures for 1996 are imputed based on the rate of change observed between 1993 and 1995 data.

EXHIBIT 1-6
Percent Change in Total and Net Prices, 1987 to 1996
Private Four-Year Colleges and Universities

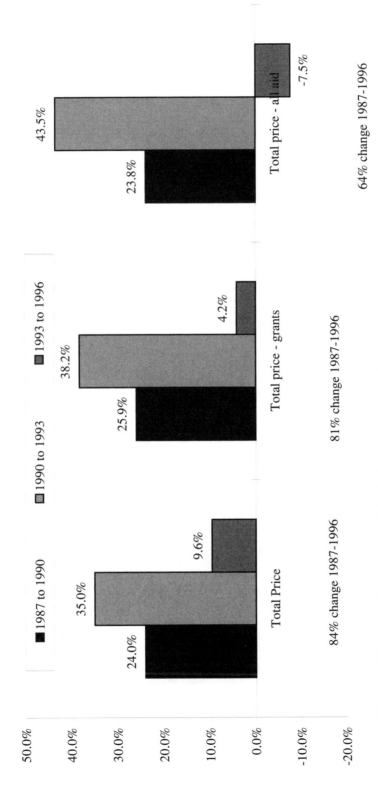

"Total price" includes tuition, room, board, books, transportation, and other expenses.
"Total price - all aid" equals total price minus grants, loans, work study, and other aid.

Source: National Center for Education Statistics, *National Postsecondary Student Aid Study,* 1987, 1990, 1993, and 1996.

Note: Total and net price estimates from NPSAS data were adjusted in order to be comparable with the 1996 "Budget" variable.

EXHIBIT 1-6a
Total and Net Prices, 1987 to 1996
Private Four-Year Colleges and Universities

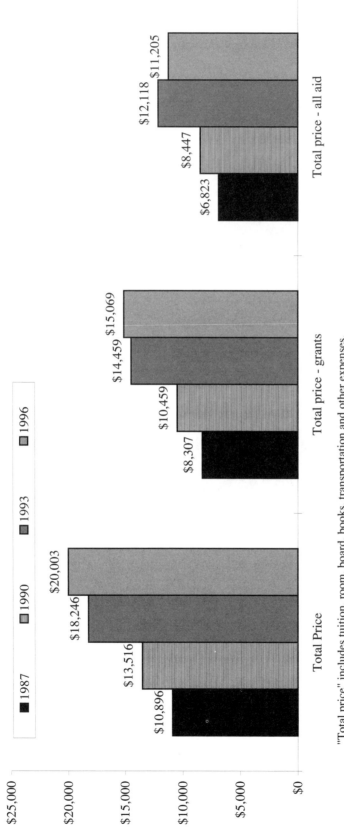

Legend: ■ 1987 ▥ 1990 ▦ 1993 ▨ 1996

Total Price
- $10,896
- $13,516
- $18,246
- $20,003

Total price - grants
- $8,307
- $10,459
- $14,459
- $15,069

Total price - all aid
- $6,823
- $8,447
- $12,118
- $11,205

"Total price" includes tuition, room, board, books, transportation and other expenses.
"Total price - all aid" equals total price minus grants, loans, work study, and other aid.

Source: National Center for Education Statistics, *National Postsecondary Student Aid Study*, 1987, 1990, 1993, and 1996.

Note: Total and net price estimates from NPSAS datta were adjusted in order to be comparable with the 1996 "Budget" variable.

EXHIBIT 1-7

Percent Change in Cost, Sticker Price, and Subsidy 1987 to 1996
Public Two-Year Colleges and Universities

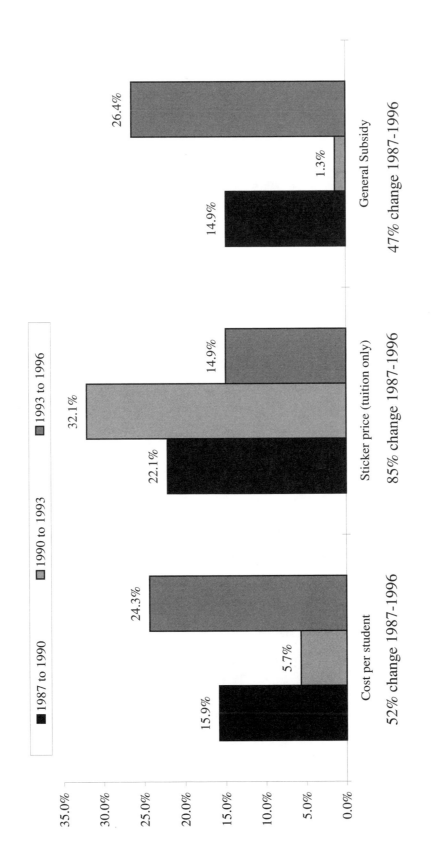

Source: National Center for Education Statistics, *National Postsecondary Student Aid Study*, 1987, 1990, 1993, and 1996.

Note: Cost per student estimates are derived from IPEDS financial and enrollment data. The cost per student figures for 1996 are imputed based on the rate of change observed between 1993 and 1995 data.

EXHIBIT 1-7a
Cost per Student, 1987 to 1996
Public Two-Year Colleges and Universities

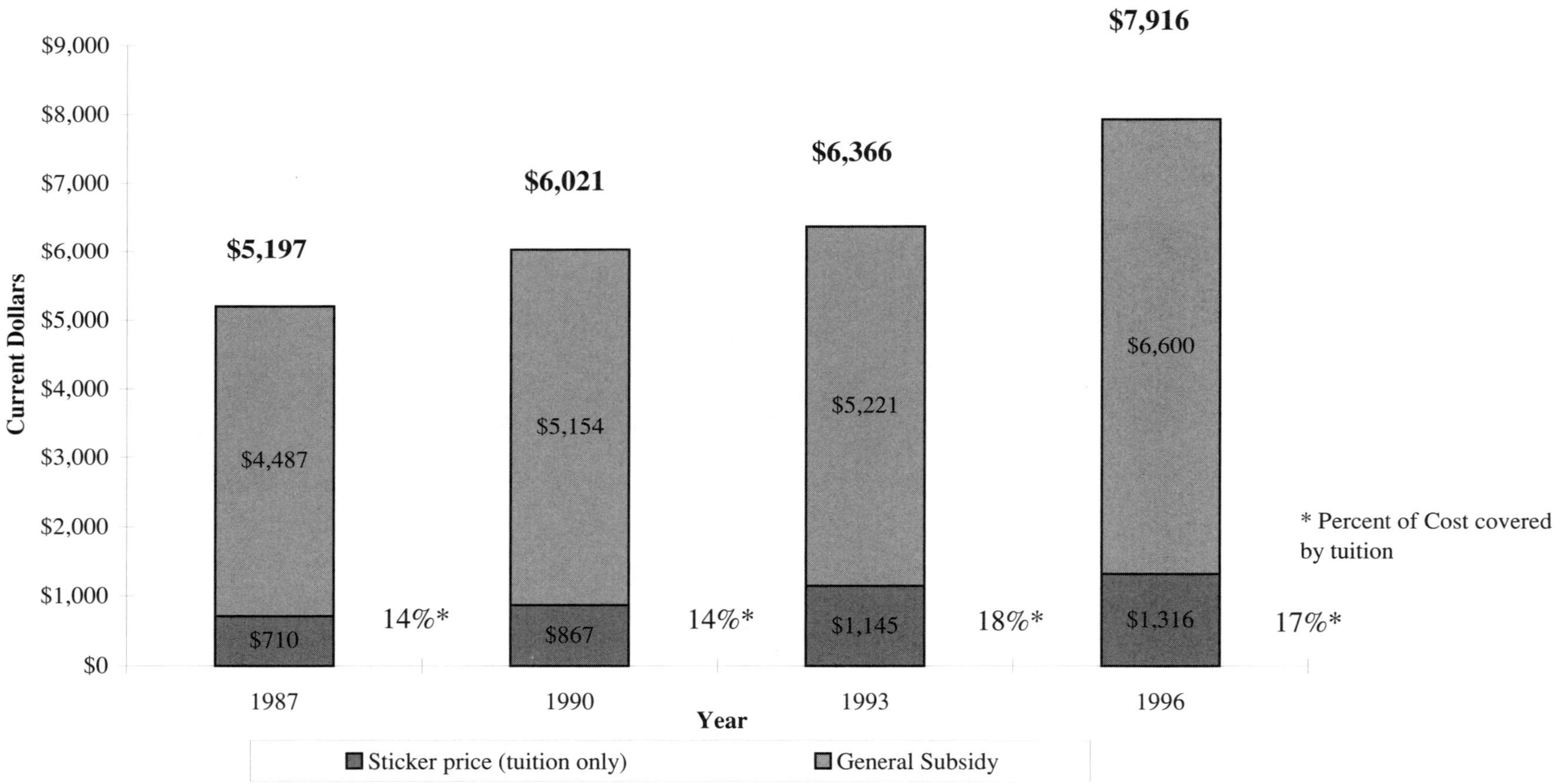

* Percent of Cost covered by tuition

Source: National Center for Education Statistics, *National Postsecondary Student Aid Study*, 1987, 1990, 1993, and 1996.

Note: Cost per student estimates are derived from IPEDS financial and enrollment data. The cost per student figures for 1996 are imputed based on the rate of change observed between 1993 and 1995 data.

EXHIBIT 1-8

Percent Change in Total and Net Prices, 1987 to 1996
Public Two-Year Colleges and Universities

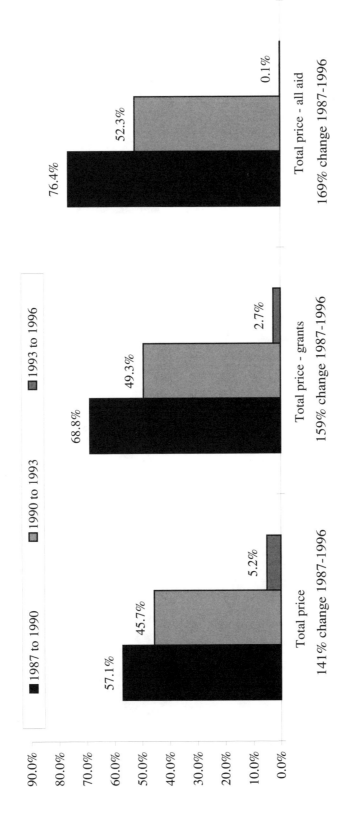

"Total price" includes tuition, room, board, books, transportation, and other expenses.
"Total price - all aid" includes total price minus grants, loans, work study, and other aid.

Source: National Center for Education Statistics, *National Postsecondary Student Aid Study*, 1987, 1990, 1993, and 1996.

Note: Total and net price estimates from NPSAS data were adjusted in order to be comparable with the 1996 "Budget" variable.

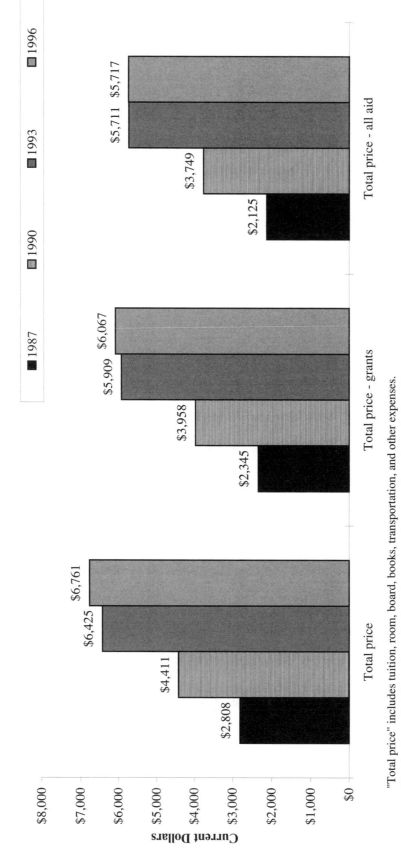

EXHIBIT 1-8a
Total and Net Prices, 1987 to 1996
Public Two-Year Colleges and Universities

"Total price" includes tuition, room, board, books, transportation, and other expenses.
"Total price - all aid" equals total price minus grants, loans, work study, and other aid.

Source: National Center for Education Statistics, *National Postsecondary Student Aid Study*, 1987, 1990, 1993, and 1996.

Note: Total and net price estimates from NPSAS data were adjusted in order to be comparable with the 1996 "Budget" variable.

EXHIBIT 1-9a

Net Price for All Institutions by Dependency Status and Income Level in Current Dollars: 1987
(For All Students—Aided and Unaided)

	Total Price	Tuition and fees	Non-Tuition Price	Grant Aid				Other Financial Aid			Net Price Formulas	
				Federal Grants	Inst. Grants	State Grants	Other Grants	Total Loans	Total work-study	Total Other**	Price-All Grants	Price-Federal Grants
Dependent students	$6,293	$2,881	$3,412	$347	$520	$243	$93	$674	$109	$27	$5,089	$5,946
Income Level***												
Low	5,733	2,462	3,271	811	577	475	110	882	187	29	3,759	4,922
Middle	5,968	2,627	3,341	159	581	214	95	754	93	23	4,920	5,809
Upper Middle	6,510	2,993	3,517	66	529	83	99	602	67	26	5,732	6,444
Upper	7,440	3,765	3,675	54	345	36	58	298	35	31	6,946	7,386
Independent students	4,648	1,730	2,919	1,039	309	301	100	976	144	74	2,898	3,609
Income Level ****												
Low	5,300	1,821	3,479	1,520	344	388	90	1,108	229	36	2,957	3,779
Middle	4,710	1,718	2,992	977	323	340	108	1,149	129	72	2,961	3,733
Upper	3,750	1,585	2,164	298	238	116	110	579	18	141	2,988	3,452

*Unsubsidized loans = unsubsidized Stafford (formerly SLS) and PLUS loans

**Aid not classified as grants, loans, or work-study. Includes assistantships, veterans benefits, military tuition aid, vocational rehabilitation and JTPA

*** Income levels for dependent students (1996 dollars): Low= less than $40,000; Middle = $40-59,999; Upper Middle= $60-79,999; Upper=greater than $80,000

****Income level for independent students (1996 dollars): Low= less than $10,000; Middle = $10-24,999; Upper = greater than $25,000

Source: NCES, NPSAS:87 Undergraduates 5/23/97

EXHIBIT 1-9b

Net Price for All Institutions by Dependency Status and Income Level in Current Dollars: 1990
(For All Students—Aided and Unaided)

	Total Price	Tuition and fees	Non-Tuition Price	Grant Aid				Other Financial Aid						Net Price Formulas		
				Federal Grants	Inst. Grants	State Grants	Other Grants	Loans excl. PLUS	PLUS	Total Loans	Total work-study	Other incl. PLUS	Total Other**	Price-All Grants	Price-Federal Grants	Price-All Aid
Dependent students	$8,240	$4,076	$4,164	$335	$676	$259	$98	$642	$98	$740	$119	$265	$167	$6,871	$7,905	$5,846
Income Level***																
Low	7,560	3,520	4,040	930	789	534	106	967	55	1,022	208	232	177	5,201	6,630	3,794
Middle	7,554	3,433	4,121	133	707	212	100	656	112	768	111	297	186	6,402	7,421	5,337
Upper Middle	8,084	3,938	4,147	35	676	109	96	506	144	650	77	299	155	7,169	8,049	6,288
Upper	10,092	5,661	4,431	11	491	66	87	303	100	403	43	243	142	9,438	10,081	8,849
Independent students	9,010	2,482	6,527	944	340	317	155	1,175	9	1,184	113	145	136	7,254	8,066	5,822
Income Level ****																
Low	8,434	2,741	5,693	1,262	414	336	101	1,203	15	1,218	167	178	162	6,322	7,172	4,774
Middle	8,643	2,298	6,345	862	286	347	196	1,239	7	1,246	94	118	111	6,952	7,781	5,501
Upper	10,388	2,255	8,133	455	277	237	198	1,027	0	1,027	37	121	121	9,221	9,933	8,036

*Unsubsidized loans = unsubsidized Stafford (formerly SLS) and PLUS loans

**Aid not classified as grants, loans,or work-study. Includes assistantships, veterans benefits, military tuition aid, vocational rehabilitation and JTPA

*** Income levels for dependent students (1996 dollars): Low= less than $40,000; Middle = $40-59,999; Upper Middle= $60-79,999; Upper=greater than $80,000

****Income level for independent students (1996 dollars): Low= less than $10,000; Middle = $10-24,999; Upper = greater than $25,000

Source: NCES, NPSAS:90 Undergraduates 8/14/95

EXHIBIT 1-9c

Net Price for All Institutions by Dependency Status and Income Level in Current Dollars: 1993
(For All Students—Aided and Unaided)

	Total Price	Tuition and fees	Non-Tuition Price	Grant Aid				Other Financial Aid						Net Price Formulas		
				Federal Grants	Inst. Grants	State Grants	Other Grants	Loans excl. PLUS	PLUS	Total Loans	Total work-study	Other incl. PLUS	Total Other**	Price-All Grants	Price-Federal Grants	Price-All Aid
Dependent students	$11,391	$5,209	$6,182	$374	$951	$228	$120	$856	$188	$1,044	$153	$263	$75	$9,718	$11,017	$8,446
Income Level*																
Low	10,436	4,408	6,028	1,221	1,142	549	136	1,442	173	1,615	293	257	84	7,389	9,215	5,397
Middle	10,291	4,273	6,017	145	1,166	208	158	979	239	1,218	163	338	99	8,614	10,146	7,134
Upper Middle	11,872	5,551	6,321	25	925	83	112	617	195	811	97	262	67	10,726	11,847	9,751
Upper	13,380	6,962	6,418	14	697	52	95	479	188	666	55	245	57	12,523	13,367	11,745
Independent students	10,208	3,197	7,010	1,125	392	308	108	1,618	45	1,663	139	230	185	8,274	9,083	6,286
Income Level****																
Low	10,341	3,415	6,926	1,777	543	442	91	1,781	67	1,848	215	292	224	7,489	8,564	5,202
Middle	10,118	3,069	7,050	893	326	251	91	1,590	39	1,629	106	237	198	8,557	9,225	6,624
Upper	10,089	2,995	7,095	323	225	158	162	1,382	15	1,397	53	116	101	9,222	9,767	7,671

*Unsubsidized loans = unsubsidized Stafford (formerly SLS) and PLUS loans

**Aid not classified as grants, loans, or work-study. Includes assistantships, veterans benefits, military tuition aid, vocational rehabilitation and JTPA

*** Income levels for dependent students (1996 dollars): Low= less than $40,000; Middle = $40-59,999; Upper Middle= $60-79,999; Upper=greater than $80,000

**** Income level for independent students (1996 dollars): Low= less than $10,000; Middle = $10-24,999; Upper = greater than $25,000

Source: NCES, NPSAS:93 Undergraduate Students 11/20/97

EXHIBIT 1-9d

Net Price for All Institutions by Dependency Status and Income Level in Current Dollars: 1996
(For All Students—Aided and Unaided)

	Total Price	Tuition and fees	Non-Tuition Price	Grant Aid				Other Financial Aid						Net Price Formulas		
				Federal Grants	Inst. Grants	State Grants	Other Grants	Loans excl. PLUS	PLUS	Total Loans	Total work-study	Other incl. PLUS	Total Other**	Price-All Grants	Price-Federal Grants	Price-All Aid
Dependent students	$11,688	$6,057	$5,631	$450	$1,266	$351	$191	$1,557	$398	$1,955	$176	$537	$139	$9,429	$11,238	$7,159
Income Level***																
Low	10,668	5,327	5,341	1,159	1,503	651	224	1,913	210	2,123	243	345	135	7,131	9,509	4,629
Middle	11,442	5,655	5,787	90	1,478	324	201	1,790	457	2,247	207	604	147	9,350	11,352	6,748
Upper Middle	11,791	5,938	5,853	11	1,154	137	176	1,364	479	1,843	121	617	138	10,312	11,780	8,210
Upper	13,433	7,649	5,784	7	791	71	143	937	578	1,516	85	717	138	12,421	13,426	10,682
Independent students	8,161	3,732	4,428	1,075	425	382	146	2,683	0	2,683	147	473	473	6,133	7,086	2,829
Income Level ****																
Low	9,185	3,812	5,373	1,667	548	518	85	3,052	0	3,052	238	472	472	6,368	7,518	2,606
Middle	8,086	3,500	4,586	901	384	358	128	2,690	0	2,690	98	405	405	6,315	7,185	3,122
Upper	6,903	3,874	3,030	233	256	171	277	2,021	0	2,021	46	558	558	5,966	6,671	3,341

*Unsubsidized loans = unsubsidized Stafford (formerly SLS) and PLUS loans

**Aid not classified as grants, loans, or work-study. Includes assistantships, veterans benefits, military tuition aid, vocational rehabilitation and JTPA

*** Income levels for dependent students (1996 dollars): Low= less than $40,000; Middle = $40-59,999; Upper Middle= $60-79,999; Upper=greater than $80,000

****Income level for independent students (1996 dollars): Low= less than $10,000; Middle = $10-24,999; Upper = greater than $25,000

Source: NCES, NPSAS:96 Undergraduate Students 11/20/97

EXHIBIT 1-10a

Net Price for Public Universities by Dependency Status and Income Level in Current Dollars: 1987
(For All Students—Aided and Unaided)

	Price			Grant Aid				Other Financial Aid			Net Price Formulas		
	Total Price	Tuition and fees	Non-Tuition Price	Federal Grants	Inst. Grants	State Grants	Other Grants	Total Loans	Total work-study	Total Other**	Price-All Grants	Price-Federal Grants	Price-All Aid
Dependent students	$5,559	$1,850	$3,710	$284	$268	$145	$83	$569	$73	$34	$4,779	$5,275	$4,104
Income Level***													
Low	5,484	1,761	3,723	775	356	328	101	915	156	33	3,924	4,709	2,819
Middle	5,401	1,754	3,647	107	291	121	83	625	53	33	4,798	5,294	4,087
Upper Middle	5,732	1,920	3,813	40	268	47	97	454	33	28	5,281	5,693	4,766
Upper	5,693	2,007	3,686	42	126	18	45	151	17	40	5,461	5,651	5,253
Independent students	4,855	1,560	3,294	1,111	337	192	99	1,248	149	185	3,115	3,744	1,533
Income Level****													
Low	5,406	1,628	3,779	1,578	388	255	59	1,399	246	77	3,127	3,828	1,405
Middle	4,722	1,558	3,164	971	305	174	200	1,507	70	186	3,072	3,751	1,308
Upper	3,977	1,422	2,556	269	266	77	71	632	30	413	3,294	3,708	2,218

*Unsubsidized loans = unsubsidized Stafford (formerly SLS) and PLUS loans

**Aid not classified as grants, loans, or work-study. Includes assistantships, veterans benefits, military tuition aid, vocational rehabilitation and JTPA

*** Income levels for dependent students (1996 dollars): Low= less than $40,000; Middle = $40-59,999; Upper Middle= $60-79,999; Upper=greater than $80,000

****Income level for independent students (1996 dollars): Low= less than $10,000; Middle = $10-24,999; Upper = greater than $25,000

Source: NCES, NPSAS:87 Undergraduate Students 5/23/97

EXHIBIT 1-10b

Net Price for Public Universities by Dependency Status and Income Level in Current Dollars: 1990
(For All Students—Aided and Unaided)

	Price			Grant Aid				Other Financial Aid			Net Price Formulas		
	Total Price	Tuition and fees	Non-Tuition Price	Federal Grants	Inst. Grants	State Grants	Other Grants	Total Loans	Total work-study	Total Other**	Price-All Grants	Price-Federal Grants	Price-All Aid
Dependent students	$7,370	$2,452	$4,918	$294	$295	$154	$69	$580	$73	$145	$6,558	$7,076	$5,760
Income Level***													
Low	7,147	2,290	4,857	914	339	346	78	948	168	121	5,470	6,233	4,232
Middle	7,024	2,292	4,732	107	340	120	80	584	59	209	6,377	6,917	5,524
Upper Middle	7,340	2,453	4,888	13	261	54	60	449	31	135	6,953	7,328	6,338
Upper	7,978	2,801	5,177	6	226	53	56	260	14	116	7,636	7,972	7,246
Independent students	8,975	2,062	6,912	905	283	232	140	1,422	100	127	7,414	8,070	5,766
Income Level****													
Low	8,364	2,042	6,322	1,175	323	248	93	1,353	147	120	6,525	7,189	4,904
Middle	8,646	2,058	6,588	758	198	238	198	1,717	48	86	7,254	7,888	5,403
Upper	11,214	2,131	9,083	335	316	171	179	1,100	50	219	10,212	10,879	8,843

*Unsubsidized loans = unsubsidized Stafford (formerly SLS) and PLUS loans

**Aid not classified as grants, loans, or work-study. Includes assistantships, veterans benefits, military tuition aid, vocational rehabilitation and JTPA

*** Income levels for dependent students (1996 dollars): Low= less than $40,000; Middle = $40-59,999; Upper Middle= $60-79,999; Upper=greater than $80,000

****Income levels for independent students (1996 dollars): Low= less than $10,000; Middle = $10-24,999; Upper = greater than $25,000

Source: NCES, NPSAS:90 Undergraduate Students 8/14/95

EXHIBIT 1-10c

Net Price for Public Universities by Dependency Status and Income Level in Current Dollars: 1993
(For All Students—Aided and Unaided)

	Price			Grant Aid				Other Financial Aid			Net Price Formulas		
	Total Price	Tuition and fees	Non-Tuition Price	Federal Grants	Inst. Grants	State Grants	Other Grants	Total Loans	Total work-study	Total Other**	Price-All Grants	Price-Federal Grants	Price-All Aid
Dependent students	$10,211	$3,408	$6,802	$316	$421	$176	$96	$961	$98	$47	$9,201	$9,895	$8,095
Income Level***													
Low	9,844	3,006	6,838	1,131	458	459	98	1,751	224	63	7,698	8,713	5,660
Middle	9,923	3,175	6,748	143	695	142	121	1,331	112	49	8,822	9,780	7,330
Upper Middle	10,268	3,446	6,822	17	329	79	89	529	48	27	9,755	10,251	9,152
Upper	10,617	3,766	6,852	17	290	61	88	528	20	48	10,161	10,600	9,565
Independent students	10,476	2,896	7,581	1,126	269	266	73	2,205	128	161	8,741	9,350	6,248
Income Level ****													
Low	10,319	2,873	7,446	1,693	347	374	94	2,443	183	188	7,810	8,625	4,997
Middle	10,553	2,937	7,616	753	231	207	52	2,060	88	160	9,311	9,800	7,002
Upper	10,754	2,877	7,878	328	136	92	58	1,846	57	91	10,141	10,426	8,147

*Unsubsidized loans = unsubsidized Stafford (formerly SLS) and PLUS loans

**Aid not classified as grants, loans,or work-study. Includes assistantships, veterans benefits, military tuition aid, vocational rehabilitation and JTPA

*** Income levels for dependent students (1996 dollars): Low= less than $40,000; Middle = $40-59,999; Upper Middle= $60-79,999; Upper=greater than $80,000

****Income level for independent students (1996 dollars): Low= less than $10,000; Middle = $10-24,999; Upper = greater than $25,000

Source: NCES, NPSAS:93 Undergraduate Students 10/2/97

EXHIBIT 1-10d

Net Price for Public Universities by Dependency Status and Income Level in Current Dollars: 1996
(For All Students—Aided and Unaided)

	Price			Grant Aid				Other Financial Aid			Net Price Formulas		
	Total Price	Tuition and fees	Non-Tuition Price	Federal Grants	Inst. Grants	State Grants	Other Grants	Total Loans	Total work-study	Total Other**	Price-All Grants	Price-Federal Grants	Price-All Aid
Dependent students	$11,447	$4,261	$7,186	$386	$590	$322	$170	$1,965	$97	$107	$9,979	$11,061	$7,810
Income Level***													
Low	11,006	3,933	7,072	1,084	938	655	212	2,425	163	115	8,116	9,921	5,412
Middle	11,055	3,931	7,124	84	578	250	200	2,287	107	84	9,943	10,970	7,464
Upper Middle	11,371	4,134	7,237	10	410	139	147	1,714	56	124	10,666	11,361	8,772
Upper	12,340	5,004	7,336	4	291	91	111	1,330	37	101	11,843	12,336	10,376
Independent students	11,978	3,418	8,560	1,022	317	350	113	4,018	107	466	10,175	10,956	5,585
Income Level****													
Low	11,796	3,421	8,375	1,547	364	465	76	4,394	174	504	9,344	10,249	4,272
Middle	11,672	3,201	8,472	817	374	370	162	4,123	40	370	9,949	10,855	5,416
Upper	12,746	3,699	9,047	232	148	92	126	3,120	57	515	12,148	12,514	8,456

*Unsubsidized loans = unsubsidized Stafford (formerly SLS) and PLUS loans

**Aid not classified as grants, loans,or work-study. Includes assistantships, veterans benefits, military tuition aid, vocational rehabilitation and JTPA

*** Income levels for dependent students (1996 dollars): Low= less than $40,000; Middle = $40-59,999; Upper Middle= $60-79,999; Upper=greater than $80,000

****Income level for independent students (1996 dollars): Low= less than $10,000; Middle = $10-24,999; Upper = greater than $25,000

Source: NCES, NPSAS:96 Undergraduate Students 10/1/97

EXHIBIT 1-11a

Net Price for Public Colleges by Dependency Status and Income Level in Current Dollars: 1987
(For All Students—Aided and Unaided)

	Price			Grant Aid				Other Financial Aid			Net Price Formulas		
	Total Price	Tuition and fees	Non-Tuition Price	Federal Grants	Inst. Grants	State Grants	Other Grants	Total Loans	Total work-study	Total Other**	Price-All Grants	Price-Federal Grants	Price-All Aid
Dependent students	$4,409	$1,395	$3,014	$373	$117	$182	$54	$552	$91	$17	$3,683	$4,036	$3,022
Income Level***													
Low	4,432	1,404	3,028	881	135	390	69	763	173	24	2,957	3,551	1,997
Middle	4,376	1,371	3,005	84	151	86	74	593	60	9	3,981	4,292	3,318
Upper Middle	4,464	1,453	3,011	36	76	31	30	402	39	6	4,291	4,427	3,844
Upper	4,342	1,348	2,994	13	69	15	16	171	9	27	4,228	4,328	4,020
Independent students	4,337	1,205	3,132	1,098	120	295	90	1,005	154	43	2,735	3,238	1,532
Income Level ****													
Low	4,892	1,226	3,666	1,686	118	396	99	1,095	235	17	2,593	3,206	1,246
Middle	4,437	1,278	3,160	826	154	326	57	1,265	134	57	3,075	3,611	1,619
Upper	3,519	1,099	2,419	222	92	74	101	601	19	81	3,029	3,296	2,328

*Unsubsidized loans = unsubsidized Stafford (formerly SLS) and PLUS loans

**Aid not classified as grants, loans,or work-study. Includes assistantships, veterans benefits, military tuition aid, vocational rehabilitation and JTPA

*** Income levels for dependent students (1996 dollars): Low= less than $40,000; Middle = $40-59,999; Upper Middle= $60-79,999; Upper=greater than $80,000

****Income level for independent students (1996 dollars): Low= less than $10,000; Middle = $10-24,999; Upper = greater than $25,000

Source: NCES, NPSAS:87 Undergraduate Students 5/23/97

EXHIBIT 1-11b

Net Price for Public Colleges by Dependency Status and Income Level in Current Dollars: 1990
(For All Students—Aided and Unaided)

	Price			Grant Aid				Other Financial Aid			Net Price Formulas		
	Total Price	Tuition and fees	Non-Tuition Price	Federal Grants	Inst. Grants	State Grants	Other Grants	Total Loans	Total work-study	Total Other**	Price-All Grants	Price-Federal Grants	Price-All Aid
Dependent students	$5,728	$2,036	$3,692	$358	$176	$175	$55	$529	$90	$112	$4,965	$5,370	$4,233
Income Level***													
Low	5,621	1,912	3,709	964	198	406	71	724	181	135	3,982	4,657	2,942
Middle	5,672	2,022	3,650	94	202	83	55	557	65	111	5,238	5,578	4,505
Upper Middle	5,712	2,056	3,655	27	170	44	44	443	46	140	5,426	5,684	4,797
Upper	6,033	2,253	3,780	13	103	34	37	235	13	49	5,846	6,020	5,549
Independent students	8,537	1,716	6,821	896	134	259	144	1,033	111	98	7,104	7,641	5,861
Income Level****													
Low	7,681	1,782	5,899	1,258	167	253	87	957	159	120	5,916	6,423	4,680
Middle	8,614	1,662	6,952	710	110	273	259	1,056	77	97	7,263	7,904	6,034
Upper	10,130	1,660	8,469	411	101	252	80	1,162	62	55	9,285	9,718	8,007

*Unsubsidized loans = unsubsidized Stafford (formerly SLS) and PLUS loans

**Aid not classified as grants, loans, or work-study. Includes assistantships, veterans benefits, military tuition aid, vocational rehabilitation and JTPA

*** Income levels for dependent students (1996 dollars): Low= less than $40,000; Middle = $40-59,999; Upper Middle= $60-79,999; Upper=greater than $80,000

**** Income levels for independent students (1996 dollars): Low= less than $10,000; Middle = $10-24,999; Upper = greater than $25,000

Source: NCES, NPSAS:90 Undergraduate Students 8/14/95

EXHIBIT 1-11c

Net Price for Public Colleges by Dependency Status and Income Level in Current Dollars: 1993
(For All Students—Aided and Unaided)

| | Price | | | Grant Aid | | | | | Other Financial Aid | | | Net Price Formulas | | |
	Total Price	Tuition and fees	Non-Tuition Price	Federal Grants	Inst. Grants	State Grants	Other Grants	Total Loans	Total work-study	Total Other**	Price-All Grants	Price-Federal Grants	Price-All Aid
Dependent students	$8,207	$2,580	$5,627	$428	$207	$186	$59	$866	$108	$46	$7,326	$7,779	$6,306
Income Level***													
Low	7,913	2,366	5,547	1,232	213	432	90	1,270	222	70	5,946	6,681	4,384
Middle	8,121	2,574	5,546	144	237	141	58	1,064	97	56	7,542	7,977	6,325
Upper Middle	8,401	2,725	5,676	31	205	44	53	647	35	27	8,068	8,370	7,360
Upper	8,501	2,864	5,637	12	173	49	35	437	43	32	8,233	8,490	7,721
Independent students	9,517	2,148	7,369	1,205	135	330	76	1,649	151	135	7,771	8,311	5,835
Income Level ****													
Low	9,348	2,247	7,101	1,886	207	489	81	1,785	205	169	6,686	7,463	4,527
Middle	9,628	2,099	7,529	960	79	272	46	1,719	130	139	8,271	8,668	6,283
Upper	9,641	2,051	7,590	394	98	141	114	1,303	89	70	8,893	9,246	7,432

*Unsubsidized loans = unsubsidized Stafford (formerly SLS) and PLUS loans

**Aid not classified as grants, loans,or work-study. Includes assistantships, veterans benefits, military tuition aid, vocational rehabilitation and JTPA

*** Income levels for dependent students (1996 dollars): Low= less than $40,000; Middle = $40-59,999; Upper Middle= $60-79,999; Upper=greater than $80,000

****Income level for independent students (1996 dollars): Low= less than $10,000; Middle = $10-24,999; Upper = greater than $25,000

Source: NCES, NPSAS:93 Undergraduate Students 10/2/97

EXHIBIT 1-11d

Net Price for Public Colleges by Dependency Status and Income Level in Current Dollars: 1996
(For All Students—Aided and Unaided)

	Price			Grant Aid				Other Financial Aid			Net Price Formulas		
	Total Price	Tuition and fees	Non-Tuition Price	Federal Grants	Inst. Grants	State Grants	Other Grants	Total Loans	Total work-study	Total Other**	Price-All Grants	Price-Federal Grants	Price-All Aid
Dependent students	$9,436	$3,257	$6,178	$501	$314	$310	$126	$1,779	$123	$73	$8,183	$8,934	$6,207
Income Level***													
Low	9,105	3,117	5,988	1,173	395	604	130	1,923	173	94	6,804	7,932	4,613
Middle	9,450	3,254	6,196	85	380	200	120	2,207	146	81	8,665	9,365	6,231
Upper Middle	9,422	3,235	6,186	3	220	76	151	1,544	69	52	8,972	9,419	7,307
Upper	10,190	3,603	6,586	5	149	21	99	1,165	37	40	9,916	10,185	8,674
Independent students	10,707	2,993	7,714	1,207	248	412	87	2,795	182	414	8,752	9,500	5,361
Income Level ****													
Low	10,540	3,018	7,522	1,806	361	509	71	3,130	293	325	7,793	8,735	4,046
Middle	10,745	2,867	7,878	943	168	386	82	3,027	111	549	9,167	9,802	5,479
Upper	11,037	3,089	7,948	172	89	224	132	1,751	16	450	10,419	10,864	8,203

*Unsubsidized loans = unsubsidized Stafford (formerly SLS) and PLUS loans

**Aid not classified as grants, loans,or work-study. Includes assistantships, veterans benefits, military tuition aid, vocational rehabilitation and JTPA

*** Income levels for dependent students (1996 dollars): Low= less than $40,000; Middle = $40-59,999; Upper Middle= $60-79,999; Upper=greater than $80,000

****Income level for independent students (1996 dollars): Low= less than $10,000; Middle = $10-24,999; Upper = greater than $25,000

Source: NCES, NPSAS:96 Undergraduate Students 10/1/97

EXHIBIT 1-12a

Net Price for Public Two-Year Colleges by Dependency Status and Income Level in Current Dollars: 1987
(For All Students—Aided and Unaided)

	Price			Grant Aid				Other Financial Aid			Net Price Formulas		
	Total Price	Tuition and fees	Non-Tuition Price	Federal Grants	Inst. Grants	State Grants	Other Grants	Total Loans	Total work-study	Total Other**	Price-All Grants	Price-Federal Grants	Price-All Aid
Dependent students	$2,808	$710	$2,098	$244	$90	$87	$43	$175	$38	$6	$2,345	$2,564	$2,125
Income Level***													
Low	2,930	682	2,248	482	104	152	68	210	76	11	2,124	2,448	1,827
Middle	2,954	733	2,220	53	95	49	19	216	8	5	2,738	2,901	2,509
Upper Middle	2,666	745	1,921	1	64	15	38	94	5	0	2,548	2,665	2,449
Upper	2,560	719	1,841	35	43	0	6	9	0	0	2,476	2,525	2,467
Independent students	3,089	611	2,478	863	77	158	56	486	110	15	1,935	2,226	1,323
Income Level****													
Low	3,581	685	2,896	1,218	56	213	81	518	174	4	2,014	2,364	1,319
Middle	3,263	575	2,688	960	101	208	54	636	133	0	1,939	2,303	1,170
Upper	2,494	546	1,947	301	82	39	25	305	4	44	2,046	2,193	1,692

*Unsubsidized loans = unsubsidized Stafford (formerly SLS) and PLUS loans

**Aid not classified as grants, loans,or work-study. Includes assistantships, veterans benefits, military tuition aid, vocational rehabilitation and JTPA

*** Income levels for dependent students (1996 dollars): Low= less than $40,000; Middle = $40-59,999; Upper Middle= $60-79,999; Upper=greater than $80,000

****Income level for independent students (1996 dollars): Low= less than $10,000; Middle = $10-24,999; Upper = greater than $25,000

Source: NCES, NPSAS:87 Undergraduate Students 5/23/97

EXHIBIT 1-12b

Net Price for Public Two-Year Colleges by Dependency Status and Income Level in Current Dollars: 1990
(For All Students—Aided and Unaided)

	Price			Grant Aid				Other Financial Aid			Net Price Formulas		
	Total Price	Tuition and fees	Non-Tuition Price	Federal Grants	Inst. Grants	State Grants	Other Grants	Total Loans	Total work-study	Total Other**	Price-All Grants	Price-Federal Grants	Price-All Aid
Dependent students	$4,411	$867	$3,544	$228	$87	$112	$26	$115	$46	$48	$3,958	$4,183	$3,749
Income Level***													
Low	4,295	814	3,481	534	109	250	25	174	83	64	3,377	3,762	3,057
Middle	4,782	887	3,895	39	117	23	14	118	36	63	4,589	4,743	4,372
Upper Middle	4,257	934	3,322	28	31	31	31	31	14	7	4,136	4,228	4,084
Upper	4,948	872	4,077	38	9	22	59	41	0	22	4,820	4,910	4,757
Independent students	6,936	866	6,070	886	59	179	120	574	87	69	5,692	6,050	4,962
Income Level ****													
Low	6,229	924	5,305	1,189	80	190	4	720	141	72	4,767	5,041	3,835
Middle	6,444	855	5,589	899	55	221	162	530	97	83	5,107	5,545	4,397
Upper	7,737	815	6,922	531	42	114	199	465	12	51	6,850	7,205	6,322

*Unsubsidized loans = unsubsidized Stafford (formerly SLS) and PLUS loans

**Aid not classified as grants, loans,or work-study. Includes assistantships, veterans benefits, military tuition aid, vocational rehabilitation and JTPA

*** Income levels for dependent students (1996 dollars): Low= less than $40,000; Middle = $40-59,999; Upper Middle= $60-79,999; Upper=greater than $80,000

****Income level for independent students (1996 dollars): Low= less than $10,000; Middle = $10-24,999; Upper = greater than $25,000

Source: NCES, NPSAS:90 Undergraduate Students 8/14/95

EXHIBIT 1-12c

Net Price for Public Two-Year Colleges by Dependency Status and Income Level in Current Dollars: 1993
(For All Students—Aided and Unaided)

	Price			Grant Aid				Other Financial Aid			Net Price Formulas		
	Total Price	Tuition and fees	Non-Tuition Price	Federal Grants	Inst. Grants	State Grants	Other Grants	Total Loans	Total work-study	Total Other**	Price-All Grants	Price-Federal Grants	Price-All Aid
Dependent students	$6,425	$1,145	$5,280	$260	$125	$96	$35	$133	$50	$14	$5,909	$6,165	$5,711
Income Level***													
Low	6,396	1,137	5,259	809	219	231	68	235	127	28	5,070	5,588	4,681
Middle	6,382	1,138	5,243	57	110	56	27	111	28	15	6,132	6,325	5,978
Upper Middle	6,761	1,288	5,474	1	86	38	4	109	0	0	6,633	6,760	6,523
Upper	6,523	1,117	5,407	3	19	0	49	9	6	0	6,453	6,520	6,438
Independent students	7,338	1,193	6,146	985	45	147	89	552	84	206	6,073	6,354	5,231
Income Level ****													
Low	7,399	1,172	6,227	1,661	53	241	50	648	172	247	5,394	5,738	4,327
Middle	7,400	1,282	6,118	830	52	104	125	434	53	275	6,288	6,569	5,527
Upper	7,188	1,122	6,066	263	27	68	102	553	4	75	6,727	6,925	6,095

*Unsubsidized loans = unsubsidized Stafford (formerly SLS) and PLUS loans

**Aid not classified as grants, loans,or work-study. Includes assistantships, veterans benefits, military tuition aid, vocational rehabilitation and JTPA

*** Income levels for dependent students (1996 dollars): Low= less than $40,000; Middle = $40-59,999; Upper Middle= $60-79,999; Upper=greater than $80,000

****Income level for independent students (1996 dollars): Low= less than $10,000; Middle = $10-24,999; Upper = greater than $25,000

Source: NCES, NPSAS:93 Undergraduate Students 11/20/97

EXHIBIT 1-12d

Net Price for Public Two-Year Colleges by Dependency Status and Income Level in Current Dollars: 1996
(For All Students—Aided and Unaided)

	Price			Grant Aid				Other Financial Aid			Net Price Formulas		
	Total Price	Tuition and fees	Non-Tuition Price	Federal Grants	Inst. Grants	State Grants	Other Grants	Total Loans	Total work-study	Total Other**	Price-All Grants	Price-Federal Grants	Price-All Aid
Dependent students	$6,761	$1,316	$5,445	$383	$145	$122	$44	$274	$33	$43	$6,067	$6,378	$5,717
Income Level***													
Low	6,556	1,258	5,298	892	177	220	65	273	70	60	5,202	5,664	4,798
Middle	6,894	1,411	5,483	17	131	98	37	371	7	58	6,611	6,877	6,174
Upper Middle	6,970	1,323	5,647	0	128	23	18	289	8	15	6,801	6,970	6,489
Upper	6,875	1,316	5,559	0	100	4	26	106	3	1	6,744	6,875	6,634
Independent students	8,242	1,440	6,803	1,002	114	158	59	853	144	452	6,909	7,240	5,460
Income Level****													
Low	8,211	1,424	6,787	1,567	143	219	25	925	237	453	6,257	6,643	4,643
Middle	8,448	1,435	7,013	957	45	163	61	1,045	115	257	7,222	7,491	5,804
Upper	8,041	1,468	6,573	240	157	64	107	520	44	682	7,473	7,801	6,227

*Unsubsidized loans = unsubsidized Stafford (formerly SLS) and PLUS loans

**Aid not classified as grants, loans,or work-study. Includes assistantships, veterans benefits, military tuition aid, vocational rehabilitation and JTPA

*** Income levels for dependent students (1996 dollars): Low= less than $40,000; Middle = $40-59,999; Upper Middle= $60-79,999; Upper=greater than $80,000

****Income level for independent students (1996 dollars): Low= less than $10,000; Middle = $10-24,999; Upper = greater than $25,000

Source: NCES, NPSAS:96 Undergraduate Students 10/1/97

EXHIBIT 1-13a

Net Price for Private Universities by Dependency Status and Income Level in Current Dollars: 1987
(For All Students—Aided and Unaided)

	Price			Grant Aid				Other Financial Aid			Net Price Formulas		
	Total Price	Tuition and fees	Non-Tuition Price	Federal Grants	Inst. Grants	State Grants	Other Grants	Total Loans	Total work-study	Total Other**	Price-All Grants	Price-Federal Grants	Price-All Aid
Dependent students	$12,147	$7,640	$4,507	$462	$1,659	$440	$192	$1,210	$202	$53	$9,395	$11,685	$7,930
Income Level*													
Low	11,693	7,351	4,342	1,137	2,362	1,036	217	1,682	340	87	6,940	10,556	4,831
Middle	11,807	7,278	4,529	438	2,112	531	239	1,559	240	48	8,487	11,369	6,640
Upper Middle	12,195	7,699	4,496	195	1,748	215	222	1,266	196	44	9,815	12,000	8,309
Upper	12,609	8,046	4,563	109	794	54	128	603	75	36	11,525	12,500	10,811
Independent students	8,739	5,221	3,518	1,197	1,314	723	203	1,510	125	106	5,303	7,542	3,562
Income Level**													
Low	9,788	5,879	3,908	1,738	1,573	1,056	195	1,732	115	87	5,225	8,049	3,290
Middle	8,735	4,885	3,850	1,184	1,401	732	141	1,621	283	128	5,277	7,551	3,246
Upper	7,291	4,588	2,703	467	916	246	273	1,056	0	116	5,388	6,824	4,216

*Unsubsidized loans = unsubsidized Stafford (formerly SLS) and PLUS loans

**Aid not classified as grants, loans, or work-study. Includes assistantships, veterans benefits, military tuition aid, vocational rehabilitation and JTPA

*** Income levels for dependent students (1996 dollars): Low= less than $40,000; Middle = $40-59,999; Upper Middle= $60-79,999; Upper=greater than $80,000

****Income level for independent students (1996 dollars): Low= less than $10,000; Middle = $10-24,999; Upper = greater than $25,000

Source: NCES, NPSAS:87 Undergraduate Students 5/23/97

EXHIBIT 1-13b

Net Price for Private Universities by Dependency Status and Income Level in Current Dollars: 1990
(For All Students—Aided and Unaided)

	Price			Grant Aid				Other Financial Aid			Net Price Formulas		
	Total Price	Tuition and fees	Non-Tuition Price	Federal Grants	Inst. Grants	State Grants	Other Grants	Total Loans	Total work-study	Total Other**	Price-All Grants	Price-Federal Grants	Price-All Aid
Dependent students	$16,124	$11,081	$5,043	$353	$2,170	$382	$244	$1,380	$234	$365	$12,975	$15,771	$10,996
Income Level***													
Low	15,565	10,478	5,087	1,199	3,283	855	248	2,189	423	488	9,981	14,366	6,880
Middle	15,589	10,552	5,037	338	3,113	640	299	1,917	310	428	11,198	15,251	8,544
Upper Middle	15,036	10,255	4,782	79	2,378	235	278	1,494	226	350	12,067	14,958	9,996
Upper	17,009	12,010	5,000	10	1,066	77	204	655	100	277	15,652	16,999	14,620
Independent students	15,291	8,253	7,037	990	1,731	621	380	2,213	168	447	11,569	14,301	8,742
Income Level ****													
Low	15,010	8,911	6,099	1,203	1,888	548	497	1,917	235	632	10,875	13,808	8,091
Middle	14,785	7,459	7,327	951	1,612	745	280	2,421	129	143	11,198	13,835	8,505
Upper	17,519	7,874	9,645	498	1,520	602	243	2,638	56	476	14,656	17,021	11,486

*Unsubsidized loans = unsubsidized Stafford (formerly SLS) and PLUS loans

**Aid not classified as grants, loans, or work-study. Includes assistantships, veterans benefits, military tuition aid, vocational rehabilitation and JTPA

*** Income levels for dependent students (1996 dollars): Low= less than $40,000; Middle = $40-59,999; Upper Middle= $60-79,999; Upper=greater than $80,000

**** Income levels for independent students (1996 dollars): Low= less than $10,000; Middle = $10-24,999; Upper = greater than $25,000

Source: NCES, NPSAS:90 Undergraduate Students 8/14/95

EXHIBIT 1-13c

Net Price for Private Universities by Dependency Status and Income Level in Current Dollars: 1993
(For All Students—Aided and Unaided)

	Price			Grant Aid				Other Financial Aid			Net Price Formulas		
	Total Price	Tuition and fees	Non-Tuition Price	Federal Grants	Inst. Grants	State Grants	Other Grants	Total Loans	Total work-study	Total Other**	Price-All Grants	Price-Federal Grants	Price-All Aid
Dependent students	$20,249	$13,081	$7,168	$320	$2,866	$324	$306	$1,804	$295	$224	$16,433	$19,929	$14,109
Income Level***													
Low	19,237	12,213	7,024	1,356	4,183	974	344	2,935	557	156	12,380	17,881	8,732
Middle	20,294	12,896	7,398	220	4,666	579	752	2,647	506	471	14,077	20,074	10,454
Upper Middle	20,462	13,249	7,213	30	2,721	93	267	1,633	231	300	17,351	20,433	15,187
Upper	20,632	13,491	7,141	13	1,632	26	145	1,136	114	112	18,816	20,618	17,454
Independent students	18,263	10,288	7,974	1,034	1,987	549	288	3,396	229	341	14,404	17,228	10,438
Income Level ****													
Low	18,973	11,400	7,573	1,758	2,901	826	91	3,584	361	588	13,397	17,215	8,864
Middle	18,000	10,277	7,723	870	1,783	373	177	3,706	248	183	14,798	17,130	10,661
Upper	17,461	8,743	8,719	148	874	324	692	2,863	21	138	15,424	17,313	12,401

*Unsubsidized loans = unsubsidized Stafford (formerly SLS) and PLUS loans

**Aid not classified as grants, loans,or work-study. Includes assistantships, veterans benefits, military tuition aid, vocational rehabilitation and JTPA

*** Income levels for dependent students (1996 dollars): Low= less than $40,000; Middle = $40-59,999; Upper Middle= $60-79,999; Upper=greater than $80,000

****Income level for independent students (1996 dollars): Low= less than $10,000; Middle = $10-24,999; Upper = greater than $25,000

Source: NCES, NPSAS:93 Undergraduate Students 10/2/97

EXHIBIT 1-13d

Net Price for Private Universities by Dependency Status and Income Level in Current Dollars: 1996
(For All Students—Aided and Unaided)

	Price			Grant Aid				Other Financial Aid			Net Price Formulas		
	Total Price	Tuition and fees	Non-Tuition Price	Federal Grants	Inst. Grants	State Grants	Other Grants	Total Loans	Total work-study	Total Other**	Price-All Grants	Price-Federal Grants	Price-All Aid
Dependent students	$23,898	$16,124	$7,774	$395	$3,903	$432	$493	$3,182	$403	$416	$18,674	$23,502	$14,674
Income Level***													
Low	23,329	15,714	7,616	1,287	6,067	1,065	787	3,900	684	297	14,123	22,042	9,243
Middle	23,017	15,313	7,703	123	5,493	482	635	3,649	486	634	16,284	22,894	11,514
Upper Middle	23,817	16,114	7,704	60	3,359	193	365	2,970	340	464	19,841	23,757	16,067
Upper	24,762	16,806	7,956	15	1,817	50	269	2,531	185	381	22,611	24,747	19,514
Independent students	19,589	11,467	8,122	865	2,259	626	408	4,294	202	736	15,431	18,724	10,198
Income Level****													
Low	19,668	11,900	7,768	1,476	2,804	771	377	4,790	323	768	14,241	18,193	8,359
Middle	19,305	11,019	8,286	418	1,946	598	369	4,138	125	819	15,974	18,887	10,892
Upper	19,859	11,201	8,658	201	1,532	344	540	3,430	53	531	17,242	19,658	13,228

*Unsubsidized loans = unsubsidized Stafford (formerly SLS) and PLUS loans
**Aid not classified as grants, loans,or work-study. Includes assistantships, veterans benefits, military tuition aid, vocational rehabilitation and JTPA
*** Income levels for dependent students (1996 dollars): Low= less than $40,000; Middle = $40-59,999; Upper Middle= $60-79,999; Upper=greater than $80,000
****Income levels for independent students (1996 dollars): Low= less than $10,000; Middle = $10-24,999; Upper = greater than $25,000
*****Income level for independent students (1996 dollars): Low= less than $10,000; Middle = $10-24,999; Upper = greater than $25,000

Source: NCES, NPSAS:96 Undergraduate Students 10/1/97

EXHIBIT 1-14a

Net Price for Private Colleges by Dependency Status and Income Level in Current Dollars: 1987
(For All Students—Aided and Unaided)

	Price			Grant Aid				Other Financial Aid			Net Price Formulas		
	Total Price	Tuition and fees	Non-Tuition Price	Federal Grants	Inst. Grants	State Grants	Other Grants	Total Loans	Total work-study	Total Other**	Price-All Grants	Price-Federal Grants	Price-All Aid
Dependent students	$9,843	$5,906	$3,937	$490	$1,241	$579	$151	$1,245	$224	$30	$7,381	$9,353	$5,882
Income Level***													
Low	9,226	5,547	3,679	1,140	1,443	1,138	202	1,644	370	25	5,305	8,087	3,267
Middle	9,568	5,783	3,785	340	1,493	617	160	1,481	246	26	6,958	9,228	5,205
Upper Middle	10,123	6,015	4,108	129	1,263	207	157	1,199	148	54	8,367	9,994	6,965
Upper	10,590	6,394	4,197	69	716	92	74	532	71	23	9,639	10,521	9,013
Independent students	7,586	4,899	2,688	1,224	835	824	210	1,497	224	22	4,493	6,363	2,750
Income Level ****													
Low	8,799	5,177	3,622	1,800	996	982	146	1,739	374	28	4,875	6,999	2,734
Middle	7,483	4,623	2,860	1,160	793	923	120	1,487	173	29	4,486	6,323	2,798
Upper	6,212	4,803	1,410	395	632	467	416	1,137	46	5	4,303	5,818	3,115

*Unsubsidized loans = unsubsidized Stafford (formerly SLS) and PLUS loans

**Aid not classified as grants, loans, or work-study. Includes assistantships, veterans benefits, military tuition aid, vocational rehabilitation and JTPA

*** Income levels for dependent students (1996 dollars): Low= less than $40,000; Middle = $40-59,999; Upper Middle= $60-79,999; Upper=greater than $80,000

****Income level for independent students (1996 dollars): Low= less than $10,000; Middle = $10-24,999; Upper = greater than $25,000

Source: NCES, NPSAS:87 Undergraduate Students 5/23/97

EXHIBIT 1-14b

Net Price for Private Colleges by Dependency Status and Income Level in Current Dollars: 1990
(For All Students—Aided and Unaided)

	Price			Grant Aid				Other Financial Aid			Net Price Formulas		
	Total Price	Tuition and fees	Non-Tuition Price	Federal Grants	Inst. Grants	State Grants	Other Grants	Total Loans	Total work-study	Total Other**	Price-All Grants	Price-Federal Grants	Price-All Aid
Dependent students	$11,614	$8,449	$3,166	$484	$1,679	$645	$186	$1,525	$243	$266	$8,621	$11,131	$6,587
Income Level***													
Low	10,768	7,708	3,060	1,243	1,995	1,224	234	1,995	359	319	6,072	9,525	3,399
Middle	11,423	8,272	3,151	280	1,975	686	240	1,851	311	307	8,243	11,143	5,773
Upper Middle	11,730	8,530	3,200	71	1,778	310	184	1,435	182	238	9,386	11,659	7,531
Upper	12,663	9,481	3,182	11	946	127	79	710	84	184	11,501	12,652	10,522
Independent students	12,309	6,626	5,683	1,287	973	885	194	2,066	195	260	8,970	11,022	6,449
Income Level ****													
Low	11,496	7,127	4,369	1,723	1,062	965	125	2,032	261	296	7,622	9,773	5,032
Middle	12,257	6,396	5,861	1,324	976	1,011	109	2,253	220	288	8,837	10,933	6,075
Upper	13,712	6,017	7,695	471	810	589	420	1,900	46	161	11,422	13,241	9,315

*Unsubsidized loans = unsubsidized Stafford (formerly SLS) and PLUS loans

**Aid not classified as grants, loans,or work-study. Includes assistantships, veterans benefits, military tuition aid, vocational rehabilitation and JTPA

*** Income levels for dependent students (1996 dollars): Low= less than $40,000; Middle = $40-59,999; Upper Middle= $60-79,999; Upper=greater than $80,000

****Income level for independent students (1996 dollars): Low= less than $10,000; Middle = $10-24,999; Upper = greater than $25,000

Source: NCES, NPSAS:90 Undergraduate Students 8/14/95

EXHIBIT 1-14c

Net Price for Private Colleges by Dependency Status and Income Level in Current Dollars: 1993
(For All Students—Aided and Unaided)

	Price			Grant Aid				Other Financial Aid			Net Price Formulas		
	Total Price	Tuition and fees	Non-Tuition Price	Federal Grants	Inst. Grants	State Grants	Other Grants	Total Loans	Total work-study	Total Other**	Price-All Grants	Price-Federal Grants	Price-All Aid
Dependent students	$16,146	$10,604	$5,543	$652	$2,433	$488	$184	$1,906	$343	$109	$12,389	$15,494	$10,031
Income Level***													
Low	13,999	8,588	5,411	1,768	2,805	968	214	2,566	541	161	8,244	12,231	4,976
Middle	16,348	10,806	5,542	314	3,762	575	241	2,766	470	198	11,455	16,034	8,022
Upper Middle	16,579	11,080	5,500	59	2,472	186	193	1,625	274	33	13,669	16,520	11,736
Upper	18,307	12,602	5,705	16	1,210	107	129	934	90	57	16,846	18,291	15,766
Independent students	13,978	6,985	6,993	1,414	1,120	661	189	2,550	237	177	10,594	12,564	7,630
Income Level****													
Low	14,195	7,447	6,748	2,078	1,385	785	197	2,475	330	140	9,750	12,117	6,805
Middle	14,154	7,028	7,125	1,333	1,149	720	143	2,811	179	204	10,808	12,821	7,614
Upper	13,519	6,272	7,247	483	692	419	220	2,432	151	210	11,705	13,037	8,912

*Unsubsidized loans = unsubsidized Stafford (formerly SLS) and PLUS loans

**Aid not classified as grants, loans,or work-study. Includes assistantships, veterans benefits, military tuition aid, vocational rehabilitation and JTPA

*** Income levels for dependent students (1996 dollars): Low= less than $40,000; Middle = $40-59,999; Upper Middle= $60-79,999; Upper=greater than $80,000

****Income level for independent students (1996 dollars): Low= less than $10,000; Middle = $10-24,999; Upper = greater than $25,000

Source: NCES, NPSAS:93 Undergraduate Students 10/2/97

EXHIBIT 1-14d

Net Price for Private Colleges by Dependency Status and Income Level in Current Dollars: 1996
(For All Students—Aided and Unaided)

	Price			Grant Aid				Other Financial Aid			Net Price Formulas		
	Total Price	Tuition and fees	Non-Tuition Price	Federal Grants	Inst. Grants	State Grants	Other Grants	Total Loans	Total work-study	Total Other**	Price-All Grants	Price-Federal Grants	Price-All Aid
Dependent students	$17,751	$11,589	$6,162	$628	$3,216	$643	$280	$3,171	$403	$210	$12,984	$17,123	$9,200
Income Level***													
Low	16,514	10,537	5,977	1,533	3,328	1,026	297	3,229	477	233	10,329	14,980	6,391
Middle	17,743	11,637	6,106	174	3,904	765	276	3,727	548	210	12,624	17,569	8,139
Upper Middle	18,530	12,292	6,237	7	3,786	303	338	3,569	327	212	14,096	18,522	9,988
Upper	19,245	12,779	6,466	13	1,969	134	214	2,258	196	172	16,916	19,232	14,290
Independent students	15,471	8,309	7,162	1,212	1,012	850	416	3,914	159	540	11,981	14,259	7,369
Income Level ****													
Low	15,240	8,339	6,901	1,951	1,315	1,208	152	4,319	238	605	10,614	13,290	5,451
Middle	15,409	7,826	7,584	1,036	1,057	741	224	3,414	130	508	12,352	14,374	8,300
Upper	15,872	8,737	7,135	296	523	427	991	3,805	70	473	13,635	15,576	9,287

*Unsubsidized loans = unsubsidized Stafford (formerly SLS) and PLUS loans

**Aid not classified as grants, loans,or work-study. Includes assistantships, veterans benefits, military tuition aid, vocational rehabilitation and JTPA

*** Income levels for dependent students (1996 dollars): Low= less than $40,000; Middle = $40-59,999; Upper Middle= $60-79,999; Upper=greater than $80,000

****Income level for independent students (1996 dollars): Low= less than $10,000; Middle = $10-24,999; Upper = greater than $25,000

Source: NCES, NPSAS:96 Undergraduate Students 10/1/97

EXHIBIT 1-15a

Net Price for Part-Time Students for All Institutions by Dependency Status and Income Level in Current Dollars: 1987
(For All Students—Aided and Unaided)

	Price				Grant Aid				Other Financial Aid			Net Price Formulas		
	Total Price	Converted Total Price	Tuition and fees	Non-Tuition Price	Federal Grants	Inst. Grants	State Grants	Other Grants	Total Loans	Total work-study	Total Other**	Price-All Grants	Price-Federal Grants	Price-All Aid
Dependent students	$3,601	$3,380	$793	$2,587	$116	$119	$47	$43	$158	$26	$65	$3,276	$3,485	$3,027
Income Level***														
Low	3,471	3,182	713	2,470	239	121	87	50	223	48	62	2,974	3,232	2,642
Middle	3,369	3,274	708	2,566	58	116	17	54	134	16	60	3,125	3,311	2,915
Upper Middle	3,782	3,558	874	2,684	18	154	36	30	115	5	86	3,543	3,764	3,337
Upper	4,160	3,762	1,068	2,694	7	75	7	21	73	11	58	4,050	4,153	3,908
Independent students	4,625	3,082	636	2,447	173	76	34	74	182	14	48	4,268	4,452	4,024
Income Level ****														
Low	4,824	4,011	645	3,366	490	87	80	63	376	28	89	4,104	4,334	3,609
Middle	4,654	3,385	646	2,739	245	73	46	32	295	27	54	4,257	4,409	3,882
Upper	4,553	2,691	628	2,063	51	73	16	91	84	5	33	4,322	4,502	4,199

*Unsubsidized loans = unsubsidized Stafford (formerly SLS) and PLUS loans

**Aid not classified as grants, loans,or work-study. Includes assistantships, veterans benefits, military tuition aid, vocational rehabilitation and JTPA

*** Income levels for dependent students (1996 dollars): Low= less than $40,000; Middle = $40-59,999; Upper Middle= $60-79,999; Upper=greater than $80,000

****Income level for independent students (1996 dollars): Low= less than $10,000; Middle = $10-24,999; Upper = greater than $25,000

Source: NCES, NPSAS:87 Undergraduates 5/23/97

EXHIBIT 1-15b

Net Price for Part-Time Students for All Institutions by Dependency Status and Income Level in Current Dollars: 1990
(For All Students—Aided and Unaided)

	Price				Grant Aid				Other Financial Aid			Net Price Formulas		
	Total Price	Converted Total Price	Tuition and fees	Non-Tuition Price	Federal Grants	Inst. Grants	State Grants	Other Grants	Total Loans	Total work-study	Total Other**	Price-All Grants	Price-Federal Grants	Price-All Aid
Dependent students	$6,569	$6,165	$1,642	$4,523	$135	$146	$76	$35	$247	$38	$71	$6,176	$6,433	$5,820
Income Level***														
Low	6,083	5,577	1,381	4,196	325	174	157	38	309	76	65	5,390	5,758	4,939
Middle	6,637	6,449	1,493	4,956	57	132	49	30	263	24	93	6,369	6,580	5,989
Upper Middle	6,532	6,146	1,680	4,466	4	130	22	24	207	14	67	6,353	6,529	6,065
Upper	7,390	6,683	2,255	4,428	8	129	13	45	155	7	61	7,195	7,382	6,972
Independent students	9,237	6,156	938	5,218	180	51	53	107	233	23	27	8,846	9,057	8,563
Income Level ****														
Low	8,400	6,984	1,107	5,877	516	95	109	67	453	70	40	7,613	7,884	7,050
Middle	7,954	5,785	903	4,881	208	43	58	85	266	18	30	7,559	7,746	7,245
Upper	10,210	6,035	901	5,134	54	41	31	132	142	11	21	9,952	10,156	9,779

*Unsubsidized loans = unsubsidized Stafford (formerly SLS) and PLUS loans

**Aid not classified as grants, loans,or work-study. Includes assistantships, veterans benefits, military tuition aid, vocational rehabilitation and JTPA

*** Income levels for dependent students (1996 dollars): Low= less than $40,000; Middle = $40-59,999; Upper Middle= $60-79,999; Upper=greater than $80,000

****Income level for independent students (1996 dollars): Low= less than $10,000; Middle = $10-24,999; Upper = greater than $25,000

Source: NCES, NPSAS:90 Undergraduates 8/14/95

EXHIBIT 1-15c

Net Price for Part-Time Students for All Institutions by Dependency Status and Income Level in Current Dollars: 1993
(For All Students—Aided and Unaided)

| | Price | | | | Grant Aid | | | | Other Financial Aid | | | Net Price Formulas | | |
| | Total Price | Converted | | | Federal Grants | Inst. Grants | State Grants | Other Grants | Total Loans | Total work-study | Total Other** | Price-All Grants | Price-Federal Grants | Price-All Aid |
		Total Price	Tuition and fees	Non-Tuition Price										
Dependent students	$6,870	$6,448	$1,603	$4,845	$192	$176	$71	$31	$369	$48	$16	$6,400	$6,678	$5,966
Income Level***														
Low	7,082	6,493	1,485	5,008	585	167	185	42	635	91	20	6,103	6,497	5,357
Middle	5,956	5,788	1,278	4,510	41	188	39	26	329	36	15	5,663	5,915	5,283
Upper Middle	7,551	7,104	2,155	4,949	14	205	17	23	307	31	22	7,292	7,537	6,933
Upper	8,313	7,517	2,304	5,213	6	195	9	48	200	40	6	8,056	8,307	7,810
Independent students	7,720	5,145	1,087	4,058	281	60	51	115	368	34	43	7,213	7,439	6,768
Income Level ****														
Low	8,384	6,971	1,419	5,552	1,084	97	175	26	948	127	76	7,003	7,300	5,852
Middle	7,691	5,594	1,132	4,462	337	83	58	60	450	36	54	7,153	7,354	6,613
Upper	7,575	4,477	983	3,494	58	39	17	165	187	10	29	7,296	7,517	7,070

*Unsubsidized loans = unsubsidized Stafford (formerly SLS) and PLUS loans

**Aid not classified as grants, loans, or work-study. Includes assistantships, veterans benefits, military tuition aid, vocational rehabilitation and JTPA

*** Income levels for dependent students (1996 dollars): Low= less than $40,000; Middle = $40-59,999; Upper Middle= $60-79,999; Upper=greater than $80,000

****Income level for independent students (1996 dollars): Low= less than $10,000; Middle = $10-24,999; Upper = greater than $25,000

Source: NCES, NPSAS:93 Undergraduate Students 12/4/97

EXHIBIT 1-15d

Net Price for Part-Time Students for All Institutions by Dependency Status and Income Level in Current Dollars: 1996
(For All Students—Aided and Unaided)

	Price			Grant Aid				Other Financial Aid			Net Price Formulas		
	Total Price	Tuition and fees	Non-Tuition Price	Federal Grants	Inst. Grants	State Grants	Other Grants	Total Loans	Total work-study	Total Other**	Price-All Grants	Price-Federal Grants	Price-All Aid
Dependent students	$7,462	$2,031	$5,431	$207	$159	$91	$40	$649	$48	$42	$6,965	$7,255	$6,226
Income Level***													
Low	6,848	1,652	5,196	472	155	151	32	699	65	37	6,038	6,376	5,238
Middle	7,270	1,883	5,387	27	197	66	34	726	39	16	6,946	7,243	6,164
Upper Middle	7,968	2,317	5,650	0	151	44	58	655	29	73	7,715	7,968	6,959
Upper	8,682	2,844	5,838	0	128	26	53	433	36	57	8,475	8,682	7,950
Independent students	5,910	1,291	4,619	305	66	70	140	658	28	103	5,329	5,605	4,540
Income Level****													
Low	6,573	1,480	5,093	798	128	160	44	1,182	88	137	5,443	5,776	4,037
Middle	6,111	1,184	4,927	367	72	75	65	740	27	116	5,533	5,745	4,651
Upper	5,496	1,281	4,215	56	36	29	230	381	4	81	5,147	5,440	4,681

*Unsubsidized loans = unsubsidized Stafford (formerly SLS) and PLUS loans

**Aid not classified as grants, loans, or work-study. Includes assistantships, veterans benefits, military tuition aid, vocational rehabilitation and JTPA

*** Income levels for dependent students (1996 dollars): Low= less than $40,000; Middle = $40-59,999; Upper Middle= $60-79,999; Upper=greater than $80,000

****Income level for independent students (1996 dollars): Low= less than $10,000; Middle = $10-24,999; Upper = greater than $25,000

Source: NCES, NPSAS:96 Undergraduate Students 12/9/97

EXHIBIT 1-16a

Net Price for Part-time Students Attending Public Universities by Dependency Status and Income Level in Current Dollars: 1987
(For All Students—Aided and Unaided)

	Price			Grant Aid				Other Financial Aid			Net Price Formulas		
	Total Price	Tuition and fees	Non-Tuition Price	Federal Grants	Inst. Grants	State Grants	Other Grants	Total Loans	Total work-study	Total Other**	Price-All Grants	Price-Federal Grants	Price-All Aid
Dependent students	$4,902	$1,208	$3,694	$171	$210	$56	$63	$285	$52	$161	$4,401	$4,731	$3,904
Income Level***													
Low	5,017	1,254	3,763	432	356	156	105	536	120	222	3,968	4,585	3,091
Middle	4,846	1,125	3,722	62	184	22	42	295	40	67	4,536	4,784	4,134
Upper Middle	4,648	1,158	3,490	49	207	0	71	85	10	225	4,320	4,599	4,000
Upper	5,087	1,291	3,795	17	7	0	14	90	4	106	5,048	5,069	4,848
Independent students	3,932	893	3,040	257	131	26	71	287	29	147	3,447	3,675	2,983
Income Level ****													
Low	5,024	1,026	3,998	753	215	63	40	661	45	348	3,953	4,272	2,900
Middle	4,238	933	3,304	236	212	49	6	469	86	86	3,734	4,002	3,093
Upper	3,276	825	2,451	69	65	3	109	69	1	92	3,029	3,207	2,868

*Unsubsidized loans = unsubsidized Stafford (formerly SLS) and PLUS loans

**Aid not classified as grants, loans, or work-study. Includes assistantships, veterans benefits, military tuition aid, vocational rehabilitation and JTPA

*** Income levels for dependent students (1996 dollars): Low= less than $40,000; Middle = $40-59,999; Upper Middle= $60-79,999; Upper=greater than $80,000

****Income level for independent students (1996 dollars): Low= less than $10,000; Middle = $10-24,999; Upper = greater than $25,000

Source: NCES, NPSAS:87 Undergraduate Students 5/23/97

EXHIBIT 1-16b

Net Price for Part-time Students Attending Public Universities by Dependency Status and Income Level in Current Dollars: 1990
(For All Students—Aided and Unaided)

	Price			Grant Aid				Other Financial Aid			Net Price Formulas		
	Total Price	Tuition and fees	Non-Tuition Price	Federal Grants	Inst. Grants	State Grants	Other Grants	Total Loans	Total work-study	Total Other**	Price-All Grants	Price-Federal Grants	Price-All Aid
Dependent students	$7,793	$2,066	$5,727	$182	$167	$109	$32	$405	$70	$114	$7,303	$7,611	$6,715
Income Level***													
Low	7,889	1,865	6,024	600	164	341	43	672	206	150	6,741	7,290	5,713
Middle	7,625	1,956	5,669	75	203	45	26	361	53	110	7,276	7,550	6,751
Upper Middle	7,784	2,131	5,653	0	172	13	29	339	0	101	7,570	7,784	7,130
Upper	7,788	2,342	5,446	3	127	11	28	224	0	90	7,619	7,785	7,305
Independent students	7,692	1,398	6,294	366	95	101	103	607	52	61	7,027	7,327	6,308
Income Level ****													
Low	8,206	1,733	6,473	891	161	151	71	976	127	89	6,931	7,315	5,741
Middle	7,251	1,315	5,936	281	84	72	60	674	45	37	6,754	6,970	5,998
Upper	7,613	1,242	6,371	90	62	88	153	329	8	59	7,219	7,522	6,823

*Unsubsidized loans = unsubsidized Stafford (formerly SLS) and PLUS loans

**Aid not classified as grants, loans,or work-study. Includes assistantships, veterans benefits, military tuition aid, vocational rehabilitation and JTPA

*** Income levels for dependent students (1996 dollars): Low= less than $40,000; Middle = $40-59,999; Upper Middle= $60-79,999; Upper=greater than $80,000

****Income level for independent students (1996 dollars): Low= less than $10,000; Middle = $10-24,999; Upper = greater than $25,000

Source: NCES, NPSAS:90 Undergraduates 8/14/95

EXHIBIT 1-16c

Net Price for Part-time Students Attending Public Universities by Dependency Status and Income Level in Current Dollars: 1993

(For All Students—Aided and Unaided)

	Price			Grant Aid				Other Financial Aid			Net Price Formulas		
	Total Price	Tuition and fees	Non-Tuition Price	Federal Grants	Inst. Grants	State Grants	Other Grants	Total Loans	Total work-study	Total Other**	Price-All Grants	Price-Federal Grants	Price-All Aid
Dependent students	$8,444	$2,241	$6,202	$208	$125	$70	$54	$692	$70	$24	$7,987	$8,236	$7,201
Income Level***													
Low	8,366	1,956	6,410	810	103	230	72	1,520	154	37	7,151	7,556	5,440
Middle	8,152	2,113	6,039	81	150	41	63	800	91	20	7,817	8,071	6,906
Upper Middle	8,694	2,491	6,203	6	173	19	22	338	30	38	8,473	8,688	8,068
Upper	8,749	2,446	6,303	3	110	15	63	338	30	5	8,557	8,746	8,183
Independent students	7,004	1,612	5,392	401	74	86	129	865	54	49	6,313	6,602	5,345
Income Level ****													
Low	8,485	1,887	6,599	1,237	164	211	41	1,848	115	90	6,833	7,249	4,780
Middle	7,626	1,735	5,891	362	71	91	65	1,046	78	28	7,037	7,264	5,885
Upper	5,920	1,404	4,517	47	35	26	212	297	10	45	5,601	5,873	5,249

*Unsubsidized loans = unsubsidized Stafford (formerly SLS) and PLUS loans

**Aid not classified as grants, loans, or work-study. Includes assistantships, veterans benefits, military tuition aid, vocational rehabilitation and JTPA

*** Income levels for dependent students (1996 dollars): Low= less than $40,000; Middle = $40-59,999; Upper Middle= $60-79,999; Upper=greater than $80,000

****Income level for independent students (1996 dollars): Low= less than $10,000; Middle = $10-24,999; Upper = greater than $25,000

Source: NCES, NPSAS:96 Undergraduate Students 10/1/97

EXHIBIT 1-16d

Net Price for Part-time Students Attending Public Universities by Dependency Status and Income Level in Current Dollars: 1996

(For All Students—Aided and Unaided)

	Price			Grant Aid				Other Financial Aid			Net Price Formulas		
	Total Price	Tuition and fees	Non-Tuition Price	Federal Grants	Inst. Grants	State Grants	Other Grants	Total Loans	Total work-study	Total Other**	Price-All Grants	Price-Federal Grants	Price-All Aid
Dependent students	$9,946	$3,029	$6,918	$262	$229	$151	$79	$1,371	$83	$58	$9,225	$9,684	$7,713
Income Level***													
Low	9,971	3,062	6,908	719	326	306	64	1,980	97	53	8,555	9,252	6,426
Middle	9,604	2,733	6,871	30	310	113	56	1,416	95	19	9,095	9,574	7,566
Upper Middle	10,113	3,075	7,039	0	162	73	138	1,152	46	41	9,740	10,113	8,501
Upper	10,076	3,194	6,882	0	76	21	74	631	81	112	9,906	10,076	9,082
Independent students	8,454	1,962	6,492	392	84	83	130	1,679	27	116	7,764	8,062	5,943
Income Level ****													
Low	9,284	2,460	6,824	876	73	162	68	2,570	53	186	8,106	8,408	5,297
Middle	8,687	1,922	6,765	430	100	85	104	2,224	30	114	7,968	8,257	5,599
Upper	7,769	1,667	6,101	57	80	32	188	754	8	72	7,413	7,712	6,578

*Unsubsidized loans = unsubsidized Stafford (formerly SLS) and PLUS loans

**Aid not classified as grants, loans,or work-study. Includes assistantships, veterans benefits, military tuition aid, vocational rehabilitation and JTPA

*** Income levels for dependent students (1996 dollars): Low= less than $40,000; Middle = $40-59,999; Upper Middle= $60-79,999; Upper=greater than $80,000

****Income level for independent students (1996 dollars): Low= less than $10,000; Middle = $10-24,999; Upper = greater than $25,000

Source: NCES, NPSAS:96 Undergraduate Students 11/20/97

EXHIBIT 1-17a

Net Price for Part-Time Students Attending Public Colleges by Dependency Status and Income Level in Current Dollars: 1987
(For All Students—Aided and Unaided)

	Price			Grant Aid				Other Financial Aid			Net Price Formulas		
	Total Price	Tuition and fees	Non-Tuition Price	Federal Grants	Inst. Grants	State Grants	Other Grants	Total Loans	Total work-study	Total Other**	Price-All Grants	Price-Federal Grants	Price-All Aid
Dependent students	$3,632	$903	$2,728	$148	$110	$74	$17	$240	$29	$49	$3,284	$3,484	$2,965
Income Level***													
Low	3,717	915	2,802	346	97	166	23	356	51	20	3,085	3,371	2,658
Middle	3,735	912	2,823	30	31	26	27	158	29	105	3,621	3,705	3,328
Upper Middle	3,637	966	2,671	13	246	5	0	305	10	0	3,374	3,625	3,059
Upper	3,147	788	2,359	0	98	0	4	2	0	95	3,045	3,147	2,947
Independent students	3,481	668	2,813	171	47	40	34	202	18	60	3,189	3,310	2,908
Income Level ****													
Low	4,640	808	3,832	444	59	113	10	411	34	80	4,013	4,196	3,488
Middle	3,915	692	3,223	247	52	58	19	330	14	110	3,540	3,668	3,085
Upper	2,926	619	2,307	67	42	13	47	94	14	38	2,756	2,859	2,611

*Unsubsidized loans = unsubsidized Stafford (formerly SLS) and PLUS loans
**Aid not classified as grants, loans, or work-study. Includes assistantships, veterans benefits, military tuition aid, vocational rehabilitation and JTPA
*** Income levels for dependent students (1996 dollars): Low= less than $40,000; Middle = $40-59,999; Upper Middle= $60-79,999; Upper=greater than $80,000
****Income level for independent students (1996 dollars): Low= less than $10,000; Middle = $10-24,999; Upper = greater than $25,000

Source: NCES, NPSAS:87 Undergraduates 5/23/97

EXHIBIT 1-17b

Net Price for Part-time Students Attending Public Colleges by Dependency Status and Income Level in Current Dollars: 1990
(For All Students—Aided and Unaided)

	Price			Grant Aid				Other Financial Aid			Net Price Formulas		
	Total Price	Tuition and fees	Non-Tuition Price	Federal Grants	Inst. Grants	State Grants	Other Grants	Total Loans	Total work-study	Total Other**	Price-All Grants	Price-Federal Grants	Price-All Aid
Dependent students	$6,305	$1,656	$4,648	$212	$95	$83	$35	$394	$41	$54	$5,880	$6,093	$5,390
Income Level***													
Low	6,470	1,651	4,819	487	106	182	51	489	81	30	5,645	5,983	5,045
Middle	6,748	1,657	5,091	97	89	45	45	517	10	95	6,473	6,651	5,850
Upper Middle	5,713	1,667	4,047	12	70	11	18	305	37	62	5,603	5,702	5,199
Upper	5,781	1,654	4,128	0	110	0	6	86	3	35	5,665	5,781	5,542
Independent students	7,490	1,121	6,369	267	33	69	87	371	36	28	7,033	7,222	6,598
Income Level ****													
Low	8,111	1,241	6,871	679	30	144	34	725	46	16	7,224	7,432	6,437
Middle	7,550	1,239	6,310	288	42	81	78	377	41	46	7,061	7,261	6,598
Upper	7,135	1,002	6,133	93	28	32	114	229	29	23	6,868	7,042	6,588

*Unsubsidized loans = unsubsidized Stafford (formerly SLS) and PLUS loans
**Aid not classified as grants, loans,or work-study. Includes assistantships, veterans benefits, military tuition aid, vocational rehabilitation and JTPA
*** Income levels for dependent students (1996 dollars): Low= less than $40,000; Middle = $40-59,999; Upper Middle= $60-79,999; Upper=greater than $80,000
****Income level for independent students (1996 dollars): Low= less than $10,000; Middle = $10-24,999; Upper = greater than $25,000

Source: NCES, NPSAS:90 Undergraduates 8/14/95

EXHIBIT 1-17c

Net Price for Part-time Students Attending Public Colleges by Dependency Status and Income Level in Current Dollars: 1993
(For All Students—Aided and Unaided)

	Price			Grant Aid				Other Financial Aid			Net Price Formulas		
	Total Price	Tuition and fees	Non-Tuition Price	Federal Grants	Inst. Grants	State Grants	Other Grants	Total Loans	Total work-study	Total Other**	Price-All Grants	Price-Federal Grants	Price-All Aid
Dependent students	$6,913	$1,684	$5,229	$327	$93	$110	$30	$487	$71	$13	$6,353	$6,586	$5,782
Income Level***													
Low	7,112	1,687	5,425	992	139	300	38	929	110	34	5,642	6,119	4,569
Middle	6,892	1,603	5,289	81	108	57	37	544	63	3	6,609	6,810	5,999
Upper Middle	6,505	1,631	4,874	3	17	10	8	237	17	11	6,466	6,502	6,201
Upper	7,263	2,033	5,230	5	25	0	51	109	129	0	7,182	7,258	6,944
Independent students	6,527	1,191	5,336	364	38	86	85	530	30	32	5,953	6,163	5,362
Income Level ****													
Low	7,957	1,475	6,481	1,183	60	257	41	1,535	89	78	6,415	6,773	4,713
Middle	7,153	1,240	5,913	407	49	75	91	490	22	22	6,531	6,746	5,997
Upper	5,707	1,070	4,637	77	24	38	96	232	15	23	5,471	5,629	5,200

*Unsubsidized loans = unsubsidized Stafford (formerly SLS) and PLUS loans
**Aid not classified as grants, loans,or work-study. Includes assistantships, veterans benefits, military tuition aid, vocational rehabilitation and JTPA
*** Income levels for dependent students (1996 dollars): Low= less than $40,000; Middle = $40-59,999; Upper Middle= $60-79,999; Upper=greater than $80,000
****Income level for independent students (1996 dollars): Low= less than $10,000; Middle = $10-24,999; Upper = greater than $25,000

Source: NCES, NPSAS:93 Undergraduate Students 11/20/97

EXHIBIT 1-17d

Net Price for Part-time Students Attending Public Colleges by Dependency Status and Income Level in Current Dollars: 1996
(For All Students—Aided and Unaided)

	Price			Grant Aid				Other Financial Aid			Net Price Formulas		
	Total Price	Tuition and fees	Non-Tuition Price	Federal Grants	Inst. Grants	State Grants	Other Grants	Total Loans	Total work-study	Total Other**	Price-All Grants	Price-Federal Grants	Price-All Aid
Dependent students	$8,002	$2,221	$5,782	$244	$147	$119	$22	$933	$114	$45	$7,469	$7,758	$6,377
Income Level***													
Low	8,408	2,281	6,127	721	188	241	15	1,076	286	59	7,243	7,687	5,822
Middle	7,411	2,150	5,262	33	240	106	34	955	47	35	6,998	7,379	5,962
Upper Middle	7,974	2,238	5,736	0	0	14	35	798	0	60	7,926	7,974	7,069
Upper	8,236	2,203	6,033	0	103	43	2	800	40	16	8,088	8,236	7,231
Independent students	7,320	1,688	5,632	351	79	61	120	1,153	45	94	6,709	6,969	5,418
Income Level ****													
Low	8,167	1,972	6,194	915	247	149	52	2,170	128	85	6,805	7,252	4,422
Middle	7,538	1,691	5,847	414	40	73	66	1,395	47	128	6,945	7,124	5,375
Upper	6,837	1,565	5,272	75	28	16	179	583	8	79	6,539	6,762	5,870

*Unsubsidized loans = unsubsidized Stafford (formerly SLS) and PLUS loans
**Aid not classified as grants, loans, or work-study. Includes assistantships, veterans benefits, military tuition aid, vocational rehabilitation and JTPA
***Income levels for dependent students (1996 dollars): Low= less than $40,000; Middle= $40-59,999; Upper Middle= $60-79,999; Upper=greater than $80,000
****Income level for independent students (1996 dollars): Low= less than $10,000; Middle = $10-24,999; Upper = greater than $25,000

Source: NCES, NPSAS:96 Undergraduate Students 11/20/97

EXHIBIT 1-18a

Net Price for Part-time Students Attending Public Two-Year Colleges by Dependency Status and Income Level in Current Dollars: 1987

(For All Students—Aided and Unaided)

	Price			Grant Aid				Other Financial Aid			Net Price Formulas		
	Total Price	Tuition and fees	Non-Tuition Price	Federal Grants	Inst. Grants	State Grants	Other Grants	Total Loans	Total work-study	Total Other**	Price-All Grants	Price-Federal Grants	Price-All Aid
Dependent students	$2,510	$325	$2,185	$92	$36	$23	$24	$46	$12	$36	$2,335	$2,419	$2,241
Income Level***													
Low	2,458	320	2,138	164	32	32	19	75	28	28	2,212	2,294	2,082
Middle	2,577	351	2,226	65	66	3	48	44	0	53	2,395	2,512	2,299
Upper Middle	2,539	318	2,220	4	18	52	1	0	0	51	2,464	2,535	2,413
Upper	2,414	289	2,125	2	2	0	16	1	0	0	2,395	2,412	2,393
Independent students	2,504	291	2,214	161	42	27	41	128	10	26	2,233	2,344	2,070
Income Level ****													
Low	3,337	325	3,013	431	35	64	65	274	22	29	2,742	2,906	2,418
Middle	2,786	302	2,484	243	17	31	18	195	14	41	2,477	2,543	2,227
Upper	2,181	276	1,905	46	53	14	41	58	5	19	2,027	2,135	1,945

*Unsubsidized loans = unsubsidized Stafford (formerly SLS) and PLUS loans

**Aid not classified as grants, loans,or work-study. Includes assistantships, veterans benefits, military tuition aid, vocational rehabilitation and JTPA

*** Income levels for dependent students (1996 dollars): Low= less than $40,000; Middle = $40,000; Middle= $40-59,999; Upper Middle= $60-79,999; Upper=greater than $80,000

****Income level for independent students (1996 dollars): Low= less than $10,000; Middle = $10-24,999; Upper = greater than $25,000

Source: NCES, NPSAS:87 Undergraduates 5/23/97

EXHIBIT 1-18b

Net Price for Part-time Students Attending Public Two-Year Colleges by Dependency Status and Income Level in Current Dollars: 1990
(For All Students—Aided and Unaided)

	Price			Grant Aid				Other Financial Aid			Net Price Formulas		
	Total Price	Tuition and fees	Non-Tuition Price	Federal Grants	Inst. Grants	State Grants	Other Grants	Total Loans	Total work-study	Total Other**	Price-All Grants	Price-Federal Grants	Price-All Aid
Dependent students	$4,566	$550	$4,016	$62	$20	$13	$20	$14	$8	$20	$4,451	$4,504	$4,409
Income Level***													
Low	4,198	507	3,691	133	31	24	26	9	19	38	3,985	4,066	3,918
Middle	5,345	546	4,799	18	13	6	20	33	0	14	5,288	5,327	5,241
Upper Middle	4,469	630	3,839	0	19	4	11	8	0	0	4,435	4,469	4,427
Upper	4,382	581	3,801	15	3	2	16	4	0	6	4,347	4,367	4,336
Independent students	4,965	403	4,561	117	11	20	47	67	16	10	4,769	4,848	4,676
Income Level ****													
Low	5,663	396	5,267	283	29	49	56	109	51	18	5,246	5,379	5,068
Middle	4,649	448	4,200	165	12	26	55	90	9	14	4,390	4,483	4,277
Upper	4,895	381	4,514	40	5	9	41	43	9	5	4,801	4,855	4,743

*Unsubsidized loans = unsubsidized Stafford (formerly SLS) and PLUS loans

**Aid not classified as grants, loans,or work-study. Includes assistantships, veterans benefits, military tuition aid, vocational rehabilitation and JTPA

*** Income levels for dependent students (1996 dollars): Low= less than $40,000; Middle = $40-59,999; Upper Middle= $60-79,999; Upper=greater than $80,000

****Income level for independent students (1996 dollars): Low= less than $10,000; Middle = $10-24,999; Upper = greater than $25,000

Source: NCES, NPSAS:90 Undergraduates 8/14/95

EXHIBIT 1-18c

Net Price for Part-time Students Attending Public Two-Year Colleges by Dependency Status and Income Level in Current Dollars: 1993

(For All Students—Aided and Unaided)

	Price			Grant Aid					Other Financial Aid			Net Price Formulas		
	Total Price	Tuition and fees	Non-Tuition Price	Federal Grants	Inst. Grants	State Grants	Other Grants	Total Loans	Total work-study	Total Other**	Price-All Grants	Price-Federal Grants	Price-All Aid
Dependent students	$4,937	$643	$4,295	$115	$18	$36	$8	$70	$22	$5	$4,760	$4,822	$4,663
Income Level***													
Low	5,272	672	4,600	322	25	90	17	137	53	11	4,817	4,949	4,616
Middle	4,668	606	4,061	16	13	21	7	59	11	3	4,612	4,652	4,539
Upper Middle	4,746	698	4,048	12	11	0	0	42	9	9	4,723	4,734	4,663
Upper	5,302	687	4,615	0	32	0	1	0	0	0	5,269	5,302	5,269
Independent students	4,046	528	3,518	237	20	27	75	171	29	41	3,687	3,809	3,446
Income Level ****													
Low	5,696	716	4,980	973	34	109	12	388	122	42	4,568	4,723	4,016
Middle	4,419	567	3,852	298	32	33	35	226	30	65	4,021	4,121	3,699
Upper	3,522	470	3,052	56	10	7	108	99	9	29	3,341	3,466	3,205

*Unsubsidized loans = unsubsidized Stafford (formerly SLS) and PLUS loans

**Aid not classified as grants, loans,or work-study. Includes assistantships, veterans benefits, military tuition aid, vocational rehabilitation and JTPA

*** Income levels for dependent students (1996 dollars): Low= less than $40,000; Middle= $40-59,999; Upper Middle= $60-79,999; Upper=greater than $80,000

****Income level for independent students (1996 dollars): Low= less than $10,000; Middle = $10-24,999; Upper = greater than $25,000

Source: NCES, NPSAS:93 Undergraduate Students 11/20/97

EXHIBIT 1-18d

Net Price for Part-time Students Attending Public Two-Year Colleges by Dependency Status and Income Level in Current Dollars: 1996
(For All Students—Aided and Unaided)

	Price			Grant Aid				Other Financial Aid			Net Price Formulas		
	Total Price	Tuition and fees	Non-Tuition Price	Federal Grants	Inst. Grants	State Grants	Other Grants	Total Loans	Total work-study	Total Other**	Price-All Grants	Price-Federal Grants	Price-All Aid
Dependent students	$5,599	$787	$4,813	$160	$37	$32	$11	$147	$14	$8	$5,360	$5,439	$5,192
Income Level***													
Low	5,368	747	4,621	325	37	58	8	173	24	8	4,939	5,042	4,734
Middle	5,723	813	4,909	23	36	11	22	163	10	8	5,631	5,700	5,451
Upper Middle	5,741	840	4,902	0	35	0	4	81	0	9	5,702	5,741	5,613
Upper	6,023	822	5,201	0	40	12	9	107	0	4	5,962	6,023	5,851
Independent students	4,661	608	4,053	290	30	48	62	254	26	79	4,231	4,371	3,872
Income Level ****													
Low	5,028	660	4,368	756	54	126	24	520	90	104	4,068	4,272	3,354
Middle	5,123	651	4,472	345	42	46	34	255	22	95	4,656	4,777	4,284
Upper	4,164	554	3,609	53	12	18	99	141	1	57	3,982	4,111	3,784

*Unsubsidized loans = unsubsidized Stafford (formerly SLS) and PLUS loans

**Aid not classified as grants, loans, or work-study. Includes assistantships, veterans benefits, military tuition aid, vocational rehabilitation and JTPA

*** Income levels for dependent students (1996 dollars): Low= less than $40,000; Middle = $40-59,999; Upper Middle= $60-79,999; Upper=greater than $80,000

**** Income level for independent students (1996 dollars): Low= less than $10,000; Middle = $10-24,999; Upper = greater than $25,000

Source: NCES, NPSAS:96 Undergraduate Students 11/20/97

EXHIBIT 1-19a

Net Price for Part-time Students Attending Private Universities by Dependency Status and Income Level in Current Dollars: 1987
(For All Students—Aided and Unaided)

	Price			Grant Aid				Other Financial Aid			Net Price Formulas		
	Total Price	Tuition and fees	Non-Tuition Price	Federal Grants	Inst. Grants	State Grants	Other Grants	Total Loans	Total work-study	Total Other**	Price-All Grants	Price-Federal Grants	Price-All Aid
Dependent students	$6,348	$3,267	$3,081	$133	$830	$143	$220	$496	$68	$141	$5,023	$6,216	$4,318
Income Level***													
Low	5,392	2,966	2,426	390	857	364	396	567	55	190	3,385	5,002	2,574
Middle	5,069	2,765	2,305	53	990	68	111	542	171	81	3,848	5,017	3,054
Upper Middle	7,254	3,289	3,965	13	918	84	228	898	44	168	6,012	7,241	4,902
Upper	6,918	3,907	3,011	0	632	8	111	140	23	117	6,166	6,918	5,886
Independent students	5,482	2,232	3,250	149	369	64	324	354	27	61	4,576	5,333	4,135
Income Level ****													
Low	5,690	2,301	3,388	521	443	223	51	568	37	27	4,452	5,168	3,820
Middle	5,809	2,433	3,376	227	439	84	215	699	133	0	4,844	5,581	4,011
Upper	5,274	2,161	3,113	50	338	25	409	231	1	81	4,452	5,225	4,139

*Unsubsidized loans = unsubsidized Stafford (formerly SLS) and PLUS loans

**Aid not classified as grants, loans,or work-study. Includes assistantships, veterans benefits, military tuition aid, vocational rehabilitation and JTPA

*** Income levels for dependent students (1996 dollars): Low= less than $40,000; Middle = $40-59,999; Upper Middle= $60-79,999; Upper=greater than $80,000

****Income level for independent students (1996 dollars): Low= less than $10,000; Middle = $10-24,999; Upper = greater than $25,000

Source: NCES, NPSAS:87 Undergraduate Students 5/23/97

EXHIBIT 1-19b

Net Price for Part-time Students Attending Private Universities by Dependency Status and Income Level in Current Dollars: 1990
(For All Students—Aided and Unaided)

	Price			Grant Aid				Other Financial Aid			Net Price Formulas		
	Total Price	Tuition and fees	Non-Tuition Price	Federal Grants	Inst. Grants	State Grants	Other Grants	Total Loans	Total work-study	Total Other**	Price-All Grants	Price-Federal Grants	Price-All Aid
Dependent students	$13,673	$8,076	$5,598	$272	$1,152	$329	$178	$1,006	$150	$226	$11,742	$13,401	$10,359
Income Level***													
Low	11,292	7,370	3,923	813	2,006	666	115	1,548	237	142	7,691	10,479	5,764
Middle	11,725	7,330	4,395	164	829	473	23	1,119	110	208	10,236	11,561	8,799
Upper Middle	14,417	7,992	6,425	44	1,074	202	157	1,014	143	264	12,939	14,373	11,518
Upper	14,671	8,978	5,693	9	668	67	303	536	104	281	13,624	14,663	12,703
Independent students	11,820	4,337	7,483	261	422	154	556	584	24	137	10,426	11,559	9,682
Income Level ****													
Low	11,818	5,387	6,431	902	682	344	248	1,146	110	215	9,642	10,915	8,171
Middle	11,540	4,499	7,040	273	379	275	629	741	7	199	9,983	11,266	9,036
Upper	11,828	3,907	7,921	37	351	41	632	329	1	86	10,767	11,791	10,352

*Unsubsidized loans = unsubsidized Stafford (formerly SLS) and PLUS loans

**Aid not classified as grants, loans, or work-study. Includes assistantships, veterans benefits, military tuition aid, vocational rehabilitation and JTPA

*** Income levels for dependent students (1996 dollars): Low= less than $40,000; Middle = $40-59,999; Upper Middle= $60-79,999; Upper=greater than $80,000

****Income level for independent students (1996 dollars): Low= less than $10,000; Middle = $10-24,999; Upper = greater than $25,000

Source: NCES, NPSAS:90 Undergraduates 8/14/95

EXHIBIT 1-19c

Net Price for Part-time Students Attending Private Universities by Dependency Status and Income Level in Current Dollars: 1993
(For All Students—Aided and Unaided)

	Price			Grant Aid				Other Financial Aid			Net Price Formulas		
	Total Price	Tuition and fees	Non-Tuition Price	Federal Grants	Inst. Grants	State Grants	Other Grants	Total Loans	Total work-study	Total Other**	Price-All Grants	Price-Federal Grants	Price-All Aid
Dependent students	$13,048	$7,124	$5,925	$215	$1,349	$157	$125	$1,229	$86	$103	$11,202	$12,833	$9,784
Income Level***													
Low	13,237	7,714	5,523	944	1,510	697	236	1,901	206	0	9,851	12,293	7,744
Middle	13,306	7,454	5,852	25	2,007	2	229	1,961	64	320	11,041	13,280	8,696
Upper Middle	12,667	6,584	6,084	75	1,147	58	91	1,145	76	24	11,296	12,592	10,051
Upper	13,005	7,654	5,351	58	1,118	44	39	628	56	63	11,747	12,948	10,999
Independent students	9,228	4,391	4,837	206	414	118	370	883	72	28	8,120	9,022	7,136
Income Level ****													
Low	10,086	4,625	5,461	966	254	469	0	1,254	380	10	8,397	9,120	6,754
Middle	9,973	4,728	5,246	277	571	165	121	1,245	66	86	8,840	9,697	7,443
Upper	8,757	4,208	4,549	33	378	33	545	659	17	7	7,768	8,724	7,085

*Unsubsidized loans = unsubsidized Stafford (formerly SLS) and PLUS loans

**Aid not classified as grants, loans,or work-study. Includes assistantships, veterans benefits, military tuition aid, vocational rehabilitation and JTPA

*** Income levels for dependent students (1996 dollars): Low= less than $40,000; Middle = $40-59,999; Upper Middle= $60-79,999; Upper=greater than $80,000

****Income level for independent students (1996 dollars): Low= less than $10,000; Middle = $10-24,999; Upper = greater than $25,000

Source: NCES, NPSAS:93 Undergraduate Students 11/20/97

EXHIBIT 1-19d

Net Price for Part-time Private Universities by Dependency Status and Income Level in Current Dollars: 1996
(For All Students—Aided and Unaided)

	Price			Grant Aid				Other Financial Aid			Net Price Formulas		
	Total Price	Tuition and fees	Non-Tuition Price	Federal Grants	Inst. Grants	State Grants	Other Grants	Total Loans	Total work-study	Total Other**	Price-All Grants	Price-Federal Grants	Price-All Aid
Dependent students	$15,751	$9,556	$6,195	$321	$924	$239	$245	$2,273	$156	$434	$14,022	$15,430	$11,160
Income Level***													
Low	13,123	7,242	5,880	990	811	582	546	2,820	208	221	10,194	12,133	6,946
Middle	low n	low n	low n	low n	low n	low n	low n	low n	low n	low n	low n	low n	low n
Upper Middle	17,900	11,404	6,496	0	1,433	140	63	2,333	334	1,340	16,264	17,900	12,257
Upper	17,372	10,934	6,438	0	464	5	149	1,473	18	266	16,755	17,372	14,998
Independent students	10,798	5,388	5,409	193	358	175	680	1,469	32	530	9,392	10,605	7,361
Income Level ****													
Low	11,847	6,131	5,716	630	758	267	69	2,024	46	993	10,123	11,217	7,060
Middle	11,389	5,506	5,883	249	443	313	304	1,872	70	585	10,079	11,140	7,552
Upper	10,183	5,085	5,098	20	185	83	1,052	1,104	11	349	8,843	10,163	7,380

*Unsubsidized loans = unsubsidized Stafford (formerly SLS) and PLUS loans

**Aid not classified as grants, loans, or work-study. Includes assistantships, veterans benefits, military tuition aid, vocational rehabilitation and JTPA

*** Income levels for dependent students (1996 dollars): Low= less than $40,000; Middle = $40,000-59,999; Upper Middle= $60-79,999; Upper=greater than $80,000

****Income level for independent students (1996 dollars): Low= less than $10,000; Middle = $10-24,999; Upper = greater than $25,000

Source: NCES, NPSAS:96 Undergraduate Students 11/20/97

EXHIBIT 1-20a

Net Price for Part-time Students Attending Private Colleges by Dependency Status and Income Level in Current Dollars: 1987
(For All Students—Aided and Unaided)

	Price			Grant Aid				Other Financial Aid			Net Price Formulas		
	Total Price	Tuition and fees	Non-Tuition Price	Federal Grants	Inst. Grants	State Grants	Other Grants	Total Loans	Total work-study	Total Other**	Price-All Grants	Price-Federal Grants	Price-All Aid
Dependent students	$5,406	$2,666	$2,740	$108	$294	$150	$141	$534	$55	$45	$4,713	$5,298	$4,079
Income Level***													
Low	5,407	2,848	2,559	288	307	274	219	777	89	62	4,319	5,119	3,392
Middle	5,273	2,296	2,977	23	264	116	201	479	18	0	4,670	5,250	4,172
Upper Middle	5,275	2,816	2,459	39	448	86	82	309	0	0	4,621	5,236	4,312
Upper	5,606	2,698	2,909	21	177	78	24	462	96	111	5,307	5,585	4,638
Independent students	4,407	2,004	2,403	144	141	71	266	312	10	30	3,785	4,263	3,432
Income Level ****													
Low	5,629	2,016	3,614	516	186	156	234	582	42	122	4,538	5,114	3,792
Middle	5,105	2,422	2,683	296	167	154	169	625	0	14	4,319	4,809	3,680
Upper	3,944	1,913	2,032	45	127	38	295	195	7	18	3,440	3,900	3,220

*Unsubsidized loans = unsubsidized Stafford (formerly SLS) and PLUS loans

**Aid not classified as grants, loans, or work-study. Includes assistantships, veterans benefits, military tuition aid, vocational rehabilitation and JTPA

***Income levels for dependent students (1996 dollars): Low= less than $40,000; Middle = $40-59,999; Upper Middle= $60-79,999; Upper=greater than $80,000

****Income level for independent students (1996 dollars): Low= less than $10,000; Middle = $10-24,999; Upper = greater than $25,000

Source: NCES, NPSAS:87 Undergraduate Students 5/23/97

EXHIBIT 1-20b

Net Price for Part-time Students Attending Private Colleges by Dependency Status and Income Level in Current Dollars: 1990
(For All Students—Aided and Unaided)

	Price			Grant Aid				Other Financial Aid			Net Price Formulas		
	Total Price	Tuition and fees	Non-Tuition Price	Federal Grants	Inst. Grants	State Grants	Other Grants	Total Loans	Total work-study	Total Other**	Price-All Grants	Price-Federal Grants	Price-All Aid
Dependent students	$9,645	$6,069	$3,576	$313	$793	$370	$97	$857	$93	$337	$8,072	$9,333	$6,785
Income Level***													
Low	8,652	5,901	2,751	809	1,160	720	77	1,282	176	160	5,886	7,844	4,269
Middle	10,042	5,841	4,201	188	874	370	110	859	123	867	8,500	9,854	6,651
Upper Middle	8,817	4,940	3,877	0	533	158	61	505	45	427	8,065	8,817	7,088
Upper	10,798	7,184	3,614	0	452	77	136	562	0	102	10,132	10,798	9,468
Independent students	8,844	2,937	5,907	188	194	169	474	560	8	60	7,819	8,655	7,190
Income Level ****													
Low	11,621	4,277	7,344	997	476	473	184	1,128	86	24	9,491	10,624	8,253
Middle	8,473	2,866	5,606	300	166	265	300	839	1	82	7,442	8,172	6,519
Upper	8,312	2,797	5,516	57	168	103	562	408	1	58	7,422	8,255	6,954

*Unsubsidized loans = unsubsidized Stafford (formerly SLS) and PLUS loans

**Aid not classified as grants, loans,or work-study. Includes assistantships, veterans benefits, military tuition aid, vocational rehabilitation and JTPA

*** Income levels for dependent students (1996 dollars): Low= less than $40,000; Middle = $40-59,999; Upper Middle= $60-79,999; Upper=greater than $80,000

****Income level for independent students (1996 dollars): Low= less than $10,000; Middle = $10-24,999; Upper = greater than $25,000

Source: NCES, NPSAS:90 Undergraduates 8/14/95

EXHIBIT 1-20c

Net Price for Part-time Students Attending Private Colleges by Dependency Status and Income Level in Current Dollars: 1993
(For All Students—Aided and Unaided)

	Price			Grant Aid				Other Financial Aid			Net Price Formulas		
	Total Price	Tuition and fees	Non-Tuition Price	Federal Grants	Inst. Grants	State Grants	Other Grants	Total Loans	Total work-study	Total Other**	Price-All Grants	Price-Federal Grants	Price-All Aid
Dependent students	$10,828	$6,263	$4,565	$581	$1,417	$278	$138	$1,485	$172	$44	$8,414	$10,247	$6,713
Income Level***													
Low	9,515	4,929	4,586	1,351	1,088	479	139	1,888	194	41	6,459	8,164	4,336
Middle	11,193	6,957	4,237	275	2,906	373	88	2,085	203	81	7,552	10,919	5,183
Upper Middle	11,769	6,926	4,843	22	1,026	84	136	1,096	146	55	10,501	11,747	9,203
Upper	12,363	7,862	4,501	2	894	16	223	522	96	3	11,228	12,361	10,608
Independent students	7,371	3,160	4,211	367	231	108	347	771	35	74	6,318	7,004	5,437
Income Level ****													
Low	9,538	3,953	5,584	1,383	405	278	70	1,669	160	301	7,402	8,155	5,272
Middle	8,453	3,810	4,643	578	454	170	210	1,163	33	36	7,041	7,875	5,810
Upper	6,535	2,764	3,771	73	117	50	454	442	9	38	5,840	6,462	5,351

*Unsubsidized loans = unsubsidized Stafford (formerly SLS) and PLUS loans

**Aid not classified as grants, loans,or work-study. Includes assistantships, veterans benefits, military tuition aid, vocational rehabilitation and JTPA

*** Income levels for dependent students (1996 dollars): Low= less than $40,000; Middle = $40-59,999; Upper Middle= $60-79,999; Upper=greater than $80,000

****Income level for independent students (1996 dollars): Low= less than $10,000; Middle = $10-24,999; Upper = greater than $25,000

Source: NCES, NPSAS:93 Undergraduate Students 11/20/97

EXHIBIT 1-20d

Net Price for Part-time Students Attending Private Colleges by Dependency Status and Income Level in Current Dollars: 1996 (For All Students—Aided and Unaided)

	Price			Grant Aid				Other Financial Aid			Net Price Formulas		
	Total Price	Tuition and fees	Non-Tuition Price	Federal Grants	Inst. Grants	State Grants	Other Grants	Total Loans	Total work-study	Total Other**	Price-All Grants	Price-Federal Grants	Price-All Aid
Dependent students	$12,664	$7,117	$5,548	$379	$798	$372	$139	$1,983	$112	$129	$10,976	$12,285	$8,752
Income Level***													
Low	10,730	5,428	5,302	981	800	542	34	1,823	111	247	8,374	9,749	6,193
Middle	13,285	7,705	5,580	44	964	351	76	3,138	121	46	11,851	13,242	8,546
Upper Middle	14,583	7,909	6,674	0	737	342	305	2,800	108	57	13,200	14,583	10,234
Upper	13,798	8,740	5,058	0	679	132	251	469	106	70	12,737	13,798	12,092
Independent students	8,681	3,868	4,813	280	205	203	632	1,500	25	143	7,362	8,402	5,694
Income Level ****													
Low	9,825	4,329	5,496	852	499	485	172	1,976	87	75	7,818	8,973	5,680
Middle	9,193	3,867	5,326	482	305	319	293	2,530	23	165	7,794	8,712	5,077
Upper	8,210	3,755	4,455	64	96	90	872	1,000	10	152	7,088	8,146	5,927

*Unsubsidized loans = unsubsidized Stafford (formerly SLS) and PLUS loans

**Aid not classified as grants, loans,or work-study. Includes assistantships, veterans benefits, military tuition aid, vocational rehabilitation and JTPA

*** Income levels for dependent students (1996 dollars): Low= less than $40,000; Middle = $40-59,999; Upper Middle= $60-79,999; Upper=greater than $80,000

****Income level for independent students (1996 dollars): Low= less than $10,000; Middle = $10-24,999; Upper = greater than $25,000

Source: NCES, NPSAS:96 Undergraduate Students 11/20/97

EXHIBIT 1-21
Average Household Income by Quintile: 1975-1996
(in Constant 1996 Dollars)

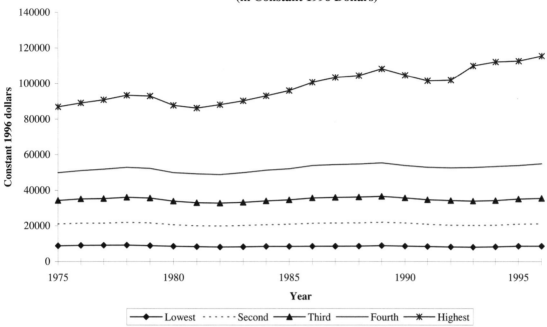

Sources: U.S. Census Bureau;
"Mean Income Received by Each Fifth and Top 5 Percent of Households, (All Races)=1967-1996;" last revised September 29, 1997
<http://www.census.gov/hhes/income/histinc/f03.html>

EXHIBIT 1-22

Ratio of Tuition to Income by Type of Institution for Selected Income Quintiles: 1975 to 1996

	1975	1980	1985	1990	1995	1996
Public Universities						
lowest quintile	0.20	0.19	0.24	0.28	0.36	0.37
middle quintile	0.05	0.05	0.06	0.07	0.09	0.09
top quintile	0.02	0.02	0.02	0.02	0.03	0.03
Public Colleges						
lowest quintile	0.15	0.15	0.19	0.22	0.30	0.31
middle quintile	0.04	0.04	0.05	0.05	0.07	0.07
top quintile	0.02	0.01	0.02	0.02	0.02	0.02
Public Two-Year						
lowest quintile	0.09	0.08	0.10	0.11	0.14	0.14
middle quintile	0.02	0.02	0.02	0.03	0.03	0.04
top quintile	0.01	0.01	0.01	0.01	0.01	0.01
Private Universities						
lowest quintile	0.86	0.85	1.18	1.44	1.74	1.81
middle quintile	0.22	0.21	0.29	0.35	0.43	0.44
top quintile	0.09	0.08	0.10	0.12	0.13	0.13
Private Colleges						
lowest quintile	0.64	0.67	0.89	1.08	1.28	1.31
middle quintile	0.17	0.17	0.22	0.26	0.31	0.32
top quintile	0.07	0.07	0.08	0.09	0.10	0.10

Sources: Tuition Data, *Digest of Education Statistics* 1996 Table 309 p. 320; Income data U.S. Census Bureau;
"Mean Income Received by Each Fifth and Top 5 Percent of Households, (All Races): 1967-1996;"
last revised September 29, 1997
<http://www.census.gov/hes/income/histinc/h03.html>

EXHIBIT 1-23

Comparison Of Net Price (Total Price - All Financial Aid) by Type of Institution to Trends in Disposal Income Per-Capita and Various Consumer Price Indices

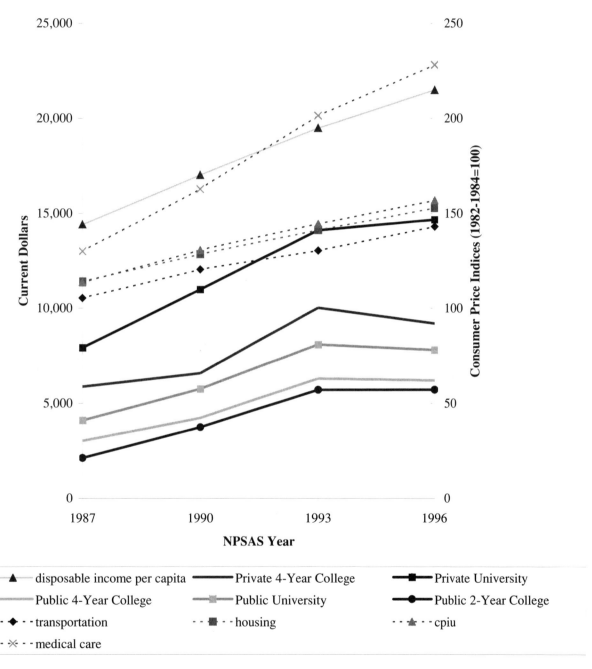

Sources: NCES, NPSAS:87 Undergraduate Students 5/23/97; NCES, NPSAS:90 Undergraduate Students 8/14/95; NCES, NPSAS:93 Undergraduate Students 10/2/97; NCES, NPSAS:96 Undergraduate Students 10/1/97; Bureau of Labor Statistics, http://stats.bls.gov/; Economic Time Series, http://bos.business.uab.edu/data/data.htm.

EXHIBIT 1-24

Undergraduate Enrollments in Four-year Institutions by Tuition Ranges: 1997

Tuition Range	Proportion of Total Undergraduate Enrollment
$20,000 or more	4.3%
18,000 - 19,999	2.3
16,000 - 17,999	2.1
14,000 - 15,999	4.1
12,000 - 13,999	5.4
10,000 - 11,999	4.2
8,000 - 9,999	3.7
6,000 - 7,999	2.8
4,000 - 5,999	15.3
2,000 - 3,999	42.2
Less than $2,000	13.6
Total	100%

Source: The College Board.

Note: The table shows the distribution of full-time undergraduates at four-year colleges by tuition charged in 1996-97. Figures include only those 1,601 public and private institutions that provided final or estimated tuition and fees by September 1, 1996.

EXHIBIT 1-25

Perceptions of the Affordability of Higher Education

The following tables are from reports conducted by the American Council on Education (ACE) and by the Sallie Mae Education Institute.

The ACE study surveyed 1,000 randomly selected adults to determine what they thought was the price (tuition and fees) of attending different types of colleges and universities. Respondents over-estimated the price of all types of institutions by $3,126 to $6,617.

Respondent Estimates of Tuition and Fees

Institution Type	Estimated Price	Actual Tuition*
Public Community College	$6,295	$1,194
Public University	$9.599	$2,982
Private Liberal Arts College	$13.824	$10,698
Private Research University	$20,410	$14,510

Note: Tuition data is for 1994-95, the most recent figures available from the Department of Education when this survey was conducted in July 1996.

Source: American Council on Education

The Sallie Mae study was based on interviews with parents of college-bound high school students; it found that parents under-estimated the price of attending college.

Estimated Price of Attending Four Years at a College or University

	Public or State College	Private College
Below Range	41 %	49 %
Average Costs	18 %	19 %
Above Range	42 %	31 %

Source: Sallie Mae Education Institute

EXHIBIT 1-26
Returns to Education: Men
Mean earnings of workers 18 years old and over by educational attainment

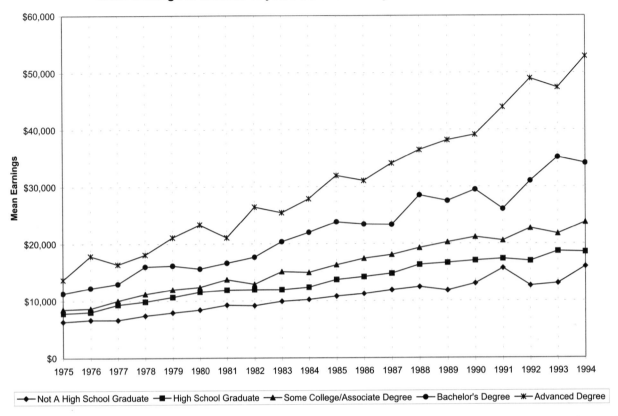

Current Population Survey, March 1995, U.S. Census Bureau, Table 19, "Mean Earnings of Workers 17 Years Old and Over, by Educational Attainment, Race, Hispanic Origin, and Sex: 1975 to 1994."

EXHIBIT 1-27
Returns to Education: Women
Mean earnings of workers 18 years old and over by educational attainment

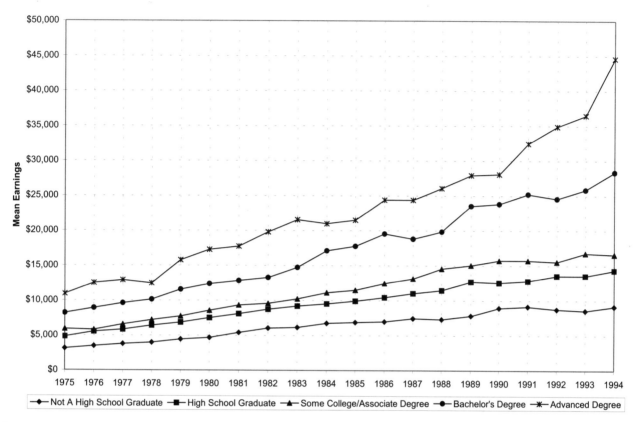

Current Population Survey, March 1995, U.S. Census Bureau, Table 19, "Mean Earnings of Workers 18 Years Old and Over, by Educational Attainment, Race, Hispanic Origin, and Sex: 1975 to 1994."

TECHNICAL NOTE

Most of the data contained in this report were previously published elsewhere. The reader should consult the original sources for further details concerning cited data. Several of the tables do contain original tabulations of recent college cost and price trends (Issue 1). This technical note provides information concerning how these figures were derived. It describes: the data sources used to produce these estimates; the classification of students; the classification of institutions; the method used to estimate what it costs colleges and universities to provide higher education to students (cost per FTE); and the derivation of "net price" estimates.

Data Sources

Multiple years of two U.S. Department of Education data sources, the National Postsecondary Student Aid Study (NPSAS) and the Integrated Postsecondary Education Data System (IPEDS) were used to estimate trends in average college costs and prices. NPSAS data were used to estimate student level information (e.g. tuition and total price of attendance) and IPEDS data were used to estimate institutional level figures (e.g. enrollment and cost to institutions of providing higher education).

NPSAS data are not collected annually, but rather every three years: 1986-87, 1989-90, 1992-93, and 1995-96. The Data Analysis Systems (DAS) software and website (http://www.pedar-das.org) maintained by MPR Associates under contract with the National Center for Education Statistics (NCES) were used to generate the NPSAS based estimates.

IPEDS finance and enrollment data were combined to derive estimates of the cost of providing higher education incurred by institutions per full-time-equivalent student. Based on the ongoing work of Gordon Winston[1], information concerning how colleges and universities spend their money as reported on the IPEDS financial form was combined to reflect the fact that these institutions are multi-product entities and produce goods and services beside instruction. The capital costs associated with the value of the land, buildings, and equipment devoted to instruction are also factored into the estimate of the cost of providing higher education. (A more detailed explanation of this calculation is provided under the "Cost per Student" discussion.)

IPEDS finance data are collected every fiscal year. Finance data from fiscal years 1987, 1990, 1993, and 1996 were desired to correspond with the student level information available from the four waves of NPSAS. Final finance data are not, however, available for 1996, so data from 1995 and 1993 were used to estimate 1996 figures. The annual rate of change in the cost of providing instruction observed for each type of institution between 1993 and 1995 was assumed to remain the same through 1996. Comparing the results of this assumption with estimates derived from early release 1996 finance data revealed similar values. Enrollment data from the fall of the academic years in questions were used to calculate full-time-equivalent enrollment (FTE). FTE is defined as the number of full-time students plus one third of the number of part-time students attending a given institution.

The first three years of IPEDS finance (1987, 1990, and 1993) and fall enrollment data (1986, 1989, and 1992) were acquired via the CASPAR website (http://caspar.nsf.gov). The 1995 finance and fall 1994 enrollment data were acquired through the NCES website (http://nces.ed.gov).

Classification of Students

Data presented in this report are for full-time, full-year dependent students attending a single institution only. These students are considered for financial aid reasons to be financially dependent on their parents. Parental as well as the student's own income and assets are considered in the determination of need-based financial aid. Approximately 74 percent of full-time, full-year undergraduates were classified as dependent in 1996. While part-time or part-year students comprise the majority, 62 percent, of all undergraduates, the price paid by full-time, full-year students is more readily interpreted and compared across years.

Classification of Institutions

Institutions were classified based on control, public or private not-for-profit, and level of degree offered. Trends in prices and costs are estimated separately for public four-year, private four-year, and public two-year institutions. In 1996, approximately 78 percent of all undergraduates attended a public institution; 46 percent were in two-year schools, 31 percent attended four-year schools, and the remaining 1 percent were enrolled in institutions offering programs lasting less than two years. Public institutions receive a share of current revenue from state appropriations; therefore tuition charged state residents at these schools is often considerably lower than in the private sector.

Cost per Student

As noted above, the derivation of the cost of instruction per full-time-equivalent student draws heavily from the work of Gordon Winston. Winston's work makes two conceptual improvements over past measures of institutions' cost of providing higher education. First, Winston recognizes that colleges and universities spend money in areas that are clearly related, areas that are partially related, and areas that are completely unrelated to instruction. Second, Winston accounts for the capital costs of the physical resources associated with providing higher education.

Based on Winston's method, instruction costs are the sum of: clearly instructional expenditures; a proportion of the partially related expenditures; and a proportion of the capital costs of all the physical assets used by the institution. The proportion used in these calculations reflects the share instruction holds in the overall operation of the institution. The specific formulation of the cost per student estimation is described below and summarized in Exhibit 1.

The two IPEDS expenditure categories of instruction and student services were treated as being clearly instructional and all the expenditures in these two categories was included in the instructional cost measure. The three IPEDS expenditure categories of institutional support, academic support, and operation of the physical plant were treated as being partially related to instruction and a proportion of the value of expenditures in these categories was added to the instructional cost measure. This proportion was calculated by dividing the sum of the two clearly instructional expenditure categories (instruction and student services) by the total current fund expenditures less mandatory and non-mandatory transfers, scholarship and fellowship expenditures, and the sum of the three partially instructional expenditure categories (institutional support, academic support, and operation of the physical plant).

EXHIBIT 1: Annotated Formula for Cost Per Student

Cost =

Clearly Instruction	+	Proportion Partially Instruction	+	Proportion Capital Costs
Current expenditures on: Instruction Student Services		Current expenditures on: Academic Support Institutional Support Operation of Physical Plant		Depreciation (2.5%): Replacement value of Buildings Replacement value of Equipment plus Opportunity Cost (9.12%) : Replacement value of Buildings Replacement value of Equipment Replacement value of Land

Where proportion equals

Current expenditures on instruction and student services
divided by
Total current fund expenditures less: current expenditures on academic support, institutional support, operation of physical plant, scholarships and fellowships, mandatory and non-mandatory transfers

Cost Per Student =
Cost divided by full-time-equivalent enrollment

Capital costs include both the real depreciation of physical assets and the opportunity costs associated with their use for higher education. IPEDS collects information concerning the replacement and book value of buildings and equipment used by colleges and universities. While the replacement value for land is not collected, book value for land used is. Land book value was converted to replacement or market value by multiplying land book value by 2.138. This correction of land value was based on the relationship observed by Winston and Yen (1995) between the book value and replacement value of buildings. Depreciation was assumed to be 2.5 percent and the opportunity cost was set to equal the average return over the past twenty years of 30 Year Treasury Bills, 9.12 percent. Land values were assumed not to depreciate in value. Hence, the value of all capital resources consumed in the provision of instructional services is computed as follows; 2.5 percent of (Building replacement value + Equipment replacement value) plus 9.12 percent (Building replacement value + Equipment replacement value + 2.138*Land Book Value).

Due to a high level of missing data in the physical asset information in the IPEDS data, the data imputation techniques discussed in the appendix of Winston and Yen (1995, p.39-40) were adopted. In order to lessen the impact of outlying cases, the highest one percent of estimated values of instructional costs per full-time-equivalent student in each year were deleted from the analysis.

Net Price Calculations

The posted tuition, the "sticker price" is not paid by a substantial portion of undergraduate students due to financial aid. Roughly half of all undergraduates receive some sort of aid. Among dependent students attending a college or university full-time for the entire academic year, the group of students that tables included in Issue 1 focus on, the percentage receiving some type of financial aid is higher still, 64 percent.

Two different definitions of net price are used. In the first version of net price, only grant aid is subtracted from the total price of attendance. In the second version, all financial aid, including loan and work study earnings, is subtracted from the total price. The first definition captures the actual price paid by students and families, regardless of the mechanisms used to finance the purchase of higher education. The second captures the actual cash outlay that students and their families encounter during the year of college attendance.

To maintain a consistent measure of total price of attendance over time, certain adjustments had to be made to the student self-reported total price information available in the NPSAS data for 1987 and 1990. The 1996 NPSAS includes a revised measure of total price, a student budget variable based on the combination of student self-reports and institution provided data. A 1996 comparable version of this student budget variable was added to the 1993 NPSAS data which also contains student self-reports of total price. Using 1993 NPSAS data, which contained both measures, ratios of the revised student budget variable to student self-reports were calculated for each type of institution addressed by the report. The institution specific ratios were then applied to the self-reported total price information available in 1987 and 1990 to make these data comparable to the 1996 student budget estimates.

[1]Primarily, on Williams Project Discussion Paper (DP)-32, "Costs, Prices, Subsidies, and Aid in U.S. Higher Education," July, 1995, written with Ivan C. Yen.

Issue 2: Innovative methods for reducing or stabilizing tuition

Concern over rising college tuition — and the affordability of higher education — has prompted states and institutions to develop innovative strategies for reducing or stabilizing tuition. Some methods target tuition levels directly, such as freezing tuition or limiting the level of tuition increases. Other strategies target tuition indirectly by attempting to minimize the total cost to the student of obtaining a degree or providing parents and students more flexible payment options. Finally, many institutions are dealing with tuition increases by reducing expenditures in order to pass along savings to students and their families.

Findings

- Three primary categories of strategies that states and institutions — both public and private — are adopting to reduce or stabilize tuition include:
  - limiting tuition increases;
  - expediting time to degree; and
  - offering payment options. (Exhibit 2-1)
- Tuition prepayment plans became increasingly popular during the tuition hikes of the early 1990s. (Exhibit 2-2) Investment consultants now caution investors of the lower return rates due to smaller increases and even decreases in tuition. (Healy, Patrick. *Financial Experts Say Smaller Tuition Increases Have Eroded the Value of Prepaid Plans.* The Chronicle of Higher Education, Nov. 21, 1997.)
- Many institutions are reducing the costs of programs and services in order to stabilize tuition prices. The National Association of College and University Business Officers (NACUBO) recognizes innovative institutional initiatives with their annual Higher Education Awards. (Exhibit 2-3)
- Many states and state university systems are redirecting specified percentages of their budgets to more efficient areas. (Exhibit 2-4)

Conclusions

To what extent have colleges and universities, as well as state legislatures and governing boards, adopted innovative methods to reduce or stabilize tuition?

There is considerable evidence to indicate that institutions of higher education have become sensitive to the prices they charge students and their families. As of August 1997, 27 states offered tuition prepayment options of various types. A number of states and institutions have limited the rate at which they increase tuition, and a few states and institutions have actually reduced the tuitions they charge. Furthermore, a number of colleges and universities have made efforts to expedite the amount of time to earn a degree, thus reducing the price for students.

EXHIBIT 2-1
Overview of Methods for Reducing or Stabilizing Tuition

The following information is taken from a General Accounting Office (GAO) publication entitled *Rising College Tuition and Costs* and from the National Association of Independent Colleges and Universities (NAICU) report *Innovative Approaches to Making College Affordable*.

Public Institutions

GAO reports three major strategies that states and institutions are adopting to reduce the burden of paying for college: (1) limiting tuition increases; (2) expediting time to degree; and (3) offering payment options.

Limiting tuition increases. This method involves holding tuition levels constant from year to year or tying tuition increases to inflation. Examples include:

- The Virginia Council of Higher Education recommended to the state legislature that tuition be held constant in school years 1996-97 and 1997-98.
- The Massachusetts Higher Education Coordinating Council cut school year 1996-97 tuition for state residents by 5 percent at 4-year state colleges.
- University of Colorado at Boulder set out-of-state tuition to reflect the local CPI.
- Washington State changed its tuition-setting policy from one based on schools' expenditures to one based on inflation.

Expediting time to degree. Expediting time to degree reduces institutional costs per student and reduces the amount of time that a student is paying tuition. Specific strategies include:

- reducing the number of credits required to graduate;
- shortening the length of a program (e.g., by allowing students to complete 4 years of work in 3 years or by offering 3-year degree programs);
- guaranteeing completion in four years (e.g., by waiving required courses that are not available);
- helping entering students avoid remedial courses (e.g., by helping high school students select the courses they need to prepare them for college);
- providing college credit through acceleration programs, such as advanced placement courses;
- facilitating the transfer of community college credits; and
- improving academic advising, to provide students with information necessary to complete their degree on time.

Offering payment options. Payment options do not reduce tuition; rather, they alleviate the burden of paying for college. GAO identified three primary types of payment programs:

- college savings plans (which may include tax-advantaged college savings bonds or special college savings accounts);
- monthly payment plans (which allow students to spread payments over the enrollment period, rather than paying in full at the beginning of each semester or quarter); and
- tuition prepayment programs (different types are outlined in Exhibit 2-2 below). The 1997-98 Almanac of Higher Education reports that 28 states offered tuition prepayment programs, as of August, 1997.

EXHIBIT 2-1 (Continued)
Overview of Methods for Reducing or Stabilizing Tuition

Independent Institutions

NAICU reports that independent colleges and universities are implementing many of the same cost-saving methods described above, including: tuition freezes, cuts, and limits on increases, payment options, and accelerated degree programs. In addition, NAICU institutions also report the following cost-saving methods:

- No tuition (some institutions, known as "work colleges", either charge no tuition or provide full tuition scholarships to all students);
- Special scholarships or tuition discounts;
- Tuition guarantees (e.g., students can "lock-in" the price of tuition for a four-year period or institutions guarantee a ceiling on tuition increases); and
- Graduation or job guarantees, in which institutions guarantee that students will be able to graduate in four years; others guarantee help in finding a job after graduation.

EXHIBIT 2-2

Overview of Major Types of Tuition Prepayment Plans

Type of plan	Selected state using the plan type	Description
Contract	Florida	The purchaser contracts for a predetermined amount of education, with the cost calculated based on current tuition levels. As of January 1995, 327,707 contracts had been purchased through the program, but approximately 14 percent had been canceled. In September 1994, over 12,000 students were attending community colleges and 4-year schools and paying at least part of their school expenses using prepaid tuition.
Tuition Credit	Pennsylvania	The purchaser starts an account into which he or she makes deposits for prepaid units of education. Between 1993, when the program began, and December 1995, nearly 14,300 accounts were opened with a total of about $45.5 million. Because participants must be in the program for at least 4 years, the earliest that credits can be used is September 1997.
Certificate	Massachusetts	Participants purchase certificates from the state redeemable for a percentage of a school's tuition and mandatory fees. However, the state commits to pay only the face value of the certificate plus interest compounded annually at a rate equal to 2 percent above the increase in CPI. The schools absorb the loss if their costs rise more than the value of the certificates. The program began in 1995.

Source: GAO/HEHS-96-154: *Rising College Tuition and Costs*, Table 5.2, p. 58.

EHXIBIT 2-3

NORTHWEST MISSOURI STATE UNIVERSITY

Culture of Quality Plan for Improving Undergraduate Education

For the past decade, Northwest Missouri State University has worked to instill a "Culture of Quality" (COQ) on campus by continually evaluating and improving quality and service through long- and short-term planning activities. Although the primary goal of this initiative is to provide a superior education for students, COQ is designed to pervade every aspect of campus life. The initiative began with the refining and sharpening of the university's mission statement from which a set of mutually supporting best practice goals were developed through a benchmarking process.

Under the COQ system, all departments on campus, both academic and service, follow a seven-step planning process model. Targets are established for faculty, staff, and administrative productivity based on national benchmarks, and each year more than $150,000 is distributed to departments that submit proposals reflecting COQ goals.

The university uses key quality indicators, external customer data, and mandates from regulatory and accrediting agencies to ensure continuous improvement in the delivery of educational programs. Future student needs and expectations are determined through environmental scanning, employer and alumni surveys, on-campus symposia, forums, and benchmarks.

The results of Northwest's COQ initiative are far-reaching. Northwest student now score above the national average on tests and competitions, parents have expressed high satisfaction with their perceptions of career planning and academic counseling, and the university's enrollment growth is at capacity. In addition, the university's bookstore sales have increased $120,000 since 1992, campus dining customer satisfaction has rated above national averages since 1991, and the Grounds Association ranked Northwest among the nation's top six campuses.

96-078 Management   Winner—$10,000

The following pages are from:

Source: National Association of College and University Business Officers (NACUBO). *1996 Higher Education Award Winners.* NACUBO, 1996.

UNIVERSITY OF CALIFORNIA—IRVINE

A Model for Sustaining Administrative Improvement

As part of efforts to become a top-ranking research university by the year 2000 the University of California—Irvine developed and implemented a model for sustaining administrative improvements. The model promotes long-lasting organizational change and process improvement through institutional and administrative goal setting, articulation of foundations and principles, use of streamlining tools, and customer-driven process improvements.

Throughout the administrative improvement model's implementation, the university strived to ensure the satisfaction of students and other customers. The implementation team used customer satisfaction surveys to substantiate process improvement outcomes, and customers provided evaluative feedback from the project's earliest stages.

Technology upgrades, skills development, human resource initiatives outsourcing, and process re-design are just a few of the many areas the university set out to tackle—and the results of this initiative were just as pervasive. The project resulted in the completion of more than 200 action plan innovations that yielded measurable performance outcomes. University paper use was reduced by 6.2 million pieces per year; the time for renovation project estimates was reduced by 33 percent; training time for low-value purchasing was reduced by 50 percent; and the cycle time for student parking permit sales was reduced from one to 30 days to less than one minute.

96-069 Management   Winner—$10,000

UNIVERSITY OF CALIFORNIA—SAN DIEGO

Beyond Reengineering: Implementing a Balanced Scorecard in Higher Education

In response to the rapid change in work processes and management philosophies occurring throughout the campus, the senior management at the University of California—San Diego (UCSD) set out to develop a system for measuring performance baselines for the customer satisfaction, internal business practices, and financial viability. In 1993 UCSD launched a balanced scorecard planning and performance measurement system for 30 institutional business functions using three primary data sources: 1) institutional financial reports; 2) NACUBO benchmarks; and 3) faculty, staff, and student customer satisfaction surveys. The university's vision, mission, and values formed the infrastructure upon which the scorecard program is built.

For each of the 30 business functions in the program, nine service attributes are measured by faculty and staff, and students measure attributes for eight support services. Throughout the scorecard system, performance goals and remedial performance action plan commitments are built into the performance review process.

The benefits of UCSD's balanced scorecard program included reorganization of the workload in the vice chancellor's area; revision of job descriptions with performance standards; continual training for user departments on-going customer assessments; and the meeting of communication needs through technology.

96-072 Management   Winner—$5,000

TROY STATE UNIVERSITY

Quality Improvement in Planning, Programs, and Services

To improve its programs, services, and planning, Troy State University created and implemented a total quality management program called the Institutional Effectiveness Cycle (IEC). The IEC is an annual evaluation process that uses established benchmarks to measure the quality of every service, program, and operation of the university—both academic and nonacademic.

The cycle begins each fall, when all of the university's administrators define six Points of Institutional Effectiveness for their areas. Plans for implementation and assessment of the six points are developed in the winter quarter, and in the spring, budgets are created for implementation. The university's Office of Institutional Research Planning and Effectiveness provides a "how to" manual to guide administrators through the IEC process.

The results of Troy State's Institutional Effectiveness Cycle are improved programs and services, the creation of a strategic plan for the year 2000, and the establishment of a total quality management program that is embraced by staff, faculty, and administrators.

96-077 Management   Winner—$5,000

THE UNIVERSITY OF WASHINGTON

Faculty Grants Management Training Program

To improve the administration of the $477 million it receives annually in externally funded grants and contracts, the University Washington developed and implemented a grants management training program. The training program, which is mandatory for every faculty member who submits a grant or contract proposal, encompasses the total grants management process from preparing a proposal to fiscal report preparation and final audit. Faculty must attend the training at least once every three years to stay up to date on grants administration processes and changes, and training sessions are continuously modified as new compliance and audit regulations occur.

To date, 1,805 University of Washington faculty members have completed the grants management training program, and efficiency and productivity have greatly improved as a result. An annual cost savings of $64,977 was realized from reductions in the number of unallowable and unallocable charges during the terms of grants. Annual interest savings totaled $31,815 due to significant reductions in grant overexpenditures.

96-057 Resource Enhancement   Winner—$5,000

THE UNIVERSITY OF WASHINGTON

U-PASS: Transportation Management Program

With fewer than 12,000 parking spaces for the more than 50,000 people on its campus each day, the University of Washington created U-PASS, a transportation management program designed to alleviate the parking shortage and provide better transportation services to commuters. The U-PASS is a sticker placed on the back of the university ID card that allows the user to take advantage of several alternative transportation modes. A quarterly rate for students and faculty entitles them to unlimited rides on two primary transit agencies, free carpool parking subsidized vanpool fares, ridematching service, night shuttle service, and merchant discounts.

The U-PASS program is funded through a combination of sources, with the administration's contribution capped at over one million each year, leaving the revenue generated by the sale of the U-PASS and the customers of the parking system to cover the cost of the program.

96-055 Resource Enhancement   Winner—$2,500

UNIVERSITY OF CALIFORNIA—IRVINE

Rethinking Energy: A Comprehensive Approach

When the opening of three new energy-intensive research buildings left the University of California—Irvine facing a major utility budget shortfall, the university took a revolutionary approach to energy management. To compensate for the shortfall, the Facilities Management department developed and implemented a multi-dimensional assessment and comprehensive redesign program to reduce energy consumption and expenditures.

The comprehensive energy approach began with a commitment from executive management to support and make long-term investments in the program, and included such efforts as retrofitting projects, management operational modifications, creation of energy efficiency design elements, development of a technology deployment plan, a forum for adopting best practices, customer support groups for feedback and process improvement a partnership with utility company, and thorough analysis of financing alternatives.

The university's initiative eliminated a projected 1.5 million deficit and generated an annual savings of $1.9 million as well as significant environmental benefits.

96-003 Resource Enhancement   Winner—$2,500

VIRGINIA COMMONWEALTH UNIVERSITY

Resource Enhancement Through Restructuring

Virginia Commonwealth University developed a unique restructuring program that combines cost cutting with revenue enhancements to generate funds for starting new programs or improving existing ones. The program's success lies in the implementation of four simultaneous initiatives: traditional and nontraditional resource allocation strategies, an administrative cost reduction program, a workforce transition plan, and an updated strategic plan. The first three initiatives generated $38 million in savings for the university, and the updated strategic plan provides direction for reallocation of this money.

As a result of its restructuring program, the university no longer depends upon increased tuition revenue and state appropriations to provide additional resources required for infrastructure changes. The resource enhancement through restructuring program has enabled the university to start a new School of Engineering, build a research park, establish new interdisciplinary centers of academic excellence, attract faculty, expand the campus library, and provide state-of-the-art technology.

96-043 Resource Enchancement   Winner—Honorable Mention

UNIVERSITY OF MISSOURI—COLUMBIA

Open Bidding on Wholesale Electricity

To reduce electricity costs, the University of Missouri—Columbia forged a contract to purchase 50 million kilowatt-hours of interruptible electricity from a local utility company. This innovative wholesale electricity contract met about one-third of the campus's electrical needs and cost less than generating the electricity through the university power plant. Purchasing the electricity instead of generating it also means less wear on university power plant equipment.

The University of Missouri—Columbia's initiative demonstrates that, with a minimal amount of effort, institutions can achieve substantial savings in utility costs. Unlike other energy-saving programs, wholesale electrical purchases require no massive workforce retraining, equipment investments, or capital improvements disruptions. To date, the contract has saved $210,000 for the first contract year, and could save at least $200,000 for each subsequent year of the program.

96-035 Resource Enhancement   Winner—Honorable Mention

UNIVERSITY OF NEBRASKA MEDICAL CENTER

Moving Beyond Boundaries: Building High-Performance Individuals and Organizations

The University of Nebraska Medical Center instituted Moving Beyond Boundaries (MBB), a leadership development process, to create new levels of decision making and enhance the medical center's long-term performance. Staff who exhibit behavior that reflects the organization's values and who have the potential for additional leadership responsibility are selected for the program.

The MBB program is a six-month process. Ten groups of 25 participants from various areas of the university attend a series of six, two-day sessions at locations off campus. Participants who complete MBB gain (1) an increased understanding of the academic health sciences center environment within the larger context of a global environment; (2) better knowledge of business processes, especially as they relate to the changing management of health care and higher education; and (3) a self-reference as university leadership, thinking beyond their departments or academic units.

This initiative has strengthened the critical thinking abilities of staff. It has also encouraged flexibility throughout the institution by empowering employees in nontraditional positions with leadership authority.

97-024 Management   Winner—$10,000

The following pages are from:

Source: National Association of College and University Business Officers (NACUBO). *1996 Higher Education Award Winners.* NACUBO, 1996.

LOYOLA COLLEGE IN MARYLAND

Self-Directed Work Teams

To improve operational efficiency, increase staff morale, and reduce operating expenses, the Physical Plant Department at Loyola College in Maryland formed highly empowered, self-directed work teams to assist with management functions. The college hired a consultant to assess the effectiveness of the change process, identify problems, and develop a training program in such areas as conflict management, customer satisfaction, and communications.

Team members are assigned lead roles in resolving problems, and they rely on open communication and feedback to handle issues. Groups are formed within the teams to address individual issues as they arise. The arrangement gives every team member a chance to participate in institutional decision making.

The proof of the teams' success is not only in the Physical Plant Department but throughout the campus: management has learned more effective management techniques; housekeeping staff have increased their duties by 50 percent, reducing overtime; and environmental services has improved the quality of the campus, making it more appealing to students, prospective students, alumni, staff, and guests. As a result of these changes, the department has saved more than $625,000 annually.

97-041 Resource Enhancement   Winner—$7,500

MIAMI-DADE COMMUNITY COLLEGE

Florida Community College Software Consortium

To replace outdated computer systems, meet state requirements for uniform reporting methods, and satisfy user demands, Miami-Dade Community College and seven other community colleges formed a partnership with the computer company Software AG. This union produced the Florida Community College Software Consortium (FCCSC). The consortium responded to its members' needs by developing a suite of applications for key administrative areas—such as personnel and payroll, finance, student affairs, and facilities.

All modules were organized using state-of-the-art applications and technology. The system developed for personnel and payroll contains modules for applicant tracking, demographics, job assignments, benefits, position control, payroll, and time accounting. Finance modules include general ledger, budget, accounts payable, accounts receivable, and purchasing. The student affairs modules integrate data from admissions, registrations, records, curriculum, fees and tuition, and degree audit. Formal and on-the-job training enhanced staff's knowledge about and comfort with the new database.

By mixing the college's personnel, financial and computer resources with those of other consortium members, Miami-Dade Community College discovered a formula for efficiently maximizing its software and administrative efforts. The modern computer system has eliminated unnecessary processes, reduced administrative costs and provided the college with the technology it needs to enter the 21st century. Miami Dade-Community College has saved over $3.5 million by participating in this partnership.

97-051 Resource Enhancement   Winner—$5,000

PURDUE UNIVERSITY

Avoiding Software Failure in the Year 2000

Purdue University's Management Information Department has developed conversion software that both identifies possible computer problems in the year 2000 and introduces solutions to those programming issues. Dates in computer programs are currently set so that only the last two digits of the year are variable. This will create data-processing anxiety for many organizations at the turn of the century.

The software has converted 74 of Purdue's 133 COBOL subsystems. And about 2.3 million lines of code have been scanned, modified, tested, and returned to production. The university has sold the distribution rights to the software. Thanks to the conversion software, many information systems will have no problem outputting December 31, 1999, and inputting January 1, 2000. Purdue's foresight in 1994 in recognizing the two-year digit problem and the approach taken has saved the university more than $630,000.

97-011 Resource Enhancement   Winner—$5,000

CORNELL UNIVERSITY

Books In Print on Campus Network

Management at Cornell University's Campus Store understood that its customers appreciated—and deserved—convenient service. The store now provides its customers with 24-hour electronic access to *Books in Print* due to a partnership with publisher R.R. Bowker. This free, automated service is the Campus Store's online connection to its faculty, staff, students, and alumni. Individuals with a Cornell network ID can obtain information on U.S. books.

With on-line *Books in Print*, the Campus Store can serve its customers in a more proactive way. Professors and department coordinators can research a book's availability before placing their orders. Students can conduct book searches using title or ISBN number. Users can also find price, copyright, and publisher information on the integrated information network. In addition, customers can place book orders using this up-to-date system. Away from campus, users can connect to *Books in Print* from their office, dormitory, or apartment desktops. On campus, users can access the network from the library or nearest kiosk.

Cornell was one of the first universities to offer such a cost- and time-saving service. The on-line version of *Books in Print* is one of the institution's most essential, and accessible, reference tools.

97-015 Process Improvement   Winner—$2,500

FLORIDA STATE UNIVERSITY

Demand Analysis System

To improve the management of its enrollment and course offerings, Florida State University created Demand Analysis System (DAS). This software program identifies the number of unfilled requests for classes, or the "unmet demand," during the telephone-registration process.

The DAS helps the university's registrar and department heads track how many students request a particular course and the student's class level. In the past, seniors complained about not getting the classes they needed to graduate. Due to the analysis system, departments are able to respond to actual student demand; the unmet demand of students has sharply decreased. The DAS has also enhanced the university's Three-year Baccalaureate Program, which accelerates the rate of graduation while lowering overall tuition costs. The three-year program would have been impossible to implement without the analysis system.

Florida State University has the best four-year graduation rate in the state university system because of the DAS. But most importantly, the program has received high marks from the university's students.

97-043 Process Improvement   Winner—$2,500

EXHIBIT 2-4
Examples of Cost Saving Initiatives by Selected Colleges and Universities

Colleges and universities nationwide are facing escalating costs and decreasing state and Federal funding. Therefore, many have implemented initiatives to save money and to reduce the need to increase tuitions too steeply. The following examples are provided.

CALIFORNIA STATE UNIVERSITY SYSTEM

In December 1996, system officials reported productivity enhancements totaling over $17 million in direct savings, avoided costs, improved services, and reallocation of expenditures. The largest cutbacks—$9.4 million—came as the result of changes in the academic program, procurement process, distribution of information, facilities management, environmental health and safety, and public safety. In dealing with those areas, the California system eliminated some positions and consolidated others and cut the costs of both utilities and workers' compensation.

The report detailed the amounts saved by:

- Increasing use of and access to technology in curriculum development and course delivery, academic support, and administrative services ($2.8 million).
- Expanding working arrangements with partners both inside and outside the system. Those outside included government agencies, private industry, and other universities and colleges. Internal collaborations avoided costs by sharing training, equipment, curriculum development, and mainframe computer support ($2.1 million).
- Refinancing bonds, lowering insurance outlays, and altering short-term financing agreements ($1.6 million).
- Improving services to students and employees involving recruitment and registration, financial aid processing, automated fee payment, advisor consultations, degree audits, and the dissemination of everyday information ($1.5 million).

BRANDEIS UNIVERSITY (MASSACHUSETTS)

Under the aegis of its Brandeis 2000 initiative, the university slashed the overall 1996-97 budget by over $500,000. Areas of reduction included the following:

- Personnel costs in such categories as dining services, physical plant, administrative affairs, and communications—$386,000.
- Life, disability and other insurance, through rebidding the contracts—$85,000.
- Outside vendors, through renegotiation of agreements—$79,000.
- Printing, publication and mailing, both reductions and eliminations—$50,000.

BOWDOIN COLLEGE (MAINE)

In 1990, this liberal-arts institution undertook what its treasurer has called a "3 R's" effort—reorganization, reallocation, and retrenchment." The plan focused on "straitjacketing revenues and cutting costs" in such areas as:

- *Early retirement*—two packages offered as an inducement to cut more than 50 administrative and support positions.
- *Staffing*—increased use of part-time and temporary positions.
- *Vacancies*—are filled only after careful review.

Implementation of these and other cost control efforts have reduced Bowdoin's budget by 30 percent in real terms since 1990.

NORTHERN MICHIGAN UNIVERSITY

In 1994-95, Northern Michigan University (NMU) limited salary increases to no more than the rate of inflation. The university also:

- Eliminated the positions of almost 30 percent of executives and senior administrators, 20 percent of administrative staff, and 10 percent of service staff.
- Reduced health care costs by making an agreement with a Preferred Provider Organization.
- Cut back sick leave and annual leave benefits for management and administrative/professional employees.

WASHINGTON STATE UNIVERSITY

Responding to demands from both the public and the state legislature, Washington State University has sought greater efficiency through initiatives ranging from library cooperatives and academic-funding reallocations to energy conservation. Some specific examples:

- Ten percent budget cuts in central administration to help offset reductions in state funding.
- Reallocation of funds from areas with declining enrollments to those that are attracting more and more students.
- Collaboration with Eastern Washington University to create and co-fund a cooperative academic library with 30,000 volumes. Both staffing and space costs have been reduced for each institution.
- Energy conservation measures that have produced annual savings of more than $1 million.

Recycling and composting programs that save money as well as protect the environment—and have drawn the praise of the state's Department of Ecology.

CLARK UNIVERSITY (MASSACHUSETTS)

Rewarding academic success is an unusual and key element in Clark's effort to attract students: the university offers students who maintain a B-plus average en route to an undergraduate degree a fifth year free to complete several masters-level programs, including a master of arts degree and the MBA.

In addition, Clark is striving to hold expenditures for administration and physical plant to about 10 percent of its total budget. Among the initiatives taken to reach that goal:

- Strategic fuel-purchasing.
- Computerized energy co-generation and management (for example, using waste energy to heat and cool buildings), resulting in an annual savings of one-third.
- Consortium purchasing: in Clark's home city of Worcester, MA., 10 higher educational institutions and 20 other nonprofit institutions have banded together to purchase bulk items, saving almost 30 percent in the process.
- "Enterprise" budgeting, which treats certain parts of the university self-contained businesses.

Additional funding through stepped-up efforts to secure research and other types of grants.

UNIVERSITY OF VIRGINIA

Faced with a 1994 legislative appropriations act requiring emphasis on minimizing costs, preparing for increased enrollments, and ensuring the effectiveness of course offerings, the University of Virginia restructured to streamline operations and use savings to enhance core academic programs. Among the university areas whose operations were revised (amount saved in parentheses):

- The central offices of personnel, purchasing, and finance: nine positions reallocated and other changes ($231,250).
- The employee health care plan: changes in coverage ($335,000).
- The bursar's office: telephone course registration ($10,000 to $20,000).

The Electronic Forms and Information Warehouse: by computerization of frequently used information; reduction of paper and processing costs ($85,000).

THE UNIVERSITY OF MISSOURI SYSTEM

The system has been moving to cut costs since 1992, when it set in motion a five-year financial plan that called for generating $125 million in savings. Among the highlights of the plan:

- A program of voluntary early-retirement incentives, coupled with attrition and layoffs, yielded a reduction of 1,300 positions.
- Computer systems on all of the campuses were consolidated.
- The university and its employees, retirees, and their families changed to managed health care, resulting in a first-year saving for all parties of $10.7 million.

Refinancing the university's debt has saved approximately $1.6 million over the past several years.

PRINCE GEORGE'S (MARYLAND) COMMUNITY COLLEGE

Faced with declining public funding, Prince George's Community College in 1991 began implementing a variety of money-saving steps:

- Eliminating cost-of-living salary increases.
- Reducing class offerings by 10 percent in 1995.
- Furloughing substantial numbers of employees, resulting in $600,000 in saved wages during a single year.
- Downsizing in 1993 yielded annual reductions of $800,000.
- Staff turnover resulted in net annual savings of over $400,000
- Renegotiating fringe benefits, for a saving of $275,000.

YORK COLLEGE OF PENNSYLVANIA

Through an on-going program of continuous improvement initiative in both quality and efficiency, York College has achieved effective cost control consistent with high quality and instruction. Some specific indicators:

- Contains total charges to less than 60 percent of the average for private colleges and universities.
- Ranks in the top 25 percent in quality in the *U.S. News and World Report* survey of regional liberal arts colleges.
- Focuses on productivity in faculty and administrative staffing.

GEORGETOWN UNIVERSITY (WASHINGTON, DC)

This fall, Georgetown initiated the "Administrative Excellence" project with the goals of improving services provided by the university and generating significant savings. The 18-month initiative will review all the university's major processes (e.g. procurement procedures and facilities use, renovation, and construction) and identify ways to increase the efficiency and effectiveness of the operations, while decreasing costs significantly. Special task forces have been assigned to the critical areas of procurement and facilities management. Although the university has not announced the targeted amount of cost reduction, officials report that savings will not come from faculty salaries, research costs, or financial aid.

SOUTH DAKOTA STATE UNIVERSITY

South Dakota State University is the land grant university within South Dakota's Unified System of Higher Education composed of six public universities. All universities are involved in a budget exercise called "Efficiency through Redirection" whereby 5 percent of the institutional funding is being directed away from support of low enrollment undergraduate (less than 10 students) and graduate (less than 7 students) courses toward the purchase of new technology and the support of campus centers of excellence which reflect the focus of each university. The University hopes to be better focused and technologically equipped without increasing spending as a result. The South Dakota Unified System also recently created a consolidated student service center for application, financial aid, housing, etc., resulting in substantial saving in student service personnel related expenses.

UNIVERSITY OF GEORGIA

The governor of Georgia, Zell Miller, requested that all government agencies identify five percent of their budget that could be redirected to achieve greater efficiency. The University of Georgia developed a cost saving plan for budget redirection which totaled well over five percent. The following actions were systemwide initiatives which redirected funds in specific areas totaling over $21 million. The thirty-four campuses also developed over $37 million in redirection plans. The areas of redirection were professional development ($901,000), instructional technology ($7,578,000), student information system ($2,885,900), strategic campus initiatives ($8,953,678), and targeted nursing programs ($837,449).

INDEPENDENT CALIFORNIA COLLEGES AND UNIVERSITIES

Golden Gate University

Golden Gate University recently implemented a Responsibility Center Management (RCM) model for its campuses. RCM is a management model that provides for decentralized decision making, the linking of planning and budgeting, a performance-based reward system, and a higher level of accountability. Targets, qualitative and quantitative, are set, results are measured and each RCM is rewarded both with bonuses for performance above the targets and opportunity funds (i.e., "profits") to lavish on that awarded unit as they see fit. Unit performance on costs has improved markedly as a result. The list of actions to reduce costs in all of the 37 units is very long. Technology is behind many of them. Responsibility center management is a management tool that empowers managers to be entrepreneurial and at the same time recognizes the cost of operations. It strengthens an appreciation of trials and tribulations of running a business.

Pepperdine University

Beginning in 1992, Pepperdine began a comprehensive planning process to reduce administrative costs in the university. Formerly, five senior administrators reported to the President. In the reorganization, positions filled by the Vice Presidents for Administration, Finance, Student Affairs and University Affairs were eliminated. University management was reassigned by the President to three senior officers: a Provost (the chief academic officer), an Executive Vice President (the chief operational officer) and an Executive Vice Chancellor (the chief development officer). Certain managers and support staff were also eliminated or reassigned as a consequence of the streamlined administrative team. Attendant expense budgets, personnel costs, and so forth, were also available for reallocation.

The goal of reallocating $1 million was met. Actually, more than $1.5 million was reallocated, but the net impact after establishing new offices and meeting resultant management needs was more than $1.1 million. A portion of those funds was allocated directly to student and academic program budgets, and the remainder continues to serve as a Strategic Initiative Fund (SIF), directed by the President and Provost, for projects serving students in the classroom or otherwise in the campus environment. The SIF has been especially useful in funding new technology.

Belmont University

In 1995, Belmont University received the Overall Innovative Management Achievement Award from the National Association of College and University Business Officers for its comprehensive management initiative in Continuous Quality Improvement. Continuous Quality Improvement at Belmont has changed the way work is done, changed the attitudes of students, and changed how Belmont is viewed in the community. Teamwork has become the way faculty and staff do business and measurement serves as the key driver to decision making. Focusing on processes that directly impact student life, Belmont staff use Continuous Quality Improvement tools to improve the way Belmont does business; and students and other stakeholders have benefited.

Stanford University

Since 1989, Stanford has made significant and sustained efforts to control its expense base and achieve efficiencies. We have gone through three major budget reduction and down-sizing efforts during this period, cutting approximately $50 million from the University's unrestricted budget of $450 million. Some of the more significant cuts were achieved by eliminating the office of the Vice President for Administrative Resources and streamlining administrative support services, outsourcing many legal services, and reducing facilities expenditures through service adjustments, productivity savings, and conservation initiatives.

During this time, Stanford has also combined unrestricted funds with a variety of other sources to create new academic initiatives and improve existing programs as well. Examples include:

- New undergraduate initiatives such as Freshman and Sophomore Seminars designed to promote close interaction with faculty; Sophomore Dialogue Tutorials, in which two to four students participate in directed readings; and Sophomore and Honors Colleges, where students come to Stanford before the start of the school year to live and work together in faculty-supervised academic programs.
- The Pacific Initiative, which includes an Asia Pacific Scholars Program modeled after the Rhodes Scholarships, a core faculty with new billets, and a restructured master's degree program in international policy with a track designed for students particularly interested in Asia and the Pacific.
- Increases in the number of undergraduate advisors, production of a training video for advisors, and creation of an Undergraduate Advising Center Web site.

EXHIBIT 2-5

A Measure of Instructional Productivity

Dr. George Waldner, President of York College of Pennsylvania, developed a "Quality Instruction Efficiency Index" for monitoring instructional productivity. A description follows.

In the normal course of institutional life in academia, there is a constant and passionate focus on qualitative improvement. That is clearly desirable and highly consistent with the overall mission of higher education. What is less prevalent, however, is a concomitant, vigorously advocated concern to attain educational quality in a highly cost-efficient way.

One approach to engendering greater emphasis on efficiency issues is an index of instructional productivity, which colleges and universities could use to measure their own productivity profile in relationship to their self-selected peer group of institutions and, especially, in reference to their institutional missions and circumstances.

Quality Instruction Efficiency Index

(QIEI)

Criteria Areas	Maximum Points
1. FTE Student: FTE Faculty Ratio (.5 score points subtracted per unit over 25)	20 (:1)
2. Average Full-time Faculty Instructional Load-Semester Hours Per Academic Year (Fall plus Spring) (.5 score points off for each hour over 25)	25
3. Percentage of Semester Hours Taught by Part-Time Faculty (.5 score points off for each percentage point over 20)	15
4. Average Section Size (.5 score points subtracted for each unit over 30)	25
5. Minimum Section Size (.5 score points off for each unit over 20)	15
Maximum Score	100

EXHIBIT 2-5 (Continued)

A Measure of Instructional Productivity

Space does not permit a full exposition of the QIEI, but the essential concepts are as follows:

Criterion #1   The Full-time Equivalent ratio of students to faculty is a foundation indicator of both efficiency and quality. The index posits 20 as a hypothetical norm. Institutions with richer (lower) ratios are penalized on this measure; institutions with much higher ratios, implying a diminution of quality, also lose some points.

Criterion #2   The QIEI focuses on instruction, since that is the principal service that students come to college to receive. Any excessive diversion of full-time faculty resources away from instruction erodes efficiency, while excessive teaching loads may impair quality. The norm is set at 25 semester hours per regular academic year, assuming that a full time faculty member teaches 12 semester hours (4 sections) in each semester, and that some faculty members opt to teach additional sections.

Criterion #3   Usage of part-time faculty, if done with appropriate support and not excessive in focused areas, can greatly enhance efficiency. The norm is set at 15%.

Criterion #4   It is widely recognized that student participation in the learning process enhances the quality of the educational experience. The norm posited is a section size of 25, with deductions beyond the level of 30.

Criterion #5   Small sections are the great bane of instructional efficiency, but sometimes essential in particular programs. Institutions need a policy (with very few exceptions permitted) on the minimum number of enrollees required for a course section to be offered. The norm is set at 15.

The point of the QIEI is not to make all colleges conform to the same "cookie-cutter" approach. Rather, it is to provide a tool for a broadly participatory campus dialogue, including faculty, administration, trustees, and students on what trade-offs the institution is making on the quality-efficiency continuum and whether the choices are producing the desired results. The QIEI can also highlight and lift up for emulation, particular peer institutions which excel at maximizing both quality and efficiency.

Note: The foregoing material may be quoted or utilized only with the author's permission.

Issue 3: Trends in college and university administrative costs, including administrative staffing, ratio of administrative staff to instructors, ratio of administrative staff to students, remuneration of administrative staff, and remuneration of college and university presidents or chancellors

Analysts examining rising higher education costs and prices typically include increased administrative costs as one of the key explanations for escalating tuitions. The need to employ more administrators to cover both expanded services and larger numbers of Federal, state, and local regulations combined with higher administrative salaries is thought to drive administrative costs up. Many contend that these costs are, in turn, passed on to students.

Findings

- Administrative expenditures increased as a share of total educational and general expenditures between 1980 and 1987 at all types of institutions — public universities, public four-year colleges, public two-year colleges, private universities, and private four-year colleges. Between 1987 and 1994, this ratio either remained steady or fell. (Exhibit 3-1)
- Administrative expenditures increased 24, 22, and 38 percent at public four-year, public two-year, and private four-year institutions respectively, between 1980 and 1987, after adjusting for inflation. Between 1987 and 1994, administrative expenditures increased at the rate of inflation. (Exhibits 3-2, 3-3, and 3-4)
- Between 1989 and 1994, the salaries for a wide variety of administrative positions increased, averaging between 5 and 6 percent a year. After 1994, only chief executives and business officers maintained this rate of increase, with deans of arts and science and directors of admissions and alumni affairs limited to cost of living adjustments. (Exhibit 3-5)

Conclusions

Have increases in college and university administrative costs affected tuition increases?

Possibly. Administrative expenditures per full-time-equivalent student have increased between the mid 1970s and mid 1990s and in some, but not all, types of institutions, the proportion of total educational and general expenditures represented by administrative costs has increased slightly. Testimony before the Commission also indicates that the administrative structure needed to support increasing numbers of state and Federal regulations has driven up administrative expenditures.

EXHIBIT 3-1

Administrative[1] Expenditures in Constant Dollars and as a Percentage of Total Educational and General Expenditures, 1976-77 to 1993-94

	Public Universities		Public Four-Yr. Colleges		Public Two-Yr. Colleges		Private Universities		Private Colleges	
	Expenditure per FTE student	Percent of Total E&G	Expenditure per FTE student	Percent of Total E&G	Expenditure per FTE student	Percent of Total E&G	Expenditure per FTE student	Percent of Total E&G	Expenditure per FTE student	Percent of Total E&G
1976-77	$1,848	13.0%	$1,728	16.7%	$1,013	18.1%	$2,918	13.2%	$2,214	20.4%
1977-78	1,889	13.2	1,748	16.7	1,091	19.4	2,908	13.4	2,225	20.6
1978-79	1,950	13.1	1,849	17.1	1,135	19.5	3,095	14.0	2,270	20.7
1979-80	1,846	12.5	1,886	17.3	1,087	19.0	3,171	14.2	2,311	20.8
1980-81	1,865	12.9	1,859	17.2	1,045	19.1	3,154	13.9	2,363	21.1
1981-82	1,871	13.1	1,892	17.6	1,040	19.0	3,120	13.8	2,423	21.4
1982-83	1,868	13.1	1,827	17.4	1,012	19.5	3,368	14.8	2,505	21.7
1983-84	1,918	13.1	1,933	18.2	1,041	19.8	3,717	15.2	2,588	21.6
1984-85	2,098	13.7	2,061	18.4	1,163	20.2	3,793	14.9	2,687	21.7
1985-86	2,212	13.9	2,133	18.4	1,227	20.7	3,956	15.0	2,784	21.7
1986-87	2,270	14.0	2,166	18.7	1,314	21.8	4,378	15.2	3,104	22.8
1987-88	2,307	13.9	2,176	18.4	1,264	21.3	4,427	15.2	3,075	22.1
1988-89	2,358	13.9	2,123	18.2	1,295	21.5	4,521	15.2	3,120	22.2
1989-90	2,326	13.8	2,188	18.7	1,255	21.5	4,438	14.7	3,129	21.9
1990-91	2,353	13.7	2,121	18.6	1,277	21.6	4,586	14.8	3,232	22.2
1991-92	2,276	13.3	2,185	18.9	1,184	20.9	4,726	14.8	3,184	21.4
1992-93	2,302	13.1	2,320	19.4	1,195	20.9	4,619	14.1	3,112	20.7
1993-94[2]	2,383	13.3	2,277	18.8	1,266	21.0	4,688	13.9	3,169	20.6

Figures were converted to constant 1993-94 dollars using The Higher Education Price Index.

Notes: [1]Includes institutional and academic support less libraries.
　　　　[2]Preliminary data.

Source: U.S. Department of Education, *Digest of Education Statistics*, 1996, Tables 338-342.

EXHIBIT 3-2

Education and General Expenditures by Type Per FTE Student
In Public Four-year Institutions: 1980, 1987, and 1994
Constant 1996 Dollars

	Instruction	Administration	Student Services	Research	Libraries	Public Service	Maintenance of Plant	Scholarships	Mandatory Transfers	Total
1979-80	$5,394	$1,918	$643	$1,801	$485	$730	$1,344	$438	$179	$12,932
1986-87	5,991	2,369	713	2,082	458	831	1,362	503	205	14,502
1993-94	6,068	2,519	777	2,540	461	982	1,263	819	244	15,674

Includes four-year colleges and universities.
Source: *Digest of Education Statistics,* Tables 196, 338, and 339.

EXHIBIT 3-3

Education and General Expenditures by Type Per FTE Student
In Public Two-year Institutions: 1980, 1987, and 1997
Constant 1996 Dollars

	Instruction	Administration	Student Services	Research	Libraries	Public Service	Maintenance of Plant	Scholarships	Mandatory Transfers	Total
1979-80	$2,951	$1,115	$507	$24	$188	$131	$688	$137	$127	$5,867
1986-87	3,104	1,363	588	7	142	136	722	140	52	6,254
1993-94	3,227	1,375	680	11	151	154	673	224	44	6,538

Source: *Digest of Education Statistics,* 1996, Tables 196 and 340.

EXHIBIT 3-4

Education and General Expenditures by Type Per FTE Student
In Private Four-year Institutions: 1980, 1987, and 1994
Constant 1996 Dollars

	Instruction	Administration	Student Services	Research	Libraries	Public Service	Maintenance of Plant	Scholarships	Mandatory Transfers	Total
1979-80	$5,540	$2,623	$845	$1,867	$548	$333	$1,521	$1,328	$276	$14,879
1986-87	6,853	3,624	1,169	2,145	560	497	1,659	2,036	346	18,889
1993-94	7,616	3,785	1,373	2,276	658	690	1,702	3,134	420	21,654

Includes four-year colleges and universities.
Source: *Digest of Education Statistics,* 1996, Tables 196, 341, and 342.

EXHIBIT 3-5

Change in Median Salaries of Selected Administrators: 1989, 1994, and 1997 (Constant 1996 Dollars)

	Academic Year		
	1988-89	1993-94	1996-97
Job Title			
Chief Executive of Single Institution	$106,103	$111,079	$119,219
Dean of Arts and Sciences	82,230	86,644	83,548
Chief Business Officer	77,173	82,109	85,756
Director of Admissions	52,388	54,291	52,326
Director of Alumni Affairs	41,221	41,912	41,743

Sources: *The Almanac of Higher Education* 1989-90 p.44-45, *The Almanac of Higher Education* 1995, p.50-53, *The Chronicle of Higher Education* 1996-97 Almanac Issue, p.24.

Issue 4: Trends of (a) faculty workload and remuneration (including the use of adjunct faculty), (b) faculty-to-student ratios, (c) number of hours spent in the classroom by faculty, and (d) tenure practices, and the impact of such trends on tuition

Because higher education is a labor-intensive industry, changes in policies that affect the number of faculty required to teach courses (workload and hours spent in the classroom), as well as the types of faculty hired (part-time vs. full-time, senior vs. junior, tenured vs. not tenured) can have a major impact on an institutions' cost of providing education. These costs, in turn, can be passed on to students in the form of tuition increases.

Tables presented in this section derive primarily from the 1988 and 1993 National Study of Postsecondary Faculty (NSOPF) conducted by the National Center for Education Statistics. This is one of the few sources of national faculty trend data that cover a broad range of issues. As a result, however, the most recent data is the fall of 1992 (the next NSOPF survey is scheduled for the fall of 1999). Other sources of faculty trend data are available on specific issues, such as compensation.

Findings

- In the fall of 1992, 58 percent of all instructional faculty and staff[1] were employed full time and 42 percent were employed part time. In the fall of 1987, 67 percent of all instructional faculty and staff were employed full time and 33 percent were employed part time. (Exhibit 4-1)
- There was a decline in the percentage of instructional faculty and staff who had tenure between the fall of 1987 and 1992 (from 58 percent to 54 percent) and an increase in the percentage of faculty who were not on a tenure track at their institution (from 8 percent to 11 percent) during this same time period. (Exhibit 4-2)
- There was an increase in the percentage of instructional faculty and staff who were instructors or lecturers between the fall of 1987 and the fall of 1992. (Exhibit 4-3)
- There was an increase in two measures of classroom workload between the fall of 1987 and the fall of 1992: student contact hours increased from 300 to 337 during this period, and the mean number of classroom hours increased from 9.8 hours to 11 hours. (Exhibit 4-5)
- Full-time instructional faculty and staff in public institutions were more likely than their counterparts in private institutions to believe that there had been pressure to increase their work load in recent years. (Exhibit 4-8)
- Faculty salaries essentially kept pace with inflation in the 1990s. (Exhibits 4-9 and 4-10)

Conclusions

Have changes in faculty composition and workload resulted in increased costs and tuition?

Probably not. Data indicate that institutions of higher education are relying more and more on part-time faculty who are paid less and often do not receive benefits. There also appears to be an increase in the use of instructors and lecturers who are also paid less than higher ranked faculty. In general, faculty salaries essentially kept pace with inflation throughout the 1990s, indicating no major cost increases.

EXHIBIT 4-1

Number and Percentage of Higher Education Instructional Faculty and Staff by Employment Status and Type and Control of Institution: Fall 1987 and Fall 1992

Type and control of institution and year	Instructional faculty and staff	Employment status	
		Full-time	Part-time
1992			
All institutions[1]	904,935	58.4	41.6
Public research	132,717	80.9	19.1
Private research	49,423	65.1	34.9
Public doctoral[2]	73,570	71.8	28.2
Private doctoral[2]	46,699	61.4	38.6
Public comprehensive	141,533	66.8	33.3
Private comprehensive	75,085	51.4	48.6
Private liberal arts	58,961	64.5	35.5
Public 2-year	276,292	39.8	60.2
Other[3]	50,654	51.7	48.3
1987			
All institutions[1]	769,825	66.9	33.1
Public research	119,334	85.6	14.4
Private research	53,120	78.3	21.7
Public doctoral[2]	67,678	83.2	16.8
Private doctoral[2]	39,793	63.0	37.0
Public comprehensive	130,341	74.5	25.5
Private comprehensive	60,457	60.9	39.1
Private liberal arts	55,391	69.4	30.6
Public 2-year	200,663	47.9	52.1
Other[3]	43,047	50.0	50.0

[1] All accredited, nonproprietary U.S. postsecondary institutions that grant a 2-year (A.A.) or higher degree and whose accreditation at the higher education level is recognized by the U.S. Department of Education.

[2] Includes institutions classified by the Carnegie Foundation as specialized medical schools.

[3] Public liberal arts, private 2-year, and religious and other specialized institutions, except medical.

SOURCE: U.S. Department of Education. National Center for Education Statistics. *[1993 National Study of Postsecondary Faculty (NSOPF-93)] Instructional Faculty and Staff in Higher Education Institutions: Fall 1987 and Fall 1992,* Table 2.1, NCES 97-447, by Rita Kirshstein, Nancy Matheson, and Zhongren Jing. Project Officer: Linda J. Zimbler. Washington, DC: 1997.

EXHIBIT 4-2

Number and Percentage of Full-time Higher Education Instructional Faculty and Staff, by Tenure Status and Type and Control of Institution: Fall 1987 and Fall 1992

Type and control of institution and year	Full-time instructional faculty and staff	Tenure status				
		Tenured	On tenure track	Not on tenure track	No tenure system for faculty status	No tenure system at institution
1992						
All institutions[1]	528,260	54.2	21.5	11.2	4.7	8.4
Public research	107,358	63.4	19.7	12.1	4.5	0.3
Private research	32,164	49.8	22.8	17.6	9.0	0.9
Public doctoral[2]	52,808	53.6	26.7	15.7	3.8	0.2
Private doctoral[2]	28,684	45.6	27.1	13.9	7.6	5.8
Public comprehensive	94,477	60.7	24.5	11.1	3.3	0.4
Private comprehensive	38,561	52.9	26.1	12.3	3.7	5.1
Private liberal arts	38,052	46.0	25.4	12.6	5.1	10.9
Public 2-year	109,957	52.7	15.2	6.0	4.3	21.8
Other[3]	26,200	28.6	14.2	7.3	7.0	42.9
1987						
All institutions[1]	515,138	58.4	21.0	7.9	3.6	9.1
Public research	102,115	66.9	19.2	8.5	4.6	0.7
Private research	41,574	52.4	29.7	13.1	3.2	1.7
Public doctoral[2]	56,294	58.1	27.1	11.6	3.0	0.2
Private doctoral[2]	25,065	43.7	28.1	2.1	6.6	19.6
Public comprehensive	97,131	65.2	22.1	8.7	2.9	1.1
Private comprehensive	36,842	54.9	29.4	8.7	3.8	3.2
Private liberal arts	38,446	49.4	24.5	8.2	5.3	12.7
Public 2-year	96,144	59.6	9.1	4.0	2.3	25.0
Other[3]	21,528	34.6	16.1	4.3	3.4	41.7

[1] All accredited, nonproprietary U.S. postsecondary institutions that grant a 2-year (A.A.) or higher degree and whose accreditation at the higher education level is recognized by the U.S. Department of Education.

[2] Includes institutions classified by the Carnegie Foundation as specialized medical schools.

[3] Public liberal arts, private 2-year, and religious and other specialized institutions, except medical.

SOURCE: U.S. Department of Education. National Center for Education Statistics. *[1993 National Study of Postsecondary Faculty (NSOPF-93)] Instructional Faculty and Staff in Higher Education Institutions: Fall 1987 and Fall 1992,* Table 2.5, NCES 97-447, by Rita Kirshstein, Nancy Matheson, and Zhongren Jing. Project Officer: Linda J. Zimbler. Washington, DC: 1997.

EXHIBIT 4-3

Number and Percentage of Full-time Higher Education Instructional Faculty and Staff in 4-year Institutions, by Tenure Status and Program Area: Fall 1987 and Fall 1992

Program area and year	Full-time instructional faculty and staff	Tenure status				
		Tenured	On tenure track	Not on tenure track	No tenure system for faculty status	No tenure system at institution
1992						
All program areas in 4-year institutions*	405,783	55.5	23.5	12.4	4.5	4.1
Agriculture/home economics	9,698	72.4	19.3	4.1	3.5	0.7
Business	28,895	51.5	29.9	10.4	3.6	4.5
Education	30,127	54.9	23.6	14.1	4.7	2.7
Engineering	20,381	61.8	27.5	6.0	1.4	3.3
Fine arts	26,874	52.9	22.1	9.7	3.4	11.9
Humanities	54,093	59.9	18.7	11.6	5.5	4.3
Natural sciences	79,663	63.7	21.4	9.0	3.1	2.8
Social sciences	48,030	63.4	23.0	8.5	2.5	2.7
All other fields	44,346	49.1	25.7	13.6	6.8	4.8
1987						
All program areas in 4-year institutions*	414,832	58.5	23.9	8.9	3.9	4.7
Agriculture/home economics	10,104	75.3	16.8	4.9	2.6	0.4
Business	28,630	42.9	36.7	11.5	3.6	5.3
Education	31,812	60.5	18.9	12.5	3.6	4.5
Engineering	20,915	61.8	29.9	4.5	2.4	1.2
Fine arts	27,628	56.5	23.0	8.1	4.7	7.7
Humanities	60,781	68.7	15.8	6.7	4.7	4.1
Natural sciences	74,852	63.3	23.2	7.2	3.2	3.2
Social sciences	47,324	67.9	21.9	5.2	1.9	3.1
All other fields	29,042	53.5	31.2	9.0	3.4	3.0

* Health sciences faculty are included in the program area but are not shown separately. See Technical Notes for details.

SOURCE: U.S. Department of Education. National Center for Education Statistics. *[1993 National Study of Postsecondary Faculty (NSOPF-93)] Instructional Faculty and Staff in Higher Education Institutions: Fall 1987 and Fall 1992,* Table 2.6, NCES 97-447, by Rita Kirshstein, Nancy Matheson, and Zhongren Jing. Project Officer: Linda J. Zimbler. Washington, DC: 1997.

EXHIBIT 4-4

Number and Percentage of Full-time Higher Education Instructional Faculty and Staff, by Academic Rank and Type and Control of Institution: Fall 1987 and Fall 1992

Type and control of institution and year	Full-time instructional faculty and staff	Academic rank				
		Full professor	Associate professor	Assistant professor	Instructor or lecturer	Other ranks/ not applicable
1992						
All institutions[1]	528,260	30.4	23.4	23.5	16.2	6.4
Public research	107,358	39.8	26.4	22.7	7.8	3.4
Private research	32,164	33.3	22.7	27.0	11.2	5.8
Public doctoral[2]	52,808	31.3	26.3	31.2	9.3	2.0
Private doctoral[2]	28,684	30.5	26.8	29.1	10.9	2.7
Public comprehensive	94,477	34.3	26.9	26.1	11.2	1.5
Private comprehensive	38,561	26.8	29.0	31.9	9.2	3.2
Private liberal arts	38,052	28.7	25.3	29.9	10.8	5.4
Public 2-year	109,957	19.1	12.9	11.3	40.1	16.7
Other[3]	26,200	27.8	23.4	21.8	13.2	13.8
1987						
All institutions[1]	515,138	32.7	23.5	23.0	13.4	7.5
Public research	102,115	44.3	27.8	21.8	5.9	0.2
Private research	41,574	37.9	25.2	29.0	5.7	2.2
Public doctoral[2]	56,294	34.2	30.4	26.9	7.8	0.7
Private doctoral[2]	25,065	33.2	27.7	30.2	9.0	0.0
Public comprehensive	97,131	36.8	26.1	23.3	12.6	1.2
Private comprehensive	36,842	31.1	28.9	32.8	6.8	0.4
Private liberal arts	38,446	30.4	22.2	31.2	10.6	5.7
Public 2-year	96,144	15.6	9.4	11.2	33.8	29.9
Other[3]	21,528	27.2	20.2	18.3	12.4	22.0

[1] All accredited, nonproprietary U.S. postsecondary institutions that grant a 2-year (A.A.) or higher degree and whose accreditation at the higher education level is recognized by the U.S. Department of Education.

[2] Includes institutions classified by the Carnegie Foundation as specialized medical schools.

[3] Public liberal arts, private 2-year, and religious and other specialized institutions, except medical.

SOURCE: U.S. Department of Education. National Center for Education Statistics. *[1993 National Study of Postsecondary Faculty (NSOPF-93)] Instructional Faculty and Staff in Higher Education Institutions: Fall 1987 and Fall 1992,* Table 2.3, NCES 97-447, by Rita Kirshstein, Nancy Matheson, and Zhongren Jing. Project Officer: Linda J. Zimbler. Washington, DC: 1997.

EXHIBIT 4-5

Mean Number of Classroom Hours and Student Contact Hours of Full-time Instructional Faculty and Staff, by Type and Control of Institution: Fall 1987 and Fall 1992

Type and control of institution and year	Full-time instructional faculty and staff	Mean classroom hours	Mean student contact hours[1]
1992			
All institutions[2]	528,260	11.0	337.4
Public research	107,358	6.9	281.3
Private research	32,164	7.1	231.7
Public doctoral[3]	52,808	9.7	337.1
Private doctoral[3]	28,684	8.3	395.6
Public comprehensive	94,477	10.9	337.0
Private comprehensive	38,561	10.6	273.6
Private liberal arts	38,052	11.0	242.4
Public 2-year	109,957	16.3	457.3
Other[4]	26,200	12.9	321.4
1987			
All institutions[2]	515,138	9.8	300.4
Public research	102,115	6.7	263.5
Private research	41,574	5.9	225.5
Public doctoral[3]	56,294	8.1	285.9
Private doctoral[3]	25,065	6.7	200.1
Public comprehensive	97,131	10.4	316.7
Private comprehensive	36,842	10.8	276.1
Private liberal arts	38,446	10.5	234.5
Public 2-year	96,144	15.1	420.8
Other[4]	21,528	10.8	322.6

[1] Number of hours per week spent teaching classes, multiplied by the number of students in those classes.

[2] All accredited, nonproprietary U.S. postsecondary institutions that grant a 2-year (A.A.) or higher degree and whose accreditation at the higher education level is recognized by the U.S. Department of Education.

[3] Includes institutions classified by the Carnegie Foundation as specialized medical schools.

[4] Public liberal arts, private 2-year, and religious and other specialized institutions, except medical.

SOURCE: U.S. Department of Education. National Center for Education Statistics. *[1993 National Study of Postsecondary Faculty (NSOPF-93)] Instructional Faculty and Staff in Higher Education Institutions: Fall 1987 and Fall 1992,* Table 3.5, NCES 97-447, by Rita Kirshstein, Nancy Matheson, and Zhongren Jing. Project Officer: Linda J. Zimbler. Washington, DC: 1997.

EXHIBIT 4-6

Mean Number of Hours Worked by Full-time Instructional Faculty and Staff, by Type and Control of Institution: Fall 1987 and Fall 1992

Type and control of institution and year	Full-time instructional faculty and staff	Mean hours worked per week
1992		
All institutions[1]	528,260	52.5
Public research	107,358	56.4
Private research	32,164	57.6
Public doctoral[2]	52,808	55.1
Private doctoral[2]	28,684	53.4
Public comprehensive	94,477	52.4
Private comprehensive	38,561	51.9
Private liberal arts	38,052	52.5
Public 2-year	109,957	46.9
Other[3]	26,200	49.0
1987		
All institutions[1]	515,138	52.7
Public research	102,115	56.8
Private research	41,574	56.1
Public doctoral[2]	56,294	54.7
Private doctoral[2]	25,065	52.2
Public comprehensive	97,131	52.7
Private comprehensive	36,842	51.2
Private liberal arts	38,446	52.5
Public 2-year	96,144	46.9
Other[3]	21,528	51.9

[1] All accredited, nonproprietary U.S. postsecondary institutions that grant a 2-year (A.A.) or higher degree and whose accreditation at the higher education level is recognized by the U.S. Department of Education.

[2] Includes institutions classified by the Carnegie Foundation as specialized medical schools.

[3] Public liberal arts, private 2-year, and religious and other specialized institutions, except medical.

SOURCE: U.S. Department of Education. National Center for Education Statistics. *[1993 National Study of Postsecondary Faculty (NSOPF-93)] Instructional Faculty and Staff in Higher Education Institutions: Fall 1987 and Fall 1992,* Table 3.1, NCES 97-447, by Rita Kirshstein, Nancy Matheson, and Zhongren Jing. Project Officer: Linda J. Zimbler. Washington, DC: 1997.

EXHIBIT 4-7

Percentage Distribution of Full-time Instructional Faculty and Staff, by Time Allocation and Type and Control of Institution: Fall 1987 and Fall 1992

Type and control of institution and year	Full-time instructional faculty and staff	Percentage of time spent			
		Teaching activities	Research activities	Administrative activities	Other activities
1992					
All institutions[1]	528,260	54.4	17.6	13.1	14.7
Public research	107,358	40.4	31.5	12.9	15.2
Private research	32,164	34.6	35.3	12.8	16.8
Public doctoral[2]	52,808	46.8	23.8	13.2	16.1
Private doctoral[2]	28,684	44.5	21.7	15.7	18.1
Public comprehensive	94,477	60.2	14.0	12.0	13.7
Private comprehensive	38,561	59.5	11.8	14.6	13.8
Private liberal arts	38,052	63.5	9.6	14.7	11.8
Public 2-year	109,957	68.7	4.5	12.0	14.6
Other[3]	26,200	60.8	10.7	14.9	13.5
1987					
All institutions[1]	515,138	57.1	17.3	13.2	12.5
Public research	102,115	43.6	30.1	13.9	12.3
Private research	41,574	42.1	30.6	13.2	14.2
Public doctoral[2]	56,294	47.8	22.8	14.7	14.7
Private doctoral[2]	25,065	41.1	26.4	12.8	19.6
Public comprehensive	97,131	63.5	12.3	12.8	11.4
Private comprehensive	36,842	63.7	11.2	14.2	11.0
Private liberal arts	38,446	66.8	10.5	13.8	9.0
Public 2-year	96,144	73.3	4.2	10.9	11.6
Other[3]	21,528	63.6	8.8	15.2	12.5

[1] All accredited, nonproprietary U.S. postsecondary institutions that grant a 2-year (A.A.) or higher degree and whose accreditation at the higher education level is recognized by the U.S. Department of Education.

[2] Includes institutions classified by the Carnegie Foundation as specialized medical schools.

[3] Public liberal arts, private 2-year, and religious and other specialized institutions, except medical.

SOURCE: U.S. Department of Education. National Center for Education Statistics. *[1993 National Study of Postsecondary Faculty (NSOPF-93)] Instructional Faculty and Staff in Higher Education Institutions: Fall 1987 and Fall 1992*, Table 3.3, NCES 97-447, by Rita Kirshstein, Nancy Matheson, and Zhongren Jing. Project Officer: Linda J. Zimbler. Washington, DC: 1997.

EXHIBIT 4-8

Percentage Distribution of Full-time Instructional Faculty and Staff, by Perception of Pressure to Increase Work Load in Recent Years and Type and Control of Institution: Fall 1992

Type and control of institution and year	Full-time instructional faculty and staff	Worsened	Stayed the same	Improved	Don't know
1992					
All institutions[1]	528,260	51.2	34.4	8.3	6.1
Public research	107,358	61.9	25.3	7.2	5.5
Private research	32,164	45.6	41.2	5.5	7.7
Public doctoral[2]	52,808	60.1	27.2	6.9	5.8
Private doctoral[2]	28,684	40.8	42.0	10.1	7.2
Public comprehensive	94,477	53.6	32.6	8.4	5.4
Private comprehensive	38,561	36.4	44.3	12.8	6.5
Private liberal arts	38,052	40.2	39.7	13.4	6.8
Public 2-year	109,957	49.3	38.6	6.4	5.8
Other[3]	26,200	45.1	36.8	10.2	7.9

[1] All accredited, nonproprietary U.S. postsecondary institutions that grant a 2-year (A.A.) or higher degree and whose accreditation at the higher education level is recognized by the U.S. Department of Education.

[2] Includes institutions classified by the Carnegie Foundation as specialized medical schools.

[3] Public liberal arts, private 2-year, and religious and other specialized institutions, except medical.

SOURCE: U.S. Department of Education. National Center for Education Statistics. *[1993 National Study of Postsecondary Faculty (NSOPF-93)] Instructional Faculty and Staff in Higher Education Institutions: Fall 1987 and Fall 1992,* Table 3.11, NCES 97-447, by Rita Kirshstein, Nancy Matheson, and Zhongren Jing. Project Officer: Linda J. Zimbler. Washington, DC: 1997.

EXHIBIT 4-9

Average Faculty Salary Levels by Sector, Institution Type, and Academic Rank: 1985-86, 1990-91, and 1996-97
(1996 Constant Dollars)

	SALARY		
	1985-86	1990-91	1996-97
Public			
Doctoral Institutions			
Academic Rank			
Professor	$66,435	$72,568	$72,220
Associate	48,747	52,820	52,110
Assistant	40,902	44,393	43,625
Instructor	29,791	31,104	32,127
Lecturer	35,623	37,562	36,989
No rank	-	36,206	38,789
All combined	52,830	57,202	59,851
General Baccalaureate Institutions			
Academic Rank			
Professor	51,926	53,901	54,614
Associate	43,381	45,077	44,935
Assistant	36,294	37,682	37,545
Instructor	29,368	31,824	30,048
Lecturer	32,430	32,544	31,137
No rank	-	43,985	34,656
All combined	41,456	43,709	43,794
Two Year Colleges with Ranks			
Academic Rank			
Professor	50,847	54,081	52,752
Associate	43,395	45,701	43,887
Assistant	37,154	38,259	38,099
Instructor	31,234	32,484	33,641
Lecturer	27,049	26,998	29,188
No rank	-	30,156	35,067
All combined	41,573	43,721	43,356
Private Independents			
Doctoral Institution			
Academic Rank			
Professor	77,561	87,573	92,112
Associate	53,019	59,327	60,360
Assistant	43,527	49,987	51,255
Instructor	34,078	38,823	39,574
Lecturer	36,250	41,368	40,337
No rank	-	41,224	44,861
All combined	60,850	68,810	72,296

EXHIBIT 4-9 (Continued)

Average Faculty Salary Levels by Sector, Institution Type, and Academic Rank: 1985-86, 1990-91, and 1996-97
(1996 Constant Dollars)

| | SALARY | | |
	1985-86	1990-91	1996-97
General Baccalaureate			
Academic Rank			
Professor	55,702	59,555	62,047
Associate	42,273	45,858	46,819
Assistant	34,471	37,898	38,393
Instructor	27,253	30,576	30,080
Lecturer	35,405	39,423	39,444
No rank	-	40,503	36,009
All combined	42,346	46,362	48,455

Source: American Association of University Professors, *Academe*, 1996-97, 90-91, 85-86, p. 26, 21, and 9.

EXHIBIT 4-10

Percentage Increases in Real Salaries for All Faculty Ranks

Year	Professor	Associate	Assistant	Instructor	All Ranks
1976-77	-0.2	-0.2	-0.2	-0.2	-0.2
1977-78	-1.4	-1.2	-1.3	-1.2	-1.3
1978-79	-3.1	-2.9	-2.8	-2.7	-2.9
1979-80	-5.1	-5.5	-5.7	-6.1	-5.4
1980-81	-3.3	-3.6	-3.3	-3.5	-3.4
1981-82	-0.1	-0.1	-0.2	-0.7	-0.1
1982-83	2.4	2.4	2.9	2.8	2.5
1983-84	-0.8	0.6	1.2	1.3	0.9
1984-85	2.7	2.4	2.6	2.2	2.6
1985-86	2.2	2	2.3	2	2.2
1986-87	4.8	4.6	4.5	3.8	4.7
1987-88	0.6	0.4	0.5	-0.6	0.5
1988-89	1.3	2.2	1.5	0.9	1.3
1989-90	1.6	1.6	1.6	0.7	1.4
1990-91	-0.6	-0.8	-0.6	-1.1	-0.7
1991-92	0.3	0.4	0.7	0.8	0.4
1992-93	-0.3	-0.6	-0.3	-0.6	-0.4
1993-94	0.3	0.4	0.3	0.5	0.3
1994-95	0.7	0.7	0.5	0.8	0.7
1995-96	0.6	0.4	0.2	0.1	0.4
1996-97	-0.4	-0.3	-0.9	-0.1	-0.3

Source: American Association of University Professors, *Academe*, March/April 1997, p.14.

EXHIBIT 4-11

Teaching Responsibilities at Yale University by Department

Department	Hours Taught by Teaching Assistants	Hours Taught by Tenured & Tenure-Track Faculty
American Studies	44.0	18.5
Art History	34.0	34.0
Economics	49.0	34.0
English	75.5	76.0
French	59.0	16.5
German	51.0	13.0
History	132.0	83.5
Italian	55.0	12.5
Latin	21.5	9.0
Music	46.5	30.0
Philosophy	36.5	36.5
Political Science	57.0	72.5
Russian	32.5	20.0
Sociology	29.0	28.5
Spanish	83.0	20.0
All Departments	864.0	765.5

SOURCE: Federation of University Employees at Yale, *Study Shows Teaching Assistants Do Majority of Teaching at Yale,* March 28, 1995.

Issue 5: Trends in (a) the construction and renovation of academic and other collegiate facilities, and (b) the modernization of facilities to access and utilize new technologies, and the impact of such trends on tuition

An often-cited explanation for increasing college tuition is a decaying physical plant exacerbated by years of deferring needed repairs and renovations. A recent National Science Foundation survey of scientific and engineering research facilities estimated that deferred maintenance costs to replace or repair existing science and engineering facilities was approximately $9.3 billion.[1] Another recent report, *A Foundation to Uphold*, estimates deferred maintenance costs for all campus facilities to be approximately $26 billion.[2]

In addition to the costs of maintaining and renovating their buildings, higher education institutions must also face the costs associated with the quality of resources located within their infrastructure. Both library expenditures and the cost of technology continue to require substantial funds from higher education institutions. Thus, not only are many college and university buildings and laboratories old and outdated in terms of computer wiring and other types of infrastructure needs, but they are also struggling to maintain quality information access within the walls of these buildings on our nation's campuses.

Findings

Academic Facilities

- An average of 27.5 percent of the gross square footage of campus buildings was renovated between 1975 and 1990. (Exhibit 5-1)
- Two-year colleges and medical schools have the newest facilities; almost three-quarters of their gross square footage was renovated or constructed between 1975 and 1990. (Exhibit 5-2)
- Half of all respondents to a recent campus facilities survey reported their accumulated deferred maintenance had increased since 1988. (Exhibit 5-3)
- The estimated average deferred maintenance (ADM) for public research institutions was $63.9 million; the average ADM for private research institutions was $59.1 million: the average ADM for public four-year colleges was $19.2 million; and for private four-year colleges the average ADM was reported to be $6.5 million. (Exhibit 5-5)

Science and Engineering Research Facilities

- The amount of science and engineering research space in need of repair generally increased in all fields between 1988 and 1996. (Exhibit 5-10)
- Colleges and universities spent $2.8 billion to construct science and engineering research facilities during fiscal years 1994 and 1995. (Exhibit 5-11)
- Colleges and universities spent $1.1 billion to repair or renovate science and engineering research facilities during fiscal years 1994 and 1995. (Exhibit 5-12)
- The total estimated cost for deferred science and engineering research construction and repair/renovation projects in 1996 was $9.3 billion. (Exhibit 5-13)

Library Expenditures by Type of Institution

- Private university libraries spent more per full-time-equivalent student than other types of institutions. (Exhibit 5-14)

- While per-full-time-equivalent student expenditures by private university libraries declined during the early 1980's, overall they rose. The average library expenditure per-full-time-equivalent student remained steady at other types of institutions. (Exhibit 5-14)

Technology Costs

- Technology costs are a growing concern for more institutions. According to *The 1997 National Survey of Information Technology in Higher Education*, 20.4 percent of survey respondents (up from 17.4 percent the previous year) identify "financing the replacement of aging hardware and software" as the most pressing information technology issue for their campus.

- Between 1994 and 1997 the percentage of courses that used technology in instruction including E-mail, Internet, and CD-Rom based materials, increased. (Exhibit 5-15)

- Growing numbers of institutions, particularly public colleges and universities, are charging mandatory user fees to help support the campus technology infrastructure and underwrite some of the operating costs associated with academic computing. (Exhibit 5-16)

- Less than a third of the campuses participating in *The 1997 National Survey of Information Technology in Higher Education* reported a working financial plan for information technology. The vast majority of US colleges and universities (70.1 percent) continue to fund most of their equipment, network, and software expenses with one-time budget allocations or special appropriations. (Exhibit 5-17)

- The total cost of incorporating information technology in education is not explicit. Some costs (i.e., monetary costs, such as computer and network hardware and software) are obvious, while others (i.e., space and time costs) are difficult to quantify. (Tissue, Brian M. The Costs of Incorporating Information Technology in Education. http://www.chem.vt. edu/archive/chemconf97/paper04.html#3

Conclusions

Have costs to construct and renovate campus facilities affected tuition increases?

Probably. Deferred maintenance costs appear to be increasing and the amount of science and engineering research space in need of repair generally rose between 1988 and 1996. Furthermore, all types of colleges and universities report large deferred maintenance costs, ranging from $4.8 million in two-year colleges to $63.9 million in public research universities. These deferred maintenance costs suggest that facilities costs will continue to exert pressure on institutions to either raise tuitions or revenue from sources other than tuition.

Have technology costs driven tuitions up?

Possibly. As is the case with elementary/secondary education, technology has become an integral part of today's college and university campus. Technology costs are a growing concern for higher education institutions, although data that explicitly specify how much colleges and universities are spending on technology are not readily available.

EXHIBIT 5-1

Percentages of Total Gross Square Footage Renovated Between 1975 and 1990 by Type of Institution

	Public Research	Private Research	Doctoral Universities	Public 4-yr/MA	Private Masters
Below 10%	38.8%	25.0%	19.0%	28.8%	25.0%
10% to 19%	25.8	25.0	28.6	32.2	12.5
20% to 29%	16.1	16.7	19.0	11.8	29.2
30% to 39%	16.1	16.7	19.0	6.8	12.5
40% to 49%	3.2	0.0	9.6	6.8	4.2
50% to 59%	0.0	8.3	0.0	3.4	8.3
60% Or More	0.0	8.3	4.8	10.2	8.3
Total	100.0%	100.0%	100.0%	100.0%	100.0%
Median	14.4%	20.0%	21.2%	16.6%	24.3%
Mean	17.2%	24.4%	23.4%	23.7%	26.3%
Number	31	12	21	59	24

	Private 4-Year	Pub/Priv HBCUs	2-Year Colleges	Medical Colleges	All Respondents
Below 10%	12.5%	28.6%	45.7%	22.2%	27.0%
10% to 19%	28.6	14.3	14.3	33.3	25.1
20% to 29%	16.1	14.3	8.6	0.0	14.9
30% to 39%	12.5	14.3	5.7	22.2	11.8
40% to 49%	7.1	0.0	5.7	0.0	5.5
50% to 59%	7.1	0.0	2.9	11.1	4.3
60% Or More	16.1	28.6	17.1	11.1	11.4
Total	100.0%	100.0%	100.0%	100.0%	100.0%
Median	25.6%	25.0%	13.0%	18.3%	19.1%
Mean	33.8%	30.8%	28.9%	30.6%	27.5%
Number	56	7	35	9	255

Source: APPA (1997), *A Foundation to Uphold*, Table II-6.

EXHIBIT 5-2

Percentage of Total Gross Square Footage Renovated and Constructed Between 1975 and 1990 by Type of Institution

	Percent Renovated	Percent Constructed	Percent Combined
Two-Year Colleges	25.6%	50.1%	75.7%
Medical Colleges	25.8	48.0	73.8
Public/Private HBCUs	28.3	31.1	59.4
Public Four-year/Masters	22.3	33.6	55.9
Private Masters Universities	24.1	28.5	52.6
Private Four-year Colleges	32.4	19.8	52.2
Private Research Universities	22.7	27.3	50.0
Doctoral Universities	22.2	23.1	45.3
Public Research Universities	16.3	25.1	41.4
All Colleges	23.2	32.3	55.5

Source: APPA (1997), *A Foundation to Uphold*, p. 94.

Note: This table does not eliminate duplicates—facilities that were constructed and renovated between 1975 and 1990. Thus, it overestimates the newness of the facilities.

EXHIBIT 5-3

Changes in Accumulated Deferred Maintenance
Since 1988, by Type of Institution

	Public Research	Private Research	Doctoral Universities	Public Four-year/MA	Private Masters
Increased	76.0%*	42.9%	57.9%	62.2%	36.4%
Decreased	8.0*	23.8	21.0	16.2	36.4
Same	14.0	23.8	15.8	13.5	18.2
No Answer	2.0	9.5	5.3	8.1	9.0
Total	100.0%	100.0%	100.0%	100.0%	100.0%
Number	50	21	38	74	33

	Private 4-Year	Pub/Priv HBCUs	2-Year Colleges	Medical Colleges	All Respondents
Increased	32.9%*	47.2%	40.3%	38.9%	49.5%
Decreased	45.2*	22.2	12.3	27.8	23.5
Same	12.3	25.0	24.6	22.2	17.5
No Answer	9.6	5.6	22.8*	11.1	9.5
Total	100.0%	100.0%	100.0%	100.0%	100.0%
Number	73	36	57	18	400

* Indicates percentages are statistically significantly different from other row percentages, at the 0.05 level of significance.

Source: APPA (1997). *A Foundation to Uphold*. Table IV-1.

EXHIBIT 5-4

Total Funding Necessary To Eliminate Accumulated Deferred Maintenance At The End Of 1994-95, By Type of Institution

Millions	Public Research	Private Research	Doctoral Universities	Public 4-YR/MA	Private Masters	Private 4-Year	Pub/Priv HBCUs	2-Year Colleges	Medical Colleges	All Respondents
Under $1.00	4.5%	11.1%	3.1%	4.5%	17.8%	23.5%	31.0%	41.4%	13.3%	17.0%
$1 to $2.9	0.0	0.0	6.2	16.4	25.0	30.9	20.7	23.9	13.3	17.2
$3 to $6.9	0.0	5.6	6.2	25.4	25.0	20.6	17.2	13.0	0.0	14.9
$7 to $10.9	2.2	0.0	18.9	11.9	3.6	7.4	6.9	2.2	13.3	7.5
$11 to $14.9	4.5	0.0	3.1	8.8	3.6	1.5	6.9	4.3	13.3	4.9
$15 to $20.9	4.5	11.1	21.9	7.5	14.3	8.8	10.3	6.6	26.7	10.3
$21 to $29.9	2.2	11.1	12.5	7.5	7.1	4.4	0	4.3	6.7	5.8
$30 to $44.9	8.8	5.6	0	6	3.6	2.9	3.5	0.0	6.7	4.0
$45 to $53.9	13.3	5.6	9.4	3	0.0	0.0	0.0	0.0	0.0	3.4
$54 to $59.9	4.5	0.0	0	1.5	0.0	0.0	0.0	0.0	0.0	0.9
$60 to $69.9	11.1	11.1	9.4	0.0	0.0	0.0	0.0	0.0	0.0	2.9
$70 to $79.9	17.8	0.0	3.1	0.0	0.0	0.0	0.0	0.0	0.0	2.6
$80 to $89.9	2.2	0.0	3.1	3.0	0.0	0.0	0.0	0.0	0.0	1.1
$90 to $99.9	0.0	5.6	0.0	0.0	0.0	0.0	0.0	0.0	0.0	0.3
$100 or More	24.4	33.2	3.1	4.5	0.0	0.0	3.5	4.3	6.7	7.2
Total	100.0%	100.0%	100.0%	100.0%	100.0%	100.0%	100.0%	100.0%	100.0%	100.0%
Median	$63.1	$48.0	$17.4	$9.2	$6.3	$2.7	$2.8	$1.7	$14.5	$7.5
Number	45	18	32	67	28	68	29	46	15	348

Source: APPA (1997), *A Foundation to Uphold,* Table IV-2.

EXHIBIT 5-5

Estimated Average and Total Accumulated Deferred Maintenance For All Colleges, By Type of Institution
[dollar amounts in millions]

	Average ADM*	Low	Middle	High
Public Research	$63.9	$5,160	$5,432	$5,703
Private Research	59.1	2,190	2,305	2,420
Doctoral Universities	24.6	2,524	2,657	2,790
Public 4-Year/Masters	19.2	5,890	7,392	7,762
Private Masters	8.4	1,557	2,108	2,213
Private 4-Year	6.5	2,224	3,263	3,426
Public/Private HBCUs	6.3	481	617	648
2-Year Colleges	4.8	4,549	6,864	7,207
Medical Colleges	19.7	1,033	1,418	1,489
All Colleges		$25,608	$32,056	$33,658

*Averages are for the responding colleges.

Source: APPA (1997), *A Foundation to Uphold,* Table IV-3.

EXHIBIT 5-6
Additions to Public Institutions Physical Plants by Type of Addition: 1969-1994

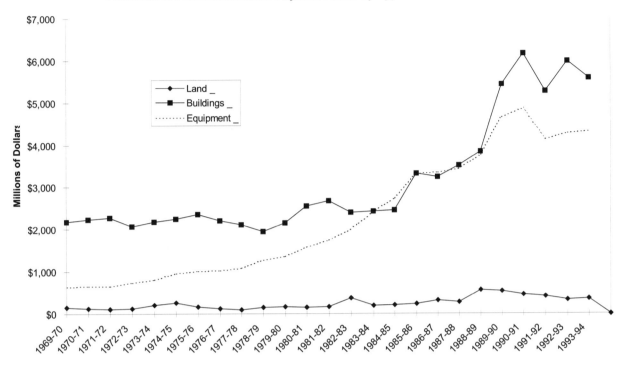

Source: National Center for Education Statistics, "Financial Statistics of Institutions of Higher Education" surveys and IPEDS "Finance" surveys.

EXHIBIT 5-7
Additions to Private Institutions Physical Plants by Type of Additions, 1969-1994

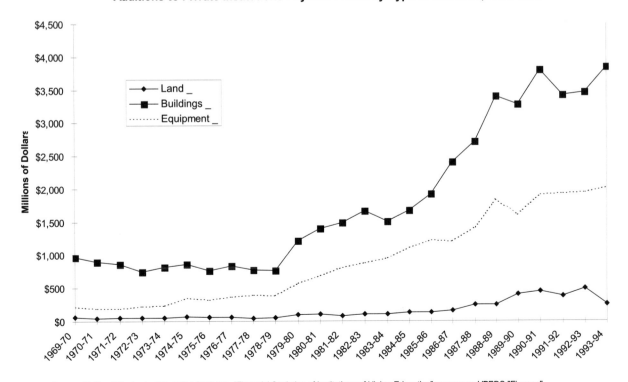

Source: National Center for Education Statistics, "Financial Statistics of Institutions of Higher Education" surveys and IPEDS "Finance" surveys.

EXHIBIT 5-8

Value of Physical Plant by Type of Property: 1899-1900 to 1993-1994

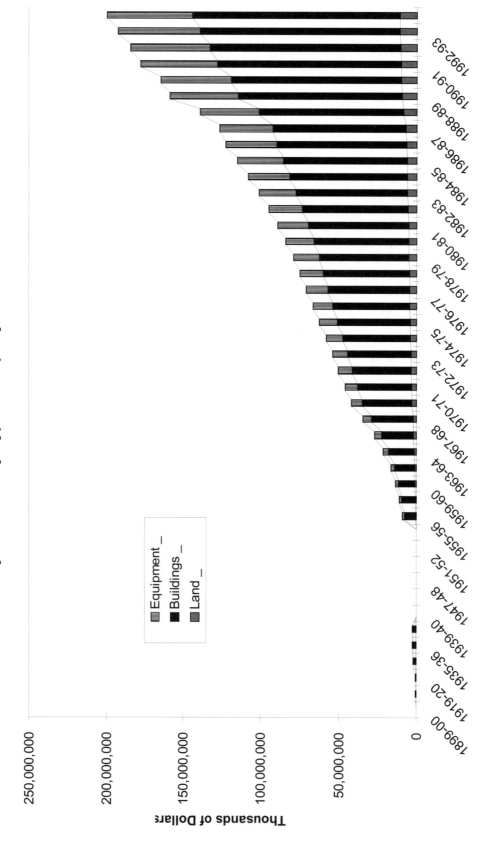

Source: National Center for Education Statistics, "Financial Statistics of Institutions of Higher Education" surveys and IPEDS "Finance" surveys.

EXHIBIT 5-9

Sources of Funds for Construction and Renovation, by Sector: 1994

PUBLIC

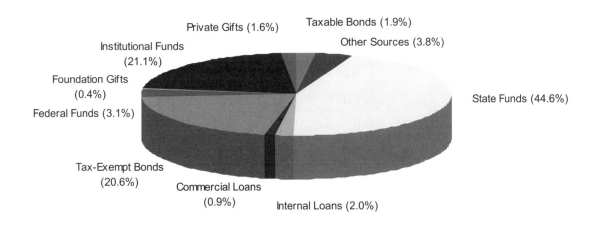

PRIVATE

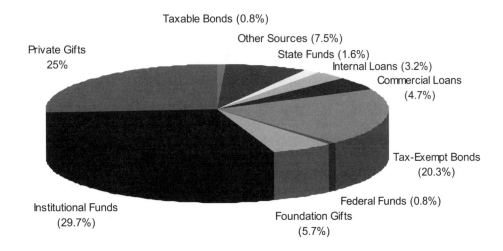

Source: APPA (1997). *A Foundation to Uphold*. Figure 10.

EXHIBIT 5-10

Trends in the Amount of Science and Engineering Research Space Requiring Repair/Renovation or Replacement by Field: 1988-1996
[net assignable square feet in millions]

Field	1988	1990	1992 [1]	1994 [1]	1996
Biological sciences—outside medical school	2.4	2.5	2.6	3.2	3.4
Physical sciences	2.9	2.7	2.4	3.1	3.4
Psychology	0.4	0.4	0.3	0.4	0.4
Social sciences	0.3	0.3	0.4	0.3	0.5
Mathematics	0.1	0.1	0.1	0.1	0.1
Computer sciences	0.2	0.1	0.1	0.1	0.2
Earth, atmospheric, and ocean sciences	0.9	0.9	0.8	1.3	1.3
Engineering	2.2	2.6	2.3	3.2	4.0
Agricultural sciences	3.6	4.6	5.2	4.4	5.3
Medical sciences—outside medical school	0.8	0.9	1.0	1.0	1.5
Medical sciences—medical school	2.4	1.9	2.7	2.9	3.6
Biological sciences—medical school	1.0	1.2	1.6	1.6	1.6

[1]Includes both "require major repair or renovation" and "requires replacement."

Source: National Science Foundation (1996). *Scientific and Engineering Research Facilities at Colleges and Universities.*

EXHIBIT 5-11

Trends in Expenditures to Construct Science and Engineering Research Facilities by Institution Type: 1986-1995

[Constant 1995 dollars in millions][1]

Institution Type	1986-1987	1988-1989	1990-1991	1992-1993	1994-1995
Total	$2,570	$2,874	$3,353	$3,040	$2,768
Doctorate-granting	2,365	2,700	3,207	2,940	2,437
Top 100 in research expenditures	2,003	1,817	2,278	2,193	2,007
Other	361	883	931	747	430
Nondoctorate-granting	204	175	144	99	331

[1]Current dollars have been adjusted to 1995 constant dollars using the Bureau of the Census's Composite Fixed-Weighted Price Index for Construction.

Source: National Science Foundation (1996). *Scientific and Engineering Research Facilities at Colleges and Universities.*

EXHIBIT 5-12

Trends in Expenditures for Capital Projects Costing Over $100,000 to Repair/Renovate Science and Engineering Research Facilities by Institution Type: 1986-1995

[Constant 1995 dollars in millions][1]

Institution Type	1986-1987	1988-1989	1990-1991	1992-1993	1994-1995
Total	$1,050	$1,178	$931	$905	$1,058
Doctorate-granting	993	1,142	895	868	981
Top 100 in research expenditures	747	563	713	673	755
Other	246	578	182	195	226
Nondoctorate-granting	56	35	36	37	77

[1]Current dollars have been adjusted to 1995 constant dollars using the Bureau of the Census's Composite Fixed-Weighted Price Index for Construction.

Source: National Science Foundation (1996). *Scientific and Engineering Research Facilities at Colleges and Universities.*

EXHIBIT 5-13

Expenditures for Deferred Capital Projects to Construct or Repair/Renovate Science and Engineering Research Facilities by Institution Type, Type of Project, and whether Project was Included in Institutional Plans [dollars in millions]

Institution Type	Included in Institutional Plans		Not included in Institutional Plans		Total
	To construct new S&E research facilities	To repair/renovate existing S&E research facilities	To construct new S&E research facilities	To repair/renovate existing S&E research facilities	
Total	$4,629	$2,790	$1,046	$876	$9,341
Doctorate-granting	4,307	2,495	1,004	763	8,569
Top 100 in research expenditures	3,480	1,653	904	601	6,638
Other	827	842	101	162	1,932
Nondoctorate-granting	322	295	42	113	772

Source: National Science Foundation/SRS, 1996 Survey of Scientific and Engineering Research Facilities at Colleges and Universities.

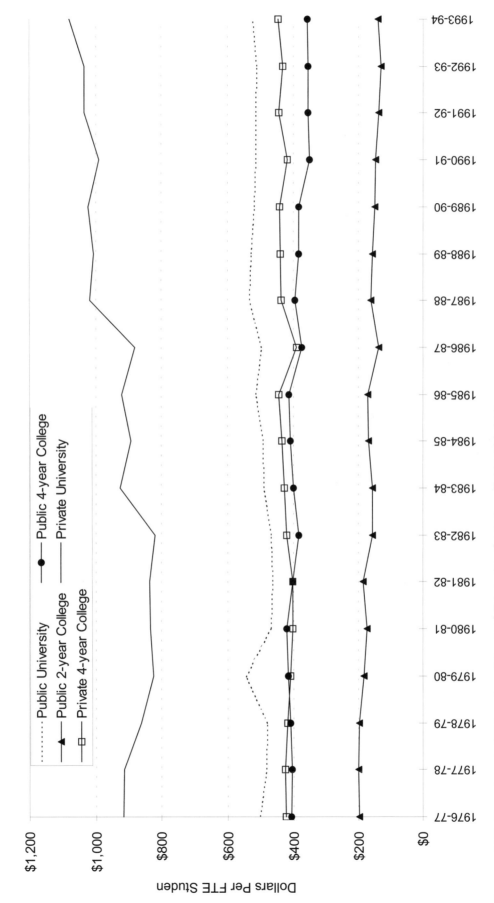

EXHIBIT 5-14
Library Expenditures Per Full-Time-Equivalent Student, 1976-77 to 1993-94
(in constant 1993-94 dollars)

Dollars Per FTE Studen

····· Public University   —●— Public 4-year College   —— Private University
—▲— Public 2-year College   —□— Private 4-year College

Source: U.S. Department of Education, Digest of Education Statistics, Table 338-342.

EXHIBIT 5-15

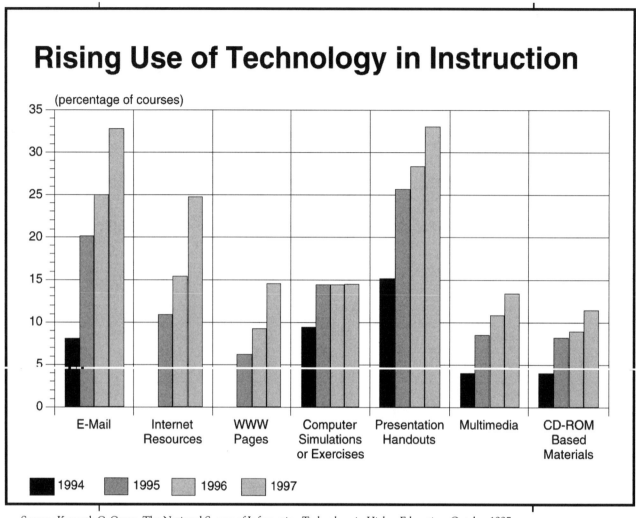

Rising Use of Technology in Instruction

(percentage of courses)

Legend: 1994, 1995, 1996, 1997

Categories: E-Mail, Internet Resources, WWW Pages, Computer Simulations or Exercises, Presentation Handouts, Multimedia, CD-ROM Based Materials

Source: Kenneth C. Green, The National Survey of Information Technology in Higher Education, October 1997.

EXHIBIT 5-16

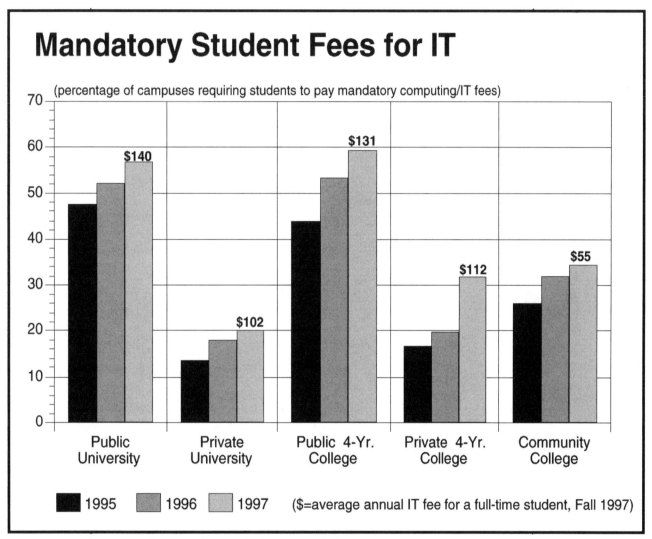

Mandatory Student Fees for IT

(percentage of campuses requiring students to pay mandatory computing/IT fees)

Source: Kenneth C. Green, The National Survey of Information Technology in Higher Education, October 1997.

EXHIBIT 5-17

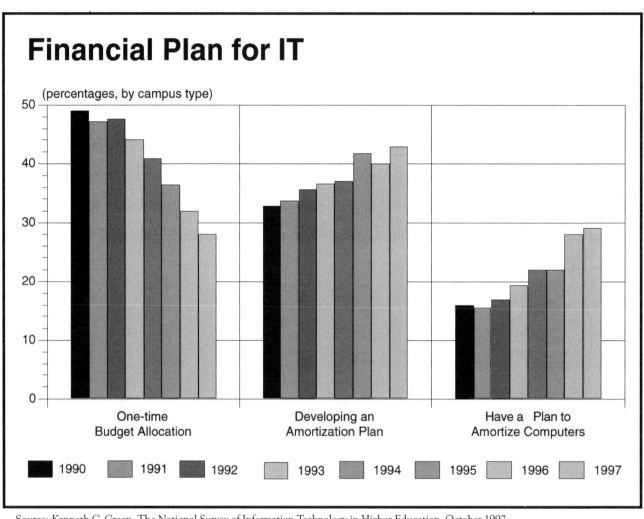

Financial Plan for IT

(percentages, by campus type)

One-time Budget Allocation · Developing an Amortization Plan · Have a Plan to Amortize Computers

1990 · 1991 · 1992 · 1993 · 1994 · 1995 · 1996 · 1997

Source: Kenneth C. Green, The National Survey of Information Technology in Higher Education, October 1997.

Issue 6: The extent to which increases in institutional aid and discounting have affected tuition increases, (including the demographics of students receiving such aid, the extent to which such aid is provided to students with limited need in order to attract such students to particular institutions or major fields of study, and the extent to which Federal financial aid, including loan aid, has been used to offset such increases)

Changes in tuition can result from many different factors. One of the factors thought to increase tuition is institutional aid, which is most frequently offered in the form of tuition discounts and fee waivers. It is contended that tuition is increased to help fund this internal source of student financial assistance. While the data seem to support this observation, the trigger for this action seems to be that external sources of financial assistance (in the form of Federal and state student aid) have failed to keep pace with increasing student need.

Findings

- Between 1987-88 and 1996-97, institutional aid increased in inflation-adjusted dollars by over 100 percent. During the same period, inflation-adjusted tuition increased by 34 percent at private four-year institutions and by 46 percent at public-four year colleges. (Exhibit 6-1)

- Most of the resources required for institutional aid are generated from tuition. It is noteworthy, therefore, that tuition and fees have increased faster than the total price of attendance (tuition, room, board, etc.). In inflation-adjusted dollars, while the total price of attendance at private four-year institutions increased by 28 percent between 1987-88 and 1996-97, tuition and fees increased by 34 percent. A similar, but more extreme pattern, is observed at public four-year institutions. In this sector, the total price of attendance increased by 24 percent in inflation-adjusted dollars, but tuition and fees increased by 46 percent. (Exhibit 6-2)

- Traditionally, Federal student aid has provided the largest share of financial assistance to students, and still does. However, during the last decade, the share of total student financial assistance provided by institutional aid has increased from about 15 percent to 20 percent. In inflation-adjusted dollars, between 1987-88 and 1996-97, institutional aid increased by 102 percent. During the same period, Federal aid increased by only 59 percent. (Exhibit 6-1)

- Increased institutional aid appears to be targeted toward dependent students. In inflation-adjusted dollars, the average institutional aid awarded to independent students changed relatively little between 1987 and 1996. (Exhibit 6-4)

- At public four-year institutions, institutional aid for dependent students appears to be directed at relatively low-income families (i.e., those with incomes less than $40,000). For these students, average institutional aid approximately doubled between 1986-87 and 1995-96. (Exhibit 6-4)

- At private four-year institutions, average institutional aid per dependent student increased by over 75 percent in inflation-adjusted dollars between 1986-87 and 1995-96. At these institutions, increased institutional aid appears to be less targeted toward students from low-income families, with students from all economic backgrounds experiencing substantial increases in institutional grants.

Conclusions

Have increases in institutional aid affected tuition increases?

Possibly. Institutional aid, in both public and private four-year institutions, increased considerably faster than tuition between 1986-87 and 1995-96. However, it is difficult to determine whether tuition increases can be attributed to increases in this type of financial aid. Work currently in progress will help to address this issue.

EXHIBIT 6-1

Sources of Aid Awarded to Postsecondary Students

Current Dollars (in millions)	1987-88	1988-89	1989-90	1990-91	1991-92	1992-93	1993-94	1994-95	Prelim. 1995-96	Estim. 1996-97	Percent change
Institutional aid	3,808	3,978	4,951	5,761	6,329	7,091	7,839	8,660	9,567	10,569	177.5
Federal aid	18,573	19,943	20,628	21,235	23,796	25,421	31,397	34,947	37,606	40,465	117.9
State aid	1,503	1,581	1,719	1,860	1,968	2,215	2,374	2,773	3,236	3,492	132.3
Total aid	23,885	25,502	27,298	28,856	32,092	34,637	41,611	46,380	50,409	54,526	128.3

Constant 1996 Dollars (in millions)	1987-88	1988-89	1989-90	1990-91	1991-92	1992-93	1993-94	1994-95	Prelim. 1995-96	Estim. 1996-97	Percent change
Institutional aid	5,157	5,151	6,115	6,743	7,179	7,799	8,403	9,026	9,712	10,432	102.3
Federal aid	25,150	25,823	25,475	24,855	26,991	27,961	33,656	36,421	38,178	39,941	58.8
State aid	2,035	2,047	2,123	2,177	2,232	2,338	2,545	2,890	3,285	3,447	69.4
Total aid	32,342	33,021	33,712	33,775	36,401	38,098	44,604	48,337	51,176	53,820	66.4

Source: The College Board, *Trends in Student Aid: 1987-1997*, Table 1 and Table 2. New York, 1997.

EXHIBIT 6-2

Changes in Tuition and Fees, Total Price of Attendance, and Family Incomes: 1987-1997

	Private Four-Year Institutions		Public Four-Year Institutions		Public Two-Year Institutions		Incomes		
	Tuition and fees	Total price of attendance	Tuition and fees	Total price of attendance	Tuition and fees	Total price of attendance	Median family income	Median family ages 45-54	Disposable (per capita)
Current Dollars									
1987-88	7,048	10,455	1,485	4,199	739	N.A.	30,970	41,413	13,896
1988-89	8,004	11,660	1,578	4,455	799	N.A.	32,191	42,192	14,905
1989-90	8,663	12,557	1,696	4,715	841	N.A.	34,213	46,101	15,789
1990-91	9,340	13,476	1,908	5,074	906	N.A.	35,353	47,164	16,721
1991-92	9,812	14,188	2,107	5,452	1,022	N.A.	35,939	49,606	17,242
1992-93	10,449	15,028	2,334	5,834	1,116	N.A.	36,812	50,079	18,113
1993-94	11,007	15,795	2,535	6,212	1,245	N.A.	36,959	52,034	18,706
1994-95	11,719	16,698	2,705	6,527	1,310	N.A.	38,752	54,379	19,381
1995-96	12,216	17,382	2,811	6,774	1,330	N.A.	40,611	55,029	20,349
1996-97	12,994	18,357	2,975	7,142	1,465	N.A.	42,559	55,687	21,117
Percent change	84.4	75.6	100.3	70.1	98.2		37.4	34.5	52.0
Constant 1996 Dollars									
1987-88	9,544	14,157	2,011	5,686	1,001	N.A.	42,752	57,167	19,182
1988-89	10,364	15,098	2,043	5,769	1,035	N.A.	42,696	55,961	19,769
1989-90	10,698	15,507	2,094	5,823	1,039	N.A.	43,288	58,330	19,977
1990-91	10,932	15,773	2,233	5,939	1,060	N.A.	42,410	56,579	20,059
1991-92	11,129	16,093	2,390	6,184	1,159	N.A.	41,368	57,099	19,846
1992-93	11,493	16,530	2,567	6,417	1,228	N.A.	41,125	55,947	20,235
1993-94	11,779	16,931	2,717	6,659	1,335	N.A.	40,102	56,458	20,297
1994-95	12,213	17,403	2,819	6,802	1,365	N.A.	40,979	57,504	20,495
1995-96	12,402	17,646	2,854	6,877	1,350	N.A.	41,795	56,633	20,942
1996-97	12,826	18,119	2,936	7,049	1,446	N.A.	42,559	55,687	21,117
Percent change	34.4	28.0	46.0	23.9	44.5		-0.5	-2.6	10.1

Source: The College Board, *Trends in Student Aid: 1987-1997*, Table 3. New York, 1997.

EXHIBIT 6-3

Number of Recipients and Aid Awarded Per Recipient

Number of recipients (in thousands)	1987-88	1988-89	1989-90	1990-91	1991-92	1992-93	1993-94	1994-95	Prelim. 1995-96	Estim. 1996-97	Percent change
FFEL/FDSL*	4,371	4,595	4,546	4,588	4,935	5,120	6,394	7,015	7,550	8,191	87.4
Pell Grants	2,882	3,198	3,322	3,422	3,781	4,177	3,743	3,675	3,612	3,601	24.9
Other Federal Programs	1,995	2,044	2,101	2,108	2,232	2,359	2,465	2,421	2,473	2,407	20.7
State Grant and SSIG	1,554	1,571	1,605	1,673	1,652	1,739	1,859	1,558	1,577	N.A.	1.5

Aid Awarded per Recipient (in Current Dollars)	1987-88	1988-89	1989-90	1990-91	1991-92	1992-93	1993-94	1994-95	Prelim. 1995-96	Estim. 1996-97	Percent change
FFEL/FDSL*	2,604	2,608	2,680	2,762	2,835	2,913	3,112	3,411	3,627	3,677	41.2
Pell Grants	1,287	1,398	1,435	1,442	1,528	1,479	1,510	1,502	1,515	1,572	21.2
Other Federal Programs	932	943	958	973	952	943	915	954	960	950	1.9
State Grant and SSIG	996	930	980	1,059	1,090	1,092	1,084	1,081	1,087	1,066	15.1

Aid Awarded per Recipient (in Constant 1996 Dollars)	1987-88	1988-89	1989-90	1990-91	1991-92	1992-93	1993-94	1994-95	Prelim. 1995-96	Estim. 1996-97	Percent change
FFEL/FDSL*	3,527	3,378	3,301	3,233	3,216	3,204	3,550	3,673	3,700	3,546	0.5
Pell Grants	1,756	1,870	1,772	1,688	1,733	1,627	1,618	1,565	1,538	1,552	-12.6
Other Federal Programs	1,262	1,218	1,183	1,138	1,080	1,038	981	995	976	938	-25.7
State Grant and SSIG	1,376	1,362	1,377	1,343	1,394	1,390	1,411	1,374	1,341	N.A.	-2.5

Note: * The numbers reported are based on the number of loans, not the number of recipients.

Source: The College Board, *Trends in Student Aid: 1987-1997*, data derived from Table 4. New York, 1997.

EXHIBIT 6-4

Average Institutional Grant By Type of Institution, Dependency, and Income Level in Constant Dollars: 1987-1996
(For All Students-Aided and Unaided)

	Public Four-Year		Public Two-Year		Private Four-Year	
	1987	1996	1987	1996	1987	1996
Dependent students	$295	$495	$124	$145	$1,966	$3,468
Income Level*						
Low	364	728	144	177	2,483	4,141
Middle	331	506	131	131	2,393	4,396
Upper Middle	281	345	89	128	2,051	3,624
Upper	151	255	60	100	1,044	1,895
Independent students	341	286	106	114	1,350	1,330
Income Level **						
Low	381	363	77	143	1,610	1,719
Middle	341	285	140	45	1,323	1,309
Upper	260	122	113	157	1,000	721

* Income levels for dependent students (1996 dollars): Low= less than $40,000; Middle = $40-59,999; Upper Middle= $60-79,999; Upper=greater than $80,000

**Income level for independent students (1996 dollars): Low= less than $10,000; Middle = $10-24,999; Upper = greater than $25,000

Sources: NCES, NPSAS:96 Undergraduate Students 10/1/97
　　　　　　 NCES, NPSAS:87 Undergraduate Students 5/23/97

Issue 7: The extent to which Federal, State, and local laws, regulations, or other mandates contribute to increasing tuition, and recommendations on reducing those mandates

Institutions of higher education—like organizations in other industries—are required to comply with Federal, state, and local laws, regulations, or other mandates. Many of these laws and regulations, designed to ensure accessibility, job security, or healthy environments, translate into increased expenditures on the part of the institutions. The increased expenditures, in turn, may be passed on in part to students in the form of increased tuition and fees.

Findings

[Note: the tables presented in this section focus on the American with Disabilities Act, largely because more data exist on this legislation than other types of regulations. Other information in this section is less quantifiable; it comes from testimony presented to the Commission.]

- Respondents to a recent survey on college and university facilities issues reported spending nearly $97 million, or an average of $286,000, on ADA compliance construction and renovation during the 1993-1994 academic year (338 respondents).
- Almost 61 percent of research universities indicated that they would need to spend over $6 million to achieve compliance with ADA. However, only 10 percent of respondents in other types of institutions reported that they would have to spend this much.

Conclusions

Do Federal, state, and local laws, regulations, and mandates contribute to increased tuition?

Probably. Although higher education institutions should comply with regulations and mandates to ensure safe operation, such compliance clearly increases institutional costs.

EXHIBIT 7-1
Summary of Commission's Findings Related to Laws, Regulations and Mandates

The Commission has heard testimony related to three major areas of laws, regulations, and mandates: environmental, toxic material, and occupational safety regulations; regulations under the Higher Education Act; and regional and specialized/professional accreditation. What follows are highlights of the testimony presented to the Commission.

Environmental, Toxic Material and Occupational Safety Regulations

Colleges should be required to handle toxic and hazardous materials properly and safely, and they should meet basic safe operating standards. However, the laws and regulations governing these issues are written for application in factory settings where tons of materials are handled and where operations involve supervisor-employee relations. Examples of the application of such regulations to academic settings include:

- Research and teaching at a major university produces 25,000 small containers of chemical waste a year. Under state law, an error in labeling any of these containers may lead to sanctions and fines.

- A major university reports that regulations bar incorporating waste treatment into the curriculum. A chemistry experiment may not add the steps necessary to render waste non-hazardous. Regulations require that only licensed and heavily regulated facilities carry out such work.

- A major university will have 1,000 to 3,000 individual laboratories. Many are required under the Clean Air Act to track and report fuel usage from each piece of combustion equipment, *regardless of size*, and report it to regulatory agencies. The universities are not required to install pollution devices or modify operations; they are only required to report the number. One university reports that it spent $150,000 on the first phase of meeting these standards.

- The EPA is proposing new controls on air emissions from chemical laboratories. Retrofitting hoods for the new regulation is estimated to cost $8,000 to $20,000 per hood. Major universities with thousands of hoods are looking at an additional capital cost of up to $20 million with annual operating costs of $1-3 million.

The Higher Education Act

Colleges and universities are responsible for the proper handling of more than $30 billion annually in Federal student aid grants and loans. Most of this activity is governed by Parts G and H of Title IV of the Higher Education Act (HEA). Unfortunately, the regulations to implement Federal student aid programs and to assure appropriate stewardship of taxpayer funds have become so extensive and internally inconsistent that excessive cost is incurred by institutions and the Department of Education.

The redundancy and inconsistency of the regulations also make compliance and enforcement difficult. Since the regulations are often inconsistent, no institution in the country can be sure it is in compliance. In several sections of the HEA, the Congress has mandated that institutions make available to students, prospective students, and employees certain kinds of information, (e.g., campus crime statistics, graduation rates, etc.). There are now 14 redundant, but slightly different, reporting requirements for campus crime.

The Commission heard presentations focusing on the litigation costs of colleges fighting the Program Review (audit) function of the Department of Education and the difficulty of obtaining effective due process. Claims for multiple millions of dollars are often decided at the $100,000 level when an administrative law judge finds that Program Review failed to consider a reasonable interpretation of regulation from the college. The litigation cost, however, is high.

EXHIBIT 7-1 (Continued)
Summary of Commission's Findings Related to Laws, Regulations
and Mandates

Regional and Special Accreditation

Accreditation was created by colleges and universities, but over the years it has taken on its own life. There is general concern throughout higher education that accreditation, particularly specialized and professional accreditation, needs to be rethought, because the cost in direct dollars, and more substantially in the diversion of faculty and staff resources, is too high.

EXHIBIT 7-2

List of Federal and State Legislation with Potential Impact on Tuition and Fees

Federal Legislation
- Americans with Disabilities Act (1990)
- Animal Research Space Regulations
- Tax-exempt bond limitations ($150 million limit for private institutions)
- Balanced Budget Act of 1997 (covers the following programs)
  - TRIO
  - State Student Incentive Grants (eliminate program)
  - Supplemental Educational Opportunity Grant
  - Veterans Education Outreach Program
  - Federal Work-Study (increase funding)
  - Perkins Loans Capital Contributions (reduce funding)
  - Education Investment Accounts (IRA's)
  - Pell Grant Expansion to $3000 (up $300)
  - Hope Scholarship & Lifelong Learning Tax Credits
  - Loan Interest Deductibility ($2,500 deduction)
  - Loan Forgiveness
  - TIAA-CREF Tax-exempt status eliminated
  - Scholarship & Fellowship Programs (increase funding)
  - AmeriCorp (threats to cut funding)
- 1993 Pell-Grant Modifications
- Increase in Minimum Wage
- Family and Medical Leave Act of 1993
- Employee Education Assistance Act (tax-exemption of employee education benefits)
- Student Right-to-Know and Campus Security Act of 1990
- Affirmative Action (elimination of mandatory retirement)
- Environmental Legislation (waste disposal, asbestos abatement)
- Telecommunications Act of 1996
- Title IX (Gender Equity—particularly as it relates to funding of sports)

State Legislation
- Land Grant Institutions (Cooperative Extension Requirements)
- State Tuition & Fees Policies
- Remediation Services
- Child Care Facilities (Mandates regarding the accessibility and quality of child care facilities)
- Distance Learning & Technology Requirements

EXHIBIT 7-3

Expenditures for ADA Compliance in 1993-94 by Type of Institution

	Public Research	Private Research	Doctoral Universities	Public Four-yr/MA	Private Masters
Nothing	0.0%	0.0%	0.0%	9.1%	3.9%
Under $25,000	4.8	0.0	5.9	19.7	34.6
$25,000 to $49,999	2.4	7.1	17.6	10.6	19.2
$50,000 to $74,999	4.8	7.1	11.8	15.2	3.8
$75,000 to $99,999	0.0	0.0	8.8	4.5	0.0
$100,000 to $149,999	2.4	14.3	23.6	9.1	19.2
$150,000 to $299,999	19.0	35.8	14.7	15.2	7.7
$300,000 to $499,999	19.0	7.1	2.9	10.6	7.7
$500,000 to $999,999	19.0	14.3	11.8	4.5	0.0
$1 Million or More	28.6	14.3	2.9	1.5	3.9
Total	100.0%	100.0%	100.0%	100.0%	100.0%
Median	$450,000	$233,000	$112,500	$67,500	$40,000
Mean	$1,089,000	$402,900	$238,000	$146,000	$128,500
Number of Institutions	**42**	**14**	**34**	**66**	**26**

	Private Four-year	Public/Private HBCUs	Two-year Colleges	Medical Colleges	All Respondents
Nothing	15.3%	3.6%	10.2%	0.0%	6.8%
Under $25,000	30.8	10.7	40.8	21.4	21.3
$25,000 to $49,999	13.8	10.7	16.4	0.0	11.8
$50,000 to $74,999	10.8	17.9	6.1	21.4	10.7
$75,000 to $99,999	7.7	7.1	2.0	7.1	4.4
$100,000 to $149,999	7.7	10.7	8.2	7.1	10.4
$150,000 to $299,999	6.2	10.7	10.2	21.4	13.3
$300,000 to $499,999	6.2	0.0	6.1	0.0	7.7
$500,000 to $999,999	0.0	17.9	0.0	14.3	7.1
$1 Million or More	1.5	10.7	0.0	7.1	6.5
Total	100.0%	100.0%	100.0%	100.0%	100.0%
Median	$31,900	$100,000	$24,400	$100,000	$73,600
Mean	$92,200	$400,800	$63,500	$285,400	$286,300
Number of Institutions	**65**	**28**	**49**	**14**	**338**

Source: APPA (1997), *A Foundation to Uphold*, Table V-3.

EXHIBIT 7-4

Estimated Total Costs of Achieving
Compliance with the ADA by Type of Institution

	Public Research	Private Research	Doctoral Universities	Public Four-yr/MA	Private Masters
None	0.0%	0.0%	3.6%	1.6%	0.0%
Under $500,000	13.5	0.0	14.8	25.0	33.3
$500,000 to $1,000,000	0.0	7.1	3.7	15.6	25.0
$1,000,000 to $1,999,999	0.0	7.1	25.9	17.2	25.0
$2,000,000 to $2,999,999	8.1	7.1	14.8	1.6	16.7
$3,000,000 to $5,999,999	13.5	28.6	25.9	15.6	0.0
$6,000,000 to $9,999,999	16.3	21.4	3.7	10.9	0.0
$10 Million or More	48.6	28.6	11.2	12.5	0.0
Total	100.0%	100.0%	100.0%	100.0%	100.0%
Median	$8,500,000	$6,000,000	$2,375,000	$1,455,000	$833,000
Mean	$12,867,000	$8,795,000	$4,997,000	$3,856,000	$895,000
Number of Institutions	**37**	**14**	**27**	**64**	**24**

	Private Four-year	Public/Private HBCUs	Two-year Colleges	Medical Colleges	All Respondents
None	7.1%	0.0%	2.1%	0.0%	2.0%
Under $500,000	37.5	17.6	60.4	18.2	29.5
$500,000 to $1,000,000	16.1	23.5	16.7	18.2	13.8
$1,000,000 to $1,999,999	23.2	5.9	8.3	0.0	14.4
$2,000,000 to $2,999,999	8.9	17.6	4.2	18.2	8.4
$3,000,000 to $5,999,999	5.4	5.9	8.3	7.1	13.1
$6,000,000 to $9,999,999	1.8	11.9	0.0	21.4	6.7
$10 Million or More	0.0	17.6	0.0	0.0	12.1
Total	100.0%	100.0%	100.0%	100.0%	100.0%
Median	$667,000	$2,167,000	$897,000	$2,750,000	$1,326,000
Mean	$888,000	$4,281,000	$694,000	$2,529,000	$3,980,000
Number of Institutions	**56**	**17**	**48**	**11**	**298**

Source: APPA (1997). *A Foundation to Uphold*, Table V-4.

EXHIBIT 7-5

Estimated Average Per Student Costs of Achieving Compliance with the ADA by Type of Institution

	Public Research	Private Research	Doctoral Universities	Public Four-yr/MA	Private Masters
Under $100	13.5%	7.7%	18.5%	25.8%	25.0%
$100 to $199	8.2	15.4	11.1	17.7	16.7
$200 to $299	13.5	7.7	22.3	11.3	16.7
$300 to $499	18.9	7.7	29.6	12.9	8.2
$500 to $999	21.6	23.0	7.4	9.7	20.8
$1,000 to $1,199	5.4	15.4	3.7	3.2	4.2
$1,200 to $1,999	13.5	7.7	3.7	8.1	4.2
$2,000 or More	5.4	15.4	3.7	11.3	4.2
Total	100.0%	100.0%	100.0%	100.0%	100.0%
Median	$470	$750	$290	$260	$250
Mean	$705	$1,100	$515	$720	$520
Number of Institutions	**37**	**13**	**27**	**62**	**24**

	Private Four-year	Public/Private HBCUs	Two-year Colleges	Medical Colleges	All Respondents
Under $100	20.0%	0.0%	34.8%	18.2%	21.2%
$100 to $199	16.4	5.9	10.9	0.0	13.0
$200 to $299	5.4	23.5	6.5	9.1	11.6
$300 to $499	7.3	5.9	19.6	0.0	13.7
$500 to $999	20.0	17.6	15.2	27.3	16.5
$1,000 to $1,199	16.4	0.0	0.0	0.0	5.8
$1,200 to $1,999	3.6	11.8	4.3	18.1	7.3
$2,000 or More	10.9	35.3	8.7	27.3	10.9
Total	100.0%	100.0%	100.0%	100.0%	100.0%
Median	$550	$675	$265	$950	$375
Mean	$920	$1,700	$650	$2,410	$850
Number of Institutions	**55**	**17**	**46**	**11**	**292**

Source: APPA (1997). *A Foundation to Uphold*. Table V-5.

Issue 8: The establishment of a mechanism for a more timely and widespread distribution of data on tuition trends and other costs of operating colleges and universities

Analyzing tuition trends as well as the costs of operating colleges and universities is a complex phenomenon. In both public and private institutions, students do not pay the full cost of their education. Revenues other than tuition, such as state appropriations in public colleges and universities or endowments in some select institutions, contribute to the educational costs. Collecting, tracking, and making sense of these types of data is critical to understanding college costs and prices.

Available Data Sources

The U.S. Department of Education collects a considerable amount of data that inform discussions of higher education costs and prices. These data are listed below.

- **The Integrated Postsecondary Education Data System (IPEDS).** This system of surveys collects data from postsecondary institutions on a number of issues that include:
  - ⇒ Characteristics of Institutions*
  - ⇒ Fall Enrollments*
  - ⇒ Fall Enrollments in Occupationally Specific Programs
  - ⇒ Completions (degrees awarded)*
  - ⇒ Salaries, Tenure, and Benefits of Full-time Instructional Faculty*
  - ⇒ Financial Statistics*
  - ⇒ College and University Libraries
  - ⇒ Fall Staff
  - * Collected annually.

- **The National Postsecondary Student Aid Study (NPSAS).** Conducted every three years since 1986, NPSAS collects data from students enrolled in all types of postsecondary education institutions. Data from parents are also collected. A major purpose of NPSAS is to determine how students and their families pay for college. As such, considerable information on financial aid is gathered.

- **The National Study of Postsecondary Faculty (NSOPF).** This comprehensive survey of faculty was conducted in both 1988 and 1993 and is scheduled to be conducted again in 2000. Data are collected on the backgrounds and composition of faculty; workload and work-related activities; salaries; and job satisfaction.

- **Postsecondary Education Quick Information System (PEQIS).** Designed to collect data from institutions of higher education quickly, PEQIS surveys have gathered information on a number of issues related to higher education finance issues.

Additional data collected that relate to higher education finance issues include:

- **The College Board's Annual Survey of Colleges.** Institutional-level data are collected on tuition and fees charged students, financial aid awarded, and the characteristics of students who attend.

- **The National Association of State Scholarship and Grant Programs Annual Survey.** This survey collects data pertaining to the total grant aid awarded by states, need-based grants to both undergraduate and graduate students, and non-need-based grants to undergraduate and graduate students.

Conclusions

Are the data currently available adequate for understanding and monitoring college costs and prices?

Not completely. Considerable data are available, both through IPEDS and the College Board, on tuition and other price-related issues. These data are collected annually and generally released in a timely manner. Data on institutional costs, although collected annually through the IPEDS Finance Survey, are typically released several years after they are collected. Furthermore, these data do not provide the kind of information that allows for a clear understanding of where and how colleges and universities spend their money.

Issue 9: The extent to which student financial aid programs have contributed to changes in tuition

The relentless growth in student financial aid programs over the last two decades or so is considered, in some quarters, to be one of the factors causing tuitions to increase. It is sometimes argued that the additional resources made available by these programs are "appropriated" by universities and colleges in the form of higher tuition and fees. Factoring in increases in the number of students receiving aid that have accompanied increases in financial aid spending reveals, however, that the average amount of aid delivered to each college student has generally not kept up with inflation, let alone the increases in the price of attending colleges and universities. The methodologies currently used to assess the relationship between financial aid and tuition levels are inadequate.

Findings

- In current dollars, total student financial aid from all sources increased by 128 percent between 1987-88 and 1996-97. About three-fourths of this total is provided by the Federal student aid programs. (Exhibit 9-1)
- In global terms, growth in student aid has substantially outpaced growth in the price of attendance. Regardless of source, student aid increased in current dollars by well over 100 percent between 1986-87 and 1996-97. Over this same period, at private and public four-year institutions, average total price of attendance increased by 76 and 70 percent respectively. (Exhibits 9-1 and 9-2)
- The number of aid recipients has grown along with rising student aid levels. For example, although Federal loan dollars increased by 118 percent between 1986-87 and 1996-97, the number of borrowers grew by almost 88 percent. (Exhibit 9-3)
- As a result of the growth in the number of students needing aid, average awards per recipient have increased at rates substantially below the rates of increase in tuition or total price (tuition, room, board, etc.) of attendance. Moreover, average loan amounts have barely kept pace with inflation, and the value of Pell grants and awards in other state grant and Federal programs actually have failed to keep pace with inflation, sometimes substantially so. (Exhibits 9-2 and 9-3)

Conclusions

Have student financial aid programs contributed to tuition increases?

Uncertain. There has been an ongoing debate regarding whether the availability of Federal student aid is related to the rapid growth of college costs and tuitions over the past two decades. In examining this issue, it is important to distinguish between the possible impact of Federal grants and Federal loans. The maximum Pell grant has not increased substantially over time but the numbers of students borrowing money and the total amount of money borrowed has increased. Loans constitute more than half of all student aid and cover more than a third of the total price of attendance.

It is unlikely that Federal grants have had an impact on the growth of tuitions at either public or private institutions. The relationship between Federally-sponsored loans and tuition growth is more problematic, however. Researchers and policy analysts reach differing conclusions on this issue.

EXHIBIT 9-1*

Sources of Aid Awarded to Postsecondary Students

Current Dollars (in millions)	1987-88	1988-89	1989-90	1990-91	1991-92	1992-93	1993-94	1994-95	Prelim. 1995-96	Estim. 1996-97	Percent change
Institutional aid	3,808	3,978	4,951	5,761	6,329	7,091	7,839	8,660	9,567	10,569	177.5
Federal aid	18,573	19,943	20,628	21,235	23,796	25,421	31,397	34,947	37,606	40,465	117.9
State aid	1,503	1,581	1,719	1,860	1,968	2,215	2,374	2,773	3,236	3,492	132.3
Total aid	23,885	25,502	27,298	28,856	32,092	34,637	41,611	46,380	50,409	54,526	128.3

Constant 1996 Dollars (in millions)	1987-88	1988-89	1989-90	1990-91	1991-92	1992-93	1993-94	1994-95	Prelim. 1995-96	Estim. 1996-97	Percent change
Institutional aid	5,157	5,151	6,115	6,743	7,179	7,799	8,403	9,026	9,712	10,432	102.3
Federal aid	25,150	25,823	25,475	24,855	26,991	27,961	33,656	36,421	38,178	39,941	58.8
State aid	2,035	2,047	2,123	2,177	2,232	2,338	2,545	2,890	3,285	3,447	69.4
Total aid	32,342	33,021	33,712	33,775	36,401	38,098	44,604	48,337	51,176	53,820	66.4

Source: The College Board, *Trends in Student Aid: 1987-1997*, Table 1 and Table 2. New York, 1997.

* Also appears as Exhibit 6-1

EXHIBIT 9-2*

Changes in Tuition and Fees, Total Price of Attendance, and Family Incomes: 1987-1997

	Private Four-Year Institutions		Public Four-Year Institutions		Public Two-Year Institutions		Incomes		
	Tuition and fees	Total price of attendance	Tuition and fees	Total price of attendance	Tuition and fees	Total price of attendance	Median family income	Median family ages 45-54	Disposable (per capita)
Current Dollars									
1987-88	7,048	10,455	1,485	4,199	739	N.A.	30,970	41,413	13,896
1988-89	8,004	11,660	1,578	4,455	799	N.A.	32,191	42,192	14,905
1989-90	8,663	12,557	1,696	4,715	841	N.A.	34,213	46,101	15,789
1990-91	9,340	13,476	1,908	5,074	906	N.A.	35,353	47,164	16,721
1991-92	9,812	14,188	2,107	5,452	1,022	N.A.	35,939	49,606	17,242
1992-93	10,449	15,028	2,334	5,834	1,116	N.A.	36,812	50,079	18,113
1993-94	11,007	15,795	2,535	6,212	1,245	N.A.	36,959	52,034	18,706
1994-95	11,719	16,698	2,705	6,527	1,310	N.A.	38,752	54,379	19,381
1995-96	12,216	17,382	2,811	6,774	1,330	N.A.	40,611	55,029	20,349
1996-97	12,994	18,357	2,975	7,142	1,465	N.A.	42,559	55,687	21,117
Percent change	84.4	75.6	100.3	70.1	98.2		37.4	34.5	52.0
Constant 1996 Dollars									
1987-88	9,544	14,157	2,011	5,686	1,001	N.A.	42,752	57,167	19,182
1988-89	10,364	15,098	2,043	5,769	1,035	N.A.	42,696	55,961	19,769
1989-90	10,698	15,507	2,094	5,823	1,039	N.A.	43,288	58,330	19,977
1990-91	10,932	15,773	2,233	5,939	1,060	N.A.	42,410	56,579	20,059
1991-92	11,129	16,093	2,390	6,184	1,159	N.A.	41,368	57,099	19,846
1992-93	11,493	16,530	2,567	6,417	1,228	N.A.	41,125	55,947	20,235
1993-94	11,779	16,931	2,717	6,659	1,335	N.A.	40,102	56,458	20,297
1994-95	12,213	17,403	2,819	6,802	1,365	N.A.	40,979	57,504	20,495
1995-96	12,402	17,646	2,854	6,877	1,350	N.A.	41,795	56,633	20,942
1996-97	12,826	18,119	2,936	7,049	1,446	N.A.	42,559	55,687	21,117
Percent change	34.4	28.0	46.0	23.9	44.5		-0.5	-2.6	10.1

Source: The College Board, *Trends in Student Aid: 1987-1997*, Table 3. New York, 1997.

*Also appears as Exhibit 6-2.

EXHIBIT 9-3*

Number of Recipients and Aid Awarded Per Recipient

Number of recipients (in thousands)	1987-88	1988-89	1989-90	1990-91	1991-92	1992-93	1993-94	1994-95	Prelim. 1995-96	Estim. 1996-97	Percent change
FFEL/FDSL**	4,371	4,595	4,546	4,588	4,935	5,120	6,394	7,015	7,550	8,191	87.4
Pell Grants	2,882	3,198	3,322	3,422	3,781	4,177	3,743	3,675	3,612	3,601	24.9
Other Federal Programs	1,995	2,044	2,101	2,108	2,232	2,359	2,465	2,421	2,473	2,407	20.7
State Grant and SSIG	1,554	1,571	1,605	1,673	1,652	1,739	1,859	1,558	1,577	N.A.	1.5

Aid Awarded per Recipient (in Current Dollars)	1987-88	1988-89	1989-90	1990-91	1991-92	1992-93	1993-94	1994-95	Prelim. 1995-96	Estim. 1996-97	Percent change
FFEL/FDSL**	2,604	2,608	2,680	2,762	2,835	2,913	3,112	3,411	3,627	3,677	41.2
Pell Grants	1,287	1,398	1,435	1,442	1,528	1,479	1,510	1,502	1,515	1,572	21.2
Other Federal Programs	932	943	958	973	952	943	915	954	960	950	1.9
State Grant and SSIG	996	930	980	1,059	1,090	1,092	1,084	1,081	1,087	1,066	15.1

Aid Awarded per Recipient (in Constant 1996 Dollars)	1987-88	1988-89	1989-90	1990-91	1991-92	1992-93	1993-94	1994-95	Prelim. 1995-96	Estim. 1996-97	Percent change
FFEL/FDSL**	3,527	3,378	3,301	3,233	3,216	3,204	3,550	3,673	3,700	3,546	0.5
Pell Grants	1,756	1,870	1,772	1,688	1,733	1,627	1,618	1,565	1,538	1,552	-12.6
Other Federal Programs	1,262	1,218	1,183	1,138	1,080	1,038	981	995	976	938	-25.7
State Grant and SSIG	1,376	1,362	1,377	1,343	1,394	1,390	1,411	1,374	1,341	N.A.	-2.5

Note: * Also appears as Exhibit 6-3.
    ** The numbers reported are based on the number of loans, not the number of recipients.

Source: The College Board, *Trends in Student Aid: 1987-1997*, data derived from Table 4. New York, 1997.

EXHIBIT 9-4

The Relationship Between Student Aid and Tuition

Perhaps because student financial need rises with increases in tuition, to most observers it makes it *appear possible* for colleges and universities to be able to capture more Federal aid by raising tuition. To the extent that the design of Federal student aid programs is such that institutions can easily capture additional aid dollars by raising their tuition, it is reasonable to expect them to do so.[1] At a theoretical level, the validity of this contention can be evaluated by examining the extent to which the Federal student aid programs create an incentive for colleges and universities to capture Federal aid. In addition, there now exists a small body of empirical evidence to inform us about how institutions respond to changes in the Federal aid programs and the increased availability of Federal student aid.

What does theory suggest?

Whether colleges and universities in practice are able to capture more Federal aid dollars by raising tuition can be assessed by examining how the main Federal aid programs — Pell Grant, Campus-Based Aid, and the student loan programs — react to increases in tuition.

Among the potential recipients of Pell grant awards, relatively few will obtain a grant that meets full need below the maximum grant (which is $2,700 in 1997-98). Only in these relatively few cases will an increase in tuition allow students (and subsequently the school) to receive a larger Pell grant. Moreover, because a student's price of attendance effectively is no longer a factor in the Pell grant award calculation, any potential linkage between grant aid and tuition is greatly weakened.

As for the campus-based aid programs, most institutions already receive the maximum funding allowed by the regulations. Thus, higher tuition will not produce increased funds.

Of all the different Federal aid programs, the student loan program is perhaps the most likely to affect tuition. However, many students already borrow the maximum loan amount.[2] Therefore, if institutions increase tuition to qualify more students for loans, a substantial part of the cost of the loan will be incurred by these students or their families. To the extent that more students have loans under the maximum borrowing limits in the public sector than in the private, there may be some potential for Federal aid increases to fuel higher tuition in the public sector.

Based on the above expectations, *a priori* there does not appear to be any substantial incentive within the current Federal aid system for colleges and universities to increase tuition. The available empirical evidence, which is reviewed briefly below, also seems to support this view.

What does the empirical evidence suggest?

In their groundbreaking study (based on data for 1978-79 and 1985-86), McPherson and Schapiro[3] found that:

- There is no evidence that private universities increase their tuition when they receive more Federal student aid.

- Between the late 1970s and mid 1980s, public four-year institutions appeared to raise tuition as Federal student aid increases. However, McPherson and Schapiro argued more recently that the substantial increases in tuition that have occurred at these institutions since the mid 1980s will mean that far fewer of them can gain Federal student aid revenue by increasing tuition. Thus, at present, the effect of Federal student aid on public tuition may have been substantially reduced. This view is supported by a more recent study by Coopers & Lybrand which, using data from 1989-90 and 1994-95, found no statistical evidence that increases in Federal student aid produce tuition increases among public four-year institutions.[4]

- Federal student aid has no statistically significant impact on tuition at public two year institutions.

- The Coopers & Lybrand study reports that Federal grant aid has the effect of reducing tuition. However, in practice, this effect is minimal because grant aid has barely increased in real terms in recent years.

What We Know About the Relationship Between Institutional Aid and Tuition

Both the McPherson and Schapiro study and the Coopers & Lybrand report examine empirically whether increases in Federal aid reduces an institution's commitment to provide student aid from its own resources. These studies found that:

- At private institutions, spending on institutional aid actually tends to increase when Federal student aid increases. McPherson and Schapiro estimated that for every $100 increase in Federal student aid, institutional aid increases by $20. They hypothesize that the increased availability of Federal aid encourages lower income students to attend college, and this requires the institutions to draw more heavily on their own internal aid resources.

- Among public institutions, there is no evidence to suggest that Federal student aid is treated as a substitute for institutional aid.

- At private institutions, the Coopers & Lybrand study estimates that about 15 percent of tuition increases on average are earmarked for institutional student aid.

The empirically-based findings cited above demonstrate that the effect of Federal and institutional aid on tuition is not a simple issue. Viewed in a comparative sense, rather than as individual findings, the issue looks even more complicated because it also appears that:

a)   grants and loans each exert a differential impact on tuition;

b)   private and public institutions respond in different ways to increases in aid availability; and

c)   the effects of increases aid on tuition may vary over time.

Federal Aid, Institutional Aid, and Tuition: What We Don't Know

Even though there is an increasing amount of discussion about, and analysis of, the relationships between Federal aid, institutional aid, and tuition, several unresolved issues remain. These are briefly described below:

Very little empirical analysis has been conducted on the way proprietary schools respond to increases in Federal student aid. Anecdotal evidence suggests that at least some proprietary schools set tuition and other charges in relation to Pell grant awards and maximum loan limits.[5] However, in practice, any such proclivity probably has been heavily constrained because Pell grant awards, and the maximum borrowing limits for undergraduate freshmen and sophomores, have increased only modestly in recent years.

In examining the relationship between the availability of Federal student aid and tuition, there is some dispute about whether the loan subsidy value is the appropriate measure to use. The McPherson and Schapiro and

Coopers & Lybrand studies both use this measure, but others have suggested that the absolute amount of loans borrowed is a more appropriate measure.[6]

College and university tuitions increase for a complex set of reasons, and there are all kinds of interactions going on between several major actors. Many of these interactions remain unexplored and unquantified. Moreover, the studies that have been completed focus on the direct effects only, even though there are many indirect effects and associations. For instance, although there may appear to be an association between increases in Federal aid and increases in tuition, there may not be a direct causal relationship. To properly inform policy, much more work needs to be conducted to uncover the major causal paths within the complex set of relationships that determine tuition increases.

Finally, not much is known about how institutional aid is used by institutions in their competitive strategy, or of its role in revenue management. The Coopers & Lybrand study found that about 15 percent of tuition increases at private institutions is devoted to institutional aid. But is this proportion increasing and, if so, why?

[1]McPherson, S. & Schapiro, O.M. "The Student Aid Game." Princeton University Press, New Jersey, 1998, p. 81.

[2]Ibid., p. 83.

[3]McPherson, S. & Schapiro, O. M. "Keeping College Affordable: Government and Educational Opportunity." Washington, DC: Brookings Institution, 1991.

[4]Coopers & Lybrand, LLP. "The Impact of Federal Student Assistance on College Tuition Levels." Washington, DC: American Council on Education, 1997.

[5]Hauptman, A. M. & Krop, C. "Federal Student Aid and the Growth in College Costs and Tuitions: Is There a Relationship." p.4. Paper submitted to the National Commission on the Cost of Higher Education, November 1997.

[6]Ibid., p. 7.

Issue 10: Trends in State fiscal policies that have affected college costs

State fiscal policies have a significant impact on tuition, particularly at public institutions, where state appropriations fund a significant portion of educational and general expenditures. The impact of changes in state fiscal policies was felt most recently during the recession of the early 1990s, when tight state budgets, combined with competing demands for state dollars, resulted in cuts in state higher education appropriations.

To provide a background for these issues, this section presents trends in state appropriations to higher education and trends in the share of revenue funded by different sources (including state governments). One issue to consider when examining this issue is that the data presented are national averages; as such, variation in state trends may be lost in the aggregation. For example, between 1994 and 1995, five states — Alaska, Montana, New Jersey, Texas, and Washington — decreased appropriations to higher education, while six states — Alabama, Idaho, Mississippi, Missouri, New Mexico, and Rhode Island — had double digit increases in appropriations.

Findings

- State appropriations to higher education decreased between 1991 and 1992 and again between 1992 and 1993, then increased between 1993 and 1994. (Exhibit 10-1)
- The state share of current-fund revenues at higher education institutions dropped from 46 percent in 1980-81 to 36 percent in 1993-94. During this same period of time, the tuition and fees share increased from 13 percent to 18 percent. (Exhibit 10-4)
- The state share of community college revenues dropped from 50 percent in 1980 to 39 percent in 1994; the tuition share increased from 15 percent in 1980 to 21 percent in 1994. (Exhibit 10-5)
- An AASCU survey of higher education administrators indicated that cuts in state appropriations most harmed: program offerings, access, and building maintenance.

Conclusions

Have trends in state fiscal policies affected college costs?

In the language of the Commission, "costs" are the expenses of an institution to provide an education. The data examined related to state fiscal policies have not affected *costs*; however, cuts in appropriations have forced many institutions to examine their revenues and expenditures.

Cuts in state appropriations appear to be related to tuition increases in public institutions in the early 1990s. During the period in which states were cutting appropriations to higher education, tuitions in public colleges and universities increased more rapidly than they had in previous or subsequent years.

303

EXHIBIT 10-1

State Appropriations for Higher Education, in Millions: 1980-1994 (in Current Dollars)

	Total Appropriations	Percent Change from Previous Year
1980	19,219,837	
1981	21,261,805	10.6%
1982	23,417,094	10.1%
1983	24,758,748	5.7%
1984	26,261,710	6.1%
1985	28,787,388	9.6%
1986	31,162,946	8.3%
1987	32,497,326	4.3%
1988	34,514,618	6.2%
1989	36,246,499	5.0%
1990	39,337,633	8.5%
1991	40,887,720	3.9%
1992	40,066,823	-2.0%
1993	39,394,110	-1.7%
1994	40,775,658	3.5%

Source: AASCU *Report of the States*, 1994.

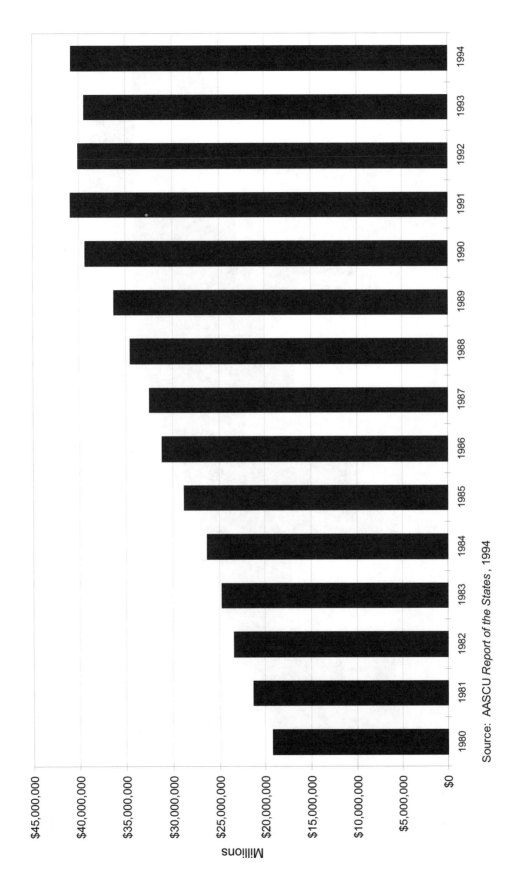

EXHIBIT 10-2
State Appropriations to Higher Education, 1980-1994
(in current dollars)

Source: *AASCU Report of the States*, 1994

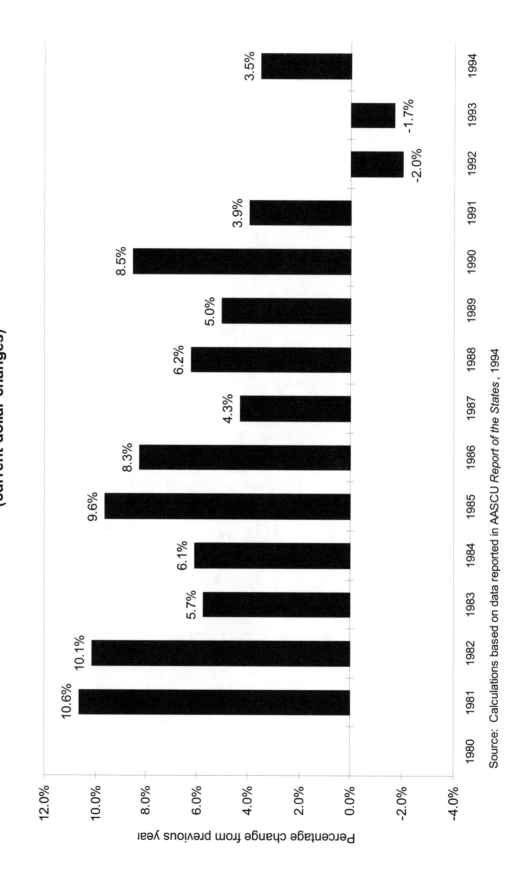

EXHIBIT 10-3

Percent Change in State Appropriations to Higher Education: 1980-1994

(current dollar changes)

Source: Calculations based on data reported in AASCU *Report of the States*, 1994

EXHIBIT 10-4

Share of Current-Fund Revenue of Public Institutions of Higher Education by Source: 1980-81 to 1993-94

	1980-81	1981-82	1982-83	1983-84	1984-85	1985-86	1986-87
Tuition and Fees	12.9	13.5	14.5	14.9	14.5	14.5	15.0
Federal Government	12.8	11.4	10.6	10.5	10.6	10.5	10.3
State Government	45.6	45.3	44.8	44.3	45.1	45.0	43.4
Sales and Service	19.6	20.4	20.6	20.6	20.0	20.0	21.2
Other	2.4	2.6	2.4	2.5	2.6	2.6	2.6
Local Governments	3.8	3.7	3.7	3.6	3.6	3.6	3.7
Private gifts, grants, and contracts	2.5	2.7	3.0	3.0	3.1	3.2	3.4
Endowment Income	0.5	0.5	0.5	0.6	0.6	0.6	0.5

	1988-89	1989-90	1990-91	1991-92	1992-93	1993-94
Tuition and Fees	15.2	15.5	16.1	17.1	18.0	18.4
Federal Government	10.3	10.3	10.3	10.6	10.8	11.0
State Government	42.5	41.7	40.3	38.3	36.8	35.9
Sales and Service	21.5	21.7	22.7	23.2	23.4	23.4
Other	2.8	2.7	2.6	2.6	2.7	2.7
Local Governments	3.7	3.7	3.7	3.7	3.7	4.0
Private gifts, grants, and contracts	3.6	3.8	3.8	4.0	4.0	4.0
Endowment Income	0.5	0.5	0.5	0.6	0.6	0.6

Source: *Digest of Education Statistics*, 1996, Table 322.

EXHIBIT 10-5

Share of Community College Revenues by Source: 1980-1994

	Federal	State	Local	Tuition	Other
1980	6.7	50.1	17.4	15.0	10.8
1983	9.4	46.3	17.2	16.6	10.6
1985	9.7	46.9	17.7	15.8	9.9
1988	9.6	45.5	18.3	16.5	10.2
1990	10.0	44.7	17.5	17.3	10.4
1992	12.2	40.3	17.3	20.0	10.2
1994	12.7	39.0	17.3	20.5	10.5

Source: AACC *National Profile of Community Colleges: Trends and Statistics*, 1997-1998, Table T5.2.

Issue 11: The adequacy of existing Federal and State financial aid programs in meeting the costs of attending colleges and universities

An assessment of the adequacy of existing financial aid programs must consider the vast difference in the price of attending different types of postsecondary institutions. This is complicated by the underlying "price-equalization" character of determining the Expected Family Contribution (EFC) which, in turn, determines financial need (total price of attendance less EFC). Such an assessment might also consider competing conceptions of the proportion of financial need Federal and state financial aid programs should meet.

Findings

- For all full-time dependent students attending public universities, 63 percent of need was met by some form of financial aid in 1996. The average dollar amount of unmet need for these students was $2,653. Federal aid programs alone met 42 percent of the need of dependent students attending public universities. Federal aid in the form of grants was primarily directed toward low-income students for whom Federal grants cover 12 percent of financial need. (Exhibit 11-1)

- At public colleges, financial aid met 65 percent of need for full-time dependent students. The amount of unmet need varied considerably by income levels: upper income level students had no need unmet by financial aid, while low, middle, and upper-middle income level students had $3,179, $1,353, and $89, respectively. (Exhibit 11-2)

- For full-time dependent students attending public two-year colleges, the average need unmet by financial aid was $2,896. Financial aid met 33 percent and Federal aid met 22 percent of need for these students. (Exhibit 11-3)

- For full-time dependent students attending private universities, the average need unmet by financial aid was $5,931. The percentage of need met by all forms of financial aid for dependent students attending private universities is the same as that of students attending public universities, 63 percent. Federal aid, however, plays a smaller relative role in the private sector, meeting 14 percent of need. (Exhibit 11-4)

- At private colleges, 74 percent of the need of dependent students is met by some form of financial aid, 24 percent by Federal sources. The average need unmet for these students was $3,273, in 1996. (Exhibit 11-5)

Conclusions

Are existing Federal and state financial aid programs adequate in meeting the financial needs of students?

It depends. There are many different ways to think about the "adequacy" of financial aid programs. Many students receive some type of financial aid; approximately two thirds of all full-time, dependent students who attended public four-year institutions in the fall of 1995 and 80 percent of these same types of students who attended private four-year institutions received some type of financial aid. Furthermore, the lower the income of the student's family, the more likely the student is to receive aid.

Students still have "unmet" financial need, however. Government, higher education institutions, the private sector and families all need to share the responsibility of assuring that the needed financial resources are available for all students wishing to pursue a postsecondary education.

EXHIBIT 11-1

Financial Aid Received by Students with Need Attending Public Universities: 1996

	Percent of All Students With Need	Average amount of need	Total Aid Amount	Total Grants	Total Loans	Total Other*	Federal Grants	Federal Loans	Federal Other*	Need Unmet by Total Aid	Need Unmet by Grants	Need Unmet by Federal Grants
Dependent students	67%	$7,251	$4,598	$1,938	$2,416	$244	$570	$2,360	$97	$2,653	$5,313	$6,680
Income Level**												
Low	98	9,389	5,652	2,933	2,436	283	1,105	2,393	126	3,738	6,457	8,285
Middle	92	5,918	3,691	1,144	2,344	203	92	2,286	90	2,228	4,775	5,827
Upper Middle	57	4,363	3,293	816	2,266	211	6	2,230	38	1,070	3,547	4,358
Upper	18	4,151	3,765	664	2,895	205	0	2,708	60	387	3,487	4,151
Independent students	93	9,849	6,738	1,915	4,235	588	1,102	4,222	90	3,112	7,934	8,747
Income Level ***												
Low	100	11,187	7,524	2,452	4,394	678	1,547	4,377	145	3,663	8,735	9,640
Middle	100	9,157	6,257	1,723	4,123	410	817	4,112	18	2,900	7,434	8,340
Upper	69	7,233	5,341	701	3,978	662	338	3,978	63	1,892	6,532	6,895

*Aid not classified as grants or loans. Includes work study, assistantships, veterans benefits, military tuition aid, vocational rehabilitation and JTPA

** Income levels for dependent students (1996 dollars): Low= less than $40,000; Middle = $40-59,999; Upper Middle= $60-79,999; Upper=greater than $80,000

***Income level for independent students (1996 dollars): Low= less than $10,000; Middle = $10-24,999; Upper = greater than $25,000

Source: NCES, NPSAS:96 Undergraduate Students 10/1/97

EXHIBIT 11-2
Financial Aid Received by Students with Need Attending Public Colleges: 1996

	Percent of All Students With Need	Average amount of need	Total Aid Amount	Total Grants	Total Loans	Total Other*	Federal Grants	Federal Loans	Federal Other*	Need Unmet by Total Aid	Need Unmet by Grants	Need Unmet by Federal Grants
Dependent students	71%	$6,204	$4,023	$1,622	$2,149	$252	$710	$1,658	$115	$2,182	$4,582	$5,494
Income Level**												
Low	99	7,703	4,524	2,325	1,931	268	1,189	1,708	137	3,179	5,378	6,514
Middle	87	4,855	3,502	848	2,405	249	97	1,747	96	1,353	4,007	4,758
Upper Middle	41	3,034	2,945	331	2,438	176	0	1,500	56	89	2,703	3,034
Upper	16	2,725	3,382	431	2,709	242	31	758	95	-658	2,294	2,694
Independent students	92	8,877	5,712	2,114	3,011	587	1,317	3,000	148	3,165	6,764	7,561
Income Level ***												
Low	100	10,099	6,495	2,759	3,121	614	1,812	3,100	231	3,605	7,340	8,288
Middle	99	8,420	5,237	1,597	3,054	586	954	3,054	67	3,183	6,823	7,466
Upper	64	5,460	3,867	829	2,546	493	267	2,546	14	1,593	4,631	5,192

*Aid not classified as grants or loans. Includes work studey, assistantships, veterans benefits, military tuition aid, vocational rehabilitation and JTPA

** Income levels for dependent students (1996 dollars): Low= less than $40,000; Middle = $40-59,999; Upper Middle= $60-79,999; Upper=greater than $80,000

***Income level for independent students (1996 dollars): Low= less than $10,000; Middle = $10-24,999; Upper = greater than $25,000

Source: NCES, NPSAS:96 Undergraduate Students 10/1/97

EXHIBIT 11-3

Financial Aid Received by Students with Need Attending Public Two-Year Colleges: 1996

	Percent of All Students With Need	Average amount of need	Total Aid Amount	Total Grants	Total Loans	Total Other*	Federal Grants	Federal Loans	Federal Other*	Need Unmet by Total Aid	Need Unmet by Grants	Need Unmet by Federal Grants
Dependent students	60%	$4,341	$1,445	$1,029	$311	$106	$635	$268	$50	$2,896	$3,312	$3,706
Income Level**												
Low	95	5,136	1,822	1,401	287	134	932	277	70	3,314	3,735	4,204
Middle	67	2,899	747	300	402	44	26	269	3	2,153	2,599	2,874
Upper Middle	11	low n	low n	low n	low n	low n	low n	low n	low n	low n	low n	low n
Upper	8	low n	low n	low n	low n	low n	low n	low n	low n	low n	low n	low n
Independent students	81	6,879	3,125	1,559	1,000	567	1,231	1,000	152	3,754	5,321	5,648
Income Level ***												
Low	100	7,721	3,568	1,953	925	690	1,567	924	224	4,153	5,768	6,154
Middle	96	6,466	2,748	1,266	1,093	389	1,001	1,093	74	3,718	5,200	5,466
Upper	37	4,897	2,574	932	1,007	634	641	1,007	117	2,324	3,965	4,256

*Aid not classified as grants or loans. Includes work study, assistantships, veterans benefits, military tuition aid, vocational rehabilitation and JTPA

** Income levels for dependent students (1996 dollars): Low= less than $40,000; Middle = $40-59,999; Upper Middle= $60-79,999; Upper=greater than $80,000

***Income level for independent students (1996 dollars): Low= less than $10,000; Middle = $10-24,999; Upper = greater than $25,000

Source: NCES, NPSAS:96 Undergraduate Students 10/1/97

EXHIBIT 11-4
Financial Aid Received by Students with Need Attending Private Universities: 1996

	Percent of All Students With Need	Average amount of need	Total Aid Amount	Total Grants	Total Loans	Total Other*	Federal Grants	Federal Loans	Federal Other*	Need Unmet by Total Aid	Need Unmet by Grants	Need Unmet by Federal Grants
Dependent students	86%	$16,197	$10,265	$5,915	$3,436	$914	$458	$1,441	$387	$5,931	$10,282	$15,739
Income Level**												
Low	99	21,540	14,134	9,261	3,885	988	1,297	2,431	556	7,406	12,279	20,243
Middle	98	17,802	11,634	6,825	3,674	1,135	125	1,851	428	6,168	10,977	17,677
Upper Middle	95	14,389	8,097	4,157	3,094	846	63	1,039	313	6,293	10,233	14,326
Upper	66	10,346	6,456	2,730	3,000	726	16	323	218	3,890	7,616	10,331
Independent students	97	16,688	9,654	4,265	4,417	972	897	4,374	182	7,033	12,423	15,791
Income Level ***												
Low	100	19,136	11,309	5,427	4,790	1,092	1,476	4,760	280	7,827	13,709	17,660
Middle	100	15,637	8,413	3,331	4,138	944	418	4,054	107	7,224	12,306	15,219
Upper	83	12,073	7,548	2,902	3,943	703	242	3,943	63	4,525	9,171	11,831

*Aid not classified as grants or loans. Includes work studey, assistantships, veterans benefits, military tuition aid, vocational rehabilitation and JTPA

** Income levels for dependent students (1996 dollars): Low= less than $40,000; Middle = $40-59,999; Upper Middle= $60-79,999; Upper=greater than $80,000

***Income level for independent students (1996 dollars): Low= less than $10,000; Middle = $10-24,999; Upper = greater than $25,000

Source: NCES, NPSAS:96 Undergraduate Students 10/1/97

EXHIBIT 11-5
Financial Aid Received by Students with Need Attending Private Colleges: 1996

	Percent of All Students With Need	Average amount of need	Total Aid Amount	Total Grants	Total Loans	Total Other*	Federal Grants	Federal Loans	Federal Other*	Need Unmet by Total Aid	Need Unmet by Grants	Need Unmet by Federal Grants
Dependent students	87%	$12,676	$9,403	$5,301	$3,434	$668	$724	$1,896	$364	$3,273	$7,375	$11,952
Income Level**												
Low	99	15,066	10,192	6,260	3,216	716	1,554	2,399	420	4,874	8,806	13,512
Middle	99	12,876	9,696	5,175	3,757	764	176	2,024	440	3,180	7,700	12,699
Upper Middle	91	9,890	9,109	4,737	3,796	576	8	1,423	255	781	5,153	9,883
Upper	51	8,243	6,734	3,208	3,068	457	15	657	181	1,509	5,035	8,227
Independent students	91	13,362	8,603	3,674	4,198	731	1,325	4,121	152	4,759	9,688	12,037
Income Level***												
Low	99	14,849	9,823	4,650	4,320	853	1,972	4,309	221	5,026	10,199	12,876
Middle	99	13,273	7,166	3,077	3,445	644	1,045	3,407	124	6,107	10,195	12,228
Upper	73	10,518	8,071	2,516	4,950	604	405	4,688	53	2,447	8,002	10,113

*Aid not classified as grants or loans. Includes work study, assistantships, veterans benefits, military tuition aid, vocational rehabilitation and JTPA.
** Income levels for dependent students (1996 dollars): Low= less than $40,000; Middle = $40-59,999; Upper Middle= $60-79,999; Upper=greater than $80,000
***Income level for independent students (1996 dollars): Low= less than $10,000; Middle = $10-24,999; Upper = greater than $25,000

Source: NCES, NPSAS:96 Undergraduate Students 10/1/97

EXHIBIT 11-6

The Contribution of Federal, State, and Institutional Financial Aid to Student Need by Type and Sector of Institution: 1996*

	Total Costs	Need**	Federal Aid	State Aid	Institutional Aid	Need not met by Financial Aid
Full-time students						
Institution type						
Public 4-year	$10,842	$7,393	$4,785	$602	$758	$1,248
Public 2-year	7,366	5,350	2,594	318	269	2,168
Private 4-year	18,856	13,319	5,598	886	4,299	2,536
Private 2-year	13,226	9,976	4,766	889	786	3,536
Part-time students						
Institution type						
Public 4-year	9,583	6,626	4,331	280	379	1,636
Public 2-year	5,942	3,912	1,822	166	114	1,811
Private 4-year	12,509	8,596	4,806	627	1,142	2,021
Private 2-year	10,839	7,380	3,327	662	366	3,025

Source: *National Postsecondary Student Aid Study*, 1996.

* Only includes full-year students with financial need
** Total Cost - Expected Family Contribution

The Unfinished Agenda

Colleges and universities are complex institutions serving millions of students. In the relatively short period of time since the establishment of the National Commission on the Cost of Higher Education, numerous issues have been identified that could contribute to rising college tuitions. Time, as well as the availability of data, did not allow for the thorough review of all of these issues.

- **Graduate Education.** How has the price of graduate education changed over time? What are the relative costs of graduate education as compared to undergraduate education? How can we distinguish these costs? Are undergraduate tuitions paying for graduate programs? Is the time to obtain a Ph.D. increasing?

- **Part-time Students.** How much do part-time students pay to attend a postsecondary institution? What is their price of attendance? How much and what types of financial aid do they receive? How much does it cost institutions to educate part-time students? Do part-time students need special types of services that differ from those of full-time students?

- **Nontraditional Students.** (Often considered to be students over the age of 22 who do not necessarily attend full-time; part-time students can be subsumed under nontraditional students). What types of financial aid do nontraditional students receive? What types of additional supports do they need?

- **Faculty Workload.** How do faculty spend their time? How can we improve upon current methods of obtaining data on faculty work? How much are they asked to teach? How frequently are faculty able to substitute activities for actual classroom teaching? Are there more efficient ways to teach?

- **Persons Who Do Not Attend.** Why do some high school graduates not pursue a college education? To what extent do financial concerns keep persons from enrolling?

- **Proprietary Schools.** How much do proprietary students pay to attend their institutions? What does it cost a proprietary school to educate students? How much and what types of financial aid do proprietary school students receive? Has the availability of Federal aid, both loans and grants, influenced tuition growth in proprietary schools?

- **Costs and Quality.** To what extent are changes in higher education costs related to changes in the quality of higher education? How are higher education products affected by changes in costs? How can quality be improved and costs reduced?

- **Technology.** How can advances in technology change the delivery of higher education? How can technology help colleges and universities to reduce their costs?

- **Saving to Pay for College.** How can students and their families save more efficiently to pay for college? What types of incentives might encourage families to save?

- **Higher Education and the Business Community.** How can businesses become more involved to help reduce some of the costs of higher education? To what extent are businesses currently providing tuition benefits for employees?

- **Remedial Education.** What does it cost colleges and universities to offer remedial education? How can higher education work with elementary and secondary schools to ensure that students are better prepared for college work?

- **Tuition Remission.** Does offering faculty tuition remission for family members drive up institutional costs?

- **Information Needs.** What kinds of information and publications would assist parents and students to make informed decisions about attending college?

EXHIBIT A

Institutions Offering Remedial Courses in Fall 1995, by Subject Area and Institutional Characteristics

Institutional characteristic	Number of higher education institutions with freshmen	Percent of higher education institutions enrolling freshmen that offer remedial courses in:			
		Reading, writing, or mathematics	Reading	Writing	Mathematics
All institutions	3,060	78	57	71	72
Type					
Public 2-year	950	100	99	99	99
Private 2-year	350	63	29	61	62
Public 4-year	550	81	52	71	78
Private 4-year	1,200	63	34	52	51
Minority enrollment					
High	340	94	87	85	93
Low	2,720	76	53	70	70

Note: Data are for higher education institutions in the 50 states, the District of Columbia, and Puerto Rico that enroll freshmen. The numbers of institutions have been rounded to the nearest 10. Numbers of institutions with freshmen may not sum to total because of rounding.

Source: U.S. Department of Education, National Center for Education Statistics, Postsecondary Education Quick Information System, Survey on Remedial Education in Higher Education Institutions, 1995.

EXHIBIT B

Freshman Remedial Enrollment in Fall 1995, by Subject Area and Institutional Characteristics

Institutional characteristic	Number of first-time freshmen (in thousands)	Percent of all entering first-time freshmen that enrolled in remedial courses in:			
		Reading, writing, or mathematics	Reading	Writing	Mathematics
All institutions	2,128	29	13	17	24
Type					
Public 2-year	943	41	20	25	34
Private 2-year	56	26	11	18	23
Public 4-year	726	22	8	12	18
Private 4-year	403	13	7	8	9
Minority enrollment					
High	338	43	25	29	35
Low	1,790	26	11	15	21

Note: Data are for higher education institutions in the 50 states, the District of Columbia, and Puerto Rico that enroll freshmen. Institutions that offered remedial reading, writing, and mathematics courses were asked about the percent of entering freshmen that enrolled in any remedial course in one or more of these subject areas, and that enrolled in remedial courses in each subject area. This information about the percent of entering freshmen enrolled in remedial courses was then combined with information about the total number of first-time freshmen (both full and part time) enrolled at all institutions with freshmen to obtain national estimates of the number of entering first-time freshmen enrolled in remedial courses. The total number of first-time freshmen was obtained from the Integrated Postsecondary Education Data System (IPEDS) 1994 Fall Enrollment file (the most recent year for which data were available). The percent of first-time freshmen enrolled in remedial courses was then calculated by dividing the sum of first-time freshmen taking remedial courses by the sum of all first-time freshmen enrolled at all institutions with freshmen.

Source: U.S. Department of Education, National Center for Education Statistics, Postsecondary Education Quick Information System, Survey on Remedial Education in Higher Education Institutions, 1995.

EXHIBIT C

Approximate Average Length of Time a Student Takes Remedial Courses at the Institution, by Institutional Characteristics: 1995

(Percent of higher education institutions offering remedial courses)

Institutional characteristic	Less than 1 year	1 Year	More than 1 year
All institutions	67	28	5
Type			
Public 2-year	46	44	10
Private 2-year	95	5	0
Public 4-year	69	27	3
Private 4-year	84	14	2
Minority enrollment			
High	53	34	13
Low	69	27	4

Note: Data are for higher education institutions in the 50 states, the Distirct of Columbia, and Puerto Rico that enroll freshmen. Percents are based on institutions that offered at least one remedial reading, writing, or mathematics course in fall 1995. Percents are computed across each row, but may not sum to 100 because of rounding. Zeros indicate that no institution in the sample gave the indicated response.

Source: U.S. Department of Education, National Center for Education Statistics, Postsecondary Education Quick Information System, Survey on Remedial Education in Higher Education Institutions, 1995.

EXHIBIT D

Reasons Institutions Did Not Offer Remedial Courses in Fall 1995

(Percent of higher education institutions not offering remedial courses)

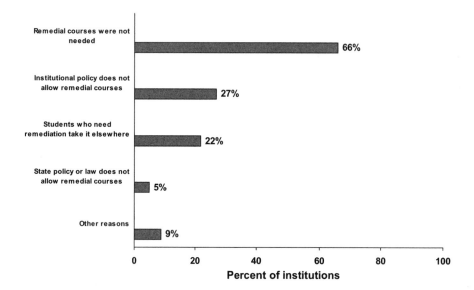

Note: Data are for higher education institutions in the 50 states, the District of Columbia, and Puerto Rico that enroll freshmen. Percents are based on those institutions that did not offer any remedial reading, writing, or mathematics courses in fall 1995.

Source: U.S. Department of Education, National Center for Education Statistics, Postsecondary Education Quick Information System, Survey on Remedial Education in Higher Education Institutions, 1995.

EXHIBIT E

Whether State Policies or Laws Affect Higher Education Institutions' Remedial Education Offerings, and How Those Policies or Laws Affect Remedial Offerings, By Institutional Characteristics: 1995

Institutional characteristics	State policies or laws affect remedial offerings at institutions offering remedial courses	How state policies or laws affect remedial offerings[*]				
		Required to offer	Encouraged to offer	Discouraged from offering	Offerings are restricted	Other
All institutions	33	59	19	4	7	10
Type						
Public 2-year	57	71	19	1	4	6
Private 2-year	3	(#)	(#)	(#)	(#)	(#)
Public 4-year	40	35	24	15	14	13
Private 4-year	7	(#)	(#)	(#)	(#)	(#)
Minority enrollment						
High	43	55	19	6	10	10
Low	31	60	20	4	6	10

[*]Percents are based on those institutions offering remedial courses with state policies or laws that affect remedial offerings. Percents are computed across each row, but may not sum to 100 because of rounding.

(#) Too few cases for a reliable estimate.

Note: Data are for higher education institutions in the 50 states, the District of Columbia, and Puerto Rico that enroll freshmen. Percents in the first column are based on institutions that offered at least one remedial reading, writing, or mathematics course in fall 1995.

Source: U.S. Department of Education, National Center for Education Statistics, Postsecondary Education Quick Information System, Survey on Remedial Education in Higher Education Institutions, 1995.

EXHIBIT F

The Cost of Remedial Education in Four States

♦ City University of New York reports that the combined cost of remedial education for four-year and two-year colleges is approximately $35 million a year. This is roughly 2.9 percent of their $1.2 billion budget (*The New York Times*, March 19, 1997).

♦ Texas's Higher Education Coordinating Board reported that state spending on remedial education rose from $39 million in 1988-89 to $153 in the biennium. The largest increase was in community colleges, raising state spending from $30 million dollars in 1988-89 to $127 million in 1996 (*The Chronicle of Higher Education,* August 2, 1996).

♦ The Florida House of Representatives Committee on Higher Education reported that with nearly 70 percent of community college freshman requiring remedial education courses, community colleges are spending $53 million dollars a year on providing this type of instruction (*The New York Times*, February 13, 1996).

♦ In 1993-94 California spent $9.3 million, approximately .6 percent of California State University expenditures ($1.446) on remedial courses for students on its 22 campuses (Board of Trustees Report, California State University, January 24-25, 1995).